CALIFORNIA CRIMINAL LAW MANUAL

Sixth Edition

Derald D. Hunt

Director, Emeritus
Administration of Justice Education
Coast Community College District
Orange County, California

Consulting Legal Editors

Martin G. Engquist

Deputy District Attorney
Orange County, California

Michael A. Horan

Attorney at Law
Santa Ana, California

Gary M. Pohlson

Attorney at Law
Santa Ana, California

 **Burgess Publishing Company**
Minneapolis, Minnesota

Copyright © 1984, 1980, 1976, 1974, 1970 by Burgess Publishing Company
Copyright © 1967 by Jack A. Fleming and Derald D. Hunt
Printed in the United States of America

Library of Congress Cataloging in Publication Data

Hunt, Derald D.
   California criminal law manual.

   Includes index.
   1. Criminal law—California—Outlines, syllabi, etc.
2. Criminal procedure—California—Outlines, syllabi,
etc. I. Engquist, Martin G. II. Horan, Michael A.
III. Pohlson, Gary M. IV. Title.
KFC1100.Z9H86 1984   345.794   83–23147
ISBN 0–8087–4749–5   347.9405

Burgess Publishing Company
7108 Ohms Lane
Minneapolis, MN 55435

J I H G F E D C B A

To Ruby,

my dearest friend, greatest advocate,

and loving wife

ACKNOWLEDGMENTS

I wish to acknowledge the welcome support received from many friends and colleagues in scores of California community colleges and state universities who are currently using *California Criminal Law Manual* in their classrooms.

These instructors' suggestions for making the text more complete and useful for themselves and their students have been gratefully adopted for the current edition.

I am especially appreciative of the valuable suggestions made by Nathan F. Iannone, Chairman, Criminal Justice, Fullerton Junior College.

Finally, I am most grateful to Arland R. Bassett, Professor of Criminal Justice, Golden West College, for his valuable contributions to Appendix D, Basic Legal Research.

D.D.H.

PREFACE

Up-dates and Changes. This revised sixth edition of *California Criminal Law Manual* reflects the most recent changes in California criminal law.

New Code Sections, as revised and added by the legislature (including penalty "enhancements"), as well as the most recent appellate court decisions, have been added throughout the text.

Controlled Substances. The chapter on dangerous drugs and controlled substances has been up-dated in this edition of the *California Criminal Law Manual*, making it more complete than ever.

Meets "Standardized" Core Curriculum. The California Community College Chancellor's office recently revised the recommended administration of justice core curriculum. The new sixth edition of *California Criminal Law Manual* is designed to address the objectives, scope, and topics as outlined in both the revised **"Concepts of Criminal Law"** course and the **"Substantive Law"** course.

Basic Legal Research. Appendix D covers an easy-to-understand segment on how to find case law and how to write a legal brief. A sample brief, showing proper format, is included.

Scope and Purpose. *California Criminal Law Manual* is designed to provide the Administration of Justice student with a thorough foundation and basic understanding of criminal law. The text is sufficiently comprehensive to stand by itself as a combination textbook and student workbook for both pre-service and in-service programs. Emphasis is on basic criminal law as it applies to law enforcement, corrections, security, criminology, and the general administration of justice.

Adequate in scope for either one or two semesters (or quarters) of criminal law instruction, the manual contains the most recent code changes, prevailing case citations, examples to illustrate salient points of law, and the *corpus delicti* of the offenses covered.

At the instructor's discretion, this manual may be used in conjunction with the *California Penal Code* or other code books. However, a supplemental text is usually not required.

Recruit Academy Training. *California Criminal Law Manual* includes large segments of instruction as specified by the Commission on Peace Officer Standards and Training (POST) for the Basic Recruit Academy. Therefore, the manual would be most applicable as a workbook and text for appropriate criminal law and laws of arrest performance objectives in a POST basic course (Functional Area 3).

TO THE STUDENT

How to Use *California Criminal Law Manual.* If you will use the "Seven-Step Plan" which follows you will learn more in less time and retain it longer with less effort.

Step 1: Read the "Terminology Defined" list related to each chapter to make sure you understand those terms with which you are not already familiar. Note those terms which may take on a slightly different meaning when applied to the study of law. You will need to know these terms in order to clearly understand what is being read in each chapter.

Step 2: Read the True-False and Essay-Discussion questions at the end of each chapter. This will help you to recognize the answer when you later read the text.

Step 3: Make a preliminary survey. Get an idea of what the material is about—what the key concepts are—*before you read*. Do this by noting section headings and subheadings.

Step 4: Read for understanding, formulating questions as you read. Look for answers to the True-False and Essay/Discussion questions as you read.

Step 5: Test yourself to be sure you can answer the questions you will find at the end of each chapter.

Step 6: Take notes in the margins of your *California Criminal Law Manual* and in your notebook on what you have read. Write brief answers to the end-of-chapter test questions.

Step 7: Review the major points of the assignment and re-read any sections you do not understand. Make notes on questions you can ask at the next class meeting.

TO THE INSTRUCTOR

This revised edition of *California Criminal Law Manual* includes several new features designed for the increased convenience and effectiveness of the instructor. Included in the new edition you will find:

1. **Basic legal research techniques**. Case law, how to find it and how to write a legal brief (format included).
2. **List of appropriate terms** and their definitions applicable to each chapter.
3. **A matching type "Terminology Quiz"** (based on item above) at the end of each chapter. Students may be instructed to complete this quiz in their text or on a separate sheet for submission. This test makes an excellent weekly (or periodic) quiz and assures the instructor that the student is "learning the language" and technical terminology of the discipline.
4. **A true-false quiz** covering key points relative to each chapter. This test, which may be answered on a separate machine-scored answer sheet, provides excellent weekly (or periodic) feedback for diagnostic and review purposes.
5. **An essay-discussion test** appropriate to each chapter, which may be used for either weekly class discussion items or more comprehensive testing such as the mid-term and final examination, or for both.
6. **Instructor's Guide.** Answers to all test questions, including essay-question items, are in the *Instructor's Guide* which can obtained without charge by written request to **Burgess Publishing Company, 7108 Ohms Lane, Minneapolis, MN 55435** on your college letterhead.

Contents

*A Terminology List, a True-False Quiz, a series of Essay-Discussion Questions, and a Terminology Quiz appear at the end of each chapter.

CHAPTER 1

Scope and Source of Criminal Law

1.1 INTRODUCTION

Criminal law, both substantive (laws defining crimes) and procedural (rules of criminal procedure) as found in the various California State codes and as interpreted by our courts, is the foundation of all administration of criminal justice in our democratic society. It is from these two primary sources, (i.e., California Code books and court interpretations) that peace officers and others in our justice system get their legal authority and responsibility. The law also provides limitations and controls. It is imperative, therefore, that professionals already in the system and students preparing for modern-day law enforcement, corrections, or security employment be well grounded in the fundamentals of criminal law. This foundation provides the framework within which each must function.

If each of us lived in a state of isolation from all other human beings, there would be little, if any, need for criminal laws, or any law at all, for that matter. Obviously, most of us do not exist as hermits but rather we live in a complex society requiring daily interaction with many other people.

In such a society, each person must know what he or she can and cannot do regarding our frequent contacts and dealings with others. In order to avoid societal chaos, we must have rules to govern our personal activities just as we must have rules to govern the operation of vehicles on our crowded streets and highways.

Even in a complex society such as ours, if everyone did the "right" thing in relation to all other members of society, we would need few criminal laws. Unfortunately, there will always be individuals who attempt to oppress the helpless, who steal the possessions of others, or in one way or another violate the life, liberty, or property of others by force or fear.

Historically, our first criminal laws came into being as a result of society's struggle to control those persons whose antisocial activity was destructive of a desirable environment in which people wanted to live. Safety, stability, and integrity are necessary for the healthy growth and benefit of the community as a whole.

We may think of crime as a violation of the basic controls of society, and we may think of criminal law as necessary to deter misconduct and otherwise deal with those individuals who would disrupt society. Criminal law is an instrument of social control. Without laws, criminal or civil, we would have no protection from the whims of others.

In order to gain the protection of society's laws, the law-abiding members must be willing to give up a small part of their freedom to do just as they wish at all times. This is especially true when one individual's activities interferes with the rights of others. With the above in mind, we may define crime as social conduct considered harmful to individuals and to our institutions and therefore made punishable by law.

1.2 ORIGIN AND DEVELOPMENT OF LAW IN GENERAL

Law in general, which includes both civil and criminal law, may be described as a collection of regulations covering the behavior of society and individuals therein.

Most of our early criminal law was based on custom or other recognized patterns of human behavior which appeared to be beneficial to the group as a whole. Even today, laws pertaining to incestuous marriages (between closely related blood relatives) can be traced to early tribal taboos. Other crimes relating to theft, murder, child molesting, etc., have a similar basis.

Law, especially criminal law, is almost as ancient in one form or another as is mankind on earth. No doubt early caveman eventually established some sort of basic rules as to who would eat first, who had to tend the fire, who was to stand guard, etc. Also, no doubt, those who didn't conform to the "law" were punished in some way by the rest of the group whose survival was based on being able to depend on one another to follow the rules. Of course, these rules or laws were not written, but were undoubtedly well understood by each member of the group.

As family groups eventually joined one another to form tribes, new rules or laws were developed to avoid conflict and to assure the peaceful functioning of the group. Children were no doubt taught local customs and taboos by parents and other members of the tribe.

As society developed and began to place its thoughts in writing, there emerged the concept of statutory (written) law. This was to have a profound effect on the entire civilized world.

The first "written" law was in the form of cuneiform symbols chiselled into rock tablets or impressed on wet clay tablets which were then baked or sun-dried hard. One of the most famous examples is the Code of Hammurabi. The Code of Hammurabi (a large stone tablet preserved in the Louvre Museum in Paris) was believed by scholars to have been written by King Hammurabi of Babylonia about 2100 B.C.

We can trace many of our legal concepts back to the Code of Hammurabi. These include: perjury, written contracts, "swearing in" of witnesses, jurys, and judges. While the bulk of our modern law is based on English jurisprudence (body of law), we have also inherited traces of Roman law (Latin medical-legal terms) as well as French and Spanish legal concepts.

As civilization developed, we find concepts such as trial by jury emerging in early England during the 12th century. We also begin to see the emergence of representative government—that is, the election or appointment of representatives who were granted authority to pass laws. These "legislatures" adopted new laws as society and modes of conduct changed. And so it is today with our California State Legislature and Congress passing new laws and rescinding old ones as the need is perceived. We also find our courts placing new interpretations on old laws.

There are no common law (unwritten) crimes in this state. On the contrary, for an act or omission to constitute a crime in California, it must be in violation of (1) a written statute, (2) in the English language and (3) must provide a penalty for its violation. Those laws passed by authorized bodies of local, state and federal governments make up our statutory law. The order of precedence is:

1. **United States Constitution**
2. **Treaties and acts of Congress**
3. **California State Constitution**
4. **State laws**
5. **Locals laws (city and county ordinances)**
6. **Court decisions**

1.3 THE PURPOSE AND NATURE OF CRIMINAL LAW

Crimes are prohibited and punished on the grounds of public policy to prevent injury to the public. Injury to the public may include destruction or interference with government, human life, private property, or other valued institutions or interests. Such considerations as desire for vengeance or compensation for injury may also be involved.

Punishment is oftentimes said to be the purpose of the criminal law; however, this is not quite true. The purpose of criminal law is to define socially intolerable conduct, and to hold conduct within limits which are reasonably acceptable from the social point of view (*Sauer v. United States, 241 F. 2d 640, 648*).

Perhaps it may be said that whatever purpose is served by punishment, one minor purpose of criminal law is that of compelling persons to cease or refrain from committing crime and forcing or persuading them to conform to established rules of conduct designed for the protection of government, life, and property.

Definition of Crime. A crime is a public offense against the state. Penal Code, Section 15, defines a crime as "an act committed or omitted in violation of a law forbidding or commanding it, and to which is annexed, upon conviction, either of the following penalties:

1. **Death**
2. **Imprisonment**
3. **Fine**
4. **Removal from office**
5. **Disqualification to hold and enjoy any office of honor, trust or profit in this state."**

The word "crime" in its more extended sense comprehends every violation of public laws. A general course of conduct, practices, habits, mode of life, or status which is prejudicial to public welfare may be prohibited by law, and punishment therefore may be provided by the state, and every course of conduct or practice or habit or mode of life or status falling within that class of wrongs is covered by the term "crime" (*People v. Babb, 103 C.A. 2d 326*).

All public offenses or crimes in California are statutory, and the court cannot have recourse to common law to determine prohibited acts (*Ex parte Harder, 9 C.A. 2d 153*). That a criminal action is being prosecuted by the People, and not in the interest of any person injured, is a fundamental principal of criminal law (*People v. Clark, 117 C.A. 2d 134*).

All crimes are against the state, and no affirmative action to prevent commission of a public offense is required to be taken by any citizen except officials charged with such duty (*People v. Weber, 84 C.A. 2d 126*)

1.4 SOURCES OF CRIMINAL LAW

In a broad sense, reason, conscience, etiquette, honor, conventions, customs, morality, and Christianity are all considered to be sources of the criminal law. More specifically, these general sources may be more effective as a means of social control than law itself. However, while such sources may, among particular groups of people, constitute the prohibition of particular acts by the common law or by statute, it must be remembered that an act is not a crime simply because it is immoral or in any sense contrary to above sources.

That the general sources stated above are actually a part of our common law is true only in a limited sense, for the law must prohibit the commission of an act in writing and must provide punishment therefor, both elements being essential in order that there may be a crime.

All criminal law in this country is based on the following four sources:
1. **English common law**
2. **Federal and State Constitution**
3. **Legislation (laws) passed by Congress and state legislatures**
4. **Prevailing decisions of the courts in criminal cases**

English Common Law. With the exception of Louisiana, the United States can trace the foundations of its criminal law to early English common law. However, even Louisiana, which had a French and Spanish heritage, adopted the common law of England by passage of a statute in 1805.

Norman Period. In 1066, William the Conqueror, a Norman military leader from France, conquered the British Isles and declared himself king. William found various individual courts in existence which were dominated by the sheriff.

Prior to 1066, no action had been taken by the various kings of Britain to reduce the laws to writing. Rather they allowed the sheriff to enforce the various tribal or village rules as he saw fit to keep order. Criminal courts *per se* were as yet unknown. William, who demonstrated a genius for organization, gradually took measures to reduce the arbitrary power of the sheriff and commanded the sheriff to act, henceforth, only in the king's name. He thus established some degree of uniformity. Additionally, William placed all courts under royal control and issued a proclamation inviting the common people of the country to seek justice in his courts.

In time, English courts became more centralized and uniform in their administration of the law. Within one hundred years following William's conquest, the known common law crimes were being more or less equally enforced throughout the country. The various acts which constituted crime were enforced by the courts based on reason and human experience of the past. Certain acts, therefore, constituted crimes by "common understanding" or by public consent of the people.

Gradually during the Westminster period in England (1285-1500), procedures became more formal. As such, the known or general custom of the kingdom became more rigid. For example, to establish that a certain practice was "custom" and therefore "law", lawyers found it useful to give examples and illustrations from their own experience and from other trials that they could personally recall. These illustrations of what had been known before were not binding on the court, but were forerunners of what we know as "precedent" in contemporary society.

With the passing of time and creation of the English Parliament, new crimes were added to the "list" and we see both the legislature (Parliament) and the courts adding to the body of common law.

The Adoption of Common Law in America. As the first settlers from England arrived, they formed agreements among themselves called "compacts," in which they adopted much of the common law of England for their governance.

Following the Declaration of Independence, many states either adopted the common law outright, or passed criminal statutes which, in fact, incorporated into written law most of the basic principles of the old common law.

The Common Law. The common law precedes our statute law. It is the total of maxims, doctrines, decisions, precedents, reasonings and practices comprising the legal heritage of Anglo-American law and the source of our legal thinking.

The common law, in the sense in which it is used here, is a body of law which derives its authority not from express enactments of the legislature like the statute law, but from the fact that it has existed from time immemorial. It is preserved and evidenced by judgments of the courts applying it to particular cases as they arise.

In another sense, the common law is used to distinguish the science of jurisprudence prevailing in England and America from other great systems such as the Roman law or the law of continental Europe known as "civil law." It may further be used to denote that law which is common to the country as a whole in contrast to laws of purely local application, or to distinguish the law enforced by the state from "canon [church] law."

According to Blackstone, the common law consists of doctrines that are not set down in any written statute or ordinance, but depend merely upon immemorial usage.

Common Law in United States.   There are today no common law offenses against the United States government (*U.S. v. Britton, 108, U.S. 199*). A statutory authority must exist for declaring any act or omission a criminal offense. It is equally true that the statute must provide punishment, and a failure to do so results in the discharge of a person accused thereunder. However, it has been decided that, when Congress has by statute referred to or adopted a common law offense, without further definition, the common law definition must be followed. This is not the case in California, however, since the law is wholly statutory in this state and there are no common law crimes (*Penal Code, Section 6; People v. Harris, 191 C.A. 2d 754*).

It is expressly provided by statute in a number of states that no act or omission is criminal or punishable, except as prescribed or authorized by code or statute. In some states, such as California, it is required that the crime must be defined by the statute to be punishable.

The Federal and State Constitute as Sources of Criminal Law.   As a second source of our criminal laws, we recognize the United States Constitution as well as the constitution of our own state as the fundamental written "law of the land." These two documents provide the framework for our criminal justice system in that they: (1) define and limit the powers of government and (2) provide for establishment and maintenance of our court system.

The U.S. Congress and State Legislature as Sources of Criminal Statutes.   From our early beginnings in this country, our courts have consistently ruled that both Congress and the State Legislature have the inherent power to pass laws defining, prohibiting, and punishing criminal conduct. The only restriction is that they may not pass any laws that conflict with and thus violate constitutional restrictions and limitations.

The United States Congress and our own California State Legislature are the two most prolific sources of our criminal law. They are both in a position to respond to changing needs of society. When a criminal law becomes outdated, it can be repealed and thus eliminated. When new technology or new societal needs are identified, new laws may be passed, or previously existing laws may be amended and updated.

Decisions of the Courts.   Our appellate courts constitute the fourth source of our criminal statutes both substantive and adjective (procedural). Once a law is passed by the legislature, it becomes subject to the need for interpretation. The law may not be clear to everyone. Different words or terms may mean different things to different people. Obviously, if we are to have a "government of laws" some entity must have the authority to define the statute as to the legislature's meaning and intent. This is the role of the court and can be recognized as an extension of the old English common law. The result of this procedure is known as case law or precedent and is based on the legal principal of *stare decisis,* which is discussed below.

1.5   CONCEPTS OF *STARE DECISIS*

The peculiarity of the common law doctrine of precedent is simply that even a single case once decided must be considered binding. This doctrine, called *stare decisis* (pronounced "star-ray-dee-sigh-sis") originated during the eighteenth century in England and is supposed to be the very essence of common law. The basic theory of *stare decisis,* which means "to rigidly adhere to precedent," is that laws by which people are governed should be fixed, definite, and known. The concept here is that persons should be informed as to what will happen to them when they commit a crime.

A commentary, published in 1761, written by the English legal scholar and professor, Blackstone, made reference to the concept of *stare decisis* as "rigidly finding precedent." This simply meant that previously decided cases were to have a great impact and influence on the decisions in contemporary cases. At the time, opinions of judges were becoming more and more available in printed form, so that it was possible for one judge to know how another judge had ruled. To establish a fair and consistent manner of adjudicating like cases, application of the rule of precedent became more and more rigid. Finally, near the end of the nineteenth century, a lower court was not considered to be bound by a series of decisions of a higher court.

However, a higher court was considered to be bound to abide by and rule in accordance with a single decision made previously in that same court.

The concept of *stare decisis* has been relaxed considerably in recent years, so that it is no longer uncommon for a court to reverse a previous decision when the reasons for the rule have changed. Contemporary courts have more recently reversed themselves as to decisions previously made by their predecessors due to a dissatisfaction with the old rule.

Two recent examples wherein the court has reversed itself involve: (1) Husband and wife may now be found guilty of conspiracy (*People v. Pierce, 61 Cal. 2d 879*). Previously husband and wife were considered one person in marriage and could not be guilty (*People v. Miller, 82 Cal. 107*, decided in 1889). (2) In unlawful sexual intercourse, PC 261.5, ignorance as to the female's age was previously no defense. The court recently changed its position in such a case with the result that good faith believe that the female was 18 years of age or more is now a valid defense to the crime (*People v. Hernandez 61 Cal. 2d 529*).

In setting precedent, the courts do not enact rules or laws as is characteristic of the state legislature. They only make rules in the sense that they explain why and how they were led to make a particular decision in a particular case. Judges will inherently refer to the same principles in a previously decided case when trying similar cases today.

1.6 CLASSIFICATION OF LAWS

Classification of Laws. Laws are classified in a number of ways. The first broad heading would consist of the *substantive* law. This, in effect, defines the relationship between individuals, and between the state and individuals. Public law applies to relations between individuals and property. Also included under substantive law are constitutional law, corporation law, and international law.

Substantive Criminal Law is much narrower in scope than the broad concept of "the administration of criminal justice." The latter encompasses all phases of criminal procedure from arrest to adjudication. Substantive law, on the other hand, has been defined as "the positive law of duties and rights," or "that part of the law which the courts are established to administer," as opposed to the rules according to which the substantitive law itself is administered.

Substantive criminal law relates to the definition and classification of crimes generally, the criminal act, the criminal intent, the capacity to commit crime and exemptions from criminal liability, the parties to crime, and finally a consideration of the important elements (*corpus delicti*) or characteristics of various offenses.

Procedural or Adjective Law is a second broad classification. This area of jurisprudence covers matters of procedure, carrying out remedies, redress, classification of crimes, and punishment. Additionally there are two other more familiar divisions of law which are of concern to those in education and social welfare. The first is penal law, which concerns an individual and his relations with the community, with appropriate definitions of crime and punishment. In these actions, the appropriate political subdivision takes action against the individual in behalf of the state of California. The second division parallel to penal law is civil law. This relates to actions between individuals of a noncriminal nature.

Criminal vs. Civil Law. Criminal law, as the term implies, concerns itself with defining those specific acts and omissions (failure to act) which constitute a crime in our society. The most common crimes are described and defined in the California Penal Code. However, many other crimes are also found in approximately forty other California Code books. These other codes include the Education Code, Welfare and Institutions Code, Health and Safety Code, Vehicle Code and the Business and Professions Code, just to name a few. The penalty for committing a crime, which is doing that which a criminal code section prohibits, or not doing that which a criminal code requires one to do, is usually a fine or a jail term (see Section 1.3 for a list of all possible penalties for a crime).

Civil law has to do mostly with describing or establishing guidelines for various routine and legal relationships and contacts between people. Laws describing the way a contract is drawn up or the terms of a promisory note, are examples. A civil wrong, such as failure to comply with the terms of a legal contract, is called a *tort*. A complaint against someone who commits a tort is filed in small claims court, municipal court, or superior court. In such cases, a judge or jury decides whether the plaintiff (the one who files suit) or the defendant was at fault. The penalty for committing a tort is civil damages which are awarded to the plaintiff and which the defendant must pay. (See Section 1.13 for an additional discussion of the difference between crimes and torts.)

1.7   STATUTE OF LIMITATIONS

The statute of limitations (PC 799-802.5) places a limit on the amount of time which may legally pass between the time the crime was either committed or discovered and the start of prosecution (*People v. Chapman, 47 C.A. 3d 597*).

In 1982, the State Legislature revised the statute of limitations in an unusual way. The current law, as given below in your text, is to remain in effect until either (1) the court of appeal or the California Supreme Court rules, or (2) the California Constitution is amended, to provide that a person indicted for a felony is not also entitled to a preliminary hearing. Currently, persons indicted by a Grand Jury have the right to a preliminary hearing following an indictment (*Hawkins v. Superior Ct 22 C. 3d 584*).

By way of introduction, it is necessary to consider the statute of limitations on certain offenses in order to know how soon after the commission or discovery of a public offense a suspect can still be prosecuted. In some cases, a Grand Jury indictment must be returned or a criminal complaint filed within a certain time after the crime is *discovered*. In other instances, the statute of limitations starts running when the crime is *committed*. There is also a difference as to the statute of limitations between felonies and misdemeanors, and even between certain felonies.

Misdemeanors: One–Year Limitation. A complaint must be filed in municipal court, or an information must be filed in superior court, or a Grand Jury indictment must be returned within one year after the *commission* of a misdemeanor (PC 801). If this time limit is not adhered to, the suspect cannot be prosecuted. Note: if the suspect has been out of the State during any part of this one year, such time does not count against the running of the statute of limitations (PC 802).

Computation of Time if Defendant Is Out of State. If, when or after the offense is committed, the defendant is out of the state, an indictment may be found, a complaint or information filed, or a case certified to the superior court, in any case originally triable in the superior court, or a complaint may be filed in any case originally triable in any other court, within the term limited by law; and no time during which the defendant is not within this state, is a part of any limitation of the time for commencing a criminal action (PC 802).

Time Limitation Period. The time limitations provided in this Chapter for the commencement of a criminal action shall be started upon the issuance of an arrest warrant or the finding of an indictment, and no time during which a criminal action is pending is a part of any limitation of the time for recommencing that criminal action in the event of a prior dismissal of that action, subject to the provisions of PC 1287 (PC 802.5).

Indictment Found When Presented and Filed. An indictment is "found," within the meaning of this Chapter, when it is presented by the Grand Jury in open court and there received and filed (PC 803).

No Statute of Limitation. There are now four crimes for which there is no statute of limitations and charges can be filed at any time after the crime is committed, discovered or the suspect arrested. They are:

1. Murder, PC 187
2. Embezzlement of public money, PC 424, PC 514
3. Kidnapping for ransom, PC 209
4. Falsification of public records, PC 115

There is no limitation of time within which a prosecution for murder, the embezzlement of public funds, kidnapping for ransom or the falsification of public records must be commenced. Prosecution for murder may be commenced at any time after the death of the person killed. Prosecution for the embezzlement of public funds, kidnapping for ransom, or the falsification of public records may be commenced at any time after the discovery of the crime (PC 799).

Three Year Limit—Felonies in General. An indictment for any felony, except those for which there is no statute of limitations (PC 799, above), or for those listed below, shall be found, or an arrest warrant issued by the municipal court, or where appropriate, the justice court, within three years after its *commission* (PC 800(a)).

Three Year Limit Following Discovery. An indictment for each of the following crimes must be found, or an arrest warrant issued by the municipal or justice court within three years after its *discovery* (PC 800(c)).

1. Grand theft, PC 487
2. Felony welfare fraud, W&I Code 11483
3. Felony Medi-Cal fraud, W&I Code 14107
4. Voluntary manslaughter, PC 192
5. Involuntary manslaughter, PC 192
6. Presenting false claims, PC 72
7. Perjury, PC 118
8. False affidavit, PC 118a
9. False documentary evidence, PC 132
10. Preparing false evidence, PC 134
11. Stock sale fraud, Corporations Code 25540, 25541

12. Conflict of interest, Government Code 1090, 27443.

Six Year Limit Following Commission. An indictment must be found, or an arrest warrant issued by the municipal or justice court for each of the following crimes within six years after its *commission.*

1. Rape, PC 261
2. Rape, aiding and abetting, PC 264.1
3. Penetration of genitals or anus with foreign object, PC 289
4. Forced sodomy, PC 286(c), (d), or (f)
5. Forced oral copulation, PC 288a, (c), (d), or (f)
6. Child molesting, PC 288
7. Public officials and employees accepting bribes, PC 68

1.8   CASE CITATIONS AND APPEALS

When a superior court case is taken up on appeal, the appeal is usually heard first by the District Court of Appeal. The person making the appeal is known as the appellant and is, in essence, asking the appeals court to consider a question of fact or law with respect to the adjudication of his case in the trial court. The appellant will usually be the defendant in a criminal action; however, the prosecution may also appeal in certain cases (PC 1238). In such cases, the prosecution is known as the appellant, and the adverse party is the respondent.

When either of the appeals courts (State Supreme Court or District Court of Appeals) makes a decision, a written opinion is filed, explaining the reasoning of that court. These written opinions are later published and appear in the *California Appellate Reports,* abbreviated *Cal. App.* or *C.A. 2d.* A typical example of a case citation reflecting a published opinion by the District Court of Appeal would be *People v. Jones, 65 C.A. 2d 381.* This citation refers to volume 65, *California Appellate Reports,* second series, page 381 (fictitious case).

If the decision of an appellate court is further appealed, it is heard by the seven justices of the California Supreme Court. The written decisions reflected by this court are published in *California Reports,* abbreviated *Cal.* or *C. 2d.* An example of a case citation of a published opinion of this court would be *People v. Smith, 51 Cal. 2d 152.* This designation refers to volume 51, *California Reports,* second series, page 152 (fictitious case).

The two Preliminary reports of cases decided by the appellate courts are subsequently published in bound volumes. However, since it generally takes a year to publish the case reports in volume form, advance copies are published within a few weeks of being filed. The *Advance California Reports* (abbreviated *A.C.*) are bound in a green pamphlet. The *Advance California Appellate Reports* (abbreviated *A.C.A.*) are bound in a salmon pamphlet. The advance reports are not completely reliable in that they are often changed in part or even completely stricken from final publication in bound volume.

1.9   ATTORNEY GENERAL OPINIONS

The California State Attorney General is the lawyer for the State. By law, he must give his written opinion, when requested, to the:

1. State Senate or Assembly
2. Governor
3. Secretary of State
4. Controller
5. Treasurer
6. State Lands Commission
7. Superintendent of Public Instruction
8. Any district attorney in the State.

Opinions of the Attorney General are expressions by him of his conclusions on legal questions which are presented to him by those persons whom he represents. Government Code section 12519 provides that the Attorney General shall render these opinions to the various state officials and agencies listed above, when requested, upon any questions of law relating to their respective offices.

Section 13 of the California State Constitution designates the Attorney General the "chief law officer of the State." Government Code sections 12550 and 12560 give him ". . . direct supervision over the district attorneys of the various counties of the State and . . . over the sheriffs of the several counties of the State."

There are generally two types of opinions rendered by the Attorney General:

1. Formal—This opinion is rendered when it is determined that the question presented is of general statewide interest. These opinions are published in a series of books called *Opinions of the Attorney General of California.*
2. Informal—This opinion will reflect a problem or problems not generally of state-wide interest. It will be a letter opinion which is sent to the individual organization or official presenting the problem. These opinions do not appear in published form; however, copies are maintained in the various offices of the Attorney General. While the informal opinions are usually not

available to the general public, copies may generally be obtained by interested persons.

Authority of Attorney General Opinions. The opinions of the Attorney General do not have the same authority as the opinions of the court. As the courts themselves have stated, "although not of controlling authority, the Attorney General opinions are, in view of his relation to the general government and the nature of his duties, regarded as having a quasi-judicial character and are entitled to great respect." (*People v. Shearer, 30 Cal. 645; People v. Berry (1956), 147 C.A. 2d 33; Santa Clara County v. Sunnyvale City Council, 168 C.A. 2d 89*).

1.10   POLICE POWER

Police power of the states is a term that does not appear in the U.S. Constitution; however, its significance is evident from the authority that it reserves to the state. The legislatures of the different states, including California, have the inherent power to prohibit and punish any act, provided they do not violate the restrictions of the Federal and State Constitutions. Under this power, the state can legislate in the following areas: (1) public health; (2) safety; (3) morals; (4) general welfare; and (5) general prosperity.

No state can make any law or enforce any law which shall abridge the privileges or immunities of citizens of the United States, nor can any state deprive any person of life, liberty, or property without due process of law, or deny to any person within its jurisdiction the equal protection of the law (*U.S. Const. Amend 14, par. 1*).

After the state legislature expressly prohibits an act and makes it a crime, there is no longer any test of public policy to be applied. The legislature has presumably enacted the law for the public good, and the courts cannot look further into its propriety than to ascertain whether the legislature had the power to pass it. As previously stated, the constitutional limitations upon the power of Congress have no application to state legislatures so far as criminal law is concerned. Even the Fourteenth Amendment, which insures to all citizens the rights guaranteed to them in the First Amendment, does not nullify the police power of the states. Moreover, the federal government itself cannot exercise the exclusive authority given to it by the states without taking into consideration this important power.

Police power is defined in Article XI, Section VII, of the California Constitution and states, "Any county, city, town or township may make and enforce within its limits all such local police, sanitary, and other regulations as are not in conflict with general laws."

The following are some examples of the police power of the state:

1. Requiring pupils to be vaccinated in schools.
2. Required registration of sexual psychopaths.
3. Prohibiting ex-convicts and drug addicts from possessing concealable firearms.

Police power is as broad as the legislative power of the state, with two exceptions: (1) The laws must be confined to local regulations and (2) The local laws are subject to general laws. Such laws shall not be unreasonable, arbitrary, or capricious, and they must provide equal protection to all citizens.

1.11   THE CONCEPT OF PRE-EMPTION

The concept of pre-emption is based on the premise that state law is superior to local ordinances and takes precedence over them when both are concerned with the same subject matter.

The principle of pre-emption has been established solely by the courts as evidenced by opinions rendered by them in such cases as *In re Lane, In re Hubbard, 62 A.C. 116,* and *People v. Lopez, 59 Cal. 2d 653.* The basic premise offered in the decisions of these cases is that a municipality may not legislate in regard to matters occupied by the state law if:

1. The subject matter is one of state concern and the general law occupies the entire field.
2. The local legislation is in conflict with a state law.
3. The subject matter is of such statewide concern that it can no longer be deemed to be merely a municipal affair.

Thus, a municipality may exercise its legislative power to enact local ordinances, provided such ordinances are not in conflict with the state law or the state has not fully occupied the field of law defined in the local ordinances. As stated in the case of *Professional Fire Fighters, Inc. v. the City of Los Angeles, 60 Cal. 2d 276* "... there are innumerable authorities holding that general law prevails over local enactments of a chartered city, even in regard to matters which would otherwise be deemed to be strictly municipal affairs, where the subject matter of the general law is of a statewide concern."

In the past, local ordinances were held to be valid when they enumerated criminal acts in greater detail than did state laws written on the same subject. More recent court decisions, however, indicate that the courts now feel that when the state legislature intended to occupy an entire field of subject matter, local ordinances concerning the same subject are invalid (*People v. Benson, 20 Cal. 2d 366*). This reasoning exists between the two statutes, and the local ordinance merely is intended to supplement the state law.

An example of the foregoing philosophy would be in the case of the state enacting only one statute covering the area of public intoxication (PC 647f). The courts have held this field to be totally occupied by state law and have thus declared local ordinances which go beyond the state law and which enumerate more specific circumstances of intoxication to be invalid. In contradistinction, many state laws have been enacted through the years covering the field of gambling, and it would appear that the state had also occupied that field of legislation. Yet, the courts have recently held that local gambling ordinances are not pre-empted and are, therefore, valid. It is obvious then, that the court's well-established position on pre-emption has not consistently been followed.

1.12 *EX POST FACTO*

The Constitution of the United States expressly prohibits Congress or any state from passing an *ex post facto* law (*Const. U.S. Art. 1, sections 9 and 10*). The California Constitution has a similar provision (*Art. 1, section 16*). Such a law is one passed after the commission of an act which changes the legal consequences of the act to the wrongdoer's prejudice. The term *ex post facto* includes:

1. Every law which makes an act committed before its passage, which was innocent when done, criminal.
2. Or which makes a crime greater than when it was committed.
3. Or which inflicts a greater punishment to a crime.
4. Or which changes the rules of evidence so that less or different testimony is sufficient to convict than was required when the act was committed. The legislature cannot increase the punishment nor may an accused's defense be taken away. However, a statute is not within the prohibition if it makes the act a less aggravated crime than when committed and makes the punishment less severe, or if it merely changes the method of procedure, unless it thereby deprives the accused of a substantial right which is vital for his protection.

Repeal of Statutes. The outright repeal or the repeal by amendment of a criminal statute after the commission of a crime (but before trial and conviction) does not bar a prosecution for such an offense unless the intent to bar further prosecutions is expressly declared in the repealing act (Gov. Code 9608).

1.13 DISTINCTION BETWEEN CRIMES AND TORTS

A crime is a public wrong, while a tort is a private wrong or an injury to another. It is safe to say that, in general, a tort or civil wrong may accompany practically every criminal wrong, subjecting the wrongdoer to punishment at the hand of the state and rendering him liable to financial damages in a civil suit by the individual immediately injured. The two proceedings are distinct, however, and have a different objective. The criminal law seeks to punish, while the civil action is designed to obtain redress for injury. Neither proceeding is a bar to the other; however, it should be noted that a *nole contendere* plea by a defendant in criminal court cannot be used against a defendent as an admission of wrong doing in any civil suit based upon or growing out of the act upon which the criminal prosecution is based. A *nolo contendere* plea (no contest) by a defendant has the same effect in court as a guilty plea, with the exception noted.

Another distinction between a crime and a tort would be the element of intent (refer to the section on *Corpus Delicti*—Act and Intent). To render one criminally liable for an act, such a person must have a criminal intent as provided by PC 20. The contrary theory underlies the law of torts. For example, a lunatic or very young child, not being able to entertain such an intent, is incapable of committing crime but may be liable for damages as a result of a wrongful act. In the case of *Ellis v. D'Angelo, 116 C.A. 2d 310* (1953), the court held that a minor is liable for all his own torts in the same manner as if he were an adult. In this case, the parents and their four-year-old child were held liable for damages caused when the child attacked a babysitter and inflicted serious injury.

There are, then, really two separate actions involved in crime. The first is represented by the *People of the State of California v. Defendant*. The second is a civil action which may be brought by the victim in a civil court against the defendant for a tort. Recovery is in payment of money for loss suffered and punitive damages, if such is allowable (*Civil Code, 1714*). Thus, if a person steals an automobile, the wrongdoer may be prosecuted in a criminal court for a violation of Section 10851 of the Vehicle Code (auto theft). The victim may also sue the wrongdoer in a civil court for damages in a tort action. Similarly, a person may strike another, and the injured party may sign a complaint and have the wrongdoer prosecuted for battery in a criminal court. The victim may also sue in the civil court for money damages in tort action.

1.14   DEFINITION OF TERMS

Crimes *Mala in Se* and *Mala Prohibita*. For the purpose of this publication it is perhaps sufficient to say that crimes *mala in se* are those serious crimes which are wrong from their very nature, such as murder, robbery, rape, etc. They are inherently so serious in their effects on society as to call for the practically unanimous condemnation of those who commit these acts.

Crimes considered to be *mala prohibita* are wrong merely because they are prohibited by statute. These are characteristically those offenses which are enacted under police power of the government and for control of the conduct of citizens.

Moral Turpitude. "Moral turpitude" is a term which the courts have had great difficulty in applying. One definition holds that "moral turpitude involves an act of baseness, vileness, or depravity in the social duties which a man owes to his fellow man or to society in general, contrary to the accepted and customary rule of right and duty between man and man." Moral turpitude then relates to that which may be deemed "shamefully immoral" and suggests a lack of honesty, integrity, modesty, and good morals on the part of a criminal perpetrator.

Crimen Falsi. The term *crimen falsi* is used to describe any class of crime that involves falsification. Examples of such crimes would be forgery, perjury or subornation of perjury, counterfeiting or false coinage, alteration of instruments, and other frauds. The term originated from Roman civil law.

Infamous Crimes. Infamous crimes are generally those which are inconsistent with the common principles of honesty and humanity. At common law, infamous crimes were treason, felony, all fraudulent offenses including those of a *crimen falsi* nature. More recently, the term is associated with an act of vileness or moral depravity, such as in the infamous crime against nature (sodomy, buggery, or bestiality) as defined in PC 286.

1.15   VENUE AND JURISDICTION

Venue has to do with the physical or geographical location of the court in which a case is to be filed or tried. Venue should *not* be confused with *jurisdiction* which has to do with the court's legal authority to act in a specific case.

Usually the case is tried in the county in which the crime was committed. Such is only logical because the county in which the crime occurred is most likely where the victim, witnesses, and investigating officers are all located.

Sometimes a defendant may legally request and receive a "change of venue." Request for a change of venue must be based on valid grounds such as: (1) pretrial publicity precludes a fair trial; (2) the defendant is such a well-known or prominent citizen (or notorious and intensely hated) that a fair trial cannot be had in the court where the case would normally be tried; or (3) the feelings of the community are such that a fair and impartial jury cannot be selected from the area. Changes of venue are not granted lightly. The burden of proof is on the party (usually the defendant) requesting the change.

Jurisdiction has to do with the court's legal authority over the defendant and the crime he is accused of committing. The Juvenile Court, for example, has initial jurisdiction over crimes committed by juveniles. Federal courts have jurisdiction over crimes in violation of the Government Code and other federal statutes.

Jurisdiction also has to do with where the crime was committed. Generally, a court has jurisdiction if *any part* of a crime was committed or occurred within its geographical boundaries. The question of where to try such crimes as conspiracy, for example where the planning took place in one jurisdiction, preparation in another, and actual accomplishment in a third jurisdiction, is therefore no major problem. The defendant(s) may legally be tried in any of the above three jurisdictions. As a practical matter, the case would most likely be tried where the crime was "completed." Completed, in this case, could mean: (1) where the money was stolen from; (2) where the victim was kidnapped from; or (3) where the victim was killed, if his body was found elsewhere.

TERMINOLOGY DEFINED—CHAPTER 1

Each of the following terms is important for a clear understanding of the text. See the Terminology Quiz at the end of this chapter.

1. Abridge: circumvent, avoid.
2. Adjective law: procedural law.
3. Appellate court: a court of appeals.

4. Canon law: church law.
5. Capricious: without good (legal) reason.
6. Common law: resulting from custom and court decisions.
7. Contemporary: modern or current.
8. *Corpus delicti:* elements of a crime.
9. *Crimen falsi:* crime involving falsification.
10. Custom: behavior which has become traditional with time.
11. Doctrines: rules.
12. *Ex post facto:* after the fact.
13. Incestuous: marriage or sexual relations between close blood relatives.
14. Infamous crime: violating common principles of humanity.
15. Inherent: within, basic to, built-in.
16. Jurisdiction: court's legal authority to act.
17. Jurisprudence: field of law.
18. *Mala in se:* wrong by its very nature.
19. *Mala prohibita:* wrong because prohibited by law.
20. Moral turpitude: relating to ethics, honesty, morality.
21. Nullify: to dilute or abolish.
22. Precedent: binding court decisions.
23. Public policy: best for majority, custom.
24. Sovereign: power to act, king.
25. *Stare decisis:* rigidly adhere to precedent.
26. Statutes: written laws.
27. Substantive law: laws defining crimes and their punishments.
28. Taboos: based on tribal prohibitions and customs.
29. Tort: private or civil wrong.
30. Venue: geographical location of court hearing a case.

TRUE-FALSE QUIZ—CHAPTER 1

1. It is primarily because people live together as a society that there is a need for laws.
2. Common law refers to those laws passed by the legislature which are commonly known by most people.
3. California has only six common law crimes.
4. An act is not a crime unless it is punishable by death, imprisonment, or fine, in this state.
5. Prevailing decisions of the courts in criminal cases is one source of our criminal law.
6. By adopting the Declaration of Independence, the people of America thereby rejected almost all of the English common law concepts.
7. Our courts have held that the State Legislature has no inherent power to pass laws defining or prohibiting criminal conduct.
8. When in question, it is ultimately up to the courts to interpret new criminal laws passed by the legislature.
9. While precedent is important in deciding cases, our courts do not always strictly adhere to the concept of *stare decisis.*
10. Adjective law is the term applied to statutes defining various crimes and their attendant punishments.
11. Substantive law is the term which describes laws defining criminal procedure and the rules by which other law is administered.
12. The statute of limitations, among other things, governs the amount of maximum time for which a person can be imprisoned for a crime.
13. When a case is appealed from the superior court, it is usually heard next in the District Court of Appeals.
14. In a criminal case, only the defendant has a right to appeal.
15. Being the chief law officer of the state, the Attorney General's opinions carry the same weight as do those of a court.
16. The "police power" of the state refers to its right to pass laws relative to public health, safety, and welfare.
17. The concept of pre-emption was established by the courts.
18. A city ordinance is legal if it describes a crime, covered by state law, in greater detail than the latter.
19. A law passed making an act a crime after the act was committed is prohibited by the Constitution.
20. A tort may be defined as a "public wrong."
21. The law prohibits suing someone for personal damages if he has already been convicted of a crime for the same act.
22. The term, *mala in se,* means prohibited by law.
23. The term, *crimen falsi,* would be applicable to such crimes as forgery and perjury.
24. Jurisdiction has to do with the court's legal authority over the defendant and the crime of which he is accused.
25. To request a change of venue means to ask to have the case tried in a court in another geographical location.

ESSAY-DISCUSSION QUESTIONS—CHAPTER 1

The following may be used as either essay or class discussion questions as directed by the instructor. The student can demonstrate knowledge of this chapter by being able to answer each of the questions briefly.

1. What are the five possible penalties which may be imposed on one convicted of a crime in California?
2. What is the basic difference between a crime and a tort?
3. What is the difference between a *mala in se* and a *mala prohibita* crime?
4. Define and give an example of a crime considered *crimen falsi*.
5. What are the four general sources of criminal law?
6. What is common law and what is its impact in criminal cases?
7. Define and give an example of "police power" of the state.
8. What is an *ex post facto* law and what is its legal effect?
9. How does substantive law differ from adjective law?
10. What is the statute of limitations for (a) misdemeanors, (b) burglary, and (c) murder?
11. Whom does the Attorney General represent and what is the legal authority of his decisions?
12. What occurred during the Westminster Period (1285-1500) in English courts which has an effect on today's courts?
13. How were the concepts of English common law first adopted in America?
14. What are the two most prolific sources of criminal law today?
15. What is meant by venue and jurisdiction as it applies to the court?

TERMINOLOGY QUIZ—CHAPTER 1

Match terms and definitions by placing the correct number in the parentheses. Answers may be written on a separate sheet for submission to the instructor at the instructor's direction.

Terms	*Definitions*
1. Abridge	(16) Court's legal authority to act
2. Adjective law	(1) Circumvent, avoid
3. Appellate court	(26) Written law
4. Canon law	(28) Tribal prohibitions
5. Capricious	(10) Behavior traditional with time
6. Common law	(6) Resulting from custom and court decisions
7. Contemporary	(7) Modern or current
8. *Corpus delicti*	(22) Binding court decisions
9. *Crimen falsi*	(4) Church law
10. Custom	(3) Court of appeals
11. Doctrines	(11) Rules
12. *Ex post facto*	(19) Wrong because of laws against it
13. Incestuous	(27) Crimes and punishments
14. Infamous crime	(18) Wrong by very nature of act
15. Inherent	(2) Procedural law
16. Jurisdiction	(20) Relating to ethics, honesty, morality
17. Jurisprudence	(25) Rigidly adhere to precedent
18. *Mala in se*	(14) Violating common principles of humanity
19. *Mala prohibita*	(8) Elements of a crime
20. Moral turpitude	(30) Geographical location of court hearing
21. Nullify	(5) Without good legal reason
22. Precedent	(9) Crime involving falsification
23. Public policy	(29) Private or civil wrong
24. Sovereign	(12) After the fact
25. *Stare decisis*	(24) King, power to act
26. Statutes	
27. Substantive law	
28. Taboos	
29. Tort	
30. Venue	

14

CHAPTER 2

Classification of Crimes and Penalties

2.1 SPECIFICATION OF CRIMES— PRESCRIPTION OF PENALTIES

No act or omission is criminal or punishable as such unless, at the time, there is a valid statute declaring an act or omission to be a crime and prescribing a penalty for the violation (PC 6 and 15).

For a public offense to be committed, some statute, ordinance, or regulation must be in existence prior in time to the commission of the act and must denounce it and label it a crime. If no written statutory excuse or justification applies to the particular offense, neither the common law nor the so-called "unwritten law" may legally be used as a defense (*Keeler v. Superior Court, 2 C.3d 619*).

Thus, the so-called defenses of the "unwritten law" or "the law of necessity" have no application in California law. As such, a defendant has no recourse to interpose a defense to such a circumstance.

There are no common law or unwritten crimes in California; the law is completely statutory. In order for an act or omission to be criminal, there must be some law or ordinance covering the specific situation. This is commonly referred to as written or "codified" law; hence, California is a codified state by relying wholly on the written or statutory format of defining crimes. Since there are no common law or unwritten crimes in California, there is no common law or unwritten justification or excuse for committing an act which is denounced as being criminal.

2.2 LANGUAGE OF CRIMINAL STATUTES

The California Constitution, Article IV, Section 24, provides that all criminal statutes must be written in the English language. Accepted Latin medical terms in the law are exceptions to this principle.

When a word, whether coming from a foreign language or coined to meet a particular need of expression, has been used as an English word in speech or writing to such an extent that its meaning has become commonly understood by people dealing with the subject to which it relates, it becomes a part of the English language with the meaning attached to it by such use even though it is not in the English dictionary (*People v. Beesley, 119 C.A. 82*).

Criminal statutes may not by interpretation be extended beyond their plain meaning unless common sense or the obvious purpose of the legislature so requires it. In the interpretation of the statutes, or the construction of the words in such statutes, the defendant is entitled to the benefit of every reasonable doubt, just as he is as to the question of fact involved (*People v. Wilkinson, 1967 248 C.A. 2d Supp. 906*).

2.3 VAGUE AND INDEFINITE STATUTES

Criminal statutes which are vague and uncertain will result in a violation of the due process clause of the Fourteenth Amendment to the U.S. Constitution (*Connolly v. General Construction Company, 269 U.S. 385*).

A criminal statute which is so vague, indefinite, and uncertain that definition of crime or standard of conduct cannot be ascertained therefrom, is unconstitutional and void (*Smith v. Peterson, 131 C.A. 2d 241*).

Words such as "immoral," or "loiter," if used in a crime, would have to be clearly defined in terms of specific acts or actions to be constitutional. Otherwise, such laws would be declared void as too vague and indefinite.

2.4   CONSTRUCTION OF PENAL STATUTES

In accordance with Penal Code, Section 4, criminal statutes must not be strictly construed, but all provisions of this code must be construed according to a fair import of their terms with a view to effect objects thereof and to promote justice (*People v. Harris, 98 C.A. 2d 662*).

Once the intention of the legislature is ascertained, it will be given effect, even though it may not be consistent with the strict letter of the statute (*People v. Black, 45 C.A. 2d 87*). Similarly, when construing a statute and seeking to ascertain the intent of the Legislature, interpretation must be given which avoids any absurdity, and especially one which goes outside of the offenses sought to be prohibited (*Ex parte Davis. 18 C.A. 2d 32*).

When language which can reasonably be interpreted in two different ways is used in a penal statute, ordinarily that interpretation or construction which is more favorable to the defendant will be adopted; particularly where one of the interpretations would impose absolute criminal liability (*In re Murdock, 68 C. 2d 313*). The provisions of the Penal Code must be interpreted according to the reasonable meaning of the terminology used. The courts cannot go so far as to create an offense by enlarging a statute, by inserting or deleting words, or by giving the terms used in the law an unusual meaning (*Keeler v. Superior Court, 2 C. 3d 619*).

2.5   CONFLICT BETWEEN STATUTES

Where two legislative enactments punish exactly the same act or omission as crimes and they are obviously in conflict, the last one passed into law will control. (*People v. Lewis, 4 C.A. 2d 775*).

A later act, not containing a repealing clause, does not automatically repeal a prior law, except so far as the two are clearly inconsistent or it is quite clear that the later act is intended as a substitute for the former in all respects and is intended to cover the entire subject to which both relate.

Normally, a new law intended to amend or replace an old law will specifically so state, including the old section number.

2.6   CONSTRUCTION AND DEFINITION OF TERMS USED IN CALIFORNIA PENAL CODE

PC 7. Certain Terms Defined in the Sense in Which They Are Used in the California Penal Code. Words used in the Penal Code in the present tense include the future as well as the present; words used in the masculine gender include the feminine and neuter; the singular number includes the plural, and the plural the singular. The word "person" includes a corporation as well as a natural person; the word "county" includes "city and county"; writing includes printing and typewriting; oath includes affirmation or declaration; and every mode of oral statement. Under oath or affirmation, is embraced by the term "testify," and every written one in the term "depose"; signature or subscription includes mark, when the person cannot write, his name being written near it, by a person who writes his own name as a witness; provided that when a signature is made by mark it must, in order that the same may be acknowledged or serve as the signature of any sworn statement, be witnessed by two persons who must subscribe their own names as witnesses thereto.

The following words have in this code the signification attached to them in this section, unless otherwise apparent from the context:

1. The word "willfully," when applied to the intent with which an act is done or omitted, implies simply a purpose or willingness to commit the act, or make the omission referred to. It does not require any intent to violate law, or to injure another, or to acquire any advantage.
2. The words "neglect," "negligence," "negligent," and "negligently" impart a want of such attention to the nature or probable consequences of the act or omission as a prudent man ordinarily bestows in acting in his own concern.
3. The word "corruptly" imports a wrongful design to acquire or cause some pecuniary or other advantage to the person guilty of the act or omission referred to, or to some other person.
4. The words "malice" and "maliciously" import a wish to vex, annoy, or injure another person, or an intent to do a wrongful act, established either by proof or presumption of law.
5. The word "knowingly" imports only a knowledge that the facts exist which bring the act or omission within the provisions of this code. It does not require any knowledge of the unlawfulness of such act or omission.

6. The word "bribe" signifies anything of value or advantage, present or prospective, or any promise or undertaking to give any, asked, given, or accepted, with a corrupt intent to influence, unlawfully, the person to whom it is given, in his action, vote, or opinion, in any public or official capacity.

7. The word "vessel," when used with reference to shipping, includes ships of all kinds, steamboats, canalboats, barges, and every structure adapted to be navigated from place to place for the transportation of merchandise or persons.

8. The words "peace officer" signify any one of the officers mentioned in Chapter 4.5 (commencing with Section 830) of Title 3 of Part 2.

9. The word "magistrate" signifies any one of the officers mentioned in Section 808.

10. The word "property" includes both real and personal property.

11. The words "real property" are coextensive with lands, tenements, and hereditaments.

12. The words "personal property" include money, goods, chattels, things in action, and evidences of debt.

13. The word "month" means a calendar month, unless otherwise expressed; the word "daytime" means the period between sunrise and sunset, and the word "nighttime" means the period between sunset and sunrise.

14. The word "will" includes codicil.

15. The word "writ" signifies an order or precept in writing, issued in the name of the people, or of a court or judicial officer, and the word "process" a writ or summons issued in the course of judicial proceedings.

16. Words and phrases must be construed according to the context and the approved usage of the language; but technical words and phrases, and such others as may have acquired a peculiar and appropriate meaning in law, must be construed according to such peculiar and appropriate meaning.

17. Words giving a joint authority to three or more public officers or other persons are construed as giving such authority to a majority of them, unless it is otherwise expressed in the act giving the authority.

18. When the seal of a court or public officer is required by law to be affixed to any paper, the word "seal" includes an impression of such seal upon the paper alone, or upon any substance attached to the paper capable of receiving a visible impression. The seal of a private person may be made in like manner, or by the scroll of a pen, or by writing the word "seal" against his name.

19. The word "state," when applied to the different parts of the United States, includes the District of Columbia and the territories, and the words "United States" may include the district and territories.

20. The word "section," whenever hereinafter employed, refers to a section of this code, unless some other code or statute is expressly mentioned.

21. To "book" signifies the recordation of an arrest in official police records and the taking by the police of fingerprints and photographs of the person arrested, or any of these acts following an arrest.

2.7 FELONIES, MISDEMEANORS, AND INFRACTIONS DEFINED

Crimes are divided into (1) Felonies, (2) Misdemeanors, and (3) Infractions (PC 16).

At common law, a felony is an offense which by the statutes or by the common law itself is punishable with death, or to which the old English law attached the total forfeiture of lands or goods, or both, or which a statute expressly declares to be such.

Under PC 17, a *felony* is a crime punishable with death or imprisonment in the state prison. All other crimes are *misdemeanors or infractions*.

If a crime provides for an alternative sentence (i.e., if it is punishable as a felony by imprisonment in the state prison or as a misdemeanor by fine or by imprisonment in county jail), the offense is and remains a *felony* for all purposes up to the time of actual sentencing or granting of probation by the court. For example, a person may commit an offense such as burglary in the second degree (see PC 459) which is a felony, and which prescribes an alternate sentence of county jail or state prison. If he is sentenced to state prison, he stands convicted of a felony due to the punishment imposed. In contradistinction, if such a person is sentenced to county jail, the alternate in this case, he stands convicted of a misdemeanor even though at the time of the commission of the offense it was a felony he was committing. The offense itself is a felony up to the time the sentence other than state prison is imposed by the court (*People v. Cornell, 16 Cal. 187; People v. Rowland, 19 C.A. 2d 540*).

Where the court suspends imposition of sentence and does not pronounce judgement and instead places the defendant on probation, if the offense is punishable as a felony, the defendant retains the status of a person convicted of a felony until the record is expunged pursuant to PC 1203.4 (*People v. Banks, 53 Cal. 2d 370*). Also, see "Expungment Procedures" in Penal Code, Section 1203.45. On the other hand, where imposition of sentence is suspended on conviction of a crime punishable by imprisonment in the state prison or in the county jail, the court may declare the crime to be a misdemeanor at the time probation is granted, or thereafter on application of the defendant or the probation officer (see PC 17, text, following).

Effect on Arrest. Any crime which provides for an alternate misdemeanor-felony sentence, is and remains a *felony* for all purposes, including arrest, up to the time of actual sentencing by the court. "Alternate penalty" felonies (sometimes called "wobblers") therefore, should be treated the same as all other felonies for all purposes by the peace officer.

PC 17. Classification of Public Offenses.

a. A felony is a crime which is punishable with death or by imprisonment in the state prison. Every other crime or public offense is a misdemeanor except those offenses that are classified as infractions.

b. When a crime is punishable, in the discretion of the court, by imprisonment in the state prison or by fine or imprisonment in the county jail, it is a misdemeanor for all purposes under the following circumstances:

1. After a judgement imposing a punishment other than imprisonment in the state prison.

2. When the court upon committing the defendant to the Youth Authority, designates the offense to be a misdemeanor.

3. When the court grants probation to a defendant without imposition of sentence and at the time of granting of probation, or on application of the defendant or probation officer thereafter, the court declares the offense is a misdemeanor.

4. When the prosecuting attorney files in a court having jurisdiction over misdemeanor offenses a complaint specifying that the offense is a misdemeanor, unless the defendant at the time of his arraignment or plea objects to the offense being made a misdemeanor, in which event the complaint shall be amended to charge the felony and the case shall proceed on the felony complaint.

5. When, at or before the preliminary examination or prior to filing an order pursuant to

Section 872 (held to answer following preliminary hearing), the magistrate determines that the offense is a misdemeanor, in which event the case shall proceed as if the defendant had been arraigned on a misdemeanor complaint.

c. When a defendant is committed to the Youth Authority for a crime punishable in the discretion of the court, by imprisonment in state prison, or by fine or imprisonment in the county jail, the offense shall, upon the discharge of the defendant from the Youth Authority, thereafter be deemed a misdemeanor for all purposes.

d. A violation of any code section listed in PC 19e is an infraction subject to the procedures described in PC 19c and 19d, when:

1. The prosecutor files a complaint charging the offense as an infraction unless the defendant, at the time he is arraigned, after being informed of his rights, elects to have the case proceed as a misdemeanor, or

2. The court, with the consent of the defendant, determines that the offense is an infraction, in which event the case shall proceed as if the defendant has been arraigned on an infraction complaint.

PC 19c. Infraction: Trial by Court, Limitations. An infraction is not punishable by imprisonment. A person charged with an infraction shall not be entitled to a trial by jury. A person charged with an infraction shall not be entitled to have a public defender or other counsel appointed at public expense to represent him unless he is arrested and not released on his written promise to appear, his own recognizance, or a deposit of bail.

PC 19d. Provisions of Law Relating to Infractions. Except as otherwise provided by law, all provisions of law relating to misdemeanors shall apply to infractions, including, but not limited to, powers of peace officers, jurisdiction of courts, periods for commencing action and for bringing a case to trial and burden of proof.

PC 19e. Infractions: Classification of Offenses. You will note that in PC 17, above, if the prosecutor files a complaint charging an infraction instead of a misdemeanor, and the defendant does not object, certain offenses, listed below in PC 19e, will proceed as infractions. The same is true if the court determines that an offense may proceed as an infraction. These offenses are: PC 330, gaming; PC 415, fighting; CVC 27150.1, selling nonregulation mufflers; CVC 40508, violating promise to appear; CVC 42005, failure to attend traffic school, and sections 25658 and 25661 of the Business and Professions Code.

A conviction for any offense made an infraction, as just described, shall not be grounds for the suspension, revocation, or denial of any license, or for the revocation of probation or parole of the person convicted.

Penalty. Except where a lesser maximum fine is expressly provided for the violation of any of the above sections, any such violation which is an infraction is punishable by a fine not exceeding $250.

2.8 PUNISHMENT FOR OFFENSES WHEN NOT OTHERWISE PRESCRIBED

PC 177 states that "when an act or omission is declared by a statute to be a public offense, and no penalty for the offense is prescribed in any statute, the act or omission is punishable as a misdemeanor."

Similarly, where the law provides that a particular crime is punishable by a specified period of imprisonment but is silent as to the place of imprisonment and the offense is not declared to be either a misdemeanor or a felony, the place of imprisonment is a jail and the offense is a misdemeanor (*In re Humphrey, 64 C.A. 572*).

2.9 PUNISHMENTS—IN GENERAL

Punishment for Felony When Not Otherwise Prescribed. Except in cases where a different punishment is prescribed by any law of this state, every offense declared to be a felony, or to be punishable by imprisonment in a state prison is punishable by imprisonment in any of the state prisons for 16 months, or two or three years: provided, however, every offense which is prescribed by any law of the state to be a felony punishable by imprisonment in any of the state prisons or by a fine, but without an alternate sentence to a county jail, may be punishable by imprisonment in the county jail not exceeding one year or by a fine or by both (PC 18).

Maximum Term for Misdemeanor Offense. Except where a different punishment is prescribed for a misdemeanor it is punishable by imprisonment in the county jail not exceeding six months or by a fine of $500, or by both (PC 19).

Exceptions. (1) PC 490 provides that petty theft is punishable by a fine not exceeding one thousand dollars ($1,000), or by imprisonment in the county jail not exceeding six months, or both. (2) Punishment

for possession of less than one ounce of marijuana is a fine not to exceed one hundred dollars ($100).

Consecutive Sentences for Misdemeanor. Where a defendant is convicted of two or more misdemeanors, either in the same or in separate prosecutions, the court may commit the defendant to the county jail under each of such convictions, and an order directing that such terms of imprisonment shall run consecutively is valid (*People v. Flanagan, 7 C.A. 2d 214; PC 19a*).

2.10 VICTIM'S BILL OF RIGHTS

On June 8, 1982, the voters of California overwhelmingly adopted an important Initiative Measure entitled Proposition 8, commonly called the "Victim's Bill of Rights." Passage of this measure resulted in many major changes in our criminal justice system. The more important aspects are discussed below.

Constitutionality. Because Proposition 8 changed the California State Constitution, the measure was immediately challenged on constitutional grounds. The two issues raised had to do with (1) the so-called single subject rule and (2) whether this initiative resulted in an amendment to or a revision of the Constitution.

California Constitution Article II, Section 8, states that an initiative measure embracing more than one subject may not be submitted to the electors or have effect. Article XVIII, permits the Constitution to be *amended*, but not *revised* by the initiative process.

The constitutional validity of Proposition 8 was upheld on all counts by the California Supreme Court on September 2, 1982 (*Brasnahan v. Brown, 32 C. 3d 236; McClanahan v. Superior Court (1983) 139 C.A. 3d. 31*).

2.11 MAJOR PROPOSITION 8 CHANGES

1. Rules of Evidence. Relevant evidence shall not be excluded in any criminal proceeding including pretrial and postconviction motions and hearings or in any trial or hearing of a juvenile for a criminal offense, whether heard in juvenile or adult court. The rule excluding hearsay evidence was not affected by Proposition 8.

This is the so-called "Truth in Evidence" section of the Initiative Measure. It is obvious from the wording of the Constitutional Amendment that *relevant evidence* may no longer be excluded from a trial merely because of some technicality or honest mistake of fact. Undoubtedly, this new rule of evidence will eventually be ruled on by the Supreme Court. Currently, however, it has been uphend in *Wilson v. Superior Court, 234 C.A. 3d 1062.*

2. Bail Provisions. A person may be released on bail by sufficient sureties (bond, cash or property), except for capital crimes (death penalty) when the facts are evident or the presumption great. Excessive bail may not be required. In setting, reducing, or denying bail, the judge or magistrate shall take into consideration (1) the *protection of the public,* (2) the seriousness of the offense charged, (3) the previous criminal record of the defendant, and (4) the probability of his or her appearing at the trial or hearing of the case. Public safety shall be the primary consideration in setting bail. Previously, public safety was not a factor which had to legally be considered in setting bail (Sec. 28e).

A person may be released on his or her own recognizance (without bail) in the court's discretion, subject to the same factors considered in setting bail. However, no person charged with the commission of any serious felony (see PC 1192.7) shall be released on his or her own recognizance.

Before a person arrested for a *serious felony* may be released on bail, a hearing may be held before a magistrate and the prosecuting attorney shall be given notice and reasonable opportunity to be heard on the matter. When a judge or magistrate grants or denies bail or release on a person's own recognizance, the reasons for that decision shall be stated in the record and included in the court's minutes (Sec. 28e).

3. Use of Prior Convictions. Any prior felony conviction of any person in any criminal proceeding, whether adult or juvenile, shall subsequently be used without limitation for purposes of impeachment or enhancement in any criminal proceeding (Sec. 28).

The purpose of this amendment to the California Constitution is to overrule the decision of the California Supreme Court in *People v. Beagle (1972) 6 C. 3d 441.* In this case the Supreme Court held that a trial court has discretion to *exclude* impeachment evidence of a defendant with a prior felony conviction in a criminal case. The existing limitations on the use of prior felony convictions set forth in Evidence Code section 788 are overridden by Proposition 8.

4. Prior as Element of Offense. When a prior felony conviction is an element of any felony offense, it shall be proven to the trier of fact (judge or jury) in open court (Sec. 28f).

The obvious purpose of this provision is to overrule the California Supreme Court in *People v. Hall (1980) 28 C. 3d 143.* In *Hall,* the Supreme Court ruled that a defendant could prevent the prosecution from proving in open court to the trier of fact that the defendant in PC 12021 cases (ex-felon in possession of a concealable firearm) and in PC 666 cases (petty theft with a prior) had been convicted on a prior felony by offering to stipulate to this fact. This amendment mandates the trier of fact be advised of the prior conviction in all circumstances. This provision is not applicable (or necessary) when a plea of guilty is entered, as in such situations there is no trier of fact.

5. Diminished Capacity Abolished. The defense of diminished capacity is hereby abolished. In a criminal action, as well as any juvenile court proceeding, evidence concerning an accused person's intoxication, trauma, mental illness, disease, or defect shall *not* be admissible to show or negate capacity to form the particular purpose, intent, motive, malice aforethought, knowledge, or other mental state required for the commission of the crime charged (PC 25(a), *Added by Initiative Measure, June 8, 1982*).

Notwithstanding the foregoing, evidence of diminished capacity or of a mental disorder may be considered by the court *only* at the time of sentencing or other disposition or commitment (PC 25 (c)).

6. Insanity. In any criminal proceeding, including any juvenile court proceeding, in which a plea of not guilty by reason of insanity is entered, this defense shall be found by the trier of fact only when the accused person proves by a preponderance of evidence (greater weight of evidence in merit and worth, majority of evidence) that he or she was incapable of (1) knowing or understanding the nature and quality of his or her act and of (2) distinguishing right from wrong at the time of the commission of the offense (PC 25(b) *Added by Initiative Measure, June 8, 1982*).

Under PC 25(b), the test for legal insanity is not whether the criminal defendant proves by a preponderance of evidence that he or she was incapable of knowing or understanding the nature of his or her act and of distinguishing right from wrong at the time of the commission of the crime. Essentially, this restores the traditional "M'Naghten Rule" as to insanity (*People v. Kelly (1973) 10 C 3d 565, 574*) which was overturned by the California Supreme Court in *People v. Drew (1978) 22 C 3d 333* (See Section 4.4, Insanity as a Defense, for additional details).

7. Serious Felony Prior Conviction Enhancement. Any person convicted of a *serious felony* (see PC 1192.7) who previously has been convicted of a serious felony in this state, or of any offense committed in another jurisdiction which includes all of the elements of any serious felony, shall receive, in addition to the sentence imposed by the court for the present offense, a *five year* enhancement for *each* such prior conviction on charges brought and tried separately. The terms of the present offense and each enhancement shall run consecutively (one following the other). (PC 667(a)).

This section shall not be applied when the punishment imposed under other provisions of law would result in a longer term of imprisonment. Note: There is no requirement of prior incarceration (imprisonment) or commitment for this section to apply. As used in PC 667, "serious felony" means a felony listed in PC 1192.7(c).

8. Crime Victim Rights. The victim of any crime, or the next of kin of the victim if the victim has died, has the right to attend all sentencing proceedings under this chapter and shall be given adequate notice by the probation officer of all sentencing proceedings concerning the person who committed the crime. The victim or next of kin has the right to appear, personally or by counsel, at the sentencing proceeding and to reasonably express his or her views concerning (1) the crime, (2) the person responsible, and (3) the need for restitution. The court, in imposing sentence, shall consider the statements of victims and next of kin and shall state on the record its conclusions concerning whether the defendant would pose a threat to public safety (PC 1191.1).

9. Crime Victim Defined. The definition of "victim" is found in the restitution provision of California State Constitution, Article I, Section 28(b). This section defines victims as ". . . all persons who suffer losses as a result of criminal activity." This includes all persons suffering personal injury or property loss or damage. In the case of the death of the victim, the next of kin provision would apply to the person closest to the victim. Notification of all relatives of the victim would not be required.

10. Plea Bargaining. Plea bargaining in any case in which the indictment or information charges any *serious felony* (see PC 1192.7(c), below) or any offense of driving while under the influence of alcohol, drugs, narcotics, or any other intoxicating substance, or any combination thereof, is prohibited, unless there is insufficient evidence to prove the people's case, or testimony of a material witness cannot be obtained, or a reduction or dismissal would not result in a substantial change in sentence (PC 1192.7(a).

As used in this section, "plea bargaining" means any bargaining, negotiation, or discussion between a criminal defendant or his or her counsel, and a prosecuting attorney or judge, whereby the defendant agrees to plead guilty or *nolo contendere* (no contest), in exchange for any promises, commitments, concessions, assurances, or consideration by the prosecuting attorney or judge relating to any charge against the defendant or to the sentencing of the defendant (PC 1192.7(b).

11. Serious Felony Defined. As used in this section "serious felony" means any of the following:

1. murder or voluntary manslaughter;
2. mayhem;
3. rape;
4. sodomy by force, violence, duress, menace, or threat of great bodily harm;
5. oral copulation by force, violence, duress, menace, or threat of great bodily harm;
6. lewd acts on a child under the age of 14 years;
7. any felony punishable by death or imprisonment in the state prison for life;
8. any other felony in which the defendant inflicts great bodily injury on any person, other than an accomplice, or any felony in which the defendant uses a firearm;
9. attempted murder;
10. assault with intent to commit rape or robbery;
11. assault with a deadly weapon or instrument on a peace officer;
12. assault by a life prisoner on a non-inmate;
13. assault with a deadly weapon by an inmate;
14. arson;
15. exploding a destructive device or any explosive with intent to injure;
16. exploding a destructive device or any explosive causing great bodily injury;
17. exploding a destructive device or any explosive with intent to murder;
18. burglary of a residence;
19. robbery;
20. kidnapping;
21. taking a hostage by an inmate of a state prison;
22. attempt to commit a felony punishable by death or imprisonment in the state prison for life;
23. any felony in which the defendant personally used a dangerous or deadly weapon;
24. selling, furnishing, administering or providing heroin, cocaine or phencyclidine (PCP) to a minor;

25. any attempt to commit a crime listed in this subdivision other than assault (PC 1192.7(c) *Added by Initiative Measure, June 8, 1982*).

12. CYA Commitments. Notwithstanding any other provision of law, no person convicted of (1) murder, (2) rape, or (3) any other serious felony, as defined in PC 1192.7, above, committed when he or she was 18 years of age or older shall be committed to the California Youth Authority.

There is little doubt about the intention of this provision. Any person 18 years or older at the time of commission of any of the crimes listed in PC 1192.7 is ineligible for commitment to the Youth Authority (W & I Code 1732.5).

2.12   PRIOR CONVICTION— PENALTY ENHANCEMENT

Both Proposition 8 and the Legislature have made many important changes in penalty enhancements, particularly as to "serious felonies," "violent felonies," and prior convictions. The most important are discussed below:

Petty Theft With Prior. Every person who, having been convicted of petit theft, grand theft, burglary, or robbery, and having served a term therefore in any penal institution or having been imprisoned therein as a condition of probation for such offense, is subsequently convicted of petit theft, then the person convicted of such subsequent offense is punishable by imprisonment in the county jail not exceeding one year or in the state prison (PC 666).

Defendant Armed. If one or more of the principals is armed with a firearm in the commission or attempted commission of a felony, *all* principals upon conviction shall be punished by an *additional* term of one year, unless such arming is an element of the offense such as carrying a concealed weapon. It should be noted that this additional term applies to any person who is a principal, whether or not such person is *personally* armed with a firearm (PC 12022).

Note, also, that any person who *personally uses* a dangerous or deadly weapon during the commission or attempted commission of a felony shall be punished by an *additional* and *consecutive* term of one year, unless use of the dangerous or deadly weapon is an element of the offense of which he was convicted (PC 12022(b).

Prior Serious Felony Conviction. Any person convicted of a serious felony as defined in PC 1192.7(c), in this state or another jurisdiction, shall receive an additional and consecutive sentence of 5 years in prison for each prior conviction (PC 667(a).

Prior Felony Conviction Outside of State. Every person who has been convicted in any other state government, country, or jurisdiction of an offense for which, if committed within this state, such person could have been punished under the laws of this state by imprisonment in a state prison, is punishable for any subsequent (later) offense committed within this state in the manner prescribed by law and to the same extent as if such prior conviction had taken place in a court in this state (PC 668).

A conviction of a felony in another state at a time when the act involved would have been a felony in California is a prior felony conviction in this state, provided the defendant served one year or more in prison for the offense in the other jurisdiction (PC 667.5(f).

Prior Federal Convictions. California will consider most prior federal felony convictions for the purposes of increasing the severity of an offense, as long as such federal offense would be a felony under California law (*People v. McVickers, 29 C. 2d 264*).

Violent Felonies. A consecutive and additional three-year prison term shall be imposed by the court for each prior prison term served for a violent felony upon conviction of a subsequent (later) conviction of a violent felony as listed below:

1. Murder or manslaughter.
2. Mayhem.
3. Rape as defined in PC 261(2).
4. Sodomy by force, etc.
5. Oral copulation by force, etc.
6. Lewd acts on a child under age 14 as defined in PC 288.
7. Any felony punishable by death or life imprisonment.
8. Any other felony in which the defendant has inflicted great bodily injury on any person other than an accomplice which has been proved as provided for in PC 12022.7 (PC 667.5).

A penalty of two years is added to the sentence of any person who *personally* uses a firearm in the commission or attempt to commit any felony including PC 245 (ADW) unless use of a firearm was an element of the offense of which such person was convicted (PC 12022.5).

Also, any person who, with intent to inflict such injury, inflicts great bodily injury on any person other than an accomplice, is subject to an additional three years in prison. As used in this section, "great bodily injury" means a significant or substantial physical injury. Note: this section does not apply to murder, manslaughter, PC 451 (arson) or PC 452 (unlawfully causing a fire) (PC12022.7).

Limit on Granting Probation. Generally, probation may not be granted to persons convicted of possession of dangerous or deadly weapons at the time of their arrest or during perpetration of most serious crimes such as arson, robbery, burglary, etc. Also, probation is not granted to persons who used or attempted to use a deadly weapon on another person or who willfully inflicted great bodily injury or torture on another during the perpetration of their crime. Exceptions may be made in unusual cases where the interest of justice would be served (PC 1203).

2.13 PRIOR CONVICTIONS—C.Y.A. COMMITMENT

There has been considerable confusion in the past as to the use of California Youth Authority prior convictions of a felony. C.Y.A. commitments can be used as prior convictions in all felony filings of the accusatory pleading providing that the C.Y.A. commitment was for a felony without the alternative of a county jail sentence. That is, if a juvenile was convicted in adult court of a straight felony and was thereafter committed to the Youth Authority, that commitment is a proper prior felony conviction regardless of the commitment date.

When a crime is punishable, in the discretion of the court, by imprisonment in the state prison or by fine or imprisonment in the county jail, it is a misdemeanor for all purposes under the following circumstances: When the court, upon committing the defendant to the California Youth Authority, designates the offense to be a misdemeanor (PC 17(b)(2). When a defendant is committed to the Youth Authority for a crime punishable, in the discretion of the court, by imprisonment in the state prison or by fine or imprisonment in the county jail, the offense shall, upon the discharge of the defendant from the Youth Authority, thereafter be deemed a misdemeanor for all purposes PC 17(b)(5).

Notwithstanding any other provision of law, no person convicted of
1. Murder,
2. Rape, or
3. Any other serious felony, as defined in PC 1192.7, committed when he or she was 18 years of age or older, shall be committed to the Youth Authority (Welfare and Institutions Code 1732.5).

This section was added by virtue of Proposition 8. The intent of the initiative measure is clear. Any person, 18 years or older at the time of the commission of any of the crimes enumerated in PC 1192.7, is not eligible for commitment to the California Youth Authority (C.Y.A.).

2.14 LESSER AND INCLUDED OFFENSES

In California there are several offenses, the commission of which necessarily includes lesser offenses. However, before a lesser offense may be said to constitute a necessary part of the greater offense, all of the legal elements (*corpus delicti*) of the lesser offense must be included in the elements of the greater offense (*People v. Greer, 30 Cal. 2d 589*). For example, every battery, which is a misdemeanor, includes an assault, but battery is the greater of the two offenses (*People v. McDaniels, 137 Cal. 192*).

Penal Code, Section 1159, states that "the jury or the judge, if a jury trial is waived, may find the defendant guilty of any offense, the commission of which is necessarily included in that with which he is charged, or of an attempt to commit the offense."

Examples of Lesser Included Offenses. The crime of simple assault is necessarily included in the crimes of battery, mayhem, assault with a deadly weapon, wife beating, rape, robbery, and sodomy with force. Petty theft is necessarily included in the crimes of grand theft and robbery. Contributing to the delinquency of a minor (CDM) is a necessarily included offense of statutory rape, child molesting, annoying or molesting a child under eighteen years, and using a minor to obtain and transport narcotics.

Examples of Lesser Offenses Not Included. The crime of robbery does not include the offense of receiving stolen property nor is the offense of child molesting necessarily included in the crime of oral copulation.

The crime of assault with a deadly weapon does not include battery or exhibiting a deadly weapon in an angry and threatening manner. Similarly, a charge of burglary does not include theft, attempted theft, or receiving stolen property.

2.15 WHEN JEOPARDY ATTACHES

The basic principle in the law of former jeopardy is that a person who has committed a criminal act shall be subject to but one prosecution for that act and that when that prosecution has resulted in a final judgment of conviction or if the defendant has been acquitted, or even if there is no formal verdict or finding that the defendant is not guilty, the case has proceeded to a stage equivalent in law to an acquittal, and no further prosecution of such defendant can be had for such act. Furthermore, a conviction by plea of guilty is a valid conviction which will bar a second prosecution (*People v. Golstein, 32 Cal. 432*).

In essence, the jeopardy rule prevents second prosecution for either the identical offense involved in the first trial or for another offense based upon the act constituting the offense charged in the first trial. Furthermore the defendant cannot be prosecuted a second time upon a charge of an attempt to commit such offense nor for any offense necessarily included therein, nor for an offense in which such offense is necessarily included.

When the defendant is convicted or acquitted or has been once placed in jeopardy upon an accusatory pleading, the conviction, acquittal, or jeopardy is a bar to another prosecution for the offense charged in such accusatory pleading, or for an attempt to commit the same, or for an offense necessarily included therein, of which he might have been convicted under the accusatory pleading (PC 1023).

If a defendant should be convicted of a lesser included offense and a greater offense subsequently results as an outgrowth of the lesser offense, the conviction of the lesser offense does not preclude a prosecution for the greater subsequent offense. For example, if a person is convicted of ADW, a lesser included offense to murder, and the victim subsequently expires within 3 years and a day, the defendant could be tried for the latter offense since at the time of the conviction for the assault, a homicide had not occurred and could not be charged against the defendant (PC 194).

Similarly, a conviction of a lower degree of a crime is an acquittal of the higher degree of that crime. A person charged with first-degree murder who is convicted of second-degree murder cannot, upon a reversal on appeal, be prosecuted for first-degree murder (*Green v. U.S., 335 U.S., 184*).

As previously pointed out, both the U.S. Constitution and the California Constitution state in part that "no person shall be . . . subject, for the same offense, to be twice placed in jeopardy." A similar provision is reflected in Penal Code, Sec. 687: "No person can be subjected to a second prosecution for a public offense for which he has once been prosecuted and convicted or acquitted."

Cases Where Jeopardy Does Not Attach. There can be no plea to former jeopardy in the following cases where the defendant is in pursuance of one criminal purpose or design but commits successive offenses which are actually separate:

1. Burglary will not bar a prosecution for receiving stolen property, even though such property represents the fruits of the burglary.
2. Robbery committed after an unlawful entry.
3. Possession of alcohol by a minor and public intoxication.
4. Additional assault after consummation of a robbery.
5. Soliciting perjury or subornation of perjury.
6. Rape and assault with a deadly weapon when the latter is shown to be unnecessary to commit forcible rape.
7. Abortion and practicing medicine without a license.
8. Drunkenness and drunk driving.
9. ADW and weapons violations.
10. Robbery and kidnapping for the purpose of robbery when one is not incidental to the other.

It should be noted that in the above examples, where both charges are based upon the same act, as where the kidnapping is an incident in the perpetration of the robbery, there can be but one conviction for one offense, resulting in a bar to a subsequent prosecution for the other offense.

TERMINOLOGY DEFINED—CHAPTER 2

See the Terminology Quiz at the end of this chapter.

1. Acquit: find not guilty.
2. Booking: recording an arrest, photographing, and fingerprinting.
3. Bribe: anything of value given to illegally influence another.
4. Consecutive sentences: one following after the other.
5. Due process: a legal hearing of some type.
6. Felony: a crime punishable by death or state prison.
7. Former jeopardy: previously acquitted of same crime, can't be retried.
8. Import: to imply, to signify something.
9. Infraction: an offense not punishable by imprisonment.
10. Justices: judges of appellate courts.
11. Knowingly: conscious of the act done.
12. Magistrate: any trial court judge.
13. Malice: a wish to injure, vex or annoy.
14. Misdemeanors: all crimes other than felonies and infractions.
15. Negligence: failing to use due care as required by law.
16. Ordinance: a city or county law.

17. Preponderance: majority of evidence, the most.
18. Real property: land, real estate.
19. Unwritten law: common law.
20. Willfully: willingness to do an act, intentional.

TRUE-FALSE QUIZ—CHAPTER 2

1. No act is a crime unless there is a valid statute declaring it a crime and providing a penalty for its violation.
2. The "unwritten law" is a legal defense to certain crimes involving husband and wife relationships.
3. The California Constitution provides that all crimes must be written in the English language.
4. Foreign words, even those of common usage in the U.S., may not be included in penal code statutes.
5. Vague and indefinite laws are in violation of the 14th Amendment of the U.S. Constitution.
6. When two laws punish exactly the same act as a crime, and they are in conflict, the latest in time will control.
7. According to Penal Code, Section 4, criminal statutes must be very strictly construed to be legal.
8. The word "willfully," when applied to the intent with which an act is done, requires a specific intent to violate the law.
9. The word "malice" means an intent to do a wrongful act.
10. Crime is classified into four levels of seriousness by the California Penal Code.
11. A felony is a crime punishable by death or imprisonment in the state prison.
12. The same punishment applicable to misdemeanors is also applicable to infractions in California.
13. If one commits a burglary and is sentenced to the county jail, he stands convicted of a misdemeanor.
14. Any crime which provides for punishment in either the state prison or county jail remains a felony for all purposes until the actual sentencing in court.
15. An infraction is *not* punishable by imprisonment.
16. A person charged with an infraction is *not* entitled to a trial by jury.
17. Except as otherwise provided by law, all provisions of law relating to misdemeanors shall apply to infractions.
18. When an act or omission is declared by statute to be a public offense, and no penalty is prescribed in any statute, the offense is punishable as a felony.
19. Except where a different punishment is prescribed by law for a felony, the minimum penalty is one year in state prison, or by fine or both.
20. Where a defendant is convicted of two or more misdemeanors, either in the same or separate prosecutions, consecutive sentences are valid.
21. The penalty for petty theft with a prior petty theft conviction is the same as for petty theft with a prior felony conviction.
22. The "Victim's Bill of Rights," provides that evidence, providing it is relevant, may *not* be excluded because of a mere technicality.
23. The general rule excluding hearsay evidence was not affected by the passage of Proposition Eight.
24. A jury may find a defendant guilty of any offense the elements of which are necessarily included in the offense with which he is charged.
25. If a defendant is found not guilty of a murder charge, then later he admits his guilt, he may be retried for the crime.

ESSAY-DISCUSSION QUESTIONS— CHAPTER 2

1. In order for an act or omission to be a crime, what two things must exist relative to statute law?
2. Briefly discuss the language requirements in our criminal statutes and the legal effect of vague or indefinite statutes.
3. When two laws punish exactly the same act or omission as crimes and they are in conflict, which one controls or takes precedent?
4. Briefly define the words (a) corruptly, (b) nighttime, and (c) process, as used in the Penal Code and explained in the text.
5. What is the legal difference between a felony and a misdemeanor?
6. What are the two major differences between a misdemeanor and an infraction?
7. What classification of crime does a person stand convicted of who is sentenced to the county jail following conviction of burglary?
8. What is the punishment for petty theft with a prior conviction of petty theft?
9. List five (5) of the ten (10) changes brought about by passage of Proposition 8, "Victim's Bill of Rights," as given in your text.
10. What is meant by "lesser and included in offense"?

TERMINOLOGY QUIZ—CHAPTER 2

Match terms and definitions by placing the correct number in the parentheses. Answers may be written on a separate sheet for submission to the instructor at the instructor's direction.

1. Acquit
2. Booking
3. Bribe
4. Consecutive sentence
5. Due process
6. Felony
7. Former jeopardy
8. Import
9. Infraction
10. Justices
11. Knowingly
12. Magistrate
13. Malice
14. Misdemeanor
15. Negligence
16. Ordinance
17. Preponderance
18. Real property
19. Unwritten law
20. Willfully

( ) Willingness to do an act, intentional
( ) Judges of appellate courts
( ) An offense not punishable by imprisonment
( ) Found not guilty
( ) Conscious of the act done
( ) To imply, to signify something
( ) Any trial court judge
( ) Recording an arrest, fingerprinting
( ) Anything of value to illegally influence
( ) A wish to injure, vex, or annoy
( ) One following after the other
( ) A legal hearing of some type
( ) Common law
( ) A city or county law
( ) A crime punishable by death or state prison

CHAPTER 3

The Elements of Crime—*Corpus Delicti*

3.1 THE *CORPUS DELICTI*

Corpus delicti means "the essential elements of a crime" or "the body of the crime." It has to do with the rules of evidence which govern proof of the commission of crimes, particularly as concern the "act" element thereof and the commission of the act by human agency.

The *corpus delicti,* or "substance of the crime," is applicable to any crime and relates particularly to the "act" element of criminality, i.e., that a certain prohibited act has been committed or result accomplished and that it was committed or accomplished by a criminal human agency.

As a practical matter, the Penal Code definition of a crime clearly states those essential elements necessary to the commission of that particular crime in terms of certain words used in the section. Thus, in the crime of burglary, reference is made to anyone who *enters* a certain kind of *structure with intent to commit grand or petty theft or any felony.* In this case, the certain essential elements to the commission of this crime are reflected by analysis of the crime.

Proof of *Corpus Delicti.* The prosecution must establish the *corpus delicti* of a crime, and failure to do so is a bar to further prosecution. The amount of proof, however, need not go beyond *prima facie* (on its face, on first view) proof, and the prosecution is said to have a *prima facie* case when evidence in its favor is sufficiently strong for the defendant to be called on to answer it.

Circumstantial Evidence. The *corpus delicti* of a crime may be proven solely by circumstantial evidence. Thus, as previously stated, the essential elements of the crime of murder may be established without producing the body of the victim. Similarly, a genuine, unaltered photograph depicting defendants involved in a sex act was held admissible and sufficient to prove the *corpus delicti* of the crime denounced by PC 288 (*People v. Doggett, 83 C.A. 2d 405*).

Identity of Perpetrator. The identity of the perpetrator of a criminal offense is not a necessary and essential part of the *corpus delicti,* nor is such necessary to establishing proof of the *corpus delicti.* Thus, in order to prove the *corpus delicti* of burglary, it is necessary to prove that an entry was made; however, it is not necessary that the person who entered be known to the police.

Proof by Confession or Admission of Perpetrator. The law makes no provision for establishing the *corpus delicti* of a crime solely upon the confession or admission of the accused (*People v. Mehaffey, 32 Cal. 2d 535*). Such proof must be established independently of any extrajudicial statement made by a defendant. If this were not so, undoubtedly countless individuals would be prosecuted for crimes which they in fact did not commit based merely on their confessions or admissions to the commission of such an act. For example, if a suspect is apprehended in the act of burglarizing a residence, is admonished of his constitutional rights, and thereafter admits the offense, such admission or confession may be used to support additional evidence in establishing the *corpus delicti* of the burglary offense.

If, however, the same suspect admits several additional burglaries, the location of which is unknown to himself or the police, he cannot be held criminally liable inasmuch as it would be impossible to establish the commission of these additional crimes without proving the *corpus delicti* of each independently of the suspect's extrajudicial confessions or admissions.

3.2   THE CRIMINAL ACT

Penal Code, Section 20, states that in order to constitute a crime, there must be a unity of act and intent, or criminal negligence. The joint operation of an act and general criminal intent is essential to constitute any crime (*People v. Sanche, 35 C. 2d 522*).

An act is simply defined as "an effect produced through conscious exertion of will." The act varies with each crime, and for that reason it is difficult to define. In some cases it may be a physical or muscular movement, while in others it may be an omission to act. The act may involve passive participation in crime, activity outside of this state which results in a crime within the state, a series of acts, proximate results, or just the mere doing of something, i.e., the result of some human agency. Thus, in homicide cases the act is the killing of a human being; in larceny it is the taking and carrying away of personal property of another; in arson it is the burning of real or personal property; in rape it is the having of sexual intercourse. In each of these cases the act is muscular or physical in character, however it need not always be, as in the case of omission to act or passively participating in a crime.

Omission to Act. A mere omission to act may be sufficient to complete a crime. Such omissions are generally characteristic of those crimes which involve the performance of an official duty imposed by law. In many such crimes there is a lack of physical movement on the part of the perpetrator, such as in the failure to provide a minor child with necessities (PC 270), causing a child to suffer (PC 273a), or contributing to the delinquency of a minor by omitting the performance of a legally imposed duty.

Under certain circumstances a factual situation may be sufficient to give rise to a legal duty to act for the benefits of another. For example, one who undertakes to render aid to another may not be legally bound to do so, but having commenced such an undertaking, he cannot later abandon such a purpose if the person being aided will suffer further harm as the result of partial performance. Ordinarily, however, the criminal law will recognize a negative act (omission to act) only if the one who has failed to take affirmative action was under a legal duty to do what was not done, with the explanation that such a legal duty may exist because of (1) an express provision of law, (2) a legal relation, (3) a factual situation, or (4) a contract.

The law holds that there is no distinction between a person acting wrongfully and failing to act where there is a legal duty to act, the latter being just as much manifestation of will as acting positively when there is a duty not to act.

Passive Participation. In some classes of crime, criminal liability may result from passive participation in a criminal act wherein little physical or muscular activity takes place. For example, a female who submits to an illegal abortion is a passive participant in such an act.

The Court held in *People v. Chapman, 28 NW 896, (Michigan),* that the defendant-husband of the prosecutrix was not a mere passive onlooker, but a passive participant when he, desiring to obtain a divorce, agreed with one "R" that the latter should persuade the defendant's wife to commit adultery which subsequently resulted in the crime of forcible rape.

Acts Outside the State. An act may take place outside of this state which will result in a crime within the state. PC 497 provides that "Every person who, in another state or county, steals or embezzles the property of another, or receives such property knowing it to have been stolen or embezzled, and brings the same into this state, may be convicted and punished in the same manner as if such larceny, or embezzlement, or receiving, had been committed in this state."

When the commission of a public offense, commenced outside the state, was consummated within its boundaries by a defendant, himself outside the state, through the intervention of an innocent or guilty agent or any other means proceeding directly from said defendant, he is liable to punishment therefor in this state in any competent court within the jurisdictional territory of which the offense is consummated (PC 778).

Conversely, an act may take place within this state which is not criminal in nature, but which results in a crime without the state. PC 778a states that "whenever a person, with intent to commit a crime, does any act within this state in execution or part execution of such intent, which culminates in the commission of a crime, either within or without this state, such person is punishable for such crime in this state in the same manner as if the same had been committed entirely within this state." Thus, where defendant sent a box of poisoned candy from San Francisco to a person in Delaware with intent to cause her death, which it did, the court held that the case could be prosecuted in this state for the crime of murder (*People v. Botkin, 132 Cal. 232*).

Person Who Aided Crime in State from Without, Found Here. A person who at the time is out of this state who causes, aids, advises, or encourages any person to commit a crime within this state, and is afterwards found within this state, is punishable in the same manner as if he or she had been within this state when he or she caused, aided, advised or encouraged the commission of such crime (*PC 778b*).

Jurisdiction: Offenses Committed Partly in One Jurisdiction and Partly in Another. When a public offense is committed in part in one jurisdictional territory and in part in another, or the acts or effects constituting the offense occur in two or more jurisdictions, the jurisdiction of such offense is in any competent court within either jurisdiction (*PC 781*). This section applies in cases such as kidnapping, child molesting, or even murder, where the victim is taken from one place to another. It is also applicable in cases where it is difficult to determine when and where the crime began and ended or where there are repeated assaults that occur in more than one city, county, or other jurisdictional area.

Offenses Committed on Boundary of Two or More Jurisdictions. When a public offense is committed on the boundary of two or more jurisdictional territories, or within 500 yards thereof, the jurisdiction of such offense is in any competent court within either jurisdiction (*PC 782*). As in the instance above, this section is applicable where it is difficult to determine exactly where a crime was committed relative to city, county, or state lines.

Act of Possession. A person may be guilty of a crime where his act has no immediate effect upon the person or property of another. For example, mere possession of contraband material such as narcotics without prescription, certain firearms, or burglars' tools would constitute a violation of the laws prohibiting such materials.

One Act Affecting Several Victims. Though there be but one act or action and one intent but more than one victim of the crime, there are instances in which there are as many crimes committed as there are persons victimized. For example, if one were to shoot and kill a person, and the fatal bullet continued through the first person, inflicting mortal wounds upon a second person, there is but one act resulting in two homicides (*People v. Majors, 65 Cal. 138*). Similarly, where "A" shoots at "B" but misses and hits "C" (see "Transferred Intent") there is but one act, however, "A" is guilty of an assault upon "B" and the murder of "C" based on the doctrine of transferred intent.

Several Acts Resulting in One Offense. There are some offenses which, by their very nature, require that the wrongdoer become involved in several physical acts in order to perpetrate a crime. For example, one may embezzle from his employer on several occasions for one common purpose, motive, or design, which may result in one act of grand theft rather than several acts of petty theft. Many of these acts will ultimately result in only one offense being committed and in such a case, a conviction or acquittal based on one portion of the entire act is a bar to another prosecution for the same offense which involves another portion of the act. Thus, an acquittal of the charge of receiving stolen property is a bar to another prosecution for receiving stolen property where the property is involved in the two cases, though not the same, was received by the defendant at the same time (*People v. Willard, 92 Cal. 482*).

3.3 CONCURRENCE OF ACT AND INTENT—MULTIPLE OFFENSES

Punishment for two offenses arising from the same act is prohibited by the Constitution of the United States and again by the California Constitution, Article I, Section 13. Penal Code, Section 654, states that "an act or omission which is made punishable in different ways by different provisions of this code may be punished under either of such provisions, but in no case can it be punished under more than one; an acquittal or conviction and sentence under either one bars a prosecution for the same act or omission under any other."

Dual Convictions—Multiple Punishment. Penal Code, Section 654, also prohibits multiple punishment for a single act which may violate more than one statute. The prohibition against multiple punishment of a single act, however, is not limited to necessarily included offenses (*People v. Bauer 1 C. 3d 1968*). Thus, where the defendant was charged with violation of the Vehicle Code, Section 23102(a), driving under the influence of intoxicating liquor, entered a plea of guilty, and was sentenced, and four days thereafter was subsequently charged with violating Vehicle Code, Section 14601 (driving a motor vehicle at a time when her operator's license had been revoked), the court held that both offenses were based on the same motor vehicle operation. Hence, the second prosecution was barred by Penal Code, Section 654, because that section prohibits multiple prosecutions, based upon the operation of an automobile on one occasion (*People v. Morris, 237 A.C.A. 919*).

Similarly, if only a single act is charged as the basis of the multiple convictions, only one punishment can result. Thus where one commits an illegal abortion and the victim dies, the defendant may be prosecuted for second-degree murder or for illegal abortion, but not for both offenses (*People v. Brown, 48 Cal. 2d 577*).

Penal Code, Section 654, precludes multiple punishment not only where one act is involved, but also in cases where there is a course of conduct which violates more than one statute and comprises an indivisible transaction. For example, where a burglary, robbery, and assault were all incident to and a means of obtaining the victim's possessions, it was immaterial that the burglary was complete before the robbery and the assault, and judgments of conviction must be reversed insofar as they impose multiple punishment. The court held in this case that all offenses committed by the defendant were "incident to one objective." As was pointed out in *People v. McFarland, 58 Cal. 2d 748*, the fact that the burglary was complete in each case before the robbery and the assault is immaterial (*People v. Helms, 242 A.C.A. 528*).

Penal Code, Section 654, prohibits double punishment and not double conviction (see section entitled "Former Jeopardy"). Thus, where a trial court has erroneously imposed double punishment, the Appellate Court, in considering an appeal, will eliminate the effect of the judgment only as to the penalty imposed for the lesser offense and will permit the punishment for the most serious offense to stand (*People v. McFarland*).

3.4   PROXIMATE CAUSE

Some causal relationship must exist between the defendant's act or the act of another in his behalf, and the prohibited result which constitutes the crime. This causal relationship is said to exist when a defendant's act was the proximate cause of the injury caused. To be proximate, the defendant's act need be only a contributing cause, as in the case of concurrent acts of two persons acting with a common design, or in some instances if they are concurrent but independent of each other.

Generally speaking, it may be said that the defendant in a criminal case is not liable for remote and indirect consequences of his acts; he is liable for the direct and proximate consequences for such acts. Thus, a defendant is liable criminally, assuming the requisite intent is present, if his act or omission was the proximate cause of the death of the decedent in a homicide case, if the injury sustained which ultimately causes death was a natural and probable consequence of the defendant's act.

The results intended by the perpetrator are proximate if they, in fact, take place, regardless of time or place. This fact is illustrated in the previously mentioned case wherein the defendant in California sent a box of poisoned candy to a person in Delaware, who ate the candy and died.

More Than One Proximate Cause. There may be more than one proximate cause of death. When the conduct of two or more persons contributes concurrently as proximate causes of a death, the conduct of each is a proximate cause of the death regardless of the extent to which each contributes to the death. A cause is concurrent if it was operative at the moment of death and acted with another cause to produce the death (*Witkin, California Crimes, Sections 78, 295*).

Proximate Cause—Felony-Murder Rule. A person who intentionally commits an unlawful act and, in so doing, inflicts unforeseen injury, is criminally liable for such injury. The "felony-murder rule" suggests that any felony resulting in the loss of human life is murder. Such is not currently the case in California. The leading case in California is *People v. Washington, 62 Cal. 2d*, wherein the defendant, Washington, appealed from a judgment of conviction of the offenses of robbery and murder, directing his argument primarily to the matter of the legal propriety of his conviction of the charge of murder. Defendant Washington, together with a co-suspect named James Ball, attempted to rob a service station operator who subsequently shot and killed the suspect, Ball. Defendant Washington was convicted of the murder of co-suspect Ball on the felony-murder theory that any killing done through the perpetration of first-degree murder is imputed to the co-suspect. Appellant Washington's motion for a new trial was denied by District Court of Appeal, who affirmed the trial court's judgment.

Washington later appealed to the California State Supreme Court, who thereafter reversed both the Appellate and lower court rulings. The Supreme Court held that a defendant cannot be convicted of the murder of a co-defendant (or anyone else) under the felony-murder rule where the killing is done by the victim in an attempt to resist the commission of the felony. For a defendant to be found guilty of murder under the felony-murder rule, the act of killing must be committed by the defendant or by his accomplice acting in furtherance of their common design. However, if the defendant or his accomplice initiates a gun battle, and someone is killed by the victim, or the police, in resistance of such activity, the defendant can be found guilty of first-degree murder (*People v. Antick 15C. 3d 79*).

3.5 CRIMINAL INTENT— HOW MANIFESTED

Criminal intent is the second of the two elements necessary to the commission of every offense. Intent is a mental element of the perpetrator, often referred to as *mens rea* or the guilty mind of the individual who fosters a criminal intent. Not all crimes require the same intent. Some crimes, by their very nature, require a particular designated state of mind, such as burglary, larceny (theft), assault, etc. In these crimes, the perpetrator must have manifested specific intent to do or accomplish a certain act in carrying out a criminal purpose. For example, to commit burglary, one must have intended to enter a structure *with the specific intent* to steal or to commit a felony. Entry of a structure without such intent would be insufficient to prove a *prima facie* case of burglary but might suffice to prove a case of unlawful entry, trespassing, or some other lesser included offense which does not require a specific designated state of mind to commit. A second example is seen in the crime of theft. Here there must generally exist a specific designated state of mind on the part of the perpetrator to permanently deprive the owner of his property. Thus, a temporary taking with intent to return the property is not theft; or, the taking of property in jest or as a practical joke would not constitute theft. Similarly, temporarily depriving one of a motor vehicle (joy riding) is difficult to prove as theft, since the state of mind of the perpetrator was not to permanently deprive the person of his property, which is requisite to the commission of the crime of theft.

Intent may be generally defined as "a design, resolve or determination of the mind" (*Bovier's Law Dictionary*); or as "the act or fact of intending or purposing; intent, purpose which is formed in the mind"; and similarly, "design, resolve; determination of the mind" (*Cochran's Law Dictionary*).

Penal Code, Section 21, states that "The intent or intention is manifested by the circumstances connected with the offense and the sound mind and discretion of the accused." In view of this section, it is important to note that all persons are presumed capable of committing crime with the possible exception of those listed in Penal Code, Section 26, (persons capable of committing crimes). Further, Penal Code,

Section 1026, presumes that the defendant upon trial "shall be conclusively presumed to have been sane at the time the offense is alleged to have been committed."

An unlawful act is presumed to have been done with intent to violate the law (*People v. Severino, 122 C.A. 2d 172*). Also, the intent to commit a crime can be inferred from established facts and circumstances (*People v. Ramirez, 101 C.A. 2d 50*). Intent to commit a crime may be proven by proof of surrounding circumstances and inferences drawn from proven facts (*People v. Ross, 105 C.A. 2d 235*).

3.6 TYPES OF INTENT

There are generally three types of intent which may be manifested by the perpetrator of a crime and which will accompany the criminal act.

1. General Intent. General intent is the type of intent which is inferred from the mere doing of an act, or failure to act, when prohibited or commanded by law. General intent may even exist in the presence of a belief that the act is right and lawful.

When a person acts without justification or excuse and commits an act prohibited as a crime, his intention to commit the act constitutes criminal intent. In such a case, the existence of the criminal intent is presumed from the commission of the act itself.

The intent which is necessary to the commission of a crime does not necessarily involve an intention to do a known criminal act. Thus, where an act is prohibited by law, the criminal intent necessary to violate that law is nothing more than an intention to do the act, regardless whether the wrongdoer knows that it is criminal, assuming that he is able to form such a criminal intent. Thus, if "X" beats "Y" with a hammer and kills him, "X" is presumed to have intended to kill "Y." A general criminal intent is sufficient in all cases in which a specific or other particular intent or mental element is not required by the law defining the crime. Some crimes, by their very nature, are perpetrated by the intentional doing of an act, and there is no necessity of proving the actual intent to commit the crime. General intent statutes enacted under the police power are good examples of this rule of law (*People v. Heal, 40 C.A. 2d 115*).

The law presumes that persons intend the necessary and direct consequences of their acts (*U.S. v. Dried Fruit Association of California, 4 F.R.D. 1*). The intentional doing of an act expressly prohibited by statute constitutes the offense denounced by the law regardless of good motive or ignorance of criminal character (*People v. Reznick, 75 C.A. 2d 832*). In addition, a person is presumed to intend to do things which he does, and especially so when they are done in the commission of a crime, excepting where the intent must be proved as a necessary element, such as in specific intent cases (*People v. Head, 9 C.A. 2d 647*).

The presence or absence of a specific intent constituting an element of an offense may be inferred by the jury from circumstances surrounding an unlawful act (*People v. Maciel, 71 C.A. 213*). Generally, one is presumed to have intended to have caused the immediate and natural consequences of his act, but where the act becomes criminal only when performed with a particular intent, such intent must be alleged and proven (*People v. Pineda, 41 C.A. 2d 100*).

2. Specific Intent. When a crime consists not merely in doing the act, but in doing it with a specific intent, the existence of that intent is an essential element. The existence of criminal intent is not presumed from the commission of the act, but the specific intent must be proven as an independent factor.

Depending on the particular wording of a criminal statute, a crime may be so defined as to require not merely a criminal intent on the part of the perpetrator, but a designated state of mind necessary to culminating an act. Usually such crimes are written in such a manner as to indicate the specific intent necessary by the inclusion of descriptive words such as "for the purpose of obtaining ransom." Additionally, most crimes, with the exception of the theft statute, will also include the phrase "with intent" to signify the necessity of proving, as an independent factor, the existence of *specific intent* to commit the particular crime. Thus, in the crime of burglary, specific intent is a necessary element to the crime inasmuch as the ultimate objective in the perpetration of the crime must be entry of a structure with the *intent* (specifically) *to steal* or *commit a felony*. Therefore, if a subject entered a structure, observed the interior for a time, and then decided to steal something of value within the structure, it would be difficult to prove a specific designated state of mind to steal *prior* to entry. In such a case, the perpetrator could not be guilty of burglary because the *corpus delicti* of this crime requiring specific intent is not satisfied; theft would undoubtedly be the charge instead.

Where the criminal intent which is implied from the doing of the act is not sufficient, and there must be a specific intent, the defendant, to be guilty, must have "specifically contemplated" the ultimate act,

otherwise there can be no crime, and he is not guilty (*People v. Armentrout, 118 C.A. Supp., 761*).

Certain penal statutes provide for the "assault to commit a crime" (e.g. sodomy, rape, robbery, mayhem, etc.), or the "attempt to commit a crime." In both cases, the specific intent, while not necessarily requisite to the actual commission of the consummated crime in these cases, would be necessary in proving an assault to commit or an attempt to commit such crimes. Thus, in the crime of assault with intent to commit rape (PC 220), proof must show that the assault was committed with the intent (specifically) to rape the victim. Similarly, an attempt to commit a crime requires the existence of a specific intent to commit the crime attempted (*People v. Gallardo, 41 Cal. 2d 57*).

3. Constructive (Transferred) Intent. Transferred intent, also referred to as constructive intent, involves liability or imputability on the part of the perpetrator for the unintended consequences of his acts. Thus, where a person, engaged in an unlawful act, commits another unlawful act, unintended by him, the intent to commit the first act is carried over to the act actually committed, and is called "transferred or constructive intent." Thus, it is not essential to the commission of a crime that the wrongdoer should commit the very act intended by him. Where several persons cooperate to rape another, and while accomplishing this purpose the victim is killed, all are guilty of homicide, though the killing is done unintentionally and without malice.

Where one intends to assault or kill a certain person, and by mistake or inadvertence he assaults or kills another, it is nevertheless a crime, and the intent is transferred from the party who was intended to the other party (*People v. Neal, 97 C.A. 2d 668*). In a manner of speaking, the law treats as intentional all consequences due to that form of negligence which is distinguished as recklessness.

3.7   HOW INTENT IS PROVED

Criminal intent may be proven by circumstantial evidence and may be inferred from the manner in which the unlawful act was committed (*People v. Hunt, 59 Cal. 430, 433*). General intent may also be proved by direct evidence, such as by words spoken by the defendant or by the circumstances surrounding the crime. The accused may have told someone of his intentions, for example, or he may have made a statement such as "this is a stick-up" during the commission of the crime. Words spoken by the accused during an assault may very well reveal his intent, i.e., rape, mayhem, sodomy, etc. For the purpose of proving intent, the conduct of the defendant before, during, and after the offense is admissible to prove intent (*People v. Welsh, 63 Cal. 167; People v. Collins, 60 Cal. App. 263*).

3.8 INTENT IN NEGLIGENCE CASES

In crimes which consist of negligence to observe proper care in performing an act, or in culpable (wrongful) failure to perform a duty, criminal intent consists in the state of mind which necessarily accompanies the negligent act or culpable omission.

To constitute criminal negligence, one must enter into an act with some appreciable measure of wantonness or flagrant or reckless disregard of the safety of others or willful indifference (*People v. Drigas, 111 C.A. 42*).

In some crimes the criminal act or omission to act consists in a mere neglect to observe proper caution in the performance of an otherwise lawful act or in culpable failure to perform a legally imposed duty. Traffic violations and child neglect cases are graphic examples of situations wherein the criminal intent requisite to such offenses may be supplied by the obvious lack of due care, caution, or circumspection which in essence amounts to negligence. It will be noted that this concept of intent closely resembles that of general intent referred to in the preceding paragraphs.

Negligence consists in reckless or indifferent omission to do what a reasonable and prudent person would do, or a similar reckless or indifferent doing of what a prudent person would not do under the same or similar circumstances.

There are generally five elements to consider in order to find intent from criminal negligence:
1. Defendant must have a legal duty (contractual relationship) imposed upon the defendant toward a person, group, or society in general, as a result of a natural or professional duty.
2. Defendant must know, or reasonably should know that he has a legal duty and that there is a present existing danger.
3. There must be an apparent ability upon the part of the defendant to perform the legally imposed duty.
4. It must be shown that the defendant failed to perform the duty which is legally imposed.
5. It must appear that the defendant's negligent act or omission was the cause of the injury sustained.

An operator of a motor vehicle who drove in excess of fifty miles per hour in a residential area and killed a pedestrian whom he did not see was guilty of "gross negligence" and of manslaughter (*People v. Flores, 83 C.A. 2d 11*). Also, the failure to use due care in the treatment of another where a duty to furnish such care exists is sufficient to constitute that form of manslaughter which results from an act of omission (*People v. Chavez, 77 C.A. 2d 621*).

A lack of "due caution and circumspection," referred to in PC 192 (manslaughter) places a criminal responsibility on a defendant who acts without due caution and circumspection and is equivalent to "criminal negligence" (*People v. Hurley, 13 C.A. 2d 208*).

Malice. The term "malice" has been used synonymously with general intent and is usually regarded as connoting a mental condition more intent on harm or injury than is involved in general intent to commit a crime. Malice means a wrongful act done intentionally without justification or excuse. It involves a disposition to injure another, a willful disregard of the rights or safety of others. Malice is most often used in connection with particular crimes such as murder, malicious mischief, extortion, malicious prosecution, assault with caustic chemicals, and other similar crimes.

Malice—Express and Implied. Malice is *express* when there is manifested a deliberate intention unlawfully to take away the life of a fellow creature. It is *implied,* when no considerable provocation appears, or when the circumstances attending the killing show an abandoned and malignant heart.

When it is shown that the killing resulted from the intentional doing of an act with express or implied malice, as defined above, no other mental state need be shown to establish the mental state of malice aforethought. Neither an awareness of the obligation to act within the general body of laws regulating society nor acting despite such awareness is included within the definition of malice (PC 188).

Malice requires something more than criminal negligence; it requires a greater kind of social harm than is involved in criminal negligence and yet does not require an actual intent to cause the resulting harm. In one case the courts stated that "malice may be said to exist (in a legal sense) whenever there has been a wrongful or intentional killing of another without lawful excuse or mitigating circumstances" (*State v. Williams, 185 M.C. 643*).

The state of mind required for malice, when less than an actual intent to cause the wrongful act, includes a vicious or callous disregard of the likelihood of such harm resulting from what is being done.

It is this viciousness or callousness which distinguishes malice from criminal negligence.

Malice, in a legal sense, means a wrongful act, done intentionally, without just or legal cause or excuse (*People v. Taylor 36 Cal. 255*). Where a defendant, having provoked and instigated a fist fight, subsequently draws and uses a knife on his adversary, such evidence will show malice with an intent to kill (*People v. Hoover, 107 C.A. 635*).

3.9 MOTIVE AND INTENT DISTINGUISHED

Motive is never indispensible to a crime or criminal prosecution, nor is it an essential element of a crime. Motive is the desire or inducement which incites or stimulates a person to do an act, as contrasted with intent, which is the purpose or resolve to do an act. A bad motive will not necessarily make an act a crime, nor will a good motive prevent an act from being a crime. Thus, if one administers a lethal drug to a terminal cancer patient to hasten death and to relieve pain and suffering, while the motive, in the eyes of some persons, may be good, the act itself is no less criminal homicide. Similarly, a parent who neglects to provide medical aid for a dependent child, in violation of a criminal statute, cannot thereafter excuse himself on the ground that he was actuated in such refusal by religious motives.

The law does not seek to punish a bad motive, but only the criminal acts that result from such a motive. Thus, unless one's ellicit motive to do an act denounced by statute as a crime actually results in a criminal act through the existence of a union, or joint operation of an act, intent, or criminal negligence, there is no crime. For example, one may be moved to steal a car. This is a bad motive; however, should he mistakenly steal his own car, though the motive exists and requisite acts take place, the criminal intent which is manifest to the commission of a crime is lacking.

Motive, while not a necessary element of a crime, may help to prove the intent necessary to the consummation of a crime. For example, in murder, the emotional urge of the perpetrator may not only aid in his identification, but may assist greatly in establishing the purpose or intent of his act. Or, in the crime of embezzlement, one's reason or moving cause (motive) for stealing from his employer, such as an overdue gambling debt, will help in proving the specific intent (fraudulent appropriation) necessary to the commission of the crime of embezzlement.

As stated previously, motive is *not* part of the *corpus delicti* of any crime and need not be proved

(*People v. Larrios, 220 Cal. 236*). Evidence of motive, however, is oftentimes valuable in removing doubt and completing proof which might otherwise be unsatisfactory. The motive may either be shown by direct testimony or inferred from the facts and surrounding of the act. Motive, in such cases, then becomes a circumstance to be considered by the court or jury. By the same token, *absence of motive* may be a circumstance in favor of the accused and can be given such weight as the jury deems proper.

Evidence of motive is admissible and may be used:

1. To show the intent with which the act was committed (*People v. Miller, 121 Cal. 343*).
2. To rebut a claim of self-defense (*People v. Brown, 130 Cal. 591*).
3. To rebut a claim of insanity by showing the rational nature of defendant's actions (*People v. Donlan, 135 Cal. 489*).
4. To remove doubt as to the identity of the perpetrator (*People v. Wright, 144 Cal. 161*).
5. To help determine the degree of the crime (*People v. Soeder, 150 Cal. 12*).
6. To help determine the issue of justification or excusability of the act (*People v. Soeder, 150 Cal. 12*).

3.10 INTOXICATION AS AFFECTING INTENT

In California, drunkenness, whether voluntary or involuntary, is never an excuse for the commission of a crime. However, in considering the effect upon the guilt of a defendant the law makes a distinction between intoxication at the time of the commission of the offense which is voluntary, and intoxication which is involuntary.

Voluntary Intoxication. Intoxication of a person is voluntary if it results from his willing use of any intoxicating liquor, drug or other substance, knowing that it is capable of an intoxicating effect or when he willingly assumes the risk of that effect (*People v. Wyatt, 22 Cal. App. 3d 671*). Voluntary drunkenness furnishes no ground of exemption from criminal responsibility or limitation thereof, except (a) where drunkenness has produced insanity, in which case the exemption is based on insanity and not on drunkenness, and (b) where a specific intent is essential to constitute the crime, in which case the fact of intoxication may negate its existence.

No act committed by a person while in a state of voluntary intoxication is less criminal by reason of his having been in such condition. Evidence of voluntary intoxication shall not be admitted to negate the *capacity* to form any mental states for the crimes charged, including, but not limited to (1) purpose, (2) intent, (3) knowledge, (4) premeditation, (5) deliberation, or (6) malice aforethought, with which the accused committed the act.

Evidence of voluntary intoxication is admissible *solely* on the issue of whether or not the defendant *actually formed* a required specific intent, premeditated, deliberated, or harbored malice aforethought, when a specific intent crime is charged.

Voluntary intoxication includes the voluntary ingestion, injection, or taking by any other means of any intoxicating liquor, drug, or other substance (PC 22).

While drunkenness itself is not an excuse for committing crime, it may be a defense when a particular motive, purpose, or intent constitutes a necessary element of the *corpus delicti* of the crime committed, and the defendant was in such an intoxicated state that he did not form that requisite state of mind necessary to the commission of the crime. Thus, in the case of burglary, where specific intent is a part of the *corpus delicti,* one who was in such an intoxicated state that he did not form the specific intent necessary could raise a defense to the commission of such a crime based on lack of awareness and ability to form the specific intent necessary.

When specific intent is an element of a crime, it is a matter for the jury to determine whether defendant was so intoxicated that he did not form a criminal intent (*People v. Sutton, 17 C.A. 2d, 561*).

Involuntary Intoxication. Intoxication is said to be involuntary when a person does not willingly and knowingly consume intoxicants, but is either fraudulently induced to partake of intoxicants, or does so in such a manner that he is not cognizant of such a fact. Where a person becomes involuntarily intoxicated, the law recognizes the fact that such a person cannot be held criminally responsible for his acts. Rather, he is placed in the category of those who under Penal Code, Section 26, are incapable of committing crimes because they are not fully conscious thereof. However, depending on the extent or degree of intoxication, a person involuntarily intoxicated may have a greater or lesser ability to appreciate what he is doing, and his intoxication may be considered in the same manner and to the same extent as if he were voluntarily intoxicated.

3.11 DIMINISHED CAPACITY

The defense of "diminished capacity" was abolished by passage of Proposition 8. Defendants utilizing this defense in the past maintained that due to intoxication, trauma, mental illness, or the effect of too much blood sugar on the brain, they did not have the *capacity* to form the necessary criminal intent to commit the crime of which they were accused.

Evidence of diminished capacity or of a mental disorder may still be considered by the court, but only at the time of sentencing or other disposition or commitment after the issue of guilt or innocence has already been determined (PC 25(c)).

TERMINOLOGY DEFINED—CHAPTER 3

See the Terminology Quiz at the end of this chapter.

1. Abet: encourage or assist another in committing a crime.
2. Accessory: aiding or concealing a *felon after* the crime.
3. Accomplice: one who aids a principal in committing a crime.
4. Concurrent: at the same time, e.g., concurrent sentences.
5. Confession: statement including acknowledgment of guilt.
6. Constructive (transferred) intent: liability for unintended consequences of an act.
7. Consummated: completed, accomplished.
8. Crime: a public offense for which punishment is provided.
9. Embezzlement: theft by one to whom property is entrusted.
10. Extrajudicial: outside the court.
11. Intent: mental purpose of, or resolve to do an act.
12. *Mens rea:* a guilty mind or wrongful purpose.
13. Motive: reason for or moving cause.
14. Omission: failure to act, especially when required by law.
15. Perpetrator: active participant or person responsible.
16. *Prima facie:* valid on its face, literally: "first face."
17. Principal: anyone involved in the initial commission of a crime.
18. Proximate cause: direct or contributing cause.
19. Specific intent: a particular mental purpose.
20. Theft: stealing with intent to *permanently* deprive.

TRUE-FALSE QUIZ—CHAPTER 3

1. Before a defendant can be convicted of a crime, the prosecution must first establish the *corpus delicti* of the offense.
2. A defendant may be convicted solely on the basis of an extrajudicial confession without first establishing the *corpus delicti* by independent evidence.
3. In order for a conduct to constitute a crime, there must be a unity of act and intent or criminal negligence.
4. A person can legally be found guilty of theft if he in fact intended to steal another's property, but accidentally took his own.
5. In some cases a mere omission to act may constitute a crime.
6. An act may take place outside this state which will result in a crime within this state.
7. Punishment for two offenses arising from the same act is prohibited by the U.S. and State Constitutions.
8. A proximate cause need not exist between the defendant's act and the result which constitutes a crime.
9. A person who intentionally commits an unlawful act, and in so doing inflicts unforeseen injury on another is criminally liable for such injury.
10. The terms "specific intent" and "constructive intent" are synonymous.
11. General intent is that type which is presumed from the mere doing of an act prohibited by law.
12. The law presumes that a person intends the necessary and direct consequences of his acts.
13. Burglary is a good example of a crime which requires constructive intent.
14. Even though no criminal intent is present, one may still be guilty of a crime if criminal negligence is present.
15. Motive is an essential part of the *corpus delicti* of a crime.

ESSAY—DISCUSSION QUESTIONS— CHAPTER 3

1. What is the prosecution's responsibility relative to the *corpus delicti* in obtaining a conviction for any crime?
2. Can a *corpus delicti* be proven by a confession or admission of a defendant? Briefly explain.
3. A "unity" between what factors must exist in order to constitute a crime?
4. Give a brief example of omission to act as it constitutes a crime.
5. May one be charged and convicted of several crimes for one act? Explain.
6. Briefly explain "proximate cause" and its importance to a defendant's criminal act.
7. Briefly explain the "felony murder rule" as discussed in your text.
8. Define "intent" and describe the types of intent which must exist to constitute a crime.
9. What is meant by the term "criminal negligence" and what is its relationship to intent?
10. Briefly explain how intent may be proven and give a short example.
11. Give an example of a crime which involves each of the types of intent.
12. List three of the five elements to consider in order to find intent in cases involving criminal negligence.
13. Briefly distinguish between motive and intent.
14. Under what circumstances, if any, is voluntary intoxication an excuse for committing a crime?

TERMINOLOGY QUIZ—CHAPTER 3

Match terms and definitions by placing the correct numbers in the parentheses. Answers may be written on a separate sheet for submission to the instructor at the instructor's direction.

1. Abet	( ) Outside of court
2. Accessory	( ) Aiding a felon after the crime
3. Accomplice	( ) One who aids a principal in a crime
4. Concurrent	( ) Direct or contributing cause
5. Confession	( ) A particular mental purpose in mind
6. Constructive intent	( ) Theft by one to whom property entrusted
7. Consummated	( ) Completed, accomplished
8. Crime	( ) Reason for or moving cause
9. Embezzlement	( ) Statement acknowledging guilt
10. Extrajudicial	( ) Valid on its face
11. Intent	( ) Liability for unintended consequences
12. *Mens rea*	( ) Mental purpose of or resolve to do an act
13. Motive	( ) Failure to act, especially when required
14. Omission	( ) Active participant or person responsible
15. Perpetrator	( ) A guilty mind or wrongful purpose
16. *Prima facie*	
17. Principal	
18. Proximate cause	
19. Specific intent	
20. Theft	

CHAPTER 4

Capacity to Commit Crime

4.1 PERSONS CAPABLE OF COMMITTING CRIME

Penal Code, Section 26, states that "All persons are capable of committing crimes except those belonging to the following classes:

1. Children under the age of fourteen, in the absence of clear proof that at the time of committing the act charged against them, they knew its wrongfulness.
2. Idiots.
3. Persons who committed the act or made the omission charged under an ignorance or mistake of fact, which disproves any criminal intent.
4. Persons who committed the act charged without being conscious thereof.
5. Persons who committed the act or made the omission charged through misfortune or by accident, when it appears that there was no evil design, intention, or culpable (wrongful) negligence.
6. Persons (unless the crime be punishable with death) who committed the act or made the omission charged under threats or menaces sufficient to show that they had reasonable cause to and did believe their lives would be endangered if they refused."

In determining the theory of criminal responsibility the law assumes capacity upon the part of all persons, except those in certain exempted classes named above, to comply with the standards of conduct set by the criminal law. Criminal responsibility simply means liability to legal punishment. In certain situations the law exempts persons from criminal responsibility who are not entirely blameless, but who, by reason of circumstances beyond their present control, are considered not sufficiently blameworthy to merit punishment. (1981)

4.2 CHILDREN UNDER AGE FOURTEEN

The common law rule regarding the criminal responsibility of children and the fact that they are conclusively presumed to be mentally incapable of committing any crime, is completely nonexistent in this state. The age referred to in the California statute refers to chronological and not mental age.

In reality, this defense providing incapacity or inability of a minor in California to commit crime when under the statutory age of fourteen years has little practical application in that all persons in this state who are under eighteen years are subject to the provisions of the juvenile court law specifically, and penal law generally. Since the primary jurisdiction for the adjudication of criminal cases involving persons under the age of eighteen years (juveniles) rests entirely with the juvenile court, it is highly unlikely that a juvenile under the age of even *sixteen* years, who has committed a crime less than a felony, would ever be subject to the formal adversary judicial proceeedings which are reserved for adults. This is not to say that children under eighteen years are not given rights equal to adults; on the contrary, the Supreme Court, particularly in the cases of *Gault v. U.S.* and *Kent v. U.S.*, spells out the fact that juveniles are to have the same inherent constitutional rights as their elders.

Juveniles are not considered to have committed crime, but rather have a unique status of criminality which is euphemistically called "juvenile delinquency." The juvenile court, having primary jurisdiction in this state in cases involving youthful offenders under eighteen years may, as a discretionary matter, make a finding of unfitness for juvenile court adjudication in the case of any juvenile who is at least sixteen years of age and who committed what would have amounted to a felony had the same offense been committed by an adult. Thus, it can be seen that the provision of PC 26.1, relating to children under four-teen years, is more applicable to juvenile court pro-ceedings than to the adult criminal court process.

The question of the capacity of a minor under fourteen to commit a crime was the subject of a 1975 Appellate Court decision. (*In re Michael, John B. 44 Cal. App 3d 443*). Nine-year-old Michael admitted to a police officer that he had broken a sideview mirror off a Mercedes automobile so he could get his hands in to pry open a wind-wing and that one of his friends reached in and unlocked the door. The boys took a package of cigarettes from inside the car. The officer asked Michael whether he knew right from wrong and if he knew it was wrong to break into cars and steal. Michael said yes. A Welfare and Institu-tion Code petition alleging that Michael committed auto burglary was sustained by the Juvenile Court.

The question in the case was whether there was clear proof that Michael knew the wrongfulness of his acts and thus had the capacity to commit auto burglary within the meaning of PC 26. The Court of Appeal held the evidence fell far short of that neces-sary to establish "clear proof" that Michael knew the wrongfulness of his acts. In reversing the judgment of the Juvenile Court, the Court of Appeal noted that the Juvenile Court did not hear expert testimony on the issue and did not directly question Michael to gain some insight into his intelligence and his under-standing of the wrongfulness of his conduct. This decision suggests that more extensive questioning would have created a stronger court case. It also points out that in cases of minors under fourteen, clear proof must be shown that at the time of the offense, the youngster knew the wrongfulness of the act. Relevant areas of inquiry would include the minor's age, intelligence, education, experience and prior police contacts. In addition, questioning the minor's parents, teachers and friends would possibly produce evidence helpful in proving the question. It should be noted that the same factors listed above are relevant in proving a *Miranda* waiver for a minor of any age.

4.3 IDIOTS

An "idiot" is simply defined as one who is virtually without mentality—one who is without understand-ing. This defense is clearly separated from that of an insanity plea and represents the defendant's mental status from birth. Such a person is said to be incapa-ble of appreciating the character and significance of his acts. The idiot, as characterized by the Binet intelligence classification, appears lowest on the scale, having been said to possess an I.Q. of from 0 to 24. Mental retardation does not necessarily come within the purview of this defense unless it can be clearly shown that the defendant was incapable of knowing the wrongfulness of his acts.

4.4 INSANITY AS A DEFENSE

The purpose of a legal test for insanity is to identify those persons who, owing to mental illness, should not be held criminally responsible and so punished for their crime. The question, then, is what constitutes insanity?

Insanity Defined. Under Proposition 8, the test for legal insanity is now whether a criminal defendant proves by a preponderance of the evidence (greater weight or majority of evidence) that he or she was (1) incapable of knowing or understanding the nature and quality of his or her act, and (2) of distinguishing right from wrong at the time of the commission of the offense (PC 25(b)).

Essentially, this restores the traditional M'Naghten rule (referred to as the "right-wrong" test) which was in effect since first adopted by the California Supreme Court in 1864, until overturned by the California Supreme Court in 1978 in (*People v. Drew, 22 C. 3d 333*).

Current Test. The test now in California for insanity requires the defendant to clearly prove by a prepon-derance of evidence that at the time of committing the act, the defendant was (1) laboring under such a defect of reason as not to know the nature and quality of his or her act; or if the defendant did know it, that (2) he or she did not know that what they were doing was wrong. Essentially, it is the defendant's responsi-bility to prove an inability to distinguish "right from wrong" because of some form of mental disorder (*People v. Kelly, (1973) 10 C. 3d 565*).

Temporary Insanity. Legal insanity of a short dura-tion (temporary insanity) if existing at the time of the commission of the offense, is as fully recognized as a defense as that of insanity for a longer duration. For drug intoxication to be legal insanity, however, it must be "settled insanity" and not merely a tempo-rary mental condition produced by the recent use of intoxicants (*People v. Kelly, 10 Cal. 3d 565*).

Burden of Proof. The law presumes every person to be sane and free from mental illness. However, if a preponderance of evidence indicates insanity on the part of the perpetrator, the burden is upon the defendant to prove his insanity by this preponderance of evidence (*People v. Loomis, 170 C. 347; People v. Harris, 167 C. 53*).

4.5 IGNORANCE OR MISTAKE OF FACT

One who honestly and mistakenly commits or omits an act which would ordinarily result in a crime were it not for the lack of a criminal intent may usually interpose a defense under this subdivision of PC 26. This must, however, be an honest mistake of fact, which is a question of fact for the jury to resolve. For example, the California Appellate Court held in a recent case of unlawful sexual intercourse (PC 261.5) that such crime is defensible on the ground that a criminal intent is lacking. In a prosecution for unlawful sexual intercourse with a girl seventeen years and some months of age, who voluntarily engaged in an act of sexual intercourse with the defendant, it was reversible error to refuse to permit defendant to present evidence showing that he had in good faith a reasonable belief that the prosecutrix was eighteen years or more of age (*People v. Hernandez, 61 Cal. 2d, 529*). In the same case the court held that in an alleged unlawful sexual intercourse, the criminal intent exists when the perpetrator proceeds with utter disregard of, or in lack of grounds for, a belief that the female has reached the age of consent.

While ignorance of the law is no defense to a criminal prosecution, a penalty may be avoided upon proof of ignorance or mistake of fact (*People v. McLaughlin, 111 C.A. 2d 781*). However, where one does an unlawful act voluntarily and willfully, he is presumed to have intended what he did as well as all natural, probable, and usual consequences of such act (*People v. Wade, 71 C.A. 2d 646*).

One cannot interpose a defense of mistake of fact where his immediate act constitutes the requisites of crime (i.e., act and intent or criminal negligence), which proximately results in additional harm to others. Thus, setting fire to a home to defraud the insurer wherein homicide is committed inadvertently is nonetheless murder. Or, an officer using "dum-dum" bullets, in violation of departmental orders, who inadvertently shoots a bystander while seeking to arrest a fleeing felon, would be guilty of manslaughter if the innocent victim should die.

4.6 UNCONSCIOUSNESS OF ACT

One may interpose a defense to his acts under the provision of PC 26, paragraph 4, in cases where he can show that such acts were not voluntarily done by him, but were precipitated by an irrational response of which he was unconscious. Such a defense has no reference to insanity or mental disease, but relates to those cases in which there is no functioning of conscious mind and the person's acts are controlled solely by the subconscious mind (*People v. Denningham, 82 C.A. 2d 119*).

Unconscious Act Defined. An unconscious act applies to persons who are not conscious of acting, but who perform acts while asleep or while suffering from a delirium of fever or because of an attack of epilepsy, a blow on the head, the involuntary taking of drugs, the involuntary consumption of intoxicating liquor, or any similar cause. Unconsciousness does not require that a person be incapable of movement (*People v. Alexander, 182 Cal. App. 2d 281*).

It is apparent that in cases where a person is subjected to involuntary intoxication without being conscious thereof, such a person might avail himself of this defense. For example, several nondrinkers who attend a party wherein a nonalcoholic punch is being served, which is subsequently "spiked" with alcohol without their knowledge or consent, and which eventually renders them unconscious of the legal and moral significance of their behavior and conduct could result in their interposing this basic defense for a crime committed or attempted by them at the time. However, the burden is on the defendant to prove his unconscious state, through medical testimony if necessary (*People v. Coston, 82 C.A. 2d 23*).

Unconsciousness caused by voluntary intoxication is not a defense when a crime requires only a general criminal intent (*People v. Conley, 64 A.C. 321*). A person may objectively manifest discretion of free will and a sound mind and yet be without criminal intent (*People v. Gorshen, 21 Cal. 2d 716*). An act done in the absence of the will is not any more the behavior of the actor than is an act done contrary to his will (*People v. Freeman, 61 C.A. 2d 110*). This section (PC26.5) does not refer to cases of unsound mind, but only to cases of persons of sound mind who suffer from some force that leaves their acts without volition or self will (*People v. Hardy, 33 Cal. 2d 52*).

4.7 ACCIDENT AND MISFORTUNE

This defense is predicated upon the absolute lack of the requisites of a crime, i.e., a lack of criminal act, intent, negligence, or evil design on the part of the defendant. Such a defense is often offered in cases of homicide, either excusable or justifiable. For example, if a person were to drive a car in a residential area within the speed limit, and thereafter a child runs into the path of the vehicle in pursuit of a ball, the subsequent traffic death of such child would have been unintentional, with no evil design on the part of the driver, assuming that the vehicle was operationally sound and there was no negligence. However, in the same case, if the driver was traveling at a high rate of speed, driving recklessly or under the influence of a drug or intoxicant, such a defense could obviously not be used.

The majority of cases in which "accident and misfortune" have been interposed as a defense generally have to do with bodily injury or homicide. The killing of a human being is excusable and not unlawful when committed in doing any lawful act by lawful means and without any unlawful intent. Examples of such include (1) lawfully correcting a child who, following a mild swat, ran and was fatally injured falling down stairs (*People v. Forbs, 62 C. 2d 847*); (2) in defending oneself from an unprovoked attack, a single blow to an assailant's chin causes him to fall back against a sharp object which causes his death (no undue advantage or deadly weapon was used).

Excusable Homicide. Homicide is excusable in the following cases:
1. When committed by accident and misfortune
   a. in lawfully correcting a child
2. Doing any other lawful act by lawful means
   a. with usual and ordinary caution,
   b. and without any unlawful intent.
3. When committed by accident and misfortune,
   a. in heat of passion,
   b. upon any sudden and sufficient provocation,
   c. or upon sudden combat,
   d. when no undue advantage is taken,
   e. nor any dangerous weapon is used,
   f. and when the killing is not done in a cruel or unusual manner (PC 195).

4.8 CRIMES COMMITTED UNDER THREATS OR MENACES

When a person is forced to commit a crime (excluding crimes which provide for the death penalty) by being subjected to threats or menaces sufficient to show that such person would have suffered great and imminent danger to his life, they may interpose a defense under this section to the commission of such forced criminal activity. Thus, where one forces another to rob a liquor store with an unloaded gun by threatening to shoot him if he fails to comply, the innocent physical perpetrator who committed the crime under threat of certain death would not be responsible for the commission of such a crime. Threats of future danger of loss of life is no defense (*People v. Otis, 174 Cal. App 2d 119*).

By contradistinction, if "A" threatens to kill "B" if the latter fails to commit a homicide upon "C" as commanded by "A," this defense is inapplicable inasmuch as it does not apply to the commission of capital crimes even if committed by innocent persons who do so as a result of fear of impending danger to their own lives.

In the commission of any crime, evidence as to whether a person was coerced and forced to assist the perpetrator due to fear of great bodily harm, and whether such person resisted such coercion, is a question for the jury to resolve (*People v. Ellis, 137 C.A. 2d 408*).

Where the crime committed is punishable by the death penalty, no amount of threats, coercion, or duress will relieve a person who cooperates in the commission of the offense (*People v. Petro, 13 C.A. 2d 245*).

4.9 CAPITAL CRIMES

In 1976, the California Supreme Court, in *Rockwell v. Superior Court* declared California's death penalty law unconstitutional because it did not permit the trier of fact to consider mitigating circumstances.

In August, 1977, the Legislature overrode the Governor's veto and enacted a new death penalty law which is in conformity with the constitutional guidelines set up by the United States Supreme Court and followed by the California Supreme Court in the *Rockwell* case.

A defendant may be sentenced to death (if 18 years of age or older) if *first degree* murder is committed under any of the following circumstances:
1. Murder for financial gain (*PC 190.2*).
2. Treason (*PC 37*) involving murder.
3. Explosive or destructive device, use of, (*PC 189*).
4. Poison, use of, (*PC 189*), during PC 187.
5. Torture, infliction of, (*PC 189*).
6. Arson, during commission of, (*PC 451*).
7. Rape, during commission of, (*PC 261*).
8. Robbery, during commission of, (*PC 211*).
9. Burglary, inhabited dwelling, (*PC 459*).
10. Mayhem, during commission of, (*PC 203*).
11. Peace officer, murder of in performance of duty (*PC 190.2*).
12. Perjury, causing execution of innocent person (*PC 128*).
13. Witness, murder to prevent testimony, (*PC 190.2*).
14. Kidnapping, murder during, (*PC 209*).
15. Child molesting, murder during, (*PC 288*).
16. Train wrecking causing death (*PC 219*).
17. Murder by life convict (*PC 4500*).

18. Murder with prior conviction (*PC 190.2*).
19. Multiple murders (*PC 190.2*).
20. Sabotage, murder during (*Military and Veterans Code 1670-72*).
21. Conspiracy to commit capital crime. In the case of conspiracy to commit murder, the punishment shall be that prescribed for murder in the first degree, (*PC 182*).
22. Murder committed for the purpose of avoiding or preventing a lawful arrest or to perfect or attempt to perfect an escape from lawful custody (*PC 190.2*).
23. Fireman, murder of, while engaged in performance of duty, and defendant knows or should know victim performing duties (*PC 190.2*).
24. Prosecutor, murder of, and carried out in retaliation for or to prevent performance of official duties (*PC 190.2*).
25. Judge, murder of, carried out in retaliation for or to prevent performance of official duties (*PC 190.2*).
26. Elected or appointed official, murder of, and intentionally carried out in retaliation for or to prevent performance of official duties (*PC 190.2*).
27. Murder by defendant lying in wait (*PC 190.2*).
28. Victim was intentionally killed because of race, color, religion, nationality, or country of origin (*PC 190.2*).
29. Sodomy, murder committed during commission of PC 286 (*PC 190.2*).

TERMINOLOGY DEFINED—CHAPTER 4

See the Terminology Quiz at the end of this chapter.
1. Abortion: procuring or causing miscarriage, may be legal or illegal.
2. Accusation: any complaint, indictment, or infraction.
3. Admission: statement by accused, usually falls short of a confession.
4. Adultery: sexual relations with married person, not one's husband or wife.
5. Affidavit: a sworn declaration in writing.
6. Affirmation: declaration by witness that he will speak truthfully.
7. Arraignment: court appearance, defendant advised of charges and rights.
8. Arrest: taking one into custody, depriving one of freedom to leave.
9. Asportation: movement of things from one place to another as in theft.
10. Assault: an unlawful attempt to inflict injury or force on another.

11. Attempt: a "try" to commit a crime, frequently punishable as a crime.
12. Capital crime: one punishable by death.
13. Contradistinction: by contrast, having opposite qualities.
14. Chronological age: actual age in years since birth.
15. Imminent: immediate, without delay.
16. Insanity: incapable of knowing right from wrong or significance of acts.
17. Interpose: to put forth, to place between.
18. Prosecutrix: female victim, especially in rape cases.
19. Requisites: necessary requirements or conditions.
20. Subornation: procuring another to commit perjury.

TRUE-FALSE—CHAPTER 4

1. Criminal responsibility means liability to legal punishment.
2. In certain instances the law exempts persons from punishment even though they are not entirely blameless.
3. In all cases, children under fourteen years are held incapable of committing a crime in California.
4. The Supreme Court has held that children under fourteen do *not* have the same rights as adults.
5. A child under fourteen can be convicted of a crime *only* if it can be proven he knew the wrongfulness of his act.
6. An "idiot" is legally defined as one whose mental age does not match his chronological age.
7. In California, the test of insanity is based on the M'Naghten Rule.
8. The burden of proof is on the defendant if insanity is his defense.
9. A defense of "mistake of fact" is a question for a jury to decide (if it is a jury trial).
10. Generally, lack of criminal intent is missing in a true "ignorance or mistake of fact" defense.
11. When one does an unlawful act involuntarily and willfully, he is presumed to have intended *all* natural, probable, and usual consequences of such an act.
12. Unconsciousness caused by voluntary intoxication is *not* a defense for crimes requiring only general intent.
13. Irresistible and uncontrollable impulses and moral insanity constitute defenses to crime in California.

14. The killing of a human being is *not* unlawful when committed by doing a lawful act by lawful means and without unlawful intent in California.

15. Fear and coercion imposed by a husband on his wife is a defense for married women in misdemeanor cases only.

16. The defense that one committed a crime under imminent threat of great bodily harm is applicable to misdemeanors only.

17. Where a crime is punishable by the death penalty, no amount of threats, coercion, or duress will relieve a defendant who cooperates in the commission of the offense.

18. In California, there are presently only seven capital crimes.

19. Kidnapping for ransom is a capital crime in California.

20. Train wrecking resulting in injury however slight to any passenger is a capital crime in California.

ESSAY-DISCUSSION QUESTIONS— CHAPTER 4

1. Enumerate four of the six exceptions to the rule that all persons are capable of committing crimes.

2. What are the practical aspects regarding the commission of crimes by persons under fourteen years of age? Are they capable of committing a crime?

3. Is a mentally retarded person legally considered an "idiot"? What I.Q. is applicable in such defenses?

4. What legal rule is applied to "insane" persons who commit crimes?

5. Briefly define and give an example of a case involving a "mistake of fact." Is this a defense or an element of the crime?

6. What may be the legal effect of voluntary intoxication in crimes involving specific intent?

7. Briefly discuss "accident and misfortune" as a defense to a crime. In what types of cases is this defense most applicable?

8. Under what circumstances is a person excused for committing a crime? What are the limitations?

9. Discuss the legal aspects of crimes committed under threats and coercion. Is this a defense to all crimes? What will constitute a legal threat in such cases?

10. List four capital crimes in California.

TERMINOLOGY QUIZ—CHAPTER 4

Match terms and definitions by placing the correct number in the parentheses. Answers may be written on a separate sheet for submission to the instructor at the instructor's discretion.

1. Abortion	( ) A complaint, indictment, or information
2. Accusation	( ) A sworn declaration in writing
3. Admission	( ) Defendant advised of rights and charges in court
4. Adultery	( ) Procuring another to commit perjury
5. Affidavit	( ) Female victim, especially in rape cases
6. Affirmation	( ) Incapable of knowing right from wrong
7. Arraignment	( ) Statement by accused, short of confession
8. Arrest	( ) Declaration by witness to tell the truth
9. Asportation	( ) Necessary requirements of conditions
10. Assault	( ) Movement of things from place to place
11. Attempt	( ) To put forth, to put between
12. Capital crime	( ) Actual years since birth
13. Contradistinction	( ) Crime punishable by death
14. Chronological age	( ) Immediate, without delay
15. Imminent	( ) By contrast, having opposite qualities
16. Insanity	
17. Interpose	
18. Prosecutrix	
19. Requisites	
20. Subornation	

CHAPTER 5

Parties to a Crime

5.1 COMMON LAW PARTIES TO CRIME

Under the old common law, the person who overtly and actually committed the criminal act was known as a principal in the *first degree*. One who knowingly and willfully assisted the actual perpetrator was known as a principal in the *second degree*. One who was not present when the crime was committed, but procured, counseled, or abetted the actual perpetrator was known as an accessory *before* the fact. Finally, one who assisted the perpetrator to escape arrest and punishment after the crime was committed was known as an accessory *after* the fact. These distinctions no longer exist, as will be discussed later. Sometimes, the old terms are used, however, to more accurately define the role or relationship of an individual to a particular crime.

5.2 PRINCIPALS DEFINED

PC 31. "All persons concerned in the commission of a crime, whether it be felony or misdemeanor, or whether they directly commit the act constituting the offense, or aid and abet in its commission, or not being present, have advised and encouraged its commission, and all persons counseling, advising, or encouraging children under the age of fourteen years, lunatics or idiots, to commit any crime, or who, by fraud, contrivance, or force, occasion the drunkenness of another for the purpose of causing him to commit any crime, or who, by threats, menaces, command, or coercion, compel another to commit any crime, are principals in any crime so committed."

The distinction between an accessory before the fact and a principal, and between principals in the first and second degree is abrogated; and all persons concerned in the commission of a crime, who by the operation of other provisions of this code are principals therein, shall hereafter be prosecuted, tried and punished as principals and no other facts need be alleged in any accusatory pleading against any such persons than are required in an accusatory pleading against a principal (*PC 971*).

Principals—Elements of Offense. As noted in PC 31, above, all persons involved in any way in the planning, preparation or carrying out of any crime become principals. This is true even if they are not present at the time the crime is committed. The key elements are:

1. Aids and abets in the commission of a crime.
2. Advises and encourages its commission (even if not present).
3. Fraudulently gets another person drunk for the purpose of causing him to commit a crime.
4. Compels another to commit a crime by threats, menaces, or coercion.

In the first sentence of PC 31, "All persons concerned in the commission of crime, whether it be felony or misdemeanor," we find that the designation "principal" applies to all crimes, misdemeanors as well as felonies. The next portion of that sentence, "whether they directly commit the act, or aid and abet in its commission," needs some explanation. If they directly commit the act, it is self-explanatory.

5.3 CALIFORNIA PENAL CODE PROVISIONS

In addition to PC 31, (Principal Defined) and PC 32, (Accessory Defined), there are several other sections of the California Penal Code which will help give a clearer picture of who are parties to a crime and the various acts which can make them such.

Persons Liable to Punishment. The following persons are liable to punishment under the laws of this state:

1. All persons who commit, in whole or in part, any crime within this state;
2. All who commit any offense without this state which, if committed within this state, would be

larceny, (theft) robbery, or embezzlement under the laws of this state, and bring the property stolen or embezzled, or any part of it, or are found with it, or any part of it within this state;

3. All who, being without this state, cause or aid, advise or encourage, another person to commit a crime within this state, and are afterwards found therein (PC 27).

4. Perjury is punishable, also, when committed outside of California to the extent provided in PC 118.

Bringing Stolen Property Into the State. Every person who, in another state or country, steals or embezzles the property of another, or receives such property knowing it to have been stolen or embezzled, and brings the same into this state, may be convicted and punished in the same manner as if such larceny, or embezzlement, or receiving had been committed in this state (PC 497).

Acts Punishable Under Foreign Law. An act or omission declared punishable by this Code is not less so because it is also punishable under the laws of another state, government or country, unless the contrary is expressly declared (PC 655).

Foreign Conviction or Acquittal. Whenever, on the trial of an accused person, it appears that upon a criminal prosecution under the laws of another state, government, or country, founded upon the act or omission in respect to which he is on trial, he has been acquitted or convicted, it is a sufficient defense (PC 656).

Aiding in Misdemeanor. Whenever a act is declared a misdemeanor, and no punishment for counseling or aiding in the commission of such act is expressly prescribed by law, every person who counsels or aids another in the commission of such act is guilty of a misdemeanor (PC 659).

General Liability—Jurisdiction. Every person is liable to punishment by the laws of this state for a public offense committed by him therein (except for federal crimes), and except as otherwise provided by law, the jurisdiction of every public offense is in any competent court within the jurisdictional territory in which it is committed (PC 777).

Out-of-State Aider and Abbettor. Every person who, being out of this state, causes, aids, advises, or encourages any person to commit a crime within this state, and is afterwards found within this state, is punishable in the same manner as if he had been within this state when he caused, aided, advised, or encouraged the commission of such crime (PC 778b).

Principal Innocent—Accessory Guilty. It is interesting to note that an accessory to the commission of a *felony* may be prosecuted, tried, and punished, though the principal may be neither prosecuted nor tried, and though the principal may even have been acquitted (PC 972).

5.4 AID AND ABET DEFINED

Aid and Abet. A person aids and abets the commission of a crime if, with knowledge of the unlawful purpose of the perpetrator of the crime, he or she aids, promotes, encourages, or instigates by act or advice the commission of such crime (*People v. Ponce, 96 Cal. App 2d 327*).

The words "aid" and "abet" must be distinguished from the synonym "encourage." The difference is that "aid" or "abet" indicates *active* support and assistance; encourage does not. "Abet" also connotes criminal participation and furthering of the act committed (*Osborne v. Boughman, 85 Cal. App 244*).

The words "aid" and "abet" are nearly synonymous terms as generally used, but strictly speaking, the former term does not imply guilty knowledge of felonious intent, whereas the word "abet" includes knowledge of the wrongful purpose and counsel and encouragement of the commission of the crime (*People v. Dole, 122 Cal. 486; People v. Morine, 138 Cal. 626; People v. Yee, 37 C.A. 579*).

A Case Example. A striking example of the responsibility of a principal is contained in *People v. Hopkins, 101 C.A. 2d 704*. Briefly, the facts are: One Richard N. Hopkins delivered a friend, Herbert Caro, who was quite ill, to the Park Emergency Hospital in San Francisco. His case was diagnosed as narcotic poisoning, and Hopkins informed the doctor in attendance that Caro had taken heroin earlier that day. Caro died that afternoon. Hopkins made a statement to an inspector of the SFPD that he was a seaman, that he had left his ship in San Francisco in early afternoon and visited a tavern in Marin County where he met decedent whom he had known for about three years. Decedent asked him if he would "like to get high tonight" to which he assented, and they left in Hopkin's car. Hopkins gave decedent $13.00 and about fifteen minutes later decedent returned to the car, having purchased some heroin. They then drove out to Funston Avenue where they stopped, opened the package, and decedent produced an eyedropper, which he filled with water at a service station. They drove around a few blocks and then parked on 14th Avenue where they took a cap of heroin and mixed it in a spoon, heated it, and after they had it mixed, Hopkins said he took a shot in the arm, and then Caro took a shot. Hopkins wrapped a handkerchief around the decedent's arm to force Caro's veins out. Hopkins took another shot and then assisted Caro in taking his second shot in the same manner by wrapping the handkerchief around Caro's arm, as he had when he took the first shot. After Caro took the second shot, he said he felt sick so he got out of the car and attempted to vomit. He wasn't able to go, and Hopkins got out and walked around the car to Caro who was practically unconscious. He (Hopkins) then placed Caro in the back seat of the car and took him to the Park Emergency Hospital.

When the decedent injected the heroin into his own arm he violated Sections 11721 and 11009 of the Health and Safety Code and when Hopkins manipulated the handkerchief-tourniquet around the decedent's arm, he assisted him in the commission of an unlawful act not amounting to a felony. As a result of these acts, decedent died. In reviewing the case the District Court of Appeal said: "The help which Hopkins gave decedent brings him within the provisions of Section 31 of the Penal Code. That he aided is clear, that he abetted is clear, since he and decedent set out together with the purpose of doing that which Section 11721 of the Health and Safety Code denounced."

In order to charge Hopkins with manslaughter it was not necessary for testimony before the grand jury to show that he injected heroin, since Section 31 draws no line between persons who directly commit the act constituting the offense and those who aid and abet in its commission.

Not Being Present: Advised and Encouraged. (*PC 31.*) In 1908 the District Court of Appeal, in the case of *People v. Frank Lewis*, said: "To be a principal it is not necessary that the person be present at the commission of the crime." In that case the defendant was charged in the information with the crime of rape upon a child under the age of sixteen years. The jury returned a verdict of guilty as charged. Defendant appealed from the order denying his motion for a new trial and from the final judgement of conviction.

The prosecutrix was the stepdaughter of the defendant. There was no evidence that defendant had sexual intercourse with her or that he was present at the commission of the crime, but there was abundant evidence that he aided and abetted its commission by one Alan Wheeler, a youth of seventeen years of age. Defendant's contention was that since he was not present when the crime was committed, the evidence must be held to be insufficient to justify the verdict.

The evidence was that defendant on several occasions solicited Wheeler to have sexual intercourse with the defendant's stepdaughter; that he brought them together under circumstances calculated to arouse their "animal passions" and to bring about his "wicked design." He advised Wheeler to procure Vaseline to be used in the action of coition, if necessary, and he also procured medicated capsules or suppositories, gave them to the girl, and instructed her in Wheeler's presence how to use them to prevent conception.

There was evidence that defendant took his stepdaughter and Wheeler to San Francisco, as the evidence showed, in furtherance of his said design previously urged upon Wheeler. They occupied a small room in which was one bed, and all three slept in it. The second night they occupied a different room in which were two beds; defendant slept in one, and Wheeler and the girl slept in the other. The Court held that was ample evidence to convict Lewis of unlawful sexual intercourse, as a principal.

In the case of *People v. Wood, 56 C.A. 2d 431*, the court said, "Where a person provides a room for another to commit statutory rape, both are guilty as being principals to the crime of rape." In this case, defendant and one James Moore were jointly charged by information with the crime of committing statutory rape. As to Moore, the information was dismissed, and upon trial defendant Wood was convicted. He appealed from judgment whereby he was sentenced to imprisonment in the county jail for a term of nine months.

Wood's chief contention was that the verdict was not warranted by the evidence. While it is conceded that defendant did not have sexual intercourse with the girl involved, it conclusively appears from the evidence that at about 2:00 a.m., defendant met Moore and the girl together, and that he, Wood, at the request of Moore, procured a room for their use, to which he conducted them and where they spent the remainder of the night until 6:00 a.m., at which time, as agreed, defendant returned and awakened them. As shown by the evidence, he knew the illegal purpose for which the room was to be used and knowingly both aided and abetted Moore in the commission of the crime. The conviction was sustained.

We see, therefore, that a person may be convicted as a principal even though not present at the actual commission of the offense.

Again, going back to PC 31, we read: "and all persons counseling, advising, or encouraging children under the age of fourteen years, lunatics or idiots, to commit any crime"—here we have a situation where the person who commits the crime, such as a child under the age of fourteen, or an idiot, might not be guilty of any crime, as Section 26, PC, refers to those people as being incapable of committing a crime. Yet, the person who counseled, advised, or encouraged them to perform the prohibited act would be subject to prosecution as a principal by virtue of Section 31.

Use of Fraud or Force. Again looking at Section 31 of the Penal Code "or who, by fraud, contrivance, or force, occasion the drunkenness of another for the purpose of causing him to commit a crime." The causing of a person to become intoxicated by means of fraud, contrivance, or force for the purpose of causing him to participate in an act of sex perversion or causing the intoxication of a married woman to have her commit adultery, would be examples of this portion.

Uses of Threats. Section 31 continues: "or who by threats, menaces, command, or coercion, compels another to commit any crime, are principles in any crime so committed." We might group these four words—threats, menaces, command, and coercion— under one heading and call it "compulsion," for we find the phraseology of the section requires that the innocent party be compelled to commit the offense through this means. Usually, the actual perpetrator of the offense under these circumstances (unless the offense be punishable with death), would have a defense under Section 26, PC; however, the person who compelled him to perform the forbidden act would be just as guilty as he would have been had he committed the crime himself.

All principals are equally guilty. Thus, where defendants admitted the commission of the crime of murder while engaged in robbing the victim, but each sought to relieve himself by contending that the other wielded the deadly instrument, it was immaterial which struck the death blow, as each was equally guilty of the resultant crime (*People v. Gomez, 209 Ca. 296*).

In order to convict one for aiding and abetting the perpetrator of an offense, there must be proof that the accused not only aided the perpetrator, but at the same time shared in the criminal intent (*People v. Butts, 236 C.A. 2d 817*).

Evidence that the defendant aided and abetted in the commission of a robbery, although he did not strike the blows with the rolled-up kit of automobile tools, authorized his conviction as a principal in the crime (*People v. Crowl, 28 C.A. 2d 299*). Mere presence, however, at the scene of the crime and failure to take steps to prevent a crime do not establish aiding and abetting (*Pinell v. Superior Court, 232 Cal. App. 2d 284*).

5.5   CO-PRINCIPALS EQUALLY GUILTY

All parties who are legally principals under the law are equally guilty. For example, where one of the perpetrators of a robbery is armed with a deadly weapon, therefor, guilty of first degree robbery, each of his co-principals are also guilty of first degree robbery even though none of the others were armed (*People v. Perkins, 37 Cal. 2d 62*). Further, all parties to the crime are responsible for the natural, reasonable, and probable consequences of the acts of any one of the others during the commission of the crime (*People v. Godstein, 146 Cal. App. 2d 268*).

Exception—"Non-triggermen" Principals. On July 2, 1982, the United States Supreme Court struck down the death penalty for "non-triggerman" criminals who did not intend to take part in a killing, but whose crimes resulted in death. The sharply divided court ruled that the imposition of death under such circumstances violates the Constitution's ban on "cruel and unusual punishment." The 5 to 4 decision is a major victory for death penalty opponents, even though it will directly affect only a fraction of the approximately 1,000 inmates now on death row in the United States.

In overturning the death penalty imposed on Florida death-row inmate Earl Enmund, for participation in a robbery during which an elderly couple was slain, Justice Byron R. White wrote: "Putting Enmund to death to avenge two killings that he did not commit and had no intention of committing or causing does not measurably contribute to the retributive end of ensuring that the criminal gets his just desserts." White said that it must be shown that defendants like Enmund "*intended or contemplated that life would be taken.*" (*Enmund v. Florida, 42 CCH Supreme Court Bulletin, Page B5024*).

Enmund said he helped plan the robbery of Thomas and Eunice Kersey's home near Wauchula, Florida, but he did not know that his accomplices would gun down the couple. Mrs. Kersey, age 74, was shot six times. Her husband, age 86, was shot three times. Trial testimony indicated that Enmund was not in the Kersey home when the killings occurred, but was waiting in a get-away car.

Most of Justice White's opinion, because of the way state death penalty statutes are fashioned, was devoted to so-called "non-triggerman" criminals who took part in a robbery. However, the opinion strongly indicates that it would be applicable to all non-triggerman defendants in "felony-murder" cases. Examples are those who take part in a rape or kidnapping during which someone else kills the victim.

Justice Sandra Day O'Conner strongly disagreed with the decision. "I dissent from this holding not only because I believe that it is not supported by our previous decisions, but also because today's holding interferes with the state criteria for assessing legal guilt by recasting intent as a matter of federal law," she stated.

The Florida Supreme Court rejected Enmund's appeal, ruling that the Constitution does not prevent imposition of the death penalty just because the evidence does not show that the criminal defendant intended to kill anyone. The U.S. Supreme Court overturned that ruling and ordered a resentencing of Enmund.

"For the purposes of imposing the death penalty, Enmund's criminal culpability must be limited to his participation in the robbery, and his punishment must be tailored to his personal responsibility and moral guilt," Justice White said. He also noted that only a handful of states allow the imposition of the death penalty for so-called "felony-murder" during a robbery like the one for which Enmund was convicted.

5.6   ACCESSORY DEFINED

PC 32. "Every person who, after a felony has been committed, harbors, conceals, or aids a principal in such felony, with the intent that said principal may avoid or escape from arrest, trial, conviction, or punishment, having knowledge that said principal has committed such felony or has been charged with such felony or convicted thereof, is an accessory to such felony."

As has been stated, there is no longer an "accessory before the fact" in California. We only have *one* type of accessory; therefore we no longer use the terms "accessory before the fact" or "accessory after the fact," but merely the general term "accessory." We find our definition of accessory in Section 32 of the Penal Code.

Note the language used as this section begins: "Every person who, *after a felony* has been committed . . ." Section 32 of the Penal Code applies only to felonies. There is no such thing as an accessory to a misdemeanor.

Harbor Defined. To "harbor" a person means to receive clandestinely and without lawful authority a person for the purpose of so concealing him that another having the right to lawful custody of such person shall be deprived of same. It may be aptly used to describe the furnishing of shelter, lodging, or food clandestinely or with concealment, and, under certain circumstances, may be equally applicable to those acts divested of any accompanying secrecy (*U.S. v. Grant, 55F 415*).

Conceal Defined. The word "conceal," as used in PC 32 means more than a simple withholding of knowledge possessed by a party that a felony has been committed. This concealment necessarily includes the elements of some affirmative act upon the part of the person tending to or looking toward the concealment of the commission of the felony. Mere silence after knowledge of its commission is not sufficient to constitute the party an accessory. The word "charged," as used in this section, means a formal complaint, indictment, or information filed against the criminal, or possibly an arrest without warrant might be sufficient. Mere general rumors and common talk that a party has committed a felony is wholly insufficient to fill the measure required by the word "charged." (*People v. Garnett, 129 C 364.*)

Proof—Punishment—Jurisdiction. We find, then, that in order to successfully prosecute a person for the crime of accessory, we will have to establish in the evidence that he had actual knowledge that the principal has committed a felony, has been charged with a felony, or had been convicted thereof; then, with that knowledge, he either harbored, concealed, or aided such principal, assisting the principal in avoiding arrest, trial, conviction, or punishment.

Section 33 of the Penal Code provides that the punishment of an accessory is by imprisonment in the state prison not exceeding one year, or in the county jail not exceeding one year, or by a fine not exceeding five thousand dollars ($5,000), or both.

Section 791, PC reads as follows: "In the case of an accessory, as defined in Section 32, in the commission of a public offense, the jurisdiction is in any competent court within the jurisdictional territory of which the offense of the accessory was committed, notwithstanding the principal offense was committed in another jurisdictional territory."

Therefore, if a felony is committed in San Francisco, and the perpetrator flees to Los Angeles, and someone performs any act making him an accessory to such felony, the accessory would be prosecuted in Los Angeles county, notwithstanding the fact that the principal would be prosecuted in the city and county of San Francisco.

5.7   ACCOMPLICE DEFINED

To be an accomplice, the person must have aided, promoted, encouraged, or instigated by act or advice the commission of such offense with knowledge of the unlawful purpose of the person who committed the offense.

A person who knowingly, voluntarily, and with common intent with the principal offender unites in the commission of the crime is an accomplice (*People v. Sieffert, 81 Cal App. 195*).

Penal Code, Section 1111, defines an accomplice as "one who is liable to prosecution for the identical offense charged against the defendant on trial in the cause in which the testimony of the accomplice is given." The purpose of this section is to define a rule of evidence, as well as an accessory.

Corroboration Required. *PC 1111.* "A conviction cannot be had upon the testimony of an accomplice unless it be corroborated by such other evidence as shall tend to connect the defendant with the commission of the offense; and the corroboration is not sufficient if it merely shows the commission of the offense or the circumstances thereof."

The law also provides that the requirement of corroboration has *not* been satisfied in the case where two or more accomplices testify against the defendant. There must be independent evidence that tends to connect the defendant with the commission of the offense.

Juveniles: Exception. There is an exception to the above rule on corroboration. In the juvenile case of *In re Darrell Anthony (90 Cal. App. 3d 325)*, the court held that in a juvenile court prosecution, a statement by an accomplice is sufficient to convict a minor for an alleged offense.

Discussion

"An 'accomplice' is one associated with, and culpably implicated with, others in the commission of a crime, all being principals." One who could be indicated as a principal would be an accomplice. The term is used to define a situation from which certain collateral consequences flow, such as the need of corroboration of testimony or the competency of an accomplice as a witness. It is commonly applied to those testifying against their fellow criminals, and if in the course of a trial any of the latter are called as witnesses, although they are principals, they are referred to as accomplices. We might say, therefore, that any principal or any conspirator, when called upon to testify in the trial of his co-conspirators, then becomes identified as an accomplice.

There are some situations in California where a participant in crime cannot be an accomplice. In unlawful sexual intercourse, Section 261.5 of the Penal Code, for instance, the prosecutrix, being under the statutory age of consent, cannot be an accomplice (*People v. Hamilton, 88 C.A. 2d 398*). The victim of a violation of Section 288 of the Penal Code, being under age of fourteen years, cannot be an accomplice. If the offense is also a violation of PC 288a (oral copulation) and the child, under fourteen, was a willing participant in forcing another to participate, and it could be established satisfactorily in the evidence that he knew the wrongfulness of the act at the time he committed it, he would then be an accomplice insofar as the 288a was concerned (*People v. Williams, 12 C.A. 2d 207*).

The test of accomplicity, therefore, is whether one can be prosecuted as a principal. He must be liable himself for the identical crime for which the principal is on trial. He must be called as a witness in the trial, and then he will be referred to as an accomplice.

5.8   FEIGNED ACCOMPLICE

A feigned accomplice is one who, under the direction of a law enforcement officer, or upon his own initiative, feigns complicity in a crime in order to detect the perpetrator in an effort to prosecute such perpetrator. As such, there is no criminal intent on the part of a feigned accomplice, nor does his activity generally constitute entrapment (See Chapter 7, "Entrapment").

A feigned accomplice is distinguished from an accomplice in that the accomplice is one who knowingly, voluntarily, and with common intent with a principal offender, unites in the commission of a crime, whereas a feigned accomplice may cooperate in the commission of a crime for the purpose of apprehending or securing evidence against the guilty party and is not guilty of the offense committed.

TERMINOLOGY DEFINED—CHAPTER 5

See the Terminology Quiz at the end of this chapter.
1. Abrogate: abolish, nullify, repeal.
2. Autopsy: dissection or testing of a body to determine cause of death.
3. Bailiff: officer assigned to keep order in the court.
4. Battery: unlawful use of force on another.
5. Bench warrant: issued by judge for contempt or failure to appear.
6. Certiorari: order from appellate court to hear an appeal.
7. Circumstantial evidence: that from which other facts may be concluded.
8. Coition: sexual intercourse, also coitus.

9. Commitment: court order sending person to jail, hospital, etc.
10. Complaint: a criminal charge made to or issued by a court.
11. Compounding: accepting a reward not to prosecute, a crime in itself.
12. Conspiracy: crime of two or more persons planning to commit a crime.
13. Contempt: disregard of court order or disrespect toward court.
14. Contraband: goods forbidden by law to possess, import, etc.
15. Coroner's jury: appointed by coroner to hear evidence as to cause of death.
16. Corroboration: evidence which confirms, supports, substantiates.
17. Court trial: jury waived; judge determines guilt or innocence.
18. Culpable: deserving the blame, guilt or censure.
19. Decedent: one who is dead, the deceased.
20. Subpoena: court order commanding witness to appear in court.

TRUE-FALSE QUIZ—CHAPTER 5

1. Under the old common law, the person who assisted the actual perpetrator in a crime was known as an accessory after the fact.
2. The distinctions of accessory before and after the fact have now been abrogated.
3. One cannot be guilty of being a principal to a crime if he was not present when the crime was committed.
4. The term "principal to a crime" applies to felonies only.
5. One can be a principal to a crime merely by advising and encouraging its commission by another.
6. The word "abet" generally signifies guilty knowledge and wrongful purpose.
7. If "A" helps "B" to voluntarily take a shot of heroin, and "B" dies from an overdose, "A" can be charged with manslaughter as being a principal to the death.
8. One who advised and encouraged a friend to have sexual relations with a 16-year-old girl would be guilty of unlawful sexual intercourse even though he was not present when the act was committed.
9. It is possible for the one who commits an act not to be guilty of a crime, but the one who aids and encourages such act to be guilty.

10. If two persons commit a robbery and one is armed, only the one so armed is guilty of first degree robbery under the "co-principal" rule.
11. There is no such crime as an accessory to a misdemeanor.
12. One can be guilty of being an accessory by helping another to plan a robbery.
13. To be guilty of being an accessory, the accused must have actual knowledge that the principal has committed a felony.
14. An accomplice is liable to prosecution for the identical offense as that charged against the principal.
15. The testimony of an accomplice must be corroborated in all cases.
16. In those instances where required, an accomplice's testimony must be corroborated to a greater degree than merely showing that a crime was committed.
17. A "feigned accomplice" is one who did not know the wrongfulness of the act committed.
18. Feigned accomplices are guilty as principals providing they are over fourteen years of age.
19. PC 33 sets the punishment for an accessory as one-half of that for a principal.
20. The test as to whether one is an accessory is whether the latter could be prosecuted as a principal.

ESSAY-DISCUSSION QUESTIONS—CHAPTER 5

1. What "elements" make one a principal to a crime in California?
2. Briefly describe how the definition of "principal" applies to felonies and to misdemeanors.
3. How does California law regarding principals differ from the old common law provisions?
4. Briefly explain the responsibility of a principal as described in *People v. Hopkins, 101 Cal. App. 2d 704.*
5. What "elements" constitute the crime of accessory?
6. How does an accessory differ from a principal?
7. How does an accomplice's culpability compare with that of a principal?
8. Briefly discuss the applicable legal factors when using an accomplice as a witness against a principal.
9. Briefly define corroboration.
10. What is a "feigned accomplice" and what would be the purpose of such a person?

TERMINOLOGY QUIZ—CHAPTER 5

Match terms and definitions by placing the correct number in the parentheses. Answers may be written on a separate sheet for submission to the instructor at the instructor's direction.

1. Abrogate
2. Autopsy
3. Bailiff
4. Battery
5. Bench warrant
6. Certiorari
7. Circumstantial evidence
8. Coition
9. Commitment
10. Complaint
11. Compounding
12. Conspiracy
13. Contempt
14. Contraband
15. Coroner's jury
16. Corroboration
17. Court trial
18. Culpable
19. Decedent
20. Subpoena

( ) issued by a judge for failure to appear in court
( ) a criminal charge made to or issued by a court
( ) goods forbidden by law to possess
( ) court order commanding witness to appear
( ) to abolish, nullify, repeal
( ) accepting a reward not to prosecute
( ) two or more persons planning a crime
( ) disregard of court order or disrespect to court
( ) deserving of blame, guilt, censure
( ) one who is dead
( ) evidence which confirms, supports, substantiates
( ) court order sending person to jail, hospital, etc.
( ) order from appellate court to hear an appeal
( ) sexual intercourse
( ) that from which other facts may be concluded

CHAPTER 6

Attempted Crimes—Obstructing Justice— Conspiracy

6.1 ATTEMPT DEFINED

PC 664. "Every person who attempts to commit any crime, but fails, or is prevented or intercepted in the perpetration thereof, is punishable, where no provision is made by law for the punishment of such attempts as follows:

Punishment for Attempted Offenses

1. **Offenses Punishable by Imprisonment in the State Prison or Death.** If the offense so attempted is punishable by imprisonment in the state prison, the person guilty of such attempt is punishable by imprisonment in the state prison for one-half the term of imprisonment prescribed upon a conviction of the offense so attempted; provided, however, that if the crime attempted is one in which the maximum sentence is life imprisonment or death the person guilty of such attempt shall be punishable by imprisonment in the state prison for a term of five, seven, or nine years.
2. **Offenses Punishable by Imprisonment in the County Jail.** If the offense so attempted is punishable by imprisonment in a county jail, the person guilty of such attempt is punishable by imprisonment in a county jail for a term not exceeding one-half the term of imprisonment prescribed upon a conviction of the offense so attempted.
3. **Offenses Punishable by Fine.** If the offense so attempted is punishable by a fine, the offender convicted of such attempt is punishable by a fine not exceeding one-half the largest fine which may be imposed upon a conviction of the offense so attempted.
4. **Crimes Divided Into Degrees.** If a crime is divided into degrees, an attempt to commit the crime may be of any such degree, and the punishment for such an attempt shall be determined as provided by this section."

Attempts: Commission of a Different Crime. PC 664 does not protect a person who, in attempting unsuccessfully to commit a crime, accomplishes the commission of another and different crime, whether greater or less in guilt, from suffering the punishment prescribed by law for the crime committed (PC 665).

Discussion

An attempt actually consists of an act done by a perpetrator, with specific intent to commit a particular crime, such act going beyond mere preparation, and coming close to accomplishment, but which nevertheless falls short of consummation of the intended crime. Thus, criminal liability will result from an act done with intent to commit a particular crime which falls short of the commission itself.

In order to constitute an attempt there must be a direct, ineffectual act, done toward the ultimate commission of the crime (*People v. Stites, 75 Cal. 570*). Mere agreement to commit a crime will not constitute an attempt to commit that particular crime in the absence of some overt physical act. The courts have held that if acts transacted would have led to the completion of the crime had there not been some interruption, this is generally sufficient to constitute an attempted offense.

It is generally agreed that the defendant's conduct must be more than merely preparatory in character. Acts which are so remote as not even to suggest intent to commit crime would not be considered attempts. Thus where a man buys a gun and some cartridges to be used in a hold-up, such actions, at this point, would not satisfy the requirements of an attempted offense.

In order to establish an attempt to commit a particular crime, it must appear that the defendant had specific intent to commit the crime and did a direct, unequivocal act toward that end, and preparation alone is insufficient; some appreciable fragment of the crime sought to be committed must have been accomplished (*People v. McEwing, 216 C.A. 2d 33*).

Elements. The elements of an attempt are (a) intent to commit the crime and (b) a direct ineffectual act done toward the commission of the crime. As stated previously, an act of preparation, only, is not sufficient to constitute an attempted crime. The general rule is if the actual transaction has commenced which would have ended in the crime if not interrupted, there is an attempt to commit the crime. Generally, the punishment for an attempted offense is one-half the penalty of the completed crime with the differences previously noted.

In some instances, an attempt is directly declared by another Penal Code section to be a crime, e.g., attempt escape, PC 107 and attempt arson, PC 455. It should be noted that assault, PC 240, is in effect an attempt battery, PC 242. It is sufficient proof of an attempt to commit a crime where it is shown that efforts of the accused reached far enough toward accomplishment of the intended offense to amount to commencement of its consummation. Entering a car without the owner's permission and operating the starter in an apparent effort to start the motor, for example, is an attempt to commit theft of the car (*People v. Carter, 73 C.A. 3d 495*).

6.2 ABANDONMENT OF ATTEMPT

When the defendant commits acts toward the commission of a crime which thereby satisfy the *corpus delicti* of an "attempt to commit an offense," he cannot thereafter avoid responsibility by abandoning his original purpose. Thus, where a perpetrator specifically intends to commit a particular crime and commits the greater part of the act which would have resulted in the consummation of the crime had he not interrupted his efforts, or had them interrupted, he cannot rely on a subsequent abandonment of criminal purpose to negate such a criminal act; he is, in effect, guilty of an attempt to commit a crime. Abandonment is a defense if the attempt to commit a crime is freely and voluntarily abandoned before the act is put in process of final execution and when there is no outside cause prompting such abandonment (*People v. Von Hecht, 133 C.A. 2d 25*).

6.3 APPARENT POSSIBILITY OF COMPLETION

There can be no crime of attempt if there is an impossibility of its consummation. If the means are, to the defendant, apparently adapted to accomplish the intended result, there is a criminal attempt in the majority of cases. However, there are those cases where it would appear that the defendant was in a physical position to commit a crime but was unable to complete the act because of a legal ramification. Thus, where one throws red pepper in the eyes of another with the intent to blind him (PC 203, mayhem), and it can be shown that the inert material thrown was not pepper and would not destroy the eye or eyesight, the perpetrator cannot be guilty of attempted mayhem. The assailant might, however, be guilty of simple assault (PC 240) or battery (PC 242).

In another case, an adult man attempted to have voluntary sex with his adult adopted daughter, but was interrupted by his wife. The question is: are either guilty of attempted incest (PC 285)? Since PC 285 and Civil Code section 59 prohibits marriage or fornication (sexual intercourse) *only* between blood relatives, the crime of incest, and therefore the attempt, could *not* have been committed as a matter of law.

In order to determine whether a crime is apparently possible to commit or absolutely impossible to commit, it is necessary to look to court decisions, because as previously stated, if the crime can apparently be consummated, then it can be attempted. Early cases have held that the defendant's lack of knowledge of the impossibility of carrying out his intention, because of surrounding circumstances, is quite immaterial. For example, a defendant could be found guilty of attempting to steal money from an empty cash register or, in a more recent case, from the person of another who has no money in his pockets (*People v. Fiegelman, 33 C.A. 2d 100*). In another case, the court held that defendant could reasonably attempt to possess contraband in violation of the Health and Safety Code when he paid a large sum of money for common talcum powder, thinking it to be narcotics (*People v. Siu*). However, the courts have said that if a person attempts to shoot another with an unloaded gun, there can be no assault because of the impossibility of completing the crime by virtue of the gun being incapable of projecting a missile (*People v. Sylva, 143 Cal. 62*); but where a defendant fired a pistol through a roof at a location where he believed the intended victim to be, although the victim, a police officer, was some distance away, the court held this to be an assault because of the possibility of completion of the act (*People v. King, 97 Cal. 666*).

If a person attempts to do something which, even if his purpose is accomplished, will not be a crime by law, he is not guilty of criminal attempt. Thus, if a person were to shoot his mother-in-law, who was at the time reclining on a couch, but who in reality had died an hour earlier as a result of cardiac arrest, the person doing the shooting is not guilty of murder or attempted murder by reason of the absolute impossibility to kill a deceased person. Homicide is the killing of a human being by a human being, which implies that both must be living beings at or during the commission of the crime.

6.4   SOLICITATION TO COMMIT CRIME

PC 653f. Soliciting Commission of Certain Crimes: Punishment—Proof

a. Every person who solicits another to offer or accept or join in the offer or acceptance of a bribe, or to commit or join in the commission of robbery, burglary, grand theft, receiving stolen property, extortion, perjury, subornation of perjury, forgery, kidnapping, arson, or assault with a deadly weapon or instrument or by means of force likely to produce great bodily injury or, by the use of force or a threat of force, to prevent or dissuade any person who is or may become a witness from attending upon, or testifying at, any trial, proceeding, or inquiry authorized by law, is punishable by imprisonment in the county jail not more than one year or in the state prison, or by a fine of not more than five thousand dollars ($5,000), or the amount that could have been assessed for the commission of the offense itself, whichever is greater, or by both such fine and imprisonment.

b. Every person who solicits another to commit or join in the commission of murder is punishable by imprisonment in the state prison for two, four, or six years.

c. Every person who solicits another to commit rape by force or violence, sodomy by force or violence, oral copulation by force or violence, or any violations of *PC 264.1* (rape), *PC 288* (lewd act on child under fourteen) or *PC 289* (penetration of genital or anal openings by foreign object), is punishable by imprisonment in a state prison for two, three or four years.

d. An offense charged in violation of *PC 653f*, subdivision (a), (b), or (c) must be proved by the testimony of two witnesses or by one witness and corroborating circumstances.

Discussion

To ask a person to offer or join, etc., in itself consummates the crime of solicitation. The crime is further completed regardless of the response of the solicited person, and no overt act other than an honest, sincere request is necessary. Thus, it has been held a crime to solicit a public officer to take a bribe, or to solicit only those felony offenses enumerated in the statute. Soliciting a misdemeanor is not a crime under this section. If the crime solicited is committed, the offense of solicitation is merged in the greater offense.

The crime of solicitation must be proved by corroboration which consists of the testimony of two witnesses, or of one witness and corroborating circumstances. It is important to remember that in respect to such a requirement, proof that other persons were solicited to commit the same crime has been held to be sufficient corroboration. Also, corroboration in this case applies only to the trial and not the preliminary hearing.

The offense of solicitation to commit a felony does not require the commission of any overt act, and it is complete when the solicitation is made. It is immaterial that the object of the solicitation is never consummated, or that no steps are taken toward its consummation (*People v. Burt, 45 Cal. 2d 311*).

Solicitation of one to offer a bribe is a crime separate and distinct from the crime of bribery or the crime of attempt (*People v. Litt, 221 C.A. 2d 543*).

An "accomplice" is a "witness" within the meaning of this section (*People v. Rissman, 154 C.A. 2d 265*). In a prosecution for willfully, unlawfully, and feloniously soliciting certain persons to join in the commission of the crime of robbery, testimony of the person so solicited was amply sufficient to make it appear that the offense had been committed and that there was probable cause to believe the one soliciting had committed it (*Kind v. Superior Court, 143 C.A. 2d 100*).

6.5   OBSTRUCTING JUSTICE— COMPOUNDING CRIMES

Introduction. The administration of justice may be obstructed in many ways. For purposes of this section, however, we are limiting the term to include (1) compounding crimes, (2) perjury, (3) subornation of perjury, (4) bribery, and (5) falsification of evidence.

Compounding or Concealing Crimes. Every person who, having knowledge of the actual commission of a crime, takes money or property of another, or any gratuity or reward, or any engagement, or promise thereof, upon any agreement or understanding to compound or conceal such crime, or to abstain from any prosecution thereof, or to withhold any evidence thereof, except in the cases provided for by law, in which crimes may be compromised by leave of court, is punishable as follows:

1. By imprisonment in the state prison or in the county jail not exceeding one year, where the crime was punishable by death or imprisonment in the state prison for life;
2. By imprisonment in the state prison or in the county jail not exceeding six months, where the crime was punishable in the state prison for any other term than for life;
3. By imprisonment in the county jail not exceeding six months, or by fine not exceeding five hundred dollars ($500), where the crime was a misdemeanor (PC 153).

Discussion

The offense of compounding a crime is committed where one who knows that it has been committed agrees, for a consideration, not to prosecute. In order for the crime to be committed, it is necessary that a criminal offense shall first have actually been committed and that the defendant shall have knowledge of such an offense. However, the mere reimbursement to a person who has been injured by the commission of a crime is not necessarily a violation of the section. For example, where one settles out of court in respect to an injury caused through the commission of a crime, such as an assault and battery, the victim violates no law in accepting some compensation for such injury.

Where a person who has knowledge of the actual commission of a crime agrees to compound or conceal such a crime, or to abstain from any prosecution thereof, he is guilty of violating this section (*Bowyer v. Burgess, 54 Cal. 2d 97*).

Under Penal Code, Sections 1377 through 1379, provision is made for misdemeanors to be "compromised" (dismissed upon payment of damages to victim) under certain circumstances, such as when the person injured by an act constituting a misdemeanor has a remedy by civil action. Penal Code, Section 1378, provides that the court may stay proceedings when compensation for injury sustained by an individual as a result of a crime has been made to the victim. Penal Code, Section 1379, expressly prohibits the compounding or compromising of any offenses, misdemeanor or felony, except as provided in PC, Sections 1377 and 1378.

6.6   PERJURY

PC 118. Perjury Defined. Every person who, having taken an oath that he will testify, declare, depose, or certify truly before any competent tribunal, officer, or persons in any of the cases in which such an oath may by California law be administered, willfully and contrary to such oath, states as true any material matter which he knows to be false, and every person who testifies, declares, deposes, or certifies "under penalty of perjury" in any of the cases in which such testimony, declarations, or certification is permitted by California law under "penalty of perjury" and willfully states as true any material which he knows to be false, is guilty of perjury.

PC 118a. False Affidavit. Any person who, in any affidavit (written statement) taken before any person authorized to administer oaths, swears, affirms, declares, deposes, or certifies that he will testify truthfully, and in such affidavit wilfully and contrary to such oath, states as true any *material* matter (important, relevant) which he knows to be false, is guilty of perjury (briefed).

PC 119. Oath Defined. The term "oath," as used in the above section, includes an affirmation and every other mode authorized by law of attesting the truth of that which is stated.

PC 120. Oath of Office. That part of an oath of office which relates to the future performance of official duties is not an oath as defined in PC 119.

PC 121. Irregularity in Administering Oath. It is no defense to a prosecution for perjury that the oath was administered or taken in an irregular manner, or that the person accused of perjury did not go before, or was not in the presence of, the officer purporting to administer the oath, if such accused caused or procured such officer to certify that the oath had been taken or administered.

PC 122. Incompetency of Witness No Defense. It is no defense to a prosecution or perjury that the accused was not competent to give the testimony, deposition, or certificate of which falsehood is alleged. It is sufficient that he did give such testimony or make such deposition or certificate.

PC 123. Witness's Knowledge of Materiality of His Testimony Not Necessary. It is no defense to a prosecution for perjury that the accused did not know the materiality of the false statement made by him, or that it did not, in fact, affect the proceedings in or for which it was made. It is sufficient that it was material, and might have been used to affect such proceeding.

PC 124. Deposition, When Deemed to Be Complete. The making of a deposition, affidavit, or certificate is deemed to be complete, within the provisions of this chapter, from the time when it is delivered to the accused to any other person, with the intent that it be uttered or published as true.

PC 125. Statement of That Which One Does Not Know to Be True. An unqualified statement of that which one does not know to be true is equivalent to a statement of that which one knows to be false.

Discussion

Perjury at common law amounted to the willful and corrupt giving, upon a lawful oath, or in any form allowed by law to be substituted for an oath in a judicial proceeding or court of justice, of false testimony material to the issue or matter of inquiry.

California recognizes that the elements necessary to the establishment of perjury be that the defendant took an oath that he would testify truly before a competent tribunal, that the oath was taken in a case in which an oath could be lawfully administered, and that the defendant then, willfully and contrary to such oath, lied about a fact *material* to the case in which he was testifying.

The ordinary test of materiality is whether testimony given could have probably influenced the tribunal before which the cause was being tried, and even though the testimony given before the grand jury is false, it cannot support a conviction for perjury unless it influenced this body upon a material issue (*People v. Sagehorn, 140 C.A. 2d 138*).

Punishment for Perjury. Perjury is punishable by imprisonment in the state prison for two, three, or four years (PC 126).

6.7 SUBORNATION OF PERJURY

PC 127. "Every person who willfully procures another person to commit perjury is guilty of subornation of perjury, and is punishable in the same manner as he would be if personally guilty of the perjury so procured."

Discussion

The crime of subornation of perjury has two essential elements: (1) that one person shall willfully procure another person to commit perjury, and (2) that such other person shall commit perjury. However, if the evidence reveals that the testimony given by a person was done so in sincere belief in its truth and under an honest mistake, such a person is not guilty. To violate the provisions of this section, it is necessary that some person shall have committed the crime of perjury and that the perjury was committed through the procurement of the person charged with its subornation. In addition, the accused must know that the testimony given was untrue.

PC 128. Procuring the Execution of an Innocent Person. "Every person who by willful perjury or subornation of perjury, procures the conviction and execution of any innocent person, is punishable by death or life imprisonment without possibility of parole. The penalty shall be determined pursuant to Sections 190.3 and 190.4." These two sections define "mitigating" and "special" circumstances for punishment purposes.

6.8 BRIBERY

PC 67. Bribing Executive Officers. "Every person who gives or offers any bribe to any executive officer of this state with intent to influence him in respect to any act, decision, vote, opinion, or other proceeding as such officer, is punishable by imprisonment in the state prison for two, three, or four years, and is disqualified from holding any office in this state."

Bribery includes the asking, giving, receiving, or agreeing to receive of any valuable consideration for the purpose of corruptly influencing a person or official in the performance or failure to perform a public duty within the scope of his office or position.

PC 67½. Bribing Public Employees. "Every person who gives or offers as a bribe to any ministerial officer, employee, or appointee of the State of California, county or city therein or political subdivision thereof, anything the theft of which would be petty theft, is guilty of a misdemeanor; if the theft of the thing so given or offered would be grand theft, the offense is a felony."

Discussion

Under Penal Code, Section 67½, bribery or attempted bribery or any attempt to corruptly influence official action of police officers constitutes the crime (*Oppenheimer v. Clifton's Brookdale, 98 C.A. 2d 403*). The crime is complete when a police officer is offered a bribe to allow gaming to continue, whether such illegal activity does in fact continue, and the officer is guilty of accepting a bribe (*People v. Markham, 64 Cal. 157*).

It is not an essential element of the crime of bribery that the bribe be offered to an official with actual authority as long as the official's act falls within the general scope of duties of the person being bribed.

PC 70. Unauthorized Gratuities—Outside Police Work. Every executive or ministerial officer, employee or appointee of the State of California, county or city therein or political subdivision thereof, who knowingly asks, receives, or agrees to receive any emolument, gratuity, or reward, or any promise thereof excepting such as may be authorized by law for doing an official act, is guilty of a misdemeanor.

Nothing contained in this section shall preclude a peace officer, as defined in PC 830, from engaging in, or being employed in, casual or part-time employment as a private security guard or patrolman for a *public entity* while off duty from his or her principal employment and outside his or her regular employment as a peace officer of a state or local agency, and exercising the powers of a peace officer *concurrently* with such employment, provided that such peace officer is in a *police uniform* and subject to reasonable rules and regulations of the agency for which he or she is a peace officer.

Notwithstanding the above provisions, any and all civil and criminal liability arising out of the secondary employment of any peace officer shall be borne by such officer's secondary employer.

It is the intent of the Legislature by this paragraph to abrogate (repeal) the holdings in *People v. Corey, 21 C. 3d 738* and *Cervantez v. J.C. Penney Co., 24 C. 3d 579*, to reinstate criminal sanctions for assault on peace officers who are employed, on a part-time or casual basis, by a *public* entity, while wearing a police uniform as private security guards or patrolmen and to allow the exercise of peace officer powers concurrently with such employment (1982, briefed).

Discussion

This 1982 amendment to PC 70 was for the obvious purpose of nullifying the two cases cited, thus restoring peace officer powers to officers "moonlighting" on a second part-time job. Assaulting someone so employed thus becomes a more serious assault under

PC 241(b), assault of a peace officer. It should also be noted that the officer *must* be in uniform and must be working for a *public* entity (such as for a community college district at a football game) as opposed to a private entity (such as "Joe's Bar and Grill").

Blackstone pointed out in his commentaries that bribery amounted to the receiving by a judge or other officer connected with the administration of justice of "any undue reward to influence his behavior in his office." Other early legal commentaries mentioned that the gist of the offense is the tendency of the bribe to pervert justice in any of the governmental departments.

In the giving of a bribe to an executive officer, the offense is complete when the bribe is delivered to the person being bribed. In the offense of offering a bribe, it is not necessary that any particular language be used by the person offering such bribe. Any conduct by the intending corruptor which satisfies the inference that a bribe is being offered is satisfactory. Thus, in the prosecution for giving away narcotic substance and giving a bribe to a deputy sheriff, the jury could have reasonably inferred that criminal intent to offer a bribe did originate in the mind of the accused and that he was not induced by the officer to commit the crime (*People v. Sweeney, 55 Cal. 2d 27*).

It is immaterial that an arrest and subsequent search be legal in order for an officer to have been offered a bribe. Simply stated, it is no defense for a person to have offered a bribe to a policeman in consideration for an immediate release from custody upon an illegal arrest. The character of the arrest, or a seizure made thereafter has no bearing on the crime of bribery, and the latter is committed when the elements are complete (*People v. Guillory, 178 C.A. 2d 854*).

6.9 BRIBERY OF WITNESSES

PC 136½. Bribing Witnesses Not to Attend. Every person who gives or offers or promises to give any witness or person about to be called as a witness, any bribe upon any understanding or agreement that such person shall not attend upon any trial or judicial proceeding, or every person who attempts by means of any offer of a bribe to dissuade any such person from attending upon any trial or judicial proceeding, is guilty of a felony.

PC 137. Bribing or Forcing Witness to Give False Testimony. Every person who gives or offers, or promises to give to any witness, or person about to be called as a witness, or person about to give material information pertaining to a crime to a law enforcement official, any bribe, upon any understanding or agreement that the testimony of such witness or information given to such person shall be thereby influenced is guilty of a felony.

   b. Every person who attempts by force or threat of force or by the use of fraud to induce any person to give false testimony or withhold true testimony or to give false material information pertaining to a crime to, or withhold true material information pertaining to a crime from, a law enforcement official is guilty of a felony, punishable by imprisonment in state prison for two, three, or four years.

As used in this section, "threat of force" means a credible threat of unlawful injury to any person or damage to the property of another, which is communicated to a person for the purpose of inducing him to give false testimony or withhold true testimony or to give false material information pertaining to a crime to, or to withhold true material information pertaining to a crime from, a law enforcement official.

   c. Every person who knowingly induces another person to give false testimony or withhold true testimony not privileged by law, or to give false material information pertaining to a crime to a law enforcement official is guilty of a misdemeanor.

As used in this section "law enforcement official" includes any district attorney, deputy district attorney, city attorney, deputy city attorney, the Attorney General or any deputy attorney general or any peace officer included in PC 830 (PC 137(e)). The provisions of PC 137(c) shall not apply to an attorney advising a client or to a person advising a member of his or her family (PC 137(f)).

PC 138. Witness Receiving Bribes. Every person who is a witness, or is about to be called as such, who receives or offers to receive, any bribe, upon any understanding that he will absent himself from the trial or proceeding upon which his testimony is required, is guilty of a felony.

The offense of bribery also encompasses the following: Asking or receiving by such persons or by public officers, employees or appointees (Penal Code, Sections 68, 70, 73, 74, and 165); soliciting of an offer or acceptance of a bribe (PC 653f); bribery of athletic participants (PC 337b); bribery of legislators (PC 85 & 86); and giving or offering bribes to judges, jurors, referees (PC 29, 93, 95 and 69).

6.10 FALSIFYING EVIDENCE

PC 132. Offering False Evidence. This section provides that every person who upon any trial, proceeding, inquiry, or investigation whatever, authorized or permitted by law, offers in evidence as genuine or true, any book, paper, document, record, or other instrument in writing, knowing the same to have been forged or fraudulently altered or antedated, is guilty of a felony.

The term *antedated* means dated ahead in time or place. It should be noted that this section applies to *written* evidence, only, and not to all types of evidence.

PC 133. Deceiving a Witness. Every person who practices any fraud or deceit, or knowingly makes or exhibits any false statement, representation, token, or writing, to any witness or person about to be called as a witness upon any trial, proceeding, inquiry or investigation whatever, authorized by law, with intent to affect the testimony of such witness, is guilty of a misdemeanor.

PC 134. Preparing False Evidence. Every person guilty of preparing any false or antedated book, paper, record, instrument in writing, or other matter or thing, with intent to produce it, or allow it to be produced for any fraudulent or deceitful purpose, as genuine or true, upon any trial, proceeding, or inquiry whatever, authorized by law, is guilty of a felony.

PC 135. Destroying Evidence. Every person who, knowing that any book, paper, record, instrument in writing, *or other matter or thing,* is about to be produced in evidence upon any trial, inquiry, or investigation whatever, authorized by law, willfully destroys or conceals same, with intent thereby to prevent it from being produced, is guilty of a felony. (Italics added for emphasis.)

6.11 CONSPIRACY

The crime of conspiracy may be committed in any one of the following six ways.

PC 182. "If two or more persons conspire:
1. To commit *any* crime (italics added).
2. Falsely and maliciously to indict another for any crime, or to procure another to be charged or arrested for any crime.
3. Falsely to move or maintain any suit, action, or proceeding.
4. To cheat and defraud any person of any property, by means which are in themselves criminal, or to obtain money or property by false pretense

or by false promises with fraudulent intent not to perform such promises.

5. To commit any act injurious to the public health, to public morals, or to pervert or obstruct justice or the due administration of the laws.
6. To commit any crime against the person of the President or Vice President of the United States, the governor of any state or territory, any United States Justice or Judge, or the secretary of any of the executive departments of the United States."

PC 184. "No agreement amounts to a conspiracy, unless some act, besides such agreement, be done within this state to effect the object thereof, by one or more of the parties to such agreement and the trial of cases of conspiracy may be had in any county in which any act be done."

Punishment for Conspiracy. Those found guilty of conspiracy, are punishable as follows:

When they conspire to commit any crime against the person of any official specified in subdivision 6, they are guilty of a felony and are punishable by imprisonment in the state prison for five, seven, or nine years.

When they conspire to commit any other felony, they shall be punishable in the same manner and to the same extent as is provided for the punishment of the said felony. If the felony is one for which different punishments are prescribed for different degrees, the jury or court which finds the defendant guilty thereof shall determine the degree of the felony defendant conspired to commit. If the degree is not so determined, the punishment for conspiracy to commit such felony shall be that prescribed for the lesser degree, except in the case of conspiracy to commit murder, in which the punishment shall be that prescribed for murder in the first degree.

If the felony is conspiracy to commit two or more felonies which have different punishments and the commission of such felonies constitutes but one offense of conspiracy, the penalty shall be that prescribed for the felony which has the greater maximum term.

When they conspire to do an act described in subdivision 4 of this section, they shall be punishable by imprisonment in the state prison, or by imprisonment in the county jail for not more than one year, or by a fine not exceeding five thousand dollars ($5,000), or both.

When they conspire to do any of the other acts described in this section they shall be punishable by imprisonment in the county jail for not more than one year, or in the state prison, or by a fine not exceeding five thousand dollars ($5,000) or both.

All cases of conspiracy may be prosecuted and tried in the superior court of any county in which any overt act tending to effect such conspiracy shall be done (*PC 182*).

Discussion

Conspiracy is actually an agreement of two or more persons to do an act which is unlawful in itself or to do a lawful act by the use of means which are unlawful. It is essential to the commission of the crime of conspiracy that there be an agreement or understanding between two or more persons that they shall act together. It is not necessary that the agreement be a formal one; it is sufficient if the minds of the parties meet understandingly so as to bring about an intelligent and deliberate agreement.

There can be no conspiracy without two or more persons agreeing to commit an unlawful act, and while at common law, husband and wife were considered one person, such is not the case in California (*People v. Pierce, 61 Cal. 2d 879*).

6.12 OVERT ACT IN CONSPIRACY

No agreement amounts to a conspiracy, unless some act, beside such agreement, be done within this state to effect the object thereof, by one or more of the parties to such agreement, and the trial of cases of conspiracy may be had in any county in which any such act be done (*PC 184*).

Discussion

The term "overt act" means any step taken or act committed by one or more of the conspirators that goes beyond the mere planning or agreement to commit a public offense and which step or act is done in furtherance of the accomplishment of the object of the conspiracy.

To be an "overt act," the step taken or act committed need not, in and of itself, constitute the crime or even an attempt to commit the crime which is the ultimate object of the conspiracy. Nor is it required that such step or act in and of itself, be unlawful.

Mere agreement or understanding between two or more persons to do an unlawful act under PC 182 is *not* sufficient to make the crime of conspiracy complete. Before the agreement amounts to a conspiracy, at least one of the conspirators must perform some overt act, lawful or unlawful, evidencing that the parties have gone beyond mere agreement and that the conspiracy has begun an active existence. It is not necessary that the overt act amount to an attempt to perform the conspiracy, although such would clearly constitute an overt act.

Specific Intent

Conspiracy is a specific intent crime, requiring the accused to have specific intent to do an unlawful act or to do a lawful act by unlawful means (*People v. Jones, 228 C.A. 2d 74*). To sustain a conviction of conspiracy there must be proof that the accused entered into a criminal agreement with specific intent to commit a crime (*People v. Smith, 63 Cal. 2d 779*).

Criminal conspiracy exists when two or more persons agree to commit a crime and then do some overt act in furtherance of the agreement (*People v. Cockrell, 63 Cal. 2d 779*). Criminal conspiracy is a corrupt agreement between two or more persons to commit an offense prohibited by statute and which is accompanied by some overt act in furtherance of such agreement (*People v. Danielson, 203 C.A. 2d 498*).

6.13 AGREEMENT OR UNDERSTANDING NECESSARY IN CONSPIRACY

The agreement referred to in the statute must be to do some act, whether it be legal or illegal. It is not necessary that each conspirator should know all of the details of the project or that the agreement should require each conspirator to participate in carrying out every detail of the conspiracy. It is sufficient that there should be a common understanding of the end to be achieved and an agreement to do whatever may be necessary to the achievement of such end.

An agreement to commit a crime, as an element of criminal conspiracy, may be inferred from the conduct of defendants in mutually carrying out a common purpose in violation of the statute defining conspiracy (*People v. Cockrell, 63 Cal. 2d 659*).

The gist of criminal conspiracy is the formation of a combination with others to do an unlawful act or to do a lawful act by unlawful means; conspiracy is a separate and distinct offense from the crime which is the substantive object of the conspiracy (*People v. Marrone, 210 C.A. 2d 299*).

Proof that two or more individuals conspired to commit a crime and engaged in overt acts leading to its commission will sustain a conviction of conspiracy even though they failed to accomplish the object of their intrigue (*People v. Buono, 191 C.A. 2d 203*). Thus, three defendants who acted in concert with each other in transporting stolen property with an ultimate objective of disposing of it in some manner

were guilty of conspiracy (*People v. Wells, 187 C.A. 2d 324*).

It need not be shown, in order to establish a conspiracy, that the parties entered into a definite agreement, but it is sufficient that they tacitly came to an understanding to accomplish the act and unlawful design, and such agreement may be inferred from the acts and conduct of the parties in mutually carrying out a common purpose in violation of the law (*People v. Buckman, 186 C.A. 2d 38*).

Husband and wife could not, at common law, enter into a conspiracy between themselves without a third party being involved. Such is not the case in California today. Husband and wife can conspire only between themselves, without a third party, and can no longer claim immunity from prosecution for conspiracy on the basis of their marital status (*People v. Pierce, 61 Cal. 2d 879*).

6.14 ABANDONMENT OF CONSPIRACY

Unlike the crime of criminal attempt under PC 664, one can withdraw from a criminal conspiracy after once having met the requirements of a co-conspirator. In so doing, the abandoning conspirator must not only withdraw from all further activity, but must remain away from the scene at the time the crime is committed by other conspirators. Further, one who intends to withdraw from a conspiracy must make this fact known to his confederates; indicating his desire to entirely sever his relationship and no longer be a partner to the illegal enterprise (*People v. Beaumaster, 17 Cal. App. 3d 996*).

Discussion

There is little case law to date on the withdrawal of a conspirator from the crime of conspiracy. However, there is some indication that while the person who intends to abandon such a conspiracy need not make his intentions known in writing, he would certainly be more successful in notifying the authorities either before or after his withdrawal.

One who has joined a criminal conspiracy can only effectively withdraw therefrom by some affirmative act bringing home the fact of his withdrawal to his confederates. Unless there is some affirmative act bringing home the withdrawal to the knowledge of his confederates, the person will be presumed to have continued until the ultimate purpose of the conspiracy is established (*People v. Moran, 166 C.A. 2d 410*).

In a robbery prosecution, communication of defendant's withdrawal from a conspiracy to commit robbery by mere acts or words to that effect was sufficient (*People v. Wilson, 76 C.A. 688*).

6.15 CRIMINAL LIABILITY FOR CONSPIRACY

All co-conspirators are liable for the resultant circumstances and consequences that naturally flow from the conspiracy and for the acts of all who participate with them in executing the unlawful purpose. Each conspirator is said to be the agent of the other, and the acts done are, therefore, the acts of each and every co-conspirator. Moreover, if one knowing of a conspiracy, without intending to join the agreement, nevertheless aids in carrying out such a conspiracy, he becomes equally guilty with the other conspirators.

Conspirators need not all join in the agreement at the same time. Those who join in a conspiracy previously formed, and who thereafter assist in its execution, become conspirators, and are equally liable with the others, not only for acts done thereafter, but for the original agreement as well, and for all acts done in furtherance thereof (*People v. Brawley, 1 C. 3d 277*).

Each conspirator is bound by the acts of a confederate in furthering the common design of conspiracy by escaping or resisting arrest, even though such acts may have been dictated by the exigencies of the moment (*People v. Smith, 63 Cal. 2d 779*).

All members of a criminal conspiracy are bound by all of the acts of the members thereof in furtherance of an agreed-upon purpose (*People v. Scott, 224 C.A. 2d 146*). In addition, one who joins a conspiracy after its formation is liable as a conspirator just as those who originated it (*People v. Cornell, 188 C.A. 2d 668*).

Once a defendant's participation in a conspiracy is shown, it will be presumed to continue unless he is able to prove that he effectively withdrew from the conspiracy before acts toward the conspired crime commenced (*People v. Crosby, 58 Cal. 2d 713*).

TERMINOLOGY DEFINED—CHAPTER 6

See the Terminology Quiz at the end of this chapter.
1. Abstain: to refrain from, refusing to participate.
2. Attest: to bear witness, to certify as true.
3. Compromise: settlement of a dispute by agreement of the parties.
4. Contusion: a bruise or similar injury however slight.
5. Cross-examination: examination of a witness by the opposing side.
6. Cumulative: additional evidence to the same point.
7. Deposition: sworn testimony given out of court to proper official.
8. e.g.: (Latin, *exempli gratia*) means "for example."
9. Element: identifiable segment of the *corpus delicti*.
10. i.e.: (Latin, *id est*) means "that is," or "in other words."
11. Immaterial: not important, does not alter anything.
12. Impanel: the process of selecting and seating a jury.
13. Impotent: lacking in sexual ability.
14. Incompetent: unfit, legally inadmissible.
15. Irrelevant: not to the point, does not apply.
16. Oath: promise or affirmation, attesting the truth.
17. Overt act: a physical act, usually toward completing a crime.
18. Perjury: giving false evidence or testimony under oath.
19. q.v.: (Latin *quode vide*) means "which see" or "see reference."
20. Solicitation: crime of offering a bribe or asking another to participate in certain felonies.

TRUE-FALSE QUIZ—CHAPTER 6

1. An act of preparation is sufficient to make one guilty of an attempt crime.
2. Entering a car without the owner's consent and operating the starter with a stolen key constitutes an attempt theft.
3. One who abandons his original purpose after committing acts toward the commission of a crime is not guilty of any crime.
4. There can be no crime of attempt if there is an impossibility of its consummation.
5. If one attempts to shoot another with an unloaded gun, he is guilty of an assault.
6. A person could be guilty of attempting to steal money from an empty cash drawer if at the time he thought it contained money.
7. If one shoots another, not knowing the person he shot was already dead, he is not guilty of assault.
8. Merely asking another to accept a bribe legally consummates the crime of solicitation.
9. The crime of solicitation must be corroborated by two witnesses or by one witness and corroborating circumstances.

10. Soliciting one to commit a misdemeanor is a crime under PC 653f.

11. The offense of solicitation does not require an overt act other than the initial solicitation.

12. If one offers an officer a bribe, but the officer refuses, the one offering the bribe is still guilty of the crime of solicitation.

13. One is not guilty of perjury if he falsely testifies as to some immaterial fact.

14. If "A" takes money from "B" to commit perjury, but instead "A" tells the truth, "B" is still guilty of subornation of perjury.

15. Offering a teacher something of value in order to receive a better grade constitutes the crime of bribery under PC 67½.

16. Because of their marital status, husband and wife cannot commit the crime of conspiracy in California.

17. Mere agreement by two or more persons to commit a felony constitutes conspiracy.

18. Conspiracy to commit a misdemeanor is a felony under PC 182.

19. If "A" and "B" plan a burglary, and "A" buys a pry-bar as a result, both are at that time guilty of conspiracy even though they are arrested before they actually do anything else toward commission of the burglary.

20. All co-conspirators are liable for the consequences of the acts of any one of the group in carrying out the conspiracy.

ESSAY-DISCUSSION QUESTIONS— CHAPTER 6

The following may be used as either essay questions or class discussion questions at the discretion of the instructor. The student may demonstrate his knowledge of this chapter by answering each of the questions.

1. How is an attempt defined? How far must it go toward completion to constitute a crime?

2. At what point is abandonment of an attempt a defense to the crime?

3. List any ten of the thirteen crimes for which one may be guilty of solicitation under PC 653f.

4. What are the elements of conspiracy?

5. Explain the overt act discussed in your text relative to conspiracy.

6. What are the elements of compounding a crime? Under what circumstances is it a felony and when a misdemeanor?

7. What is the essence of the crime of perjury? Must the witness know he is lying and must his statement be material to the case?

8. What are the elements of subornation of perjury? How does it differ from perjury?

9. What are the elements of bribery? What effect, if any, does the value of the bribe have on the offense?

10. How does bribery of a witness differ from subornation of perjury?

TERMINOLOGY QUIZ—CHAPTER 6

Match terms and definitions by placing the correct number in the parentheses. Answers may be written on a separate sheet for submission to the instructor at the instructor's direction.

1. Abstain	( ) giving false evidence or testimony under oath
2. Attest	( ) promise or affirmation, attesting the truth
3. Compromise	( ) to bear witness, to certify as true
4. Contusion	( ) settlement of a dispute by agreement of the parties
5. Cross examination	( ) not to the point, does not apply
6. Cumulative	( ) a bruise or similar injury
7. Deposition	( ) unfit, legally inadmissible
8. e.g.	( ) lacking in sexual ability
9. Element	( ) additional evidence to the same point
10. i.e.	( ) sworn testimony given out of court
11. Immaterial	( ) Latin: "for example"
12. Impanel	( ) the process of selecting and seating a jury
13. Impotent	( ) identifiable segment of the *corpus delicti*
14. Incompetent	( ) not important, does not alter anything
15. Irrelevant	( ) Latin: meaning "that is" or "in other words"
16. Oath	
17. Overt act	
18. Perjury	
19. q.v.	
20. Solicitation	

CHAPTER 7

Laws of Arrest

7.1 ARREST DEFINED

PC 834 defines arrest simply as follows: "An arrest is taking a person into custody, in a case and in the manner authorized by law. An arrest may be made by a peace officer or by a private person."

The essential elements of an arrest are (1) the taking of a person into custody *and* (2) the actual restraint of the person *or* his submission to custody (*People v. Hatcher, 2 C.A. 3d 612*). An arrest is a "seizure" and an arrest without a warrant or probable cause is "unreasonable" within the purview of the Fourth Amendment (*Lockridge v. Superior Court 275 C.A. 2d 612*). It might also be noted that a traffic violator is, during the period immediately preceding his signing of the promise to appear, under arrest (*People v. Hubbard, 9 C.A. 3d 827*).

The term "arrest" is defined by *Black's Law Dictionary* as "the apprehending or detaining of the person in order to be forthcoming to answer an alleged or suspected crime," and by *Cochran's Law Lexicon* as "the seizing of a person and detaining him in custody by lawful authority." Other sources have variously defined the term to mean the taking or detainment of a person into custody by authority of law, or the detaining of the person in order to be forthcoming to answer an alleged or supposed crime.

In California, the terms "arrest" and "detention" are not synonymous under the law. This fact was effectively pointed out by the Appellate Court years ago when they opined that a police officer has a right to make inquiry in a proper manner of anyone upon the public streets at a late hour as to his identity and the occasion of his presence, if the surroundings are such as to indicate to a reasonable man that the public safety demands such identification (*Gisske v. Sanders, 9 C.A. 13, 1908*). Hence, there is an obvious legal difference in the physical seizure of a person and merely detaining him by legal authority.

PC 835 defined how an arrest is made and what restraint is allowed. "An arrest is made by actual restraint of the person or by submission to the custody of an officer. The person arrested may be subjected to such restraint as is reasonable for his arrest and detention."

Legality of Arrest. A proper and lawfully executed arrest will generally not be rendered illegal should there be a delay in arraigning the arrestee (*People v. Jablon, 153 C.A. 2d 456*). However, the criminal and civil liability for such delay on the part of the police officer are apparent from the discussion in Section 7.18 and 7.19 of this text.

Improper procedures during or after arrest which amount to a denial of due process of law will generally result in the defendant being freed by the court. Examples of such a condition would include failure to properly arraign the defendant, failure to allow the arrestee the use of a telephone during detention. A failure to properly admonish the arrestee of his constitutional rights per the *Miranda* decision during his arrest, may result in a dismissal of the case because any confession obtained and all subsequent evidence obtained, ("Fruit of the Poisoned Tree" Doctrine) might well be excluded by the court.

To further exemplify the need for a lawful and properly executed arrest, the United States Supreme Court has held that whenever a person is in custody, or deprived of his freedom of action in any significant way, police must warn him of his constitutional rights. The Supreme Court defined "custody" thusly: "By custodial interrogation, we mean questioning initiated by law enforcement officers after a person has been taken into custody or otherwise deprived of his freedom of action in any significant way." (*Miranda v. Arizona, 384 U.S. 436*).

7.2 LAWFUL DETENTION

Generally there is a legal difference as to what actually constitutes an arrest and what amounts to a temporary detention for questioning. In California, statutory authority for warrantless arrests is defined in two sections of the Penal Code, both of which have already been discussed: PC 834, relating to the definition of an arrest, and PC 835, relating to how the arrest is made. These two sections of the Penal Code are the only statutory definitions of arrest.

An "arrest" depends entirely upon the context in which it is used. To determine whether an "arrest" has been made, the entire circumstances surrounding the incident should be examined to determine if there has been an "actual restraint" or "submission to custody" as defined in PC 835. The same holds true for temporary detention: to establish the propriety of a stopping and questioning, the facts must be testified to fully so that a reviewing court is in a position to either approve or disapprove the conduct of the police. The officer may have to rely upon his expertise, training, or past experience as a trained observer to establish to the court his justification (reasonable cause) for both temporary detention and arrest.

Differentiation Between Arrest and Detention. Temporary detention cannot be taken out of the context of the law of arrest for there is indeed a fine line between the two. Even a temporary detention for questioning can amount to an "actual restraint" of a person if it takes an unreasonable time.

While in California there is no statutory or constitutional authority to stop and question, the right to do so has been approved only by judicial interpretation, and the leading case in this connection is *In re Tony C., 21 C. 3d 288.* In this case the courts stated that an officer in the performance of his duties has to have a "rational suspicion" that the person contacted has some connection with criminal activity.

California courts have apparently sought to retain the right of a police officer to detain and question a person without neccessarily making an arrest in an effort to preserve the peace, protect property, suppress affrays, riots, etc., to investigate public offenses and to prevent crime in general. The court states, "We do not believe that our rule permitting temporary detention for questioning conflicts with the Fourth Amendment. It strikes a balance between a person's interest in immunity from police interference and the community interest in law enforcement. It wards off pressure to equate reasonable cause to investigate with reasonable cause to arrest, thus protecting the innocent from the risk of arrest when no more than reasonable investigation is justified" (*People v. Mickelson, 59 Cal. 2d 448).*

Circumstances Under Which Police May Detain and Question. As a general rule, circumstances short of probable cause to make an arrest may justify an officer stopping a pedestrian or motorist on the street for questioning. Probable cause to detain is that state of facts which would indicate to a reasonable man in a similar situation that there is a rational suspicion that some criminal activity has taken place even though the actions may be as consistent with innocent activity as with guilty. This is a decision that must be made in the first instance by the individual police officer, subject to later review by the court. Behavior which may be regarded as ordinary by the casual observer may be extremely significant to a trained officer. Police officers and police witnesses must be able to testify to the singular conduct of a suspect which makes such conduct meaningful and distinctive, to establish probable cause.

The following are examples of other relevant factors justifying investigation and detention by police:

1. *Time:* Men talking together in front of a used car lot during the day is not unusual; at 3:00 a.m. however, an investigation may be warranted (*People v. Taylor, 6 Cal. App. 3d 51).*
2. *Location:* A subject alone at 10:00 p.m. on a residential street 100 feet from a location where shots were fired.
3. *Pedestrians or automobiles:* The high mobility of an automobile has been recognized by the courts as a justification for some relaxation of the rules for arrest and detention. For example, a suspect driving a car which matched the description of a car involved in a recent robbery could be stopped; or, the conduct of three men in an automobile at 12:30 a.m. who looked steadily at a motel across the street, turned the car lights on, then off, waited five minutes, and then drove away, was sufficiently unusual to excite suspicion and subsequent detention (*People v. Cowman, 223 C.A. 2d 109).* In another case, officers testified that the defendant's youth was inconsistent with his presence in a parked Cadillac, and that he appeared "nervous." A subsequent search revealed marijuana on the defendant's person. The court held that there was no probable cause for detention of the defendant, finding "little, if anything, to distinguish the defendant from any other harried citizen who may have parked his automobile in the same spot." The lack of probable cause for detention caused the court to exclude the marijuana from evidence (*People v. One Cadillac Coupe, 62 Cal. 2d 92).*
4. *Number of people involved:* Depending on the location, and to some extent the time of day, several people grouped together might easily invite investigation.

Note: Following a 1983 decision by the U.S. Supreme Court, PC 647(e) no longer gives an officer the right to stop and question a subject who "Loiters or wanders upon the streets or from place to place without apparent reason or business and who refuses to identify himself and to account for his presence when requested by any peace officer so to do . . ." (See PC 647(e) on page 110 of your text for more details.)

Recently Reported Crimes. A report that a recent robbery-murder had just been committed by two men seen escaping in a red Cadillac, without further description, was sufficient to warrant detaining a red Cadillac proceeding normally on the streets shortly after the reported crime even though it contained but one person (*People v. Schader, 60 Cal. 2d 716*).

The defendant's detention was held to be legal where four girls had been at the scene of a robbery and ran away together after its commission. The defendant was seen with three girls who matched the description of the suspects shortly after the robbery and one-half block away and the defendant matched the fourth suspect as to race, sex and age (*In re Lynnete G., 54 Cal. App. 3d 1087*).

The Officer's Intent in Detaining. If an officer manifests an intent to arrest from the outset of the investigation, courts will label such action an arrest, not detention. Thus, any evidence seized when there is probable cause to detain but not to arrest will be rendered inadmissible. In the case *People v. Cowman,* the officers did not have probable cause to arrest, but did have probable cause to detain. The questioning after the detention revealed an effort by the officers to determine the legality of the defendant's conduct. He could have been on legitimate business, seeking a motel at which to stay the night.

In *People v. Curtis, 70 C. 2d 347,* a uniformed police officer was investigating a report of a nighttime prowler and had received a description of a male suspect, about six feet tall, wearing a white shirt and tan trousers. As he cruised the neighborhood, the officer saw the defendant, who met that description, walking along the street. The officer pulled alongside the defendant, told him to stop, and the defendant complied. After the officer got out of the car, he told the defendant he was under arrest. The defendant had appeared cooperative, he had made no furtive or suspicious movements. The officer did not question the defendant; instead he reached for the defendant's arm. The defendant tried to back away, a violent struggle ensued, both men were injured in the battle, and it finally took several officers to subdue the defendant. Defendant was acquitted of burglary but

was convicted of a felony, assault upon a peace officer (Penal Code 245).

The California Supreme Court reversed the conviction. The Court held that there were sufficient grounds to detain and question the defendant, but the officer lacked probable cause to arrest him since there could have been more than one person similarly dressed in that neighborhood that night, defendant made no furtive movements, and the defendant lived a block from where he was arrested. The Court in support cited *People v. Mickelson (1963) 63 Cal. 2d 488* and *People v. Ingle (1960) 63 Cal. 2d 407.*

The Court upheld the prior court interpretations of Section 834a of the Penal Code, prohibiting forceful resistance to lawful or unlawful arrests if the person has knowledge, or, by the exercise of reasonable care, should have knowledge that he is being arrested by a peace officer. The statute has not altered or diminished the remedies for an illegal arrest, but now requires a person to submit peacefully to arrest. However, the section merely eliminates the common law defense of resistance to unlawful arrest and does not make such resistance a new crime.

Penal Code, Section 243 (Battery on Peace Officer), like Penal Code, Section 148, (Resisting Arrest), was intended to punish resistance to an arrest. For a discussion of resistance to arrest, both lawful and unlawful, see Section 7.10, this chapter.

The question of an officer using excessive force is separate and distinct from that of the legality of the arrest. Under Penal Code, Section 835 and 835(a), an officer may use only reasonable force to make an arrest or to overcome resistance. The Court found that Penal Code, Sections 692 and 693, allow a defendant to use reasonable force to defend life and limb against excessive force. If the resistance is not justified and the arrest lawful, then the felony provisions of Section 243 apply. If the resistance is not justified and the arrest was unlawful, the conviction may be only for a misdemeanor. In a footnote the Court stated that the same rationale would apply to the greater penalty of Penal Code, Section 245 (ADW) subdivision (b) and the lesser penalty under Section 245, subdivision (a).

The Court also discussed the need for proper jury instructions and concluded that a challenge to the constitutional validity of a prior conviction should be decided by the Court outside the presence of the jury.

Determining Length and Purpose of the Detention. In the case of a reported crime having recently occurred, the officer may request the suspect to return to the scene of the crime for identification (*People v. Hanamoto, 234 C.A. 2d 6*). As a general rule, the length of time for detention should be reasonably related to the scope of interrogation, such as in the Shaw case. It is not the length of the detention itself which is critical, but whether the detention time was reasonably required to satisfy the purposes of the investigation. Thus, where a suspect was stopped because he resembled a photograph of a man wanted for murder and was subsequently transported to the police station for questioning, and thereafter taken to his room to obtain evidence of his identity where a search of his room revealed an illegal firearm, the court concluded that the conduct of the police was investigatory up to and including the discovery of the gun (*People v. Robertson, 240 Cal. App. 2d 100*).

Traffic Stops. The California Supreme Court has held that a motorist can only be detained for a warrant check for approximately the same amount of time it would take to write an ordinary traffic citation (*People v. McGaughran, 25 C. 3d 577*).

The Cursory Search Upon Detention. If the detention is proper and the circumstances warrant it, the courts will approve a cursory search for weapons or dangerous instrumentalities which would endanger the officer. This "frisk" is not regarded as a true search such as a "skin search" but rather a self-protective device for the officer's benefit as provided by PC 833. If there is probable cause to detain, and if the investigation reveals probable cause to arrest, then a true search incident to the lawful arrest may be conducted.

In permitting officers to run their hands over the outer garments of a person being questioned, the courts adopt a commonsense approach to the need for prevention against unsuspected attacks on police. But the courts scrutinize the officer's conduct to determine whether he has acted with the purpose of self-protection in mind. If the frisk is an excuse to conduct an exploratory search, any evidence seized is inadmissible as not incidental to a lawful arrest. If weapons are discovered, they may be removed and subsequently returned, or the person may be arrested on a weapons charge. Similarly, if contraband is in plain sight during the cursory search, it may be seized and the subject may be arrested for illegal possession.

An officer has the right to forestall efforts of an arrestee to reach for a weapon, to require arrestee to keep his hands in sight and then to take and examine anything that may be found on his person (*People v. Strelich, 189 C.A. 2d 632*).

The classic justifications for the doctrine of search incident to an arrest (that is, the need to discover hidden weapons and the need to prevent defendant's destruction of evidence), are not exclusive, but simply examples of circumstances that may lead to the conclusion that the search as a whole was reasonable (*People v. Webb, 66 Cal. 2d 107*).

The failure of defendant who was simply walking down an alley to stop at the officer's first command did not suffice to supply the requisite cause to detain and frisk defendant, and the evidence produced thereby was inadmissible where, though it could be inferred that the officer had heard the victim of a prior robbery call to defendant to stop, the officer neither heard nor relied on the victim's actions (*People v. Hunt, 250 C.A. 2d 311*).

7.3 PEACE OFFICER DEFINED

Chapter 4.5 of the California Penal Code, Sections 830 and 831 (with their many subsections) defines who are peace officers in this state. PC 830. which defines "peace officer," generally reads: "Any person who comes within the provisions of this chapter and who otherwise meets all standards imposed by law on a peace officer is a peace officer, and notwithstanding any other provision of law, no person other than those designated in this chapter is a peace officer."

PC 830.1. Designated Peace Officers.
a. "Any sheriff, undersheriff, or deputy sheriff, regularly employed and paid as such, of a county, any policeman of a district authorized by statute to maintain a police department, any marshal or deputy marshal of a municipal court, or any constable or deputy constable, regularly employed and paid as such, of a judicial district, or DA's investigator, is a peace officer. The authority of any such peace officer extends to any place in the state:
  1. As to any public offense committed or which there is probable cause to believe has been committed within the political subdivision which employs him: or
  2. Where he has the prior consent of the chief of police, or person authorized by him to give such consent, if the place is within a city or of the sheriff, or person authorized by him to give such consent, if the place is within a county; or
  3. As to any public offense committed or which there is probable cause to believe has been committed in his presence, and with respect to which there is immediate danger to person or property or of the escape of the perpetrator of such offense."

b. The Deputy Director, assistant directors, chief, assistant chiefs, special agents and narcotics agents of the Department of Justice and such investigators who are designated by the Attorney General, are peace officers. The authority of any such peace officers extends to any place in the state as to a public offense committed or which there is probably cause to believe has been committed within the state.

PC 830.2(a). Authority of California Highway Patrol. Provides that members of the California Highway Patrol are peace officers whose authority extends to any place in the state; provided, that their *primary* duty shall be enforcement of the provision of the Vehicle Code or of any other law relating to the use or operation of vehicles upon the highways, as that duty is set forth in the Vehicle Code.

PC 830.2(b). State Police. Defines any member of the California State Police Division (in charge of policing state buildings and grounds) as a peace officer; provided that their primary duty shall be the protection of state properties and occupants thereof.

PC 830.2(d). University of California Police. Defines a member of the University of California Police as a peace officer pursuant to Section 92600 of the Education Code, provided that the primary duty of any such peace officer shall be the enforcement of the law within the area specified in the above Education Code.

PC 830.2(e). State College Police. Defines members of a state university and state college police department as peace officers pursuant to Education Code Section 89560 with the same authority and limitations given to University of California police described above.

PC 830.3. Miscellaneous Police. Grants peace officer powers to the following agencies:
a. Department of Alcoholic Beverage Control investigators.
b. Department of Consumer Affairs investigators.
c. Department of Forestry volunteer fire wardens.
d. Department of Motor Vehicle investigators.
e. California Horse Racing Board investigators.
f. State Fire Marshal and deputy fire marshals.
g. Food and Drug Section investigators.
h. Division of Labor Standards Enforcement investigators.
i. State Department of Health and Social Service investigators.
j. California Exposition and State Fair marshals and police.
k. Department of Insurance investigators.
l. Department of Housing and Community Development investigators.
m. State Controller's Office investigators.
n. Department of Corporations investigators.
o. State Contractors' License Board investigators.

PC 830.31. Miscellaneous Police—Carrying Firearms. The following are peace officers whose authority extends to any place in the state for the purpose of their *primary* duty or when making an arrest under PC 836, or to any public offense with respect to which there is an immediate danger to persons or property or the escape of the perpetrator. Such peace officers may carry firearms *only* if authorized by their employing agency (italics added for emphasis).

PC 830.4. Security Officers. The following persons are peace officers while engaged in the performance of their duties in or about the properties owned, operated, or administered by their employing agency, or when required by their employer to perform their duties anywhere within the political subdivision which employs them. Such officers shall also have peace officer authority anywhere in the state as to an offense committed, or which there is probable cause to believe has been committed, with respect to persons or property the protection of which is the duty of such officer or when making an arrest pursuant to PC 836 as to any public offense with respect to which there is an immediate danger to person or property or of the escape of the perpetrator of the offense.

Such peace officers may carry firearms only if authorized by and under such terms and conditions as are specified by their employing agency.
a. Security officers of the California State Police Division.
b. Sergeant at Arms of each house of the Legislature.
c. Bailiffs of the Supreme Court and the courts of appeal.
d. Treasurer's office guards.
e. State Mental Health hospital guards.
f. Railroad policemen.
g. School District security officers.
h. Security officers of the County of Los Angeles.
i. Housing authority patrol officers, city, district, or county.
j. Transit district police.
k. City, county, district airport police.
l. County court service officers.

PC 830.5. Correctional, Parole, Probation Officers. This section grants peace officer status to correctional officers, parole officers, probation officers, and California Youth Authority officers for the purpose of carrying out their primary function. Except as specified, these peace officers may carry firearms only if authorized and under the terms as specified by their employing agency. Persons permitted to carry firearms either on or off duty shall meet the training requirements of PC 832 and shall qualify with the firearm at least quarterly.

PC 830.6. Reserve Officers and Deputies. Pertains to reserve and auxiliary officers, deputy sheriffs, regional park districts, etc. Such special, reserve or auxiliary officer is a peace officer only during his or her specific assignment or tour of duty.

Posse Comitatus. PC 830.6 also provides that whenever any person is summoned to the aid of any *uniformed* peace officer, such person shall be vested with such powers of a peace officer as are expressly delegated to him by the summoning officer or as are otherwise reasonably necessary to properly assist such officer. (See Section 7.14 for details on *posse comitatus*).

PC 830.7. Persons Not Peace Officers but Having Powers of Arrest. Designated cemetary employees (H & S Code 8325), regularly employed security officers for institutions of higher education (Educ. Code 94310), and Federal criminal investigators are not California peace officers, but may exercise the powers of arrest of a peace officer as specified in PC 836 and W & I Code 5150 under limited conditions. (See PC 830.8, below for an exception).

PC 830.8. Federal Investigators—Peace Officer Exception. Duly authorized federal employees are peace officers when they are engaged in enforcing applicable state or local laws on property owned or possessed by the United States government and with the written consent of the sheriff or chief of police, respectively, in whose jurisdiction such property is situated.

Discussion—Limited Authority. It should be noted that the authority of all peace officers listed in PC 830.1 through PC 830.8 and PC 831 through 831.6 is limited to some degree. In most cases, these persons' peace officer jurisdiction is limited geographically to the property their employing agencies own, administer or have jurisdiction over (with the exceptions noted). In other instances, firearms may not be carried without the express approval of the employing agency. Chapter 4.5 of the Penal Code also lists several peace officer categories where the officer is generally limited to exercising peace officer powers to his

or her primary duty such as is the case with state hospital security officers, ABC and DMV investigators.

One should also note that PC 832 requires that every person described and designated as a peace officer must complete a course certified by the Commission on Peace Officer Standards and Training in the powers to arrest and the carrying and use of firearms within 90 days after being employed.

PC 830.10. Pertains to the required wearing of nameplate or badge clearly bearing the name or identification number of a uniformed peace officer.

Notice of Consent. Consent agreements, by letter or by form entitled "Notice of Consent" may exist between municipalities with the cooperation of the county sheriff. The notice of consent grants that all regularly sworn, salaried peace officers of one jurisdiction shall have the authority of a peace officer at all times within the other jurisdiction.

Consent is a requirement of the statute and may be obtained through the signing of a formal Notice of Consent or may be obtained verbally from the chief law enforcement administrator of a municipality or county or from his agent authorized to grant such consent to make arrests as police officers in the other jurisdiction. Following obtaining of verbal consent and after investigation is completed and arrests made, officers from an outside jurisdiction should obtain consent in writing from the chief administrative officer of the other jurisdiction granting them police powers for the particular investigation and arrests.

Status of Off-Duty Police Officers. The Attorney General has ruled that a police officer may be paid on the basis of a regularly assigned forty-hour week by a city and nevertheless be charged at all times with the performance of the duties of a peace officer. He is in fact a police officer twenty-four hours a day and subject to call both during his regularly assigned duty period and while he is off duty, and also at the termination of his regularly assigned duty hours (*AG Memo Opinion, 21 December 1960*).

A California Appellate Court decision tends to reinforce the above-stated opinion. The court said "Peace officers such as policemen, constables, etc., are under a special duty at all times, because of the nature of their employment , to use their best efforts to apprehend criminals. . . . The services rendered were within the duties of their office. All their energies had been devoted to the service of the city . . ." (*People v. Derby, 177 C.A. 2d 626*).

Carrying a Concealed Weapon Outside of Jurisdiction. The carrying and possession of concealed weapons is regulated by the Dangerous Weapons Control Law (PC 12000 et seq.). Section 12002 of that law provides that those provisions do not prohibit peace officers, special police officers, or law enforcement officers from carrying various weapons and other equipment authorized for the enforcement of the law. Members of a police department are authorized to carry concealed weapons outside the city for which they are employed.

Off-Duty Status and Private Employment. The Attorney General has ruled that off-duty peace officers who seek private employment as an incidental supplement to their public duties such as working as security officers for a public entity, do not forfeit their status as peace officers. They retain such status while privately employed to keep the peace at specific public functions, and it necessarily follows that the commission of an assault or battery against such a peace officer is a felony offense as defined in PC 241 and PC 243. Injuries suffered by a peace officer while off duty, but while performing a general duty of his office, have been held to be compensable under workmen's compensation coverage (*AG Op 66/48 March 1966*). See PC 70, Section 6.8 of this text for additional details.

Status of Reserve Peace Officers. Section 24401 of the Government Code states, "Every county or district officer, except a supervisor or judicial officer, may appoint as many deputies as are necessary for the prompt and faithful discharge of duties of his office."

With reference to Section 7 of the Government Code, which provides "Whenever a power is granted to, or a duty is imposed upon, a public officer, the power may be exercised or the duty may be performed by a deputy of the officer or by a person authorized, pursuant to law, by the officer, unless this code expressly provides otherwise." Thus, since there is no express limitation on the power of a sheriff or police chief to carry a concealed weapon, such power may be exercised by the deputy or a special police officer. The omission of such restrictive language from the concealed weapon exemption indicates an intention on the part of the legislature to extend such exemption to all deputy sheriffs and policemen without reference to their permanent status or full-time employement. Therefore, a special deputy sheriff or a special or reserve police officer is included within the exemption contained in subsection (a) of 12027 of the Penal Code. When so authorized by their superior

officer, such officers may, therefore, carry concealed weapons (*AG Memo Opionion, October 1960*).

Reserve sheriff's deputies or policemen, while performing services as employees of a private patrol operator, may not wear any uniform, badge, or insignia which would give them the appearance of being deputy sheriffs or would create the impression that they are connected with a governmental agency.

Status of Federal, State, and Private Police. Federal officers, such as FBI agents, Federal Narcotics Agents, Border Patrolmen, etc., are not peace officers when acting to enforce state laws. However, as previously stated, members of the California Highway Patrol are peace officers within the meaning of PC 830.2 under the circumstances noted.

Private patrolmen, private patrol operators, and private detectives or investigators are not peace officers. In making arrests they must follow the provisions as outlined in PC 837 relative to arrests by private persons (*27 Ops. Atty. Gen. 213*).

7.4 ARRESTS BY PEACE OFFICERS WITHOUT WARRANT

The majority of arrests made by law enforcement officers are made without warrant and frequently under circumstances where thoughtful and effective judgment is far too often hampered by emotional conflicts. The officer stands in a crossfire between the obligation to bring offenders to justice and the equally binding obligation of not violating one's constitutional rights in so doing. This dilemma is a familiar occupational hazard in police work, and when caught in such a circumstance, the defense is a level head, and knowledge of the law.

Warrantless Arrests in Home. The California Supreme Court held on February 25, 1976 that warrantless arrests of people within their homes are invalid unless emergency circumstances exist. The 5-2 decision established the rule of law for the state that the constitutional protection against violation of the right of people to be secure in their persons and houses against unreasonable seizure applies to arrests within their home.

The court said, "Warrantless arrests within the home are *per se* unreasonable in the absence of exigent circumstances." The court explained the term "exigent circumstances" as meaning an emergency situation requiring swift action to prevent imminent danger to life or serious damage to property or to forestall the imminent escape of a suspect or destruction of evidence.

The ruling stems from the arrest of one Michael Ramey on August 17, 1973, by Sacramento police. Ramey was arrested at his home by officers who had no warrant, in a case involving allegedly stolen goods and marijuana (*People v. Ramey, 16 C. 3d 263*).

Arrest by Peace Officers. *PC 836.* A peace officer may make an arrest in obedience to a warrant, or may, pursuant to the authority granted him by provisions of Chapter 4.5 (commencing with Section 830) of Title 3 or Part 2, without a warrant, arrest a person:

1. Whenever he has reasonable cause to believe that the person to be arrested has committed a public offense in his presence.
2. When a person arrested has committed a felony, although not in his presence.
3. Whenever he has reasonable cause to believe that the person to be arrested has committed a felony, whether or not a felony has in fact been committed.

In analyzing the subsection 1 above, three factors must be considered: (1) reasonable cause, (2) presence, (3) public offense. A peace officer can make an arrest without a warrant if he has "reasonable cause" to believe that the arrestee has committed a felony. Some guidelines were discussed relative to establishing reasonable cause; however, subsection 1 of PC 836 relates solely to misdemeanor arrests and is the only definitive portion of the Penal Code covering this area.

An officer must have reasonable cause to believe that the person to be arrested has committed a misdemeanor *in his presence.* The term "in his presence" is not limited to proximity but relates to the person's senses, i.e., what is perceived by the person making the arrest (*People v. Lavender, 137 C.A. 582*). Thus, regardless of the distance between the officer and the person to be arrested, conduct on the part of the arrestee may very well be apparent through senses of sight, smell, taste, touch, and hearing.

Under subdivision 1, the term "public offense" refers to misdemeanor and felony offenses; however, it will be noted again that this is the only section which covers misdemeanors arrests by a peace officer without a warrant.

In subsection 2 of PC 836 the legislative intent is somewhat ambiguous; however, it is apparent that this provision is applicable only to those felonies which have actually been committed by the person who is arrested. A peace officer may, without a warrant, arrest a person for a felony not committed in the officer's presence when the criminal is fleeing from the scene of the crime (*People v. Poole, 27 Cal. 572*).

Subsection 3 of PC 836 appears to be the most practical in regard to arrests for felony offenses. This provision deals with felony arrests whether within or out of the officer's presence and has the requirement of reasonable cause to believe that the arrestee has committed a felony, whether or not a felony has in fact been committed. Thus, it is clear that any valid arrest under this subsection must be based on the reasonable and probable cause factors discussed in Section 7.7 of your text.

PC 836.5. Arrest Without a Warrant on Reasonable Cause

a. A public officer or employee, when authorized by ordinance, may arrest a person without a warrant whenever he has reasonable cause to believe that the person to be arrested has committed a misdemeanor in his presence which is a violation of a statute or ordinance which such officer or employee has the duty to enforce.

b. There shall be no civil liability on the part of, and no cause of action shall arise against, any public officer or employee acting pursuant to subdivision (a) and within the scope of his authority for false arrest or false imprisonment arising out of any arrest which is lawful or which the public officer or employee, at the time of the arrest, had reasonable cause to believe was lawful. No such officer or employee shall be deemed an aggressor or lose his right to self-defense by the use of reasonable force to effect the arrest, prevent escape, or overcome resistance.

c. In any case in which a person is arrested pursuant to subdivision (a) and the person arrested does not demand to be taken before a magistrate, the public officer or employee making the arrest shall prepare a written notice to appear and release the person on his promise to appear, as prescribed by Chapter 5C (commencing with Section 853.6) of this title. The provisions of such chapter shall thereafter apply with reference to any proceeding based upon the issuance of a written notice to appear pursuant to this authority.

d. The governing body of a local agency, by ordinance, may authorize those of its officers and employees who have the duty to enforce a statute or ordinance to arrest persons for violations of such statute or ordinance as provided in subdivision (a).

e. For the purpose of this section, "ordinance" includes an order, rule, or regulation of any air pollution control district.

f. For purposes of this section, a "public officer or employee" includes an officer or employee of a nonprofit transit corporation wholly owned by a local agency and formed to carry out the purpose of the local agency.

PC 849. Duty to Take Accused Before Magistrate, on Arrest Without a Warrant

a. When an arrest is made without a warrant by a peace officer or private person, the person arrested, if not otherwise released, shall without unnecessary delay, be taken before the nearest or most accessible magistrate in the county in which the offense is triable, and a complaint stating the charge against the arrested person shall be laid before such magistrate.

Release from Custody. Penal Code, Section 849(b), provides that "Any peace officer may release from custody, instead of taking such person before a magistrate, any person arrested without a warrant whenever:

1. He is satisfied that there are insufficient grounds for making a criminal complaint against the person arrested.
2. The person arrested was arrested for intoxication only, and no further proceedings are desirable.
3. The person was arrested only for being under the influence of a narcotic , drug, or restricted dangerous drug and such person is delivered to a facility or hospital for treatment and no further proceedings are desirable.

c. Any record of arrest of a person released pursuant to paragraphs (1) and (3) of subdivision (b) shall include a record of release. Thereafter, such arrest shall not be deemed an arrest, but a detention only."

PC 825. Appearance Before Magistrate—Maximum Time.

The defendant must, in all cases, be taken before the magistrate without unnecessary delay, and in any event, within two days after his arrest, excluding Sundays and holidays; provided, however, that when the two days prescribed herein expire at a time when the court in which the magistrate is sitting is not in session, such time shall be extended to include the duration of the next regular court session on the judicial day immediately following.

After such arrest, any attorney at law entitled to practice in the courts of record of California, may, at the request of the prisoner or any relative of such prisoner, visit the person so arrested.

Any officer having charge of the prisoner so arrested who willfully refuses or neglects to allow such attorney to visit a prisoner is guilty of a misdemeanor.

Any officer having a prisoner in charge, who refuses to allow any attorney to visit the prisoner when proper application is made therefor, shall forfeit and pay to the party aggrieved the sum of five hundred dollars ($500), to be recovered by action in any court of competent jurisdiction.

PC 851.6. Certificate Describing Arrest Without Warrant as Detention

a. In any case in which a person is arrested and released pursuant to paragraph (1) or (3) of subdivision (b) of Section 849, the person shall be issued a certificate, signed by the releasing officer or his superior officer, describing the action as a detention. The Attorney General shall prescribe the form and content of such certificate.
b. In any case in which a person is arrested and released and no accusatory pleading is filed charging him with an offense, the person shall be issued a certificate by the law enforcement agency which arrested him describing the action as a detention.
c. The Attorney General shall prescribe the form and content of such certificate.
d. Any reference to the action as an arrest shall be deleted from the arrest records of the arresting agency and of the Bureau of Criminal Identification and Investigation of the Department of Justice. Thereafter, any such record of the action shall refer to it as a detention.

7.5 PRIVATE PERSON ARRESTS

Private Persons; Authority to Arrest. A private person may arrest another:

1. For a public offense committed or attempted in his presence.
2. When the person arrested has committed a felony, although not in his presence.
3. When a felony has been in fact committed, and he has reasonable cause for believing the person arrested to have committed it (PC 837).

A private citizen, unlike a peace officer, may not arrest *solely on reasonable cause* to believe that the person to be arrested has committed a public offense in his presence, or whenever he has reasonable cause to believe that such a person has committed a felony, *unless* a felony *has in fact* been committed (*People v. Martin, 225, C.A. 2d 91*).

The subject of a citizen's arrest is reviewed in *People v. Burgess, 170 C.A. 2d 36 (1953)*,and the court discusses what circumstances must exist for the offense to have been committed "in the presence" of the arresting citizen. The term "in the presence," as used in PC 837 (authorizing an arrest by a private person without a warrant for a public offense committed or attempted in his presence) is liberally construed. "Presence" is not merely physical proximity, but also includes the senses of hearing and smell, if the noise or odor is apparent to the arresting person's senses. It should also be noted that when a citizen sees an offense committed in his presence, the arrest must be made promptly thereafter (*Ogulin v. Jeffries, 121 C.A. 2d 211* and *Hill v. Levy, 117 C.A. 2d 667*).

Use of Force. A private person is justified in using only reasonable force (as is a peace officer) in making an arrest. The citizen making an arrest may not use any more force than is absolutely necessary to overcome resistance, if any. Of course, if the person being arrested does not resist, then no force may be used. A private citizen is not justified in using lethal force in making an arrest for crimes against property, unless his or another person's life is in immediate danger. Even in felony crimes, deadly force may not be used to stop a fleeing felon unless the fleeing felon is at the moment an actual threat to other persons' lives. An example might be a fleeing bank robber who is firing a gun as he runs from the scene.

Private Person; Duty After Arrest. A private person who has arrested another for the commission of a public offense must, without unnecessary delay, take the person arrested before a magistrate or deliver him to a peace officer. There shall be no civil liability on the part of, and no cause of action shall arise against, any peace officer acting within the scope of his authority, for false imprisonment arising out of any arrest when:

1. Such arrest was lawful or when such peace officer, at the time of such arrest, had reasonable cause to believe such arrest was lawful; or
2. When such arrest was made pursuant to a charge, upon reasonable cause, of the commission of a felony by the person to be arrested; or
3. When such arrest was made pursuant to the requirements of Penal Code, Sections 142, 838, 839 (PC 847).

Duty of Officer to Receive or Arrest Person Charged with Crime. *Penalty.* Any peace officer who has the authority to receive or arrest a person charged with a criminal offense and willfully refuses to receive or arrest such person shall be punished by a fine not exceeding five thousand dollars ($5,000), or by imprisonment in the state prison or in a county jail not exceeding one year, or by both such fine and imprisonment. (PC 142). Note: Prosecution under this section is most unlikely.

Inquiry into Legality of Private Person Arrest. Common sense indicates that an officer should make reasonable inquiry into the facts surrounding a private person arrest. PC 847 protects an officer against civil liability for false arrest and false imprisonment when the arrest was in fact lawful, or the officer had reasonable cause to believe it was lawful. After receiving the arrested person, the officer must take him before a magistrate or may release him on a written promise to appear if it is a misdemeanor case. (See Sec. 7.6. of your text.)

Summoning Assistance. Any person making an arrest may orally summon as many persons as he deems necessary to aid him therein (PC 839).

Resistance to Private Person Arrest. A private person making an arrest has the right to use force in effecting an arrest if such arrest is lawful. If the person he is arresting physically resists the arrest, he is committing an assault upon the private person making the arrest since the latter is acting in a lawful capacity.

Liability of Private Person Assisting a Peace Officer. A private person who assists a peace officer in making an arrest is not criminally or civilly liable.

7.6   MISDEMEANOR CITATIONS

Several California codes authorize the issuance of a citation in lieu of taking an arrestee into custody, and in some instances, such as traffic violations and violations of the Alcohol Beverage Control Act, a citation must be issued. The citation, often referred to as a summons, is simply a form directing the defendant to appear at a specified time and place to answer a specific charge in a court of competent jurisdiction.

When a person is arrested for any misdemeanor offense and he does not demand to be taken before a magistrate, the arresting officer may, instead of taking such person before a magistrate, receive from him his written promise to appear in court. A peace officer may use the written notice to appear (1) for any misdemeanor offense which he has reasonable cause to believe the person to be arrested has committed in his presence, or (2) for any misdemeanor offense in which a private person had made the arrest and delivered the arrested person to the peace officer (PC 853.6).

PC 853.6(b) states that the time specified in the notice shall be at least 10 days after arrest.

PC853.6(c) specifies the place as the court of the magistrate before whom the person would be taken if the requirement of taking an arrested person before a magistrate were complied with.

PC 853.6(d) provides that the arrestee shall be given one copy of the notice to appear, and the officer is to retain the duplicate.

PC 853.6(e) provides that the officer shall file, as soon as practicable, the duplicate notice to appear with the court or prosecuting attorney.

PC 853.6(f) states that no warrant shall issue on such a charge for the arrest of a person who has given written promise to appear unless and until he fails to do so.

PC 853.6(g) provides for officer to indicate, on notice to appear, his desire for arrestee to be booked as defined in subdivision 21 of Section 7.

PC 853.6(h) provides that peace officer may use the written notice to appear procedure set forth in this section for any misdemeanor offense pursuant to PC 836 or PC 847 (Citizen's arrest).

PC 853.6(i) provides that arresting officer, booking officer, or superior officer, or other designated person shall make an immediate investigation into the background of arrestee to determine whether he should be released pursuant to the provisions of this chapter.

PC 853.6(j) provides that whenever any person is arrested by a peace officer for a misdemeanor, other than an offense described in Sections 11357 and 11360 of the Health and Safety Code (possession, transportation, sale of marijuana), and is not released with a written notice to appear in court pursuant to this chapter, the arresting officer shall indicate, on a form to be established by his or her employing law enforcement agency, which of the following was a reason for such nonrelease:

1. The person arrested was so intoxicated that he could have been a danger to himself or to others.
2. The person arrested required medical examination or medical care or was otherwise unable to care for his own safety.
3. The person was arrested for one or more of the offenses listed in Section 40302 of the Vehicle Code.
4. There were one or more outstanding arrest warrants for the person.
5. The person could not provide satisfactory evidence of personal identification.

6. The prosecution of the offense or offenses for which the person was arrested or the prosecution of any other offense or offenses would be jeopardized by immediate release of the person arrested.
7. There was a reasonable likelihood that the offense or offenses would continue or resume, or that the safety of persons or property would be imminently endangered by release of the person arrested.
8. The person arrested demanded to be taken before a magistrate or refused to sign the notice to appear.
9. Any other reason, which shall be specifically stated on the form by the arresting officer. Such form shall be filed with the arresting agency as soon as practicable and shall be made available to any party having custody of the arrested person, subsequent to the arresting officer, and to any person authorized by law to release him from custody before trial.

Vehicle Code Violations. Section 40500 of the Vehicle Code provides for the issuance of a citation in triplicate with generally the same requirements as for criminal offenses. There are, however, exceptions in this case where a mandatory appearance by the arrestee is necessary by law, such as (1) failure of arrestee to exhibit an operator's license or other satisfactory evidence of identity; (2) failure of arrestee to sign the citation; (3) when the arrestee demands to be taken forthwith to a magistrate; and (4) when the person arrested is charged with certain other Vehicle Code Violations (VC 20001, failure to stop at the scene of an accident involving bodily injury; VC 23102, misdemeanor drunk driving; VC 23105, driving under of drugs).

Citations for Alcoholic Beverage Control Violations. Section 24209 of the Business and Professions Code (Alcoholic Beverage Control Act) states in part that "when an arrest is made of any person for a violation of Sections 23000 through 26004, the arresting officer shall release such licensee or employee without taking him before a magistrate, upon such licensee or employee signing an agreement to appear in court or before a magistrate at a place and time designated by an arresting officer."

It is clear that B & P Code, Section 24209, offers no alternative to the issuance of citations for those violations contained in Section 23000 through 26004; however, two important considerations should be noted: (1) a physical arrest may be made in lieu of a citation for violations other than Sections 23000 through 26004, and (2) the officer may make a physical arrest for any Penal Code violation that is apparent in conjunction with a citable B & P violation. For example, any licensee under an on-sale license issued for public premises who in violation of 25665 B & P Code allows a minor to enter and to remain in the licensed premises without lawful business therin is guilty of a misdemeanor, such offense being only a citable offense in accordance with the above provisions. However, depending on the circumstances of the offense, the officer might possibly make a physical arrest of the licensee or employee for a violation of PC 272, contributing to the delinquency of a minor.

7.7 REASONABLE CAUSE TO ARREST

Virtually every lawful arrest is based upon reasonable or probable cause to arrest. These two terms have come to be used by the courts interchangeably although the meanings may vary from time to time depending upon the context in which they are used. For example, reasonable cause is usually associated with formulating the basis for arrest, while probable cause more often relates to the basis for detention or the issuance of a search warrant.

Definition of Reasonable Cause. An all-encompassing definition of the term "reasonable cause" is made somewhat impossible because of the many interpretations of the rule that the courts have been known to make in the past, since each case involving an arrest must be decided on its own merits. In a practical sense, however, reasonable cause has been judicially defined on many occasions since 1894 as "such a state of facts as would lead a man of ordinary care and prudence to believe and conscientiously entertain an honest and strong suspicion that the person is guilty of a crime." (*People v. Kilvington, 104 Cal. 86).*

In 1962, the courts recognized a distinction between the ordinary man and the officer experienced in certain fields, stating that "Reasonable cause should not be understood as placing the ordinary man of ordinary care and prudence, and the officer experienced in the detection of narcotics offenders in the same class. Circumstances and conduct which would not excite the suspicion of the man in the street, might be highly significant to an officer who had extensive training in the devious and cunning devices used by narcotics offenders to conceal their crimes." (*People v Symons, 210 A.C.A. 923.)*

The courts will generally inquire into two aspects of reasonableness to arrest: (1) Reasonable cause to believe that a crime was *prima facie* committed, based on the establishment of a *corpus delicti;* and (2) reasonable cause to believe that the person arrested is the perpetrator of the crime committed. (Note that identity of the perpetrator is not part of the *corpus delicti* in a criminal case.) To this end, it is requisite that police officers align themselves with the historical concept of reasonable cause offered by the California Supreme Court in the Kilvington Case.

Insufficient Reasonable Cause. The arresting officer must be in a position to articulate specific facts that constitute probable cause for an arrest. In *Cunba v. Superior Court. 2 C, 3d 352,* the court held there was no probable cause to make an arrest where a plainclothes officer observed the defendant and a companion look around to see if anyone was watching. When they stopped walking, it appeared that they exchanged money. The officer testified that the defendant was arrested to see if a narcotics sale had occurred.

Examples of Reasonable Cause. The following are but a very few of the factual situations involving reasonable cause to arrest. It must be kept in mind that judicial bodies, namely the United States Supreme Court and the California Appellate Courts, are continuously handing down reasonable cause cases which the police officer might use as guidelines for making a legal arrest. As in the past, the officer must rely upon sound judgment based on judicially approved policy and in many cases "snap decisions." By contradistinction, the appellate courts in California and the United States Supreme Court, in ruling on the legalities of a practical arrest situation may rely on the best legal resources and talents available in resolving individual conflicts relative to arrest. Additionally, their decisions reflect many months of judicial conference, intelligent appraisal, and voluminous research.

Status. The status of a defendant may be a controlling factor.
1. A parolee is considered in "constructive custody" whenever the parole officer has reasonable cause to believe the subject is in violation of parole (*People v. Taylor, 266 Cal. App. 2d 14)* .
2. A police officer may make a lawful entry in reliance on information from a parole officer (*People v. Hood, 150 C.A. 2d 197).*
3. The fact that the defendant has served a sentence in state prison, has a criminal reputation, or associates with criminals has also been considered as reasonable cause (*People v. Wickliff, 144 C.A. 2d 107).*

Emergencies. Generally, less fact need be shown to establish reasonable cause in so-called emergency situations.

1. Disturbance of the peace. Defendant ran to the rear of an open store and refused to leave. Upon arrival of police, defendant stated that he was a narcotics user and had entered the store to do some harm. Subject was arrested for disturbing the peace and subsequently escaped. The court held the original arrest lawful and subsequent fleeing an escape from lawful custody (*People v. Paul, 147 C.A. 2d 609*).

2. An officer in danger is certainly an emergency situation (*People v. Maddox, 46 Cal. 2d 301*).

3. Destruction of evidence amounts to an emergency situation. A defendant has no constitutional right to destroy evidence (*People v. Barnett, 156 C.A. 2d 803*).

Location. The location of offenses may be important when considered with other factors.

1. Officers had reasonable cause to arrest when another person, in company of the person to be arrested, made a suspicious move (*People v. Schraier, 141 C.A. 2d 600*).

2. Defendant was in company of a known narcotics addict. She was arrested and a search made in jail, where narcotics were discovered (*People v. Hickman, 143 C.A. 2d 79*).

3. To establish reasonable cause to arrest on observation, there must be more than merely seeing the suspect at night (*People v. Simon, 45 C.A. 2d 645*). Where the suspect was standing in a well-lighted doorway, left, returned, looked up and down the street, and resumed his original position, the court held these actions did not constitute reasonable cause (*People v. Harris, 146 C.A. 2d 142*).

4. The unusual character of two men parked in a known lovers' lane was held to be reasonable cause to question and subsequently arrest (*People v. Martin, 46 Cal. 2d 106*).

5. High crime rate areas where numerous burglaries had occurred supported arrest of three men standing by a car, who left as officers approached. Suspects were subsequently stopped, this being nighttime, and as they alighted from the vehicle, marijuana fell to the ground; hence reasonable cause was shown (*People v. Wiley, 162 C.A. 2d 836*).

6. In an area frequented by narcotic addicts and peddlers officer saw suspects exchange something and heard a coin drop. The court ruled these facts constituted reasonable cause (*People v. Brown, 147 C.A. 2d 352*).

7. Officers entered the wrong location. Probable cause was established by a telephone call in a bookmaking case. The officers broke into the wrong half of a duplex. The court held that the officers had reasonable cause to enter (*People v. Sakelaris, 154 C.A. 2d 244*).

Time or Distance. Both may be of prime importance in establishing reasonable cause.

1. During night hours officers observed defendant carrying a gasoline can. Suspect had a bulge under his coat and admitted he intended to siphon gas. He was arrested for burglary, and a search for weapons revealed a marijuana roach. Although defendant admitted he intended to siphon gas, there was not probable cause to make an arrest. The court held, however, that under these circumstances a search for weapons was proper, and the roach was admissible as evidence (*People v. Jackson, 164 C.A. 2d 759*).

2. Officers observed two young men walking in the vicinity of a warehouse district during late hours. Both subjects acted suspiciously. The court held that even in view of their conduct, the time of night, location, and the fact that one of the men had alcohol in his possession, did not afford reasonable cause to believe that they had committed a felony (*People v. Simon, 45 Cal. 2d 645*).

3. Suspect was observed walking in an area where numerous burglaries had occurred, carrying a bundle of clothing. He started to walk away when he saw the officer and gave false and misleading information about the clothing. There was reasonable cause to arrest him for burglary (*People v. West, 144 C.A. 2d 214*).

4. Where three young men standing one evening by a car in which the defendant was seated made a hasty retreat when officers brought their police car to a stop, which conduct, plus information that the officers had with respect to thefts and burglaries in the neighborhood, reasonably justified investigation, including a request that the two young men in car step out, and defendant's furtive act, on alighting from the car, in dropping something from his left hand and an officer's recovery of two cigarettes from the street, justified the officer in suspecting that defendant was attempting surreptitiously to dispose of contraband and in arresting him (*People v. Wiley, 162 C.A. 2d 836*).

Observation. There are numerous cases on record where observation by an officer constituted reasonable cause.

1. The court held there was probable cause to arrest where an officer saw the defendant and another person in an apparent exchange of money. The defendant "acted nervous" during the exchange, and on more than one occasion the officer had seen the defendant going to a nearby secluded place, which known to be frequented by narcotics users (*People v. Molty, 14 Cal. App. 3d 381*).

2. Officers observed the suspect throw a brown package from his car window as they approached. The court held that the police had cause to stop and investigate (*People v. Anders, 167 C.A. 2d 65*).

3. Observations while issuing a traffic citation constitutes reasonable cause. Contraband observed through a window of a car, observation of a gun protruding from beneath a seat, or seeing the suspect apparently cover something in the back seat are examples of this situation (*People v. McFarren, 155 C.A. 2d 383; People v. Zubia, 166 C.A. 2d 620*).

Establishing Reasonable Cause Through Citizens— Informants. An arrest may be based solely on information about which reliability has not been established. In these cases, the courts generally look only at the facts and circumstances presented to the officer at the time of arrest. Where there is an observation of innocent conduct and reliability is not established, there is no probable cause to act.

Information from victims of robbery: A robbery victim who identified a photograph of the defendant as the person who robbed him is reliable. The arrest in this case was made without a warrant, and wire similar to that used to tie one victim was recovered from the possession of the suspect (*People v. Villarico, 140 C.A. 2d 315*).

Information from Other Officers and Broadcasts. Information based on these sources is considered sufficient to establish reasonable cause. Broadcast information was held to be reliable where the victim of a robbery described the suspect, his car, and the gun to police. Officers eight to ten miles away from the scene stopped the suspect and told the defendant to step out of his car. The car was searched and the loot and gun recovered (*People v. Borbon, 146, C.A. 2d 315*).

Information from Reliable Informant. A police officer received information from a reliable inform-

ant that a certain described person on a certain street corner had heroin on his person. Officers went to the corner, arrested the defendant, and upon a search found four bundles of heroin strapped under his arm. The court held the arrest and search legal (*People v. Sexton, 153 C.A. 2d 803*).

Rearrest of Probationer or Parolee. Penal Code, Section 1203.2, provides for the re-arrest of a person on probation by a probation or peace officer without warrant or other process, at any time until final disposition of the probationer's case.

The Adult Authority shall have full power to suspend, cancel, or revoke any parole without notice and to order the return to prison of any prisoner under parole. The *written order* of any member of the Adult Authority shall be sufficient warrant for any peace officer to return to actual custody any conditionally released or paroled prisoner (PC 3060).

7.8 ENTRAPMENT

Black's Law Dictionary defines entrapment as the act of police in inducing a person to commit a crime not contemplated by him, for the purpose of prosecuting him. In one of the leading cases in California, the court stated, "The law does not tolerate a person, particularly a law enforcement officer, generating in the mind of a person who is innocent of any criminal purpose, the original intent to commit a crime, entrapping such person into the commission of a crime which he would not have committed or even contemplated but for such inducement." (*People v. Galvan, 208 C.A. 2d 443*).

The main purpose of the law is to prevent crime and not to encourage it. Thus the defense of entrapment is used where an officer is the procuring cause of the crime and puts the unlawful design or intent in the mind of the accused. The theory here is that, as stated in Chapter 3, there must be a union or joint operation of act, intent, or criminal negligence in the commission of every crime (PC 20); however, the fact that a defendant lacks such requisite intent in being entrapped constitutes a basic defense.

California Supreme Court Ruling. Late in 1979, the California Supreme Court made a major change in the law of entrapment with its decision in *People v. Barraga, 23 C 3d 675*. That decision set forth an entirely new standard for determining whether activities of law enforcement officers and their agents will be considered entrapment.

Barraga was charged with two sales of heroin to a female undercover agent, but claimed entrapment as to the second sale only, which followed the first by three weeks. The defendant and the undercover officer described the sale differently, but both agreed that the officer had contacted the defendant by telephone at a detoxification center where he worked, in order to set up the meeting for the sale.

The undercover agent testified that the final meeting took only a few minutes. She stated that defendant said that he was hesitant to deal because he did not want to go back to jail, but that eventually he gave her a note to present to a woman, telling her to give the agent some heroin.

According to the defendant, this last meeting lasted a full hour. He indicated that he consented to the meeting only because he was fed up with the undercover agent and wanted her to quit calling him while he was at work. He maintained that he had gotten rid of his heroin habit, was on a methadone program, had held his job for four years and did not want to become involved in heroin dealing again. He indicated that the undercover agent nevertheless persisted in her attempts to get him to sell her heroin, and that he finally gave her the note to the heroin dealer just to "get her off my back." Defendant presented himself as a person who after a long criminal history had finally gotten control of his life and was starting to function as a responsible member of the community.

The California Supreme Court, in overruling Barraga's conviction, discussed entrapment and the "origin of intent" rule, which had been the legal standard used in California to determine entrapment for many years.

The court rejected this former rule. It stated that the reason for having entrapment as a defense is to deter police misconduct. The court felt that the defense should thus focus itself on the police conduct, not on the defendant and his particular predispositions toward crime. The court stated that no matter how bad the defendant's prior record or present inclinations toward criminality were, police conduct to ensnare him into further crime could not be tolerated.

The court then formulated the following test on whether police actions are or are not entrapment:

Was the conduct of the law enforcement agent likely to induce a normally law-abiding person to commit the offense?

The court went on and further discussed the new test as follows:

". . .we presume that such a person (i.e., a normally law-abiding person) would normally resist the temptation to commit a crime presented by the simple opportunity to act unlawfully. Official conduct that does no more than

offer that opportunity to the suspect—for example, a decoy program—is therefore permissible; but it is impermissible for the police or their agents to pressure the suspect by overbearing conduct such as badgering, cajoling, importuning, or other affirmative acts likely to induce a normally law-abiding person to commit the crime."

Guiding Principles. Although the determination of what police conduct is impermissible must to some extent proceed on an ad hoc basis, guidance will generally be found in the application of one or both of two principles.

First, if the actions of the law enforcement agent would generate in a normally law-abiding person a motive for the crime other than ordinary criminal intent, entrapment will be established. An example of such conduct would be an appeal by the police that would induce such a person to commit the act because of friendship or sympathy, instead of a desire for personal gain or other typical criminal purpose.

Second, affirmative police conduct that would make commission of the crime unusually attractive to a normally law-abiding person will likewise constitute entrapment. Such conduct would include, for example, a guarantee that the act is not illegal or the offense will go undetected, an offer of exorbitant consideration, or any similar enticement.

Finally, while the inquiry must focus primarily on the conduct of the law enforcement agent, that conduct is not to be viewed in a vacuum. It should also be judged by the effect it would have on a normally law-abiding person situated in the circumstances that may be relevant for this purpose. For example, are the transactions preceding the offense, the suspect's response to the inducements of the officer, the gravity of the crime, and the difficulty of detecting instances of its commission? We reiterate, however, that under this test such matters as the character, the predisposition to commit the offense, and subjective intent of the suspect are irrelevant.

This decision has resulted in making it easier for a defendant to claim entrapement, even when he or she is known to have been involved in the crime before. Officers should thus examine their practices, and more significantly their informants' practices, to make sure they can meet the new entrapment test.

Setting Traps. Officers may set reasonable traps in an effort to apprehend criminals. This is best illustrated by an early California case in which a constable disguised himself and feigned drunkenness by lying in an alley in an effort to apprehend suspects who were "rolling" drunks in the area. The court held that there is no entrapment where an officer disguises himself, feigns drunkenness, and makes no objection when (marked) money is taken from his person (*People v. Hanselman, 76 Cal. 460).*

There are some crimes for which the arrest and diligent prosecution of the offender is a statutory requirement (treason, gambling, dueling, etc.). In such cases it may be legally difficult to wait and watch, or to set traps in an effort to apprehend offenders. However, as a general rule, officers need not act immediately in the commission of most crimes, and may, therefore, "stake out" and wait until the criminal act is committed or attempted. In addition, they may use operatives or undercover agents to facilitate the apprehension of criminals within the guidelines as discussed in *People v. Barraga,* above.

Use of Decoy. When officers of the law are informed that a person intends to commit a crime against the property or person of another, the law permits them to afford opportunities for its cimmission and to lay traps which may result in the detection of the offender. To this end a person may be engaged to act with the one who is suspected and to be present with him at the time the crime is to be committed; and if the accused, having himself originally conceived the criminal intent, commits such of the overt acts as are necessary to complete the offense, he will not be protected from punishment by reason of the fact that when the acts were done by him the person was present, with acknowledgment and approval of the authorities, and aided in and encouraged their perpetration.

Use of Deception. The courts have held that the loaning of a truck to appellants by a police officer to facilitate the commission of a burglary is not entrapment, even though the officer knew from his conversation that they intended to commit the crime (*People v. Malone, 117 C.A. 629).*

Entrapment exists only where the official has conceived and planned the crime for one who would not have done it but for the allurement, deception, or persuasions of the officer. If the doing of an act is a crime and the criminal intent originated in the mind of the accused and the offense is completed, the fact that an officer appeared to cooperate by furnishing opportunity or otherwise aiding the offender in order to facilitate the consummation of the act, is not a defense (*People v. Finkelstin, 98 C.A. 2d 545).*

Use of Informants. Use of informants both to detect crime and to gather evidence against suspects of crime is considered almost essential for detection of the so-called "vice crimes" such as narcotics, prostitution, gambling, illegal liquor, etc., because such offenses usually involve no "victim" who will complain to the police. Inevitably, the use of police informers and under cover agents involves police deception, false friendships and sometimes the buying of information against an accused. Occasionally, at the trial level, criminal charges resulting from *flagrant* police practices have been summarily dismissed. To date, however, the courts have condoned such activities on the grounds of sheer necessity as long as police practices were kept within reasonable bounds as discussed above.

In *Hoffa v. U.S., 385 U.S. 293,* the Supreme Court rejected most of the constitutional challenges to the use of informers and upheld a conviction based on incriminating statements made by the accused to an apparent colleague (who was actually an informer). The court held that defendant's expectations that his statements would be kept confidential by the "colleague" were not entitled to constitutional protection. Defendant, in effect, was held to have "assumed the risk" that his apparent colleague might turn out to be an informant. The courts have also held that paid informers are an indispensable part of law enforcement; and that relevant evidence obtained by them is admissible.

Informers "Wired for Sound." The legality of planting a transmitter or recorder on an informer, who then has a conversation with a suspect in which the latter makes incriminating statements which he clearly would not have made had he known the police were listening, is frequently raised. It is clear the informer himself could testify to the incriminating statements, but can the police agents who are listening testify? The issue arises frequently because the prosecution may be unable to get the informer to testify (he may be afraid, or he may have fled), or the informer may have a felony record so that his testimony could be impeached.

In *Lee v. U.S., 343 U.S. 747,* the court held that police who have overheard the conversation, through cooperation with an informer wired for sound, can constitutionally testify to such conversations; and such evidence is admissible as substantive evidence of guilt. In the *Lee* case, a federal agent "audited" a conversation between the defendant and acquaintance through a transmitter planted on the acquaintance. The federal agent was allowed to testify as to the statements made by defendant. The prosecution did not call the acquaintance because of his felony record which would have been brought out in cross-examination. The *Lee* case was criticized for some time on the ground that it was inconsistent with the *Katz* case holding that evidence obtained by electronic eavesdropping violates the 4th Amendment. However, the Court has recently reaffirmed the *Lee* case, holding that eavesdropping *with the consent of one party* to the conversation is not an unreasonable search and seizure under the 4th Amendment (*U.S. v. White, 401 U.S. 745*).

Admissibility of Recordings—Limitations. Since the police themselves are permitted to testify to conversations they overhear via a planted transmitter, recording of such conversations are admissible as corroboration of the police agent's testimony (*Lopez v. U.S., 373 U.S. 427*). The recordings, as a practical matter, are more trustworthy than an individual's recollection. The use of a police agent posing as a cellmate or friend after the accused had been arrested and charged with a crime would clearly be excluded on the ground that no *Miranda* warnings were given (*Massiah v. U.S., 377 U.S. 201*). See also, *People v. Lebell, 89 Cal. App. 3d 772*.

Entrapment—Summary. If the accused is actually in custody, it seems clear that any incriminating statement obtained from him through the use of a police agent posing as a cellmate (or a friend, if the defendant has been released on bail) would be excluded on the ground that no *Miranda* warnings were given. Thus the *Lee* case, above, limited the use of planted transmitters or recorders to cases where the accused has not yet been indicted or "held to answer" for the offense, and is not in custody.

Entrapment is generally recognized as a *defense* to a criminal charge in both state and federal courts. It is also an element of criminal procedure insofar as it places limitations on police procedures in the detection and apprehension of accused criminals. The current judicial test for entrapment is the "innocence" test, based on legislative intent that statutes are not to be enforced by tempting innocent person into violations. Under this test, the court will ask whether a crime was a result of the "creative activity" of the police or whether the police merely afforded an opportunity for the suspect (predisposed to commit the crime anyway) to do so.

7.9 ACCOMPLISHING THE ARREST

An arrest is made by an actual restraint of the person or by submission to the custody of an officer. The person arrested may be subjected to such restraint as is reasonable for his arrest and detention (PC 835).

Under this section, an arresting officer or private citizen has the right to pursue an arrestee or an escapee and use whatever force may be necessary for his arrest as long as such means are reasonable.

An officer is never justified in shooting one guilty of a misdemeanor in order to effect an arrest (unless in self-defense), although, being properly engaged in attempting to make an arrest on a misdemeanor charge, he has the right to resist attack made upon him, and being rightfully there and not being legally considered the aggressor, he may in his own defense take a human life (*People v. Wilson, 36 C.A. 589*).

The manner in which the arrest is made will generally depend upon the arrestee's attitude and conduct and the nature and seriousness of the crime.

Cause and Authority for Arrest. The person making the arrest must inform the person to be arrested of the intention to arrest him, of the cause of the arrest, and the authority to make it, except when the person making the arrest has reasonable cause to believe that the person to be arrested is actually engaged in the commission of or an attempt to commit an offense, or the person to be arrested is pursued immediately after its commission or after an escape. The person making the arrest must, on the request of the person he is arresting, inform the latter of the offense for which he is being arrested (PC 841).

If the officer has reasonable cause to make an arrest, a violation of PC 841 would be unrelated and collateral to the securing of evidence by a search incident to the arrest, for what the search turns up will in no way depend on whether the officer informed the person to be arrested of the intention to arrest him, of the cause of the arrest, and the authority to make it (*People v. Maddox, 46 Cal. 2d 301; People v. Romero, 156 Cal. 2d 48*).

An officer does not have to notify the accused of his official capacity before making an arrest, when it is known to the accused or when by the exercise of ordinary reason, the accused should know it, as where the officers are in a distinctive uniform, with their badges displayed. Likewise, notice of intent to make the arrest may be indicated from the circumstances. It is not necessary that notice of such intention be given by express statement, before taking the person into custody (*Allen V. McCoy, 135 C.A. 500; People v. Valenzuela, 171 C.A. 362*).

When the arrestee insists on knowing the specific charge on which he is being arrested, it is the officer's obligation to so advise the arrested person. However, the statutory declaration of intention can be dispensed with if the circumstances are such that the arrestee knows he is about to be arrested (*People v. Scott, 170 C.A. 2d 446*).

Actual and Constructive Custody. Custody is generally defined as the detention of a person against his will. Actual custody and constructive custody differ in that, as previously stated, one comes into actual custody through physical restraint or through submission to custody. On the other hand, constructive custody implies a status of the arrestee wherein more latitude is afforded in physical detention. Constructive custody would thus apply to a county jail "trusty" or an honor farm inmate. Further, it might be said that parolees are in constructive custody of their respective parole agents, or as the courts have stated, they are in a virtual "prison without bars."

Use of Reasonable Force. Any peace officer who has reasonable cause to believe that the person to be arrested has committed a public offense may use reasonable force to effect the arrest, to prevent escape, or to overcome resistance. A peace officer who makes or attempts to make an arrest need not retreat or desist from his efforts by reason of the resistance or threatened resistance of the person being arrested; nor shall such officer be deemed the aggressor or lose his right to self-defense by the use of reasonable force to effect the arrest, to prevent escape, or to overcome resistance (PC 835a).

Homicide is never justifiable in making an arrest for a misdemeanor or preventing escape of a misdemeanor arrestee (*People v. Newsome, 51 C.A. 42*). (See also Section 7.13 "Escape and Fresh Pursuit.")

In making an arrest an officer has the right to use all the force which, from the surrounding circumstances, seems to him, as a reasonable man, necessary; he has the right to arm himself and go armed; and where the offense charged is a felony, he has the right, for his own safety if apparently necessary to a reasonable man, to kill the person whom he is seeking to arrest; and he has a right and it is his duty, to arrest a man who has committed a felony, with or without a warrant (*People v. Adams, 85 Cal. 231*).

Unlawful Use of Force—Penalties. Every public officer who, under color of authority without lawful necessity, assaults or beats any person, is punishable by a fine not exceeding five thousand dollars ($5,000) or by imprisonment in the state prison or in a county jail not exceeding one year, or by both such fine and imprisonment (PC 149).

Every officer who is guilty of willful inhumanity or oppression toward any prisoner under his care or in his custody, is punishable by a fine not exceeding two thousand dollars ($2,000) and by removal from office (PC 147).

7.10   RESISTING ARREST

Prior to the legislative enactment in 1957 of PC 834a, the traditional common law provision that a person could resist an unlawful arrest, and could use all reasonable force in doing so, was not only legal, but appeared to be the policy in the case of some groups and individuals with respect to dealing with police arrests. Such is *not* the law today, and it is a complete inaccuracy and misnomer to assume that one may resist what he deems an unlawful arrest by a peace officer.

Penal Code, Section 834a, currently states that "If a person has knowledge, or by the exercise of reasonable care, should have knowledge, that he is being arrested by a *peace officer,* it is the duty of such person to refrain from using force or any weapon to resist such arrest."

This section clearly deprives a person of his right to resist any arrest, legal or illegal, which is made by a peace officer. In a practical sense, the determination of a lawful arrest is to be left to a court of law to decide and not the person being arrested.

Misdemeanor Resisting. Every person who willfully resists, delays, or obstructs any public officer, in the discharge or attempt to discharge any duty of his office, when no other punishment is prescribed, is punishable by fine not exceeding one thousand dollars, or by imprisonment in a county jail not exceeding one year or by both such fine and imprisonment (PC 148).

In a prosecution for obstructing public officers in the discharge of their duty, the burden is on the prosecution to prove all elements of the offense, including the one that officers were then discharging or attempting to discharge some official duty, (*People v. Perry, 79 C.A. 2d 906*). One who physically attacks a police officer who is engaged in quieting a public disturbance and arresting active disturbers is guilty of "obstructing a public officer" in the performance of his duty (*People v. Powell, 99 C.A. 2d 178*). Physical resistance is not absolutely necessary. Such resistance may merely amount to verbal interference for the crime to be committed (*People v. Cooks, 250 A.C.A. 392*).

Felony Resistance. Penal Code, Section 69, relates to "Resisting Executive Officers" and states, "Every person who attempts, by means of any threat or violence, to deter or prevent an executive officer from performing any duty imposed upon such officer by law, or who knowingly resists, by the use of force or violence, such officer, in the performance of his duty, is punishable by a fine not exceeding five thousand dollars ($5,000), or by imprisonment in the state prison or in a county jail not exceeding one year, or by both such fine and imprisonment."

This section relates to the deterring or prevention of an "executive officer" from doing his legal duty or knowingly resisting the performance of such duty by force or violence and is punishable as a felony (*Manss v. Superior Court, 25 C.A. 533*).

7.11   THE MIRANDA ADMONISHMENT

In the historic decision by the United States Supreme Court in the case of *Miranda v. Arizona, et al.*, decided June 12, 1966, it was held that law enforcement officers must give a warning and secure a waiver from an arrestee in order for any statements made by an accused to be admissible in court.

Historical Note. Ernesto Miranda was convicted of kidnap and rape in 1963, but the conviction was overturned in 1966 by the U.S. Supreme Court on grounds that he was not advised of his constitutional rights against self-incrimination.

Miranda was retried on the charges, was convicted, and served five years of a twenty-year sentence. He also was serving a concurrent twenty-five-year term for an unrelated knife-point robbery of $8.00 from a woman. Miranda was released on parole in 1972. He was stabbed to death the night of January 31, 1976, during an argument at a bar near downtown Phoenix, Arizona.

Procedures for Admonishment. The specific warning which must be given, in compliance with the *Miranda* decision is as follows:
1. You have the right to remain silent.
2. Anything you say can and will be used against you in a court of law.
3. You have the right to talk to a lawyer and have him present with you while you are being questioned.
4. If you cannot afford to hire a lawyer, one will be appointed to represent you before any questioning, if you wish one.

After the warning and in order to secure a waiver, the following questions should be asked and an affirmative reply secured to each question:
1. Do you understand each of these rights I have explained to you?
2. Having these rights in mind, do you wish to talk to us now?

All statements, whether confessions, admissions, incriminating statements, or exculpatory statements are subject to the warnings before they are admissible in evidence, with the exception of those circumstances previously noted, i.e. traffic citations, voluntary contact at the police station and an offer of confession, and on-the-scene general questioning.

The suspect's agreement to talk must appear affirmatively. The waiver of his right to remain silent and to have an attorney with him must be knowingly and intelligently made. Should a suspect indicate in any manner prior to or during the questioning that he wishes to remain silent, the questioning must stop. No attempt to threaten or trick a suspect may be used to have the suspect change his mind.

If a suspect wants to consult an attorney before speaking, the questioning must stop until the suspect has consulted an attorney and the attorney is present with him.

If a waiver is secured, the officer, in addition to the affirmative evidence of the waiver, should place in the arrest report his evaluation of the suspect's education, mental and physical condition, his criminal background, if known, his age and experience, and anything that would tend to show the suspect knew what he was doing when he agreed to talk to the law enforcement official.

Who Should Be Admonished. What persons are entitled to the above warning? When should it be given? Generally, the Miranda warning must be given to all potential defendants in police custody or who are otherwise deprived of their freedom of action in any significant way *prior* to their being questioned as a *suspect* in a crime.
1. The warning must be given to the suspect arrested *prior* to being interrogated.
2. The warning must be given as soon as the officer has decided to arrest a suspect (based on reasonable cause) *if* the suspect is to be questioned about the crime.
3. Minors must be admonished at the time they are taken into custody, whether they are going to be interrogated or not.

No warning need be given in the following circumstances:
1. When a person walks into the police station and states that he wishes to confess to a crime.
2. When a person calls the police to offer a confession or any other statement he desires to make.
3. When the officer is engaged in "general on-the-scene questioning" as to facts surrounding a crime or other general questioning of citizens in the fact-finding process. It is an act of responsible citizenship for individuals to give whatever information they may have to aid in law enforcement.

When to Admonish. The following policy is recommended relative to administration of the Miranda warning.

1. No suspect in custody should be warned of his rights and a waiver solicited *unless* an interrogation is to follow immediately or in the very near future. Conversely, if a suspect is given a warning and a waiver obtained, he should be interrogated immediately or in the very near future. All too often, arrest reports indicate that a suspect was advised of his rights and a waiver obtained and *no* interrogation followed. In some cases, a warning is given and no waiver solicited. In such cases, the officer who gave the *Miranda* warning has engaged in an idle act.

2. Where the suspect appears unlikely to waive *Miranda* rights, he should not be warned of them and questioning should be deferred to a later time. This will usually occur where the suspect appears to be obviously uncooperative or belligerent.

3. Where the suspect appears likely to waive *Miranda* rights and talk about the case, questioning should begin as soon as possible. Compliance with *Miranda* rules must, of course, precede the interrogation.

4. Questioning should be deferred, together with warning of *Miranda* rights, where the arresting officer is unfamiliar with the case. For example, it often happens that an officer making an arrest upon a warrant or pursuant to instructions will be unfamiliar with the case.

5. Law enforcement agencies should adopt, wherever feasible, procedures whereby investigating officers may be promptly alerted of the fact that a suspect is in custody so that an interrogation can be begun as soon as possible. Procedures should be adopted so that investigating officers will be available to conduct an interrogation as soon as possible after the arrest of a suspect.

6. It should be remembered that a person in custody or who is significantly deprived of freedom of action need not be warned of *Miranda* rights and a waiver solicited, *unless* he is to be interrogated.

7. In all cases, any officer hearing a volunteered statement made by a suspect in conversation initiated by the suspect should make notes as soon as possible of the statements and advise his supervisor or the investigating officer. A report of the volunteered statement and the circumstances should be included in the case file. The policy should apply to any officer, whether or not he is familiar with the case.

8. In all cases, an officer should promptly notify his supervisor or the investigating officer of the fact that the suspect has stated that he desires to talk about the case. The investigating officer should be immediately informed of the suspect's request.

9. Generally a suspect who initiates a conversation about the case or states that he is willing to talk about the case need not be rewarned of his rights or a waiver again solicited.

10. Where an investigating officer either knows or reasonably believes that a suspect has been advised of his *Miranda* rights and has refused to waive those rights, he should be aware that if he thereafter initiates a conversation about the case or again solicits a waiver, any statements thereafter made will ordinarily be inadmissible *against that suspect*. However, if the officer does propose to begin the questioning about the case, knowing that statements obtained will be inadmissible against the suspect (as well as any evidence obtained thereby), there is nothing unlawful or improper in questioning the suspect provided that physically or psychologically coercive tactics are not used.

11. Even if taken into temporary custody, under W & I Code 601 or 602, or for any violation, W & I Code 625 requires that the minor be advised of his or her *Miranda* rights.

Factors Affecting the Miranda Warning. A suspect who has been taken into custody, or otherwise deprived of his freedom in any significant manner, must be warned of his *Miranda* rights *only if he is to be questioned regarding his possible participation in a crime*. An exception to this arises where the suspect is a minor under age eighteen. Section 625, W.I.C., requires that a minor be admonished at the time he is taken into custody, regardless of whether he is to be interrogated or not.

Normally, a suspect need not be advised of *Miranda* rights during a field interview situation. It is only when the temporary detention has shifted from the investigatory to the accusatory state (i.e. when there is probable cause to arrest) that further interrogation should be preceded by compliance with *Miranda*. A suspect who is placed in a police vehicle for transportation to the station will normally be deemed to be in custody. Interrogation, relative to the suspect's participation in a crime, must be preceded by compliance with *Miranda*.

Apparent Custody. The existence of custody is not limited to the external fact of arrest, detention, restraint, or significant deprivation of freedom. It may be based on the reasonable belief of an individual under questioning that he or she must submit to interrogation. In *People v. Arnold, 66 C. 2d 438,* a deputy district attorney phoned the defendant and asked her to come to his office. The defendant drove her own car to the office and was thereafter questioned at length by the deputy district attorney, who had not informed her of any constitutional rights. After the questioning, the defendant left the office and was not arrested until forty days thereafter.

The court reversed the conviction, holding that "custody" occurs if the suspect is physically deprived of his or her freedom of action in any significant way, or is led to believe, as a reasonable person, that he is so deprived.

An arresting officer who has observed all of the elements of a crime, or who bases an arrest on other substantial evidence of guilt, need not, except in cases of minors, administer the *Miranda* warnings at the time of arrest. In many cases, questioning of the suspect should be deferred to the concerned investigators who may be better informed on questions involving the particular crime, other uncleared crimes, missing property, etc. Also, if an arrestee displays belligerence or hostility toward the arresting officers and an immediate interrogation is not imperative to the case, it may be advisable to delay the admonition and questioning until a later time.

However, in those cases when an immediate on-the-scene interrogation would serve to clear up obscure facts of the case, or would be psychologically advantageous in obtaining pertinent statements, the arresting officer should thoroughly pursue the interrogation after properly administering the *Miranda* warnings and obtaining a waiver.

The voluntary spontaneous statements of an adult suspect who is *not* being interrogated are admissible, whether or not he has been advised of his constitutional rights. Therefore, any such statements should always be thoroughly detailed in the arrest report. This is particularly important where an arrestee has refused to waive his rights, since under the *Fioritto* rule, investigators cannot initiate further questioning and use ensuing statements against him (*People v. Fioritto, 68 C. 2d 714*).

Where an arrest is based solely on a warrant of arrest, the arresting officer should make the following determinations prior to admonishing the suspect and questioning him:

1. Whether the investigators who obtained the warrant, or other officers having knowledge of the case, are available for further instructions.
2. If such officers are not available, the contents of the crime report, which is usually attached to the

original warrant, should be referred to by the arresting officer before questioning of the suspect is attempted.
3. If the warrant of arrest is from a foreign jurisdiction, the arresting officers should not admonish the suspect or attempt to question him before contacting Detective Headquarters Division for further instructions.

If questions are being asked of a suspect relating solely to his identity, no *Miranda* warning need be given. A person may also be submitted to physical tests bearing on his identity (fingerprints, handwriting, blood) without being advised of his constitutional rights. However, the following exceptions should be noted:

1. If a suspect is requested to speak for voice identification purposes, he should be advised that his refusal to speak for such purpose is not privileged and that his refusal may be used as evidence against him.
2. If a suspect is to be placed in a police lineup for identification purposes, he must be first advised that he is entitled to have his attorney present during the proceedings.

Effect of Suspect's Refusal to Waive His Rights. The *Fioritto* case which follows clearly precludes the admission of statements against a defendant which were obtained in a subsequent police-initiated interview on the same case. If the defendant had previously refused to waive his *Miranda* rights, the fact that a suspect had been readmonished makes no difference. His responsive statements cannot be used against him. Nevertheless, the following distinctions point to the value of conducting subsequent interviews, notwithstanding a prior refusal to speak:

1. *Fioritto* does not render inadmissible any subsequent statements *voluntarily initiated by the defendant.* If he later changes his mind and decides to talk without further prompting from the police, his subsequent statements may be used in court. In such a case, it would be advisable to obtain a recorded statement which indicates that the statement was freely given at the defendant's own volition. Consequently, an investigator should let it be known that he is available for an interview in the event that the defendant later wishes to speak to him.
2. Where a suspect, after a prior refusal to speak, has by himself decided to make a statement, he need not be readmonished of his constitutional rights. So long as the suspect appeared to clearly comprehend his rights as they were being

explained to him at the time of the first admonition, a second warning is not legally required. However, in cases where the suspect's previous physical or mental condition may raise an issue of his capacity to understand, the admonition should be repeated and an intelligent waiver obtained.

3. The same holds true where a suspect has previously waived his rights and made a preliminary statement. If a subsequent interview is desired, the *Miranda* warning need *not* be repeated if the officer who gave the first warning has indicated that the suspect appeared to clearly understand his rights and had intelligently waived them at that time.

Although, as indicated by *Fioritto,* the police cannot continue or renew an interrogation for the purpose of obtaining admissible incriminating statements to be used against a suspect who has previously refused to waive his rights, the police are *not* precluded from further questioning of the suspect for other purposes.

1. In the case of *People v. Varnum, 66 C. 2d 808,* the California Supreme Court held that there was nothing unlawful in the proper questioning of a suspect who had not been warned of his constitutional rights. Although statements made by a suspect in custody under such circumstances cannot be used against him, they may, in fact, be used by the police for other purposes such as implicating other suspects in the crime or recovering property of a valuable or evidential nature.

2. The holding of the Varnum case may be properly extended to the subsequent questioning of a suspect who has previously indicated a refusal to waive his constitutional rights. As stated in the language of the case: "In the absence of physical or psychological coercive tactics, there is no basis for excluding as a result of questioning a suspect in disregard of his Fifth and Sixth Amendment rights, when such evidence is offered at the trial of another person."

3. In conclusion, investigating officers should continue to interview arrestees for the purpose of completing an Investigator's Final Report.

Recent Court Decisions Affecting Miranda. In the case of *People v. Fioritto, 68 C. 2d 714,* defendant and two companions burglarized a market. After his apprehension, defendant was taken into the police station but had not been formally arrested. He was advised of *Miranda* rights. The detective then asked defendant to sign a waiver of his constitutional rights.

Defendant refused. Almost immediately thereafter the officers confronted defendant with his two accomplices, both juveniles, who had confessed and had implicated defendant. In the presence of the officers, one of the juveniles and the defendant engaged in a heated argument over an eight-dollar loan. The juveniles were then taken out, and the detective again advised defendant of his rights, asking anew if he would like to sign the waiver and confess. Defendant then signed the waiver and confessed to the crime.

The California Supreme Court held the confession to be inadmissible, making the following points:

1. It was necessary to advise the defendant of *Miranda* rights and obtain a waiver before interrogation, because he was "ushered into a police station and detained for questioning" although not formally arrested.

2. By his initial refusal to waive his rights, defendant indicated that he intended to assert his rights. The privilege had been once invoked, and all further attempts at police interrogation should have ceased.

3. Although the confrontation of defendant with his two juvenile accomplices, after having been advised of *Miranda* rights and after refusal to waive such rights, introduced a new factor into the questioning, the court said, "We have no alternative but to hold that the confession thereafter secured constituted inadmissible evidence at trial."

4. The Court does not disapprove use of statements, whether admissions or confessions, volunteered by a suspect. But this rule does not apply where after a refusal to waive *Miranda* rights, the police initiate resumption of interrogation or again solicit a waiver.

Voluntary Statements. Examples of situations where volunteered statements are admissible (notwithstanding failure to give constitutional rights) are:

a. A defendant is arrested. As the arresting officer reached to disarm him, defendant exclaimed, "You have the right man," and "This is the gun I had." In the police car, he initiated a conversation with one of the officers. He volunteered that had the police been a few minutes late in arresting him, he would not have been caught, as he was planning to leave for South America. He asked how long the murder victim had lived. The officer replied and than asked, "What happened to the guy (the victim) in Farah's Bar?" Defendant responded, "He tried to be a hero," and, when requested to explain, continued, "The guy wouldn't do what he was told." All of the defendant's statements were held admissible (*People v. Treloar, 64 Cal. 2d 141 (1966)*).

b. An officer arrived at defendant's residence after police received a call from a social caseworker that defendant called him and said he had just killed his child. Unable to gain entry, the officer went next door and found defendant in clothing, wet from chest to waist. He asked defendant what he had done, and the latter replied he had done nothing. After a short conversation, the officer and defendant went to the latter's residence. Defendant said the officer would "find her in the bedroom where I put her." When asked, "Who?" defendant said, "My daughter." He then volunteered that he had drowned her in the bathtub, that she had been asleep and "didn't feel a thing," and that "it was painless." The defendant's twenty-one-month-old daughter was found in the bedroom and later determined to be dead. While two ambulance attendants were passing through the house, they heard defendant tell the officer, "I killed the little bastard." The defendant's statements to the officer were held to be admissible. The court also pointed out that the officer had the privilege, at this clearly investigatory state, to ask relevant questions which might be necessary to save a life without advising a suspect of his constitutional rights as the child had not yet been found, dead or alive (*People v. Jacobson, 63 Cal 2d 319 (1965)*).

In the case of (*Michigan v. Mosley*), decided December 9, 1975, the U.S. Supreme Court ruled 6 to 2 that after a suspect exercises his right to remain silent about one crime, police may still question him about another. The ruling reversed a Michigan Supreme Court decision vacating the conviction of one Richard Bert Mosley for the January 1971 slaying of Leroy Williams in Detroit.

Mosley had been arrested for questioning about a series of robberies. He told police he wished to exercise his right to remain silent and interrogation stopped. Two hours later another officer, after properly advising Mosley of his rights, questioned him concerning the unrelated holdup and murder of Williams. Mosley did not ask to consult an attorney nor did he object to being questioned. When the police revealed he had been named by an accomplice, Mosley made self-incriminating statements.

Prior to his trial for murder, the defendant moved to suppress his incriminating statements, maintaining that under the *Miranda* decision, it was improper for the second officer to question him about the murder after he had refused to answer the first

officer's questions about the robberies. The trial court denied the motion and Mosley was convicted. The Michigan Court of Appeals reversed the conviction holding that the second officer's interrogation of Mosley was a *per se* violation of the Miranda Doctrine. Further appeal was denied by the Supreme Court of Michigan which, in effect sustained the reversal.

Upon appeal to the U.S. Supreme Court, the judgment of the Appeals Court was reversed and the case was remanded for sentence. In writing for the majority, Justice Potter Stewart said that Mosley could have cut off questioning at any time, therefore, his *Miranda* rights were preserved. See also *People v. Mack, 89 Cal. App. 3d 974*.

In yet another case (*People v. Duck Wong, 18 C. 3d 178*), the California Supreme Court held that because criminal charges had not yet been filed against the defendant, it was not necessary that his attorney be present where the defendant knowingly and intelligently waived his *Miranda* rights. The defendant, Duck Wong, a suspect in a hit-and-run manslaughter, retained an attorney prior to his being located by the police. The attorney contacted the investigating officer and advised him that he would bring his client in to speak with the police. The officer agreed to cease his own efforts to find the defendant and to work through the attorney instead. Previously, a citizen of the ethnic community in which the defendant resided had been requested by the officer to find the defendant. The officer failed to advise his informant of the agreement between the officer and the attorney and he brought the defendant in to the officer and then acted as interpreter. The officer first inquired about the attorney. It appeared that the defendant, speaking through the interpreter, was dissatisfied with his attorney, that he planned to get a new one, and waived his constitutional right to remain silent and have counsel present for interrogation.

The appellate court ruled that even in the absence of the officer's breach of faith with the attorney (which was adequate alone to overturn the conviction) the officer was under a duty to contact the attorney once he knew the suspect was represented.

The defendant, thereafter, made incriminating statements and was convicted of vehicle manslaughter and leaving the scene of an accident and not rendering aid to an injured party.

The court, said however, that after the accusatory stage of a proceeding has been reached and counsel appointed or retained, the police may not initiate interrogation of the suspect in absence of his counsel, unless a substantial reason can be demonstrated for the absence of counsel, and any waiver of rights by the suspect is invalid without counsel.

7.12 ARREST PURSUANT TO WARRANT

Affidavit for Arrest Warrant. The statutory authority permitting the issuance of a *warrant of arrest* based solely upon formal allegations in the language as required by PC 806 is unconstitutional and violates the Fourth Amendment. However, in a case in which an officer in good faith obtains a warrant for the arrest of the accused, and, additionally, has personal knowledge constituting probable cause for the arrest of the accused at the time he attempts to execute the warrant otherwise *invalid* on federal grounds, *the arrest is lawful,* and fruits of the search incidental to that arrest are admissible if material and relevant to prove any element of the offense.

Briefly what the court is saying is that the Constitution of the United States and that of California require that before a warrant shall be issued (either search or arrest warrant) the magistrate shall review, upon affidavit, the probable cause for that arrest or search. Complaints previously used to secure warrants of arrest were mere conclusions or statements that an offense had been committed but did not, upon oath, state what was the probable cause or reason for believing that the offense had been committed. Now in order to secure arrest warrants, particularly in felony cases, the courts require affidavits accompanying the complaint. *If such affidavit is not used, any evidence found as a result of a search incidental to that arrest will not be admitted into evidence.* Of course if the defendant is already in custody, no affidavit is needed with the complaint. Each court in the various judicial districts has different forms for the affidavit that may be used by that particular court. Officers should check with the particular court in which they routinely do business.

Hearsay evidence is admissible in these affidavits because it is being used to establish probable cause for the arrest, not the truth of the matter of the offense (*Chimel v. California, 396 U.S. 752).*

Complaint. The filing of a complaint must precede the issuance of a warrant of arrest. The complaint, like a indictment or information, is an accusatory pleading (PC 691). The complaint is a written document, sworn to under oath, subscribed by the complainant, and filed with a competent court, charging a person with a criminal offense. Where there is no one available who has positive knowledge of all the facts of the alleged offense, such complaint may be made upon information and belief.

Nature of Warrant Arrest. A warrant of arrest is a written order, signed by a magistrate, and directed to a peace officer, commanding the arrest of a person. If the complaint satisfied the magistrate that the offense complained of has been committed and there are reasonable grounds to believe the defendant committed it, he has a duty to issue a warrant to arrest the defendant (PC 813). The warrant may also be issued upon indictment by the grand jury, to arrest a bail-jumping fugitive from another state (PC 847.5).

Form of Warrant of Arrest. The form of an arrest warrant is set forth by statute (PC 814, felony warrants); (PC 1427, misdemeanor warrants). The following must be included in the arrest warrant:
1. Name of defendant, but if unknown he may be designated by any name. If a fictitious name is used, the warrant must contain a description or some means of identifying the person intended, otherwise the warrant is void.
2. Time of issuance.
3. City and county where issued.
4. Signature of issuing magistrate or judge with the title of his office.
5. The bail set by the magistrate, if the offense is bailable (PC 815-815a).

Warrant—To Whom Directed. A warrant of arrest must be directed generally to any peace officer in the state and may be executed by any of those officers to whom it may be delivered (PC 816).

Although no one other than a peace officer may execute a warrant of arrest, the law provides that any person making an arrest may orally summon as many persons as he deems necessary to aid him therein (PC 839).

Nighttime Service of Warrant. An arrest for the commission of a felony may be made on any day and at any time of the day or night. An arrest for the commission of a misdemeanor or an infraction cannot be made between the hours of 10 o'clock p.m. of any day and 6 o'clock a.m. of the succeeding day, unless:
1. The arrest is made without a warrant pursuant to Section 836 or 837.
2. The arrest is made in a public place.
3. The arrest is made when the person is in custody pursuant to another lawful arrest.
4. The arrest is made pursuant to a warrant which, for good cause shown, directs that it may be served at any time of the day or night (PC 840).

Also, PC 818 provides that where a misdemeanor warrant is served at night upon a person at his place of abode, and the warrant is for a traffic offense, and such warrant on its face authorizes said procedure, the arresting officer may release the defendant on a notice to appear instead of booking him.

An arrest by a peace officer acting under a warrant is lawful even though the officer does not have the warrant in his possession at the time of the arrest, but if the person arrested so requests it, the warrant shall be shown to him as soon as practicable (PC 842).

Either a telegraphic copy or an abstract of a warrant may be sent by teletype or telegraph, and in the hands of the receiving officer, he must proceed as though he had the original warrant (PC 850). A proper abstract must contain the following:
1. The charge, and whether a felony or a misdemeanor.
2. The court of issuance.
3. The subject's name, address, and description.
4. The bail.
5. The name of the issuing magistrate.
6. The warrant number.

Delay in Executing Warrant. Case law has established that the constitutional right to a speedy trial requires that a defendant be served with a warrant of arrest within a reasonable time after the filing of the complaint. An unexplained delay of sixty days has been held not to be unreasonable, but somewhere beyond that period an unexplained delay becomes unreasonable, depending on the circumstances of the case (*Rost v. Municipal Court, 184 C.A. 2d 507*).

Disposition of Arrestee Served in County Where Warrant Issued. If the offense charged is a felony, and the arrest occurs in the county in which the warrant was issued, the officer making the arrest must take the defendant before the magistrate who issued the warrant or some other magistrate of the same county (PC 821).

Disposition of Arrestee Served in County Other Than Where Warrant Issued (Felony or Misdemeanor). An officer must inform the defendant in writing of his right to be taken before a magistrate in the county where arrested and must note on the warrant that he has so informed the defendant and, if required by the defendant, must take him before a magistrate in that county.

The defendant may post bail in the amount set on the warrant (or set by bail schedule if bail not set on a misdemeanor warrant) either with the magistrate, or with the officer in charge of the jail without appearing before the magistrate. The magistrate or officer in charge of the jail may release the arrested person and set a time and place for his appearance in the proper court of the county where the warrant was issued.

If a defendant is admitted to bail by a local magistrate, the magistrate must certify that fact on the warrant, deliver it to the officer, and the officer must then discharge the defendant from arrest and deliver the warrant to the Clerk of the issuing court.

If a felony warrant has no bail set thereon, or if in any case the defendant does not demand to be taken before a local magistrate, or if he does not post bail, the arresting officer must notify the law enforcement agency requesting the arrest in the county where the warrant was issued and that agency must take custody of the defendant within five days and take him before the magistrate who issued the warrant, or another magistrate in the same county (PC 821, 822, 823 and 1296b).

Weapons Taken From Arrested Person. Any person making an arrest may take from the person arrested all offensive weapons which he may have about his person and must deliver them to the magistrate before whom he is taken (PC 846).

Making the Arrest. The other requirements for making the arrest, including what the arresting officer must say in compliance with PC 841 and the procedures for admonishment per the *Miranda* decision, together with the amount of force which can be used, are the same whether the arrest is with or without a warrant. These provisions were treated in previous sections.

Return of Warrant After Service. The arresting officer has the duty of endorsing and subscribing his "return" on the warrant and delivering it to the magistrate at the time he delivers the arrestee. Penal Code, Sections 824 and 828, prescribe the procedure for endorsing the warrant upon proper service.

Officer's Liability in Serving Warrant. There shall be no liability on the part of, and no cause of action shall arise against, any peace officer who makes an arrest pursuant to a warrant of arrest regular upon its face if such peace officer in making the arrest, acts without malice and in the reasonable belief that the person arrested is the one referred to in the warrant (*Civil Code, Section 43.5a*).

If an officer properly serves a warrant which is regular upon its face, he incurs no civil liability regardless of how many errors may have occurred in the proceedings leading to issuance of the warrant (*Downey v. Allen, 36 C.A. 2d 269*).

7.13   ESCAPE AND FRESH PURSUIT

The laws concerning the crime of escape which are pertinent to police officers are covered by Penal Code, Sections 4532(a) and 4532(b). The concept of escape and the legislative intent of these two sections has long been a source of confusion to the police officer.

Of particular significance to the statutes defining escape are the elements "arrested and booked." A 1953 amendment divided the escape section into two parts—subsections (a) and (b), and added the wording that the person had to be *formally* charged before he could commit an escape. Such is definitely not the case today.

In 1982, subsections (a) and (b) of PC 4532 were amended and the words "formally charged" were deleted and replaced with the words "arrested and booked." As a result of this change in wording, the pertinent element of the crime of escape came to be that a person had to be *arrested and booked for, charged with or convicted of, a crime before he could commit an escape.* Since this wording was entered in both PC 4532(a), pertaining to those convicted of a misdemeanor who escape custody, and PC 4532(b), pertaining to those convicted of a felony who subsequently escape, the Legislature apparently intended that neither a misdemeanor suspect nor a felony suspect could be charged with the crime of escape for unlawful departure from an officer *prior to booking.*

People v. Redmond, 55 Cal Rptr. 195. Officers noted three male occupants in a vehicle and observed that one in the right front seat was bending over and appeared to be reaching under the seat. The conduct of the three occupants was such that a consensual search followed, revealing the presence of a gun and burglar tools within the vehicle. Suspects were arrested for a violation of PC 12025, carrying a concealed firearm, a misdemeanor. Redmond, upon being arrested, fled and was pursued by one officer, who fired a warning shot at the fleeing suspect. Redmond successfully eluded the officers, but on January 14, 1965 he was arrested as a suspect in an armed robbery of a gas station in Riverside. He was charged with one count of armed robbery consequent to that arrest and with one count of escape under Penal Code, Section 4532(a), because he had fled from officers on the earlier occasion. The District Court of Appeal affirmed the conviction on the robbery count but reversed the conviction on the escape count.

The Court, in rendering its decision in the Redmond case, commented that insofar as could be determined, "the question raised by defendant in this case has never heretofore been squarely met in the several cases in which convictions for escape under Section 4532(a) for unauthorized departure from custody of arresting officers prior to booking have been before the appellate courts." The Court then concluded that the information failed to allege and prove the crime of escape in the Redmond case, and suggested that officers have other statutory means to deter persons from resisting arrest or fleeing from custody, and specifically cited Sections 148 and 69 of the Penal Code. The Court further commented that the case decision "is not to suggest that unauthorized departure of an arrestee from the custody of an arresting officer prior to booking, charge or conviction should not be made a crime of escape, but that this is a decision to be made by the Legislature."

Conclusion. The decision of the California Court of Appeal in the Redmond case should serve to clarify the misconceptions that police officers have had concerning the laws pertaining to the crime of escape. To emphasize the effect of the Court's decision, an arrested person who flees or attempts to flee from custody after being arrested but prior to being booked into jail cannot be considered as an escapee. Although the Redmond case pertained to a fleeing misdemeanant, it seems apparent that the logic of the Court can be extended to pertain to fleeing felony suspects as well. It is essential to realize that, in view of the case just cited, a fleeing misdemeanor suspect does not become a fleeing felon simply because he flees from the custody of the arresting officer.

Fresh Pursuit. "Fresh pursuit" means close pursuit or "hot pursuit" of a suspect by a police officer. Penal Code, Section 852.2, authorizes a peace officer from another state to continue in fresh pursuit of a felony suspect into this state with the same authority thereafter as a peace officer of this state. Upon arrest in this state, the foreign peace officer must take the arrestee without unnecessary delay before the magistrate of the county in which the arrest was made. If the magistrate determines the arrest was lawful, he shall commit the person arrested to await a reasonable time for the issuance of an extradition warrant or admit him to bail. If the arrest is deemed unlawful, the magistrate shall discharge the arrestee (PC 852.3).

7.14   POSSE COMITATUS

The term *posse comitatus* means "power of the county" and in this case relates to the authority of the sheriff (or any other law enforcement officer) to command any able-bodied person over eighteen years of age to aid and assist in taking or arresting any person against whom there may be issued any process, or to prevent breach of the peace or any criminal offense.

Penal Code, Section 723, states, "When a sheriff or other public officer authorized to execute process finds, or has reason to apprehend that resistance will be made to the execution of the process, he or she may command as many able-bodied inhabitants of the officer's county as he or she may think proper to assist him or her in overcoming the resistance, and, if necessary, in seizing, arresting, and confining the persons resisting, their aiders and abettors."

Penal Code, Section 150, states in part that any able-bodied person over eighteen years of age who refuses to join the *posse comitatus,* by neglecting or refusing to aid and assist in taking or arresting any escapee, or neglecting or refusing to aid and assist in preventing any breach of the peace or criminal offense, is punishable by a fine of not less than $50 or more than $1,000.

7.15   THREATENED OFFENSES

Penal Code, Section 701, provides that "An information may be laid before any of the magistrates mentioned in Section 808, that a person has threatened to commit an offense against the person or property of another."

When the information is laid before such magistrate he must examine, on oath, the informer and any witness he may produce and must take their depositions in writing and cause them to be subscribed by the parties making them (PC 702).

Penal Code, Section 703, provides for the issuance of a warrant for the arrest of a person who threatens the commission of a criminal offense; and, if it appears that there is no reason to fear such commission on the part of the arrestee, he must be discharged (PC 705).

If, however, there is just reason to fear the commission of the offense, the person complained of may be required to enter into an undertaking in such sum, not exceeding five thousand dollars, as the magistrate may direct, with one or more sufficient sureties, to keep the peace towards the people of this state, and particularly toward the informer. The undertaking is valid and binding for six months, and may, upon the renewal of the information, be extended for a longer period, or a new undertaking be required (PC 706).

If the undertaking required by the last section (PC 706) is given, the party informed of must be discharged. If he does not give it, the magistrate must commit him to prison, specifying in the warrant the requirement to give security, the amount thereof, and the omission to give the same (PC 707). If the person complained of is committed for not giving the undertaking required, he may be discharged by any magistrate, upon giving the same (PC 708).

7.16   IMMUNITY FROM ARREST

All persons are subject to arrest except where a statutory provision gives an exception. In practice, the word "immunity" is actually a misnomer inasmuch as no person is actually immune from physical arrest when such arrest is lawful. The arrestee, on the other hand, may be legally immune from prosecution under certain circumstances, which will be subsequently enumerated, but one still may be arrested, after which one may claim legal exemption to arrest before a competent court.

Any statute that covers immunity from arrest, except in cases of diplomatic immunity, in which the term "arrest" is used, is made in reference to a *civil* arrest and *not* a *criminal* arrest. Thus, by statute, certain persons are exempt from arrest under certain circumstances, but such arrest as used in the statute means civil arrest even though the word "civil" may have been ommitted.

Diplomatic Immunity. Diplomatic immunity may be broadly defined as the freedom from local jurisdiction accorded under international law by the receiving state to duly accredited diplomatic officers, their families, and servants. Such immunity is a universally recognized principle included in the body of rules known as international law, which civilized nations have accepted as binding them in their intercourse with one another which is enforceable in the United States courts.

Witness Coming Into State Exempt From Process. If a person comes into this state in obedience to a subpoena directing him to attend and testify in this state, he shall not, while in this state pursuant to the subpoena or order, be subject to arrest of the service of process, civil or criminal, in connection with matters which arose before his entrance into this state under the subpoena (PC 1334.4).

Witness Passing Through State Exempt From Process. If a person passes through this state while going to another state in obedience to a subpoena or order to attend and testify in that state, or while returning therefrom, he shall not while so passing through this state be subject to arrest or the service of process, civil or criminal, in connection with matters which arose before his entrance into this state under the subpoena (PC 1334.5).

Immunity of Legislators. Article I, Section 6, of the United States Constitution states "The Senators and Representatives shall in all cases, except treason, felony, and breach of the peace, be privileged from arrest during their attendance at the session of their respective Houses, and in going to and returning from the same."

Article IV, Section 11 of the California Constitution states the "Members of the Legislature shall, in all cases except treason, felony, and breach of the peace, be privileged from arrest, and shall not be subject to any civil process during the session of the legislature, nor for fifteen days before the commencement and after the termination of each session."

The California Appellate Court stated in a leading case that a member of the State Legislature was not immune from arrest for a criminal charge including a violation of a city ordinance, and did not have the right to resist such arrest (*In re Emmett, 120 C.A. 349*).

Immunity of Electors. Elections Code, Section 400, states "Except for an indictable offense, every voter is privileged from arrest, while at, or while going to and returning from, his polling place on election day." The same privilege which applies to legislators, but no greater, applies to voters while at, going to, and returning from the voting place.

Immunity of Mail Carriers. The exemption of the mail carrier, as claimed under the statutes of the United States giving exemption to mail carriers while on duty is substantially similar, and the same principle applies to the constitutional provision giving exemption to senators and members of Congress. It was held that while a mail carrier, when in the discharge of his duty, cannot be detained upon any civil suit, he is legally liable to arrest on a charge of any criminal offense. The defendant in that case was apprehended for violating the liquor laws of the state and resisted arrest by assaulting the officer (*In re Renny v. Walker, 64 ME 430*).

7.17 ARRESTED PERSON'S RIGHTS AFTER ARREST

Arrestee's Right to Phone Call (PC 851.5)

a. Any person arrested has, immediately after he is booked, and, except where physically impossible, no later than three hours after his arrest, the right to make, at his own expense, in the presence of a public officer or employee, at least two

phone calls from the police station or other place at which he is booked, one completed to the person called, who may be his attorney, employer, or relative, the other completed to a bail bondsman.

b. Any public officer or employee who deprives an arrested person of the rights granted by this section is guilty of a misdemeanor.

The statute means, as its plain language indicates, that the right to a phone call by the arrestee arises immediately after booking, and lasts for an indefinite time, until the accused has no more need thereof. The entire tenor of the statute is one of liberality to the accused. For instance, it grants him the right to make *at least two* telephone calls; it does not limit the number of calls that he may make if the prison authorities are amenable. Finally, the words of the statute are "who may be his attorney, etc." rather than "who must be." The inference is clear therefrom that the enumeration in the statute is permissive rather than exclusive. It is likely that the Legislature intended to indicate the kind of telephone calls that must be permitted, *giving the enumerated people merely as examples* of those with whom a prisoner might validly have business (*In re Newbern, 55 Cal. 2d 500*).

The implication of the wording of PC 835, "from the police station or other place at which he is booked," is that the arrestee has to be in the police station or booking facility within three hours after his arrest in order to exercise his right of at least two telephone calls. This is not necessarily true. When it is physically impossible to have the arrested person in the jail within *three hours from the time of his arrest,* the person has a right to complete a call from the place where he is temporarily detained or confined. It is generally inconceivable that it would be "physically impossible" to get an arrestee to the police station within three hours unless he required hospitalization. In this instance, phone calls from the hospital will satisfy the requirements of the law.

Time Within Which the Defendant Must Be Taken Before a Magistrate. The defendant must, in all cases, be taken before the magistrate without unnecessary delay, and, in any event, within two days after his arrest excluding Sundays and holidays, provided, however, that when the two days prescribed herein expire at a time when the court in which the magistratae is sitting is not in session, such time shall be extended to include the duration of the next regular court session on the judicial day immediately following. After such arrest, any attorney at law entitled to practice in the courts of record of California, may, at the request of the prisoner or any relative of such prisoner, visit the person so arrested. Any officer, having charge of the prisoner so arrested, who willfully refuses or neglects to allow such attorney to visit a prisoner is guilty of a misdemeanor. Any officer, having a prisoner in charge, who refuses to allow any attorney to visit the prisoner when proper application is made, therefore shall forfeit and pay to the party aggrieved the sum of five hundred dollars ($500), to be recovered by action in any court of competent jurisdiction (PC 825).

The accused is entitled to receive sound legal advice as to how to respond to each accusation as it arises in the course of an investigation or interrogation unless he clearly and knowingly waives that right (*People v. Nerger, 238 A.C.A. 832;* also see Chapter 4, *Miranda v. Arizona*).

Alleged unreasonable delay in taking the defendant before a magistrate is not prejudicial error, where there was no showing that alleged unnecessary delay in any way militated against the defendant at his trial, or caused an unfair trial (*People v. Hightower, 189 C.A. 2d 309*).

A delay between the time of arrest of the defendant and the time that he is brought before a magistrate must materially affect the outcome of the trial before the defendant has cause to complain (*People v. Freely, 179 C.A. 2d 100*).

7.18 LAW ENFORCEMENT PROCEDURES AND CIVIL LIABILITY

There is always a possibility that a police officer can be held liable to the person whom he has arrested in either a criminal or civil action, or possibly both. As in a criminal case, the best defense to a civil action is knowledge of the laws of arrest and those facts that constitute reasonable cause.

Nature of Civil Action Against Police Officers. The following are the more common actions brought against individual officers by citizens.

1. *Assault and battery.* An assault is an unlawful attempt, coupled with an apparent present ability to commit a violent injury on the person of another. Battery is any willful and unlawful use of force or violence upon the person of another.
2. *False arrest and false imprisonment (e.g., delay in arraignment).* False imprisonment is the unlawful violation of the personal liberty of another. An officer is not liable for damages if the precautions adopted at the time of arrest were honestly believed necessary and reasonable

under the circumstances. This is true even though it may subsequently develop that restraint was actually unneccessary (*6 C.J.S., Arrest, Section 17(c) 1, p. 619;5 C.J.S., Arrest, Section 72, p. 432*).
3. *Negligence (e.g., directing traffic, etc.).* Officers having a general duty to exercise due care. "Due care" is measured against the standard of the ordinarily prudent or reasonable person.
4. *Wrongful death (e.g., shootings).* Wrongful death civil action is initiated by survivors of the decedent. A police officer making an arrest has the right to use all force which from the surrounding circumstances seems to him as a reasonable man necessary to effect the arrest.

Defense to Civil Actions. There are four basic defenses to civil actions brought against police officers.
1. *Probable cause for the arrest.* Probable cause has been defined as "such a state of facts as would lead any man of ordinary care and prudence to believe or entertain an honest and strong suspicion that the person arrested is guilty of the offense charged."

A police officer need not have certainty in his own mind. Probable cause may exist though the officer has some doubt. In considering the question of probable cause, the court will look only at the facts and circumstances presented to the officer at the time he was required to act.

The fact that an officer stops a person and asks reasonable questions under certain circumstances does not mean necessarily that the person is arrested. The court must determine as a matter of law whether the facts and circumstances as they appear or are found to exist constitute reasonable cause.

Reasonable cause to effect an arrest may consist of information from others. In one case the arresting officer relied on information from his superior officer, who in turn had received the information from the defendant's probation officer, who in turn had received it from the defendant's wife.

In applying the rule of probable cause, the courts have taken into consideration the training and experience of the arresting officer. An officer with only a short length of employment in law enforcement and limited field experience may be subjected to intense cross examination regarding training and experience. The courts may take both affirmative and negative aspects of these two points in arriving at a decision as to whether the arresting officer acted in good faith in making the arrest.

The fact that the arrestee was not prosecuted for the violation for which he was arrested does not make the arrest unlawful, and the unlawfulness of the arrest does not depend upon the outcome of the criminal prosecution. The fact of acquittal in a criminal prosecution is immaterial in the civil action.

There shall be no liability on the part of, and no cause of action shall arise against, any peace officer who makes an arrest pursuant to a warrant of arrest regular upon its face, if such peace officer in making the arrest acts without malice and in the reasonable belief that the person arrested is the one referred to in the warrant (*Civil Code, Section 43.5a*).

2. *Reasonable force in effecting arrest.* If the force used by a police officer is reasonably necessary to effect a lawful arrest, then such police officer is not liable for any injuries that might result from the use of such force (*People v. Adams, 83 Cal. 231*).

As expressed by the Supreme Court of Indiana, "police officers are constantly confronted with difficult and trying duties in handling prisoners, many of whom are hardened and resourceful, and the courts will go far in the support of police officers who act in good faith in a legitimate effort to protect society. They may exercise reasonable means for the safekeeping of prisoners, to preserve discipline, and to secure obedience to reasonable orders" (*Bonahoon v. State, 203 Ind., 51, 178 N.E. 570*).

3. *Self-defense.* Any necessary force may be used to protect from wrongful injury the person or property of oneself (*Civil Code, Section 50*).

Homicide necessarily or inadvertently committed by a public officer or one acting under his authority, while in the exercise of his authority or duty, is generally justifiable or excusable (*People v. Mason, 72 C.A. 2d 699*).

While a peace officer, when attempting an arrest, may use all *necessary* force to effect it, or may take the life of the supposed offender, if necessary, to save his own, there must be a *real* or *apparent necessity* to justify resorting to such measure for his own safety or protection (*People v. Newsome, 51 C.A. 42*).

4. *Immunity from malicious prosecution.* A police officer acting within the scope of his authority as such is immune from civil liability for malicious prosecution.

An example of such a circumstance would be a citizen's arrest for battery. After observing apparent bruises about the head of the complainant, the officer receives the defendant into custody upon the complainant's arrest. The subsequent trial reveals that the citizen lied about the bruises and they were not inflicted by the defendant. The arresting officer is not civilly liable for the arrest and incarceration of the defendant.

7.19 FALSE ARREST

As stated in section 1 of this chapter, an arrest is made by taking a person into custody in a manner authorized by law (see PC 834). If an arrest is made without authority, a "false arrest" arises, making the arresting person liable for the crimes of false arrest and false imprisonment, and the civil wrong (tort) of false imprisonment. False arrest, which is the beginning of false imprisonment, is defined by PC 146 as the arrest or detention of any person without lawful authority. The definition of false imprisonment is the " . . . unlawful violation of the personal liberty of another," PC 236, and is the same whether treated as a crime or a civil wrong. The civil wrong of false imprisonment consists of an unlawful restraint or confinement of a person, making the arresting person liable for money damages.

In order to take advantage of the immunities granted by PC 847, the arrest must be lawful, that is, made in conformance with the provisions of PC 833. However, a lawful arrest may become a false imprisonment if the prisoner is denied a right such as not being brought before a magistrate within a reasonable period of time as commanded by PC 849. The arrest remains lawful, but the detention that ensues is a false imprisonment.

Note: For further discussion of false imprisonment, see Chapter 12, Section 5.

TERMINOLOGY DEFINED—CHAPTER 7

See the Terminology Quiz at the end of this chapter.

1. Admonish: advise of rights, usually in reference to "Miranda Warning."
2. Appellant: one who takes an appeal to a higher court.
3. Ambiguous: doubtful, not clear, having more than one meaning.
4. Covert: secretive, clandestine, disguised.
5. Cursory: superficial, such as cursory or "patdown" search.
6. Defendant: one against whom a civil or criminal action is brought.
7. Demurrer: an answer to a legal accusation claiming it is defective.
8. Diplomatic immunity: freedom from arrest under international law.
9. Direct examination: examination in court of witness by the side that calls him.

10. Entrapment: inducing one to commit a crime not previously contemplated.
11. Flagrant: openly corrupt or criminal, see Heinous.
12. Fresh pursuit; "hot pursuit" of a suspect shortly after a crime.
13. Heinous: hateful, a repulsive crime, brutal, see Flagrant.
14. Incriminating: tending to show guilt such as incriminating evidence.
15. Indigent: one who is destitute, without means, very poor.
16. Information: formal accusation of crime by DA to superior court.
17. Manifest: clear, plain, apparent to the sight or understanding.
18. Pursuant: as a result of, in accordance with.
19. Scrutinize: to inspect closely, to examine critically.
20. Subsequent: occurring after some other event or thing.

TRUE-FALSE QUIZ—CHAPTER 7

1. A traffic violator is technically under arrest from the time he is stopped until released on his written promise to appear.
2. The Penal Code specifically gives officers the right to stop and detain suspicious persons.
3. Evidence seized when there is probable cause to detain but not arrest, will be rendered inadmissible if an arrest is made.
4. If the detention is proper, the courts will approve a cursory search for weapons which could endanger the officer.
5. If a frisk is used as an excuse to conduct an exploratory search, any evidence found is inadmissible.
6. PC 830 (along with its sub-sections) grants full peace officer status to all those enumerated.
7. The Penal Code requires all uniformed peace officers to wear either a numbered badge or name-plate.
8. Generally speaking, members of a police department are authorized to carry concealed weapons outside of the city by which they ar employed.
9. A peace officer may arrest a person whenever he has reasonable cause to believe the person arrested has committed a public offense in his presence.
10. A peace officer may take an arrest when he has reasonable cause to believe the person arrested committed a felony, whether or not a felony in fact has been committed.

11. Once a peace officer has arrested someone, he may not legally release the arrested person without first taking him before the nearest magistrate.
12. If an officer arrests someone for a misdemeanor and subsequently releases him due to insufficient grounds to prosecute, the arrest thereafter is legally deemed a detention only.
13. Except for serving warrants, a private person has the identical powers of arrest as does a peace officer.
14. An officer may legally release a citizen-arrested misdemeanant on a signed citation rather than taking him directly to jail or court.
15. No arrest without a warrant may legally be made except on reasonable cause.
16. Entrapment is the incucing of someone to commit a crime he didn't otherwise contemplate for the purpose of arresting and prosecuting the subject.
17. If a citizen knows he is being arrested by an officer, but believes the arrest is unlawful, he is legally justified in resisting such arrest.
18. Generally, the Miranda Warning should be given just before incriminating questions are asked of a suspect of a crime.
19. Before a legal warrant can be issued, the suspect's true name must be determined and included on the warrant.
20. If an arrested person escapes from the police car shortly after being arrested, he may be charged with the crime of escape in addition to the crime for which he was initially arrested.

ESSAY-DISCUSSION QUESTIONS— CHAPTER 7

1. What are the four basic defenses to a civil action for false arrest?
2. Define "arrest." Is arrest synonymous with "detention" in California?
3. In determining "reasonable cause" for making an arrest, into what two aspects will the court generally inquire?
4. What are the four "elements" of the Miranda decision warning? When must it be given?
5. What are the three instances where a peace officer may make an arrest without a warrant?
6. What does *posse comitatus* mean? What is its practical application in law enforcement?
7. What is the essence of entrapment? How does it differ from "setting traps" or using decoys for the purpose of apprehending suspects?

8. May a suspect who has just been arrested in the field for a crime be charged with excape if he breaks and runs from the officer? What are the elements of the crime of escape?

9. Under what three circumstances may a private person make an arrest and what must he do with the suspect immediately following an arrest?

10. What is the arrestee's right relative to phone calls following his arrest?

TERMINOLOGY QUIZ—CHAPTER 7

Match terms and definitions by placing the correct number in the parentheses. Answers may be written on a separate sheet for submission to the instructor at the instructor's direction.

1. Admonish
2. Appellant
3. Ambiguous
4. Covert
5. Cursory
6. Defendant
7. Demurrer
8. Diplomatic immunity
9. Direct examination
10. Entrapment
11. Flagrant
12. Fresh pursuit
13. Heninous
14. Incriminating
15. Indigent
16. Information
17. Manifest
18. Pursuant
19. Scrutinize
20. Subsequent

( ) one who is destitute
( ) a repulsive crime, brutal
( ) superficial
( ) to inspect closely
( ) occurring after some other event
( ) freedom from arrest under international law
( ) clear, plain, apparent to the sight
( ) one who takes an appeal to a higher court
( ) as a result of, in accordance with
( ) tending to show guilt
( ) doubtful, having more than one meaning
( ) secretive, clandestine, disguised
( ) an answer to a legal accusation
( ) formal accusation of a crime by the DA
( ) to advise of rights, Miranda warning

CHAPTER 8

98   Offenses Ag

injury or ten
peace," (3
ing wor
guara
vie

Offenses Against the Pub

8.1 DISTURBING THE PEACE

PC 415. Any of the following persons shall be punished by imprisonment in the county jail for a period of not more than 90 days, a fine of not more than two hundred dollars ($200), or both such imprisonment and fine.

1. Any person who unlawfully fights in a public place or challenges another person in a public place to fight.
2. Any person who maliciously and willfully disturbs another person by loud and unreasonable noise.
3. Any person who uses offensive words in a public place which are inherently likely to produce an immediate violent reaction.

PC 415.5 Disturbing Peace—Schools. This section is very similar to PC 415, above, except that it applies only to buildings and grounds of any public school, elementary school, community college, state college, state university, etc., as defined in PC 626. The elements are otherwise the same as in PC 415. It should be noted that PC 415.5 does *not* apply to any person who is a registered student of the school where the disturbance took place.

This section, passed in 1980, was obviously designed to punish nonstudents for coming on campus and disrupting persons and classes. The advantage of this section over the older PC 415, is that PC 415.5 provides increased punishment for previous convictions of this and other school disturbance laws beginning with PC 626. (See Section 8.13 of your text for additional details.)

Discussion

At common law, any willful and unjustifiable disturbance of the public peace was a crime. The offense consisted of disturbing a neighborhood or a number of people assembled in a public meeting, or of disturbing an individual in such a manner or to such an extent as to provoke a breach of the peace.

California penal law divides the statute relative to disturbing the peace into three general areas.

Fighting or Challenging to Fight. This part of the section also has reference to persons who threaten or challenge to fight. It is particularly difficult to apply this portion of the statute in cases not observed by the officer inasmuch as at times both participants in a fight will be guilty if they are mutually involved, but on other occasions one may be a victim of an assault and battery. It is quite proper police procedure in these cases to determine the presence of a *corpus delicti*, either for this offense or for assault and battery, and thereafter disperse the participants if no formal complaints are forthcoming.

Loud and Unreasonable Noise. The courts have rather consistently stated that where evidence establishes no fact which, directly or by inference, warrants the conclusion that the defendant was making loud or unreasonable noise with the intention to disturb someone, such person cannot be said to have the requisite intent necessary to complete the crime. The statute requires that the perpetrator do the act in a willful or malicious manner, which requires a specific intent to disturb the peace by loud and reasonable noise.

Disturbing the normal activities of a business, a bank in this case, by singing and other disruptive conduct to the annoyance, disturbance, and obstruction of patrons with normal business to transact indicated beyond a reasonable doubt the existence of a disturbance of the peace as defined in PC 415 (*People v. Green*).

Offensive Words. The U.S. Supreme Court recognizes the existence of "fighting words," which is applicable to PC 415 (3). These are defined as: "those words which by their very utterance inflict to incite an immediate breach of the ...5 U.S. 568, 572). The utterance of fight-...ds is not protected by the First Amendment ...ntee of free speech. Later cases support the ...w that it is not merely the words themselves, but ...lso the context in which they are uttered, that qualify them as "fighting words," and there is often a further requirement that words be spoken with intent to have the effect of inciting the hearer to an immediate breach of the peace.

Offensive Signs. In *Cohen v. California, 403 U.S. 15,* the United States Supreme Court held that the California statute on disturbing the peace was not violated where a defendant walked through a courthouse corridor wearing a jacket bearing the words "Fuck the Draft." The court reasoned that no person who viewed the jacket could regard the words as a direct personal insult, and there was no showing that anyone was, in fact, violently aroused. Therefore, no violation was committed.

The offense known as disturbing the peace or breach of the peace embraces a great variety of conduct destroying or menacing public order and tranquility. PC 415 limits this conduct to fighting, offering to fight, loud and unreasonable noise, and offensive words in a *public* place. Note that challenging to fight or fighting or use of offensive words in private is not a violation of PC 415. We should also note that PC 415 (2) limits disturbing an individual's peace to loud and unreasonable noise. What is loud and unreasonable could be further described as that which agitates or arouses from a state of repose, or molests or interrupts. The circumstances surrounding the incident are very important. The amount of noise which would be disturbing in a quiet residential neighborhood would be much less than that required to disturb someone in a noisy public place.

A complaining witness who observed the disturbance prior to the arrival of police officers has every right to make a private person arrest upon the suspect, assuming that he has legal cause to do so (*People V. Cove, 228 C.A. 2d 466*).

Evidence authorized conviction of two members of a religious sect under the provision of this section, penalizing as a misdemeanor the willful and malicious disturbance of the peace or quiet of any person (*People v. Vaughan, 65 C.A. 2d Supp. 844*).

Joint tenants have no authority to enter and take possession from licensee of premises by using force and violence, by pounding upon licensee's door, and by using abusive language. Such activity is clearly a violation of this section (*People v. Verdier, 152 C.A. 2d 348*).

Public peace is disturbed when acts complained of disturb public peace or tranquility enjoyed by members of the community in which good order reigns, where such acts are likely to produce violence, or where they cause consternation and alarm in the individual; no act need have, in itself, any element of violence to constitute a breach of the peace (*People v. Green, 234 C.A. 2d 871*).

8.2 ASSEMBLY TO DISTURB THE PEACE AND FAILURE TO DISPERSE

PC 416. "If two or more persons assemble for the purpose of disturbing the public peace, or committing any unlawful act, and do not disperse on being desired or commanded so to do by a public officer, persons so offending are severally guilty of a misdemeanor."

Discussion

If a group assembles with no other apparent motive than to disturb the public peace, i.e., an unlawful purpose, this section is violated. If the group is assembled for a lawful purpose, this section does not apply. A willful disturbance of the peace for no lawful purpose, or to commit an unlawful act, are the chief prohibitions of this section.

If a group assembles with a lawful purpose, it does not become unlawful if the conduct or statements provoke others to a breach of the peace. Thus, large numbers of people could picket in front of a particular church during services, express vile epithets to those entering and departing, thereby provoking wrath and indignation, but no action could normally be taken by police. An assembly is not unlawful, nor does it disturb the peace, if the participants' conduct provokes breaches of peace by onlookers.

8.3 UNLAWFUL ASSEMBLY

PC 407. "Unlawful Assembly" Defined. "Whenever two or more persons assemble together to do an unlawful act, or do a lawful act in a violent, boisterous, or tumultuous manner, such assembly is an unlawful assembly."

PC 408. Penalty. "Every person who participates in any rout or unlawful assembly is guilty of a misdemeanor."

Discussion

In a prosecution for violation of PC 407, there are two distinct types of conduct. One is assembly to do an *unlawful* act. The other is assembly to do a *lawful* act in a violent, boisterous or tumultuous manner. Each is defined below.

"Assembly to Do an Unlawful Act." The statutory language that there must be an assembling to do an unlawful act only requires that there be an assembly for an unlawful purpose by those who knowingly participate. Those in the assembly must intend to commit an unlawful act or engage in an unlawful purpose.

"Or Do a Lawful Act in a Violent, Boisterous, or Tumultuous Manner." In a prosecution for a violation of this part of the statute, the courts have said that not every meeting where violent, boisterous conduct occurs may be called an unlawful assembly. The statute is intended to prevent a tumultuous disturbance of the public peace by two or more persons having no avowed, ostensible, legal, or constitutional objective, assembled under such circumstances, and acting in such a manner which produces danger to the public peace and tranquility, and which excites terror, alarm, or consternation in the neighborhood.

Evidence—Assembly to Do an Unlawful Act. Evidence of joint or common unlawful purpose, as manifested by signs, chants, statements, conduct, etc., is necessary to support a prima facie case. Adoption or concurrence by the assembly of the common purpose, by their acts, statements, and conduct will further evidence the assembly into an unlawful one.

A single act of misconduct by one person in an otherwise lawful assembly would not convert the assembly into an unlawful one.

Evidence—Assembly to Do a Lawful Act by Unlawful Means. The same evidence as indicated above is necessary. However, additional evidence of conduct which terrorizes the community or places the inhabitants in fear is necessary. Such fear is measured in such terms as would reasonably impart fear to an average man. In testing this, it is necessary to take into account the hours at which the parties meet, the language used by them, and the act done.

PC 11460. Unlawful Assembly. Paramilitary Organization Defined. Penalty. "Any two or more persons who assemble as a paramilitary organization for the purpose of practicing with weapons shall be punished by imprisonment in the county jail for not more than one year or by a fine of not more than one thousand dollars ($1,000), or by both."

As used in this section, "paramilitary organization" means an organization which is not an agency of the United States Government or of the State of California, or which is not a private school meeting the requirements set forth in Section 12154 of the Education Code, but which engages in instruction or training in guerilla warfare or sabotage, or which, as an organization, engages in rioting or the violent disruption of, or violent interference with, school activities. (Revised, 1981.)

8.4 REFUSAL TO DISPERSE

PC 409. Remaining Present at the Scene of Riot, Rout, or Unlawful Assembly. "Every person remaining present at the place of any riot, rout or unlawful assembly, after the same has been lawfully warned to disperse, except public officers and persons assisting them in attempting to disperse the same, is guilty of misdemeanor."

PC 409.5 Police Authority to Close Area During Calamity

a. Whenever a menace to the public health or safety is created by a calamity such as flood, storm, fire, earthquake, explosion, accident, or other disaster, officers of the California Highway Patrol, California State Police, police department, or sheriff's office, or any officer or employee of the Department of Forestry or Department of Parks and Recreation designated as a peace officer by PC 830.3, may close off the area where the menace exists for the duration thereof by means of ropes, markers, or guards to any and all persons not authorized by such officer to enter or remain within the closed area. If such a calamity creates an immediate menace to the public health, the local health officer may close the area where the menace exists pursuant to the conditions which are set forth above in this section.

b. Officers of the California Highway Patrol, police departments, or sheriff's office (etc.) may close the immediate area surrounding any emergency field command post or any other command post activated for the purpose of abating any calamity enumerated in this section or any riot or other civil disturbance, to any and all unauthorized persons pursuant to the conditions which are set forth in this section whether or not such field command post or other command post is located near to the actual calamity or riot or other civil disturbance.

c. Any unauthorized person who willfully and knowingly enters an area closed pursuant to subdivision (a) or (b) and who willfully remains within such area after receiving notice to evacuate or leave, shall be guilty of a misdemeanor.

d. Nothing in this section shall prevent a duly authorized representative of any news service, newspaper, or radio or television station or network from entering the areas closed pursuant to this section.

Discussion

An assembly may be unlawful even if it consists of a "sit-in." As one court has said, "There can be little doubt that Section 409 can encompass, under applicable circumstances, activity which consists in the occupying of an area, place, or establishment for the purpose of an organized protest against some grievance."

Penal Code, Section 409, making it a misdemeanor to remain at the place of any riot, rout, or unlawful assembly after being lawfully warned to disperse, can encompass under applicable circumstances, activity that consists in the occupying of an area, place, or establishment for the purpose of an organized protest against some grievance (*In re Bacon, 240 Cal. App 2d 34*).

Where students protesting university regulations knowingly remained in a university building after it became closed to the public and after being fairly and adequately notified to leave by the chancellor and by a police captain going from floor to floor announcing over a portable loudspeaker that persons gathered were participating in an unlawful assembly and were free to leave but that those who remained would be arrested for trespass, they violated PC 409 in failing to disperse though they may not have participated in the assembly (*In re Bacon, supra*).

Those convicted of unlawful assembly and trespass could also be punished under Penal Code, Section 148 (resisting arrest), providing that every person who resists a public officer is guilty of a public offense, since punishments for unlawful assembly and for trespass were not the same as the punishment for resisting arrest (*In re Bacon, supra*).

Under PC 407, the illegal purpose of a group in assembling to view a "hot-rod" race renders the action of the group knowingly participating therein an unlawful assembly (*Coverstone v. Davies, 38 Cal. 2d 315*).

8.5 SUPPRESSION OF RIOTS

PC 723. Power of Sheriff or Other Officer in Overcoming Resistance to Process. "When a sheriff or other public officer authorized to execute process finds, or has reason to apprehend, that resistance will be made to the execution of the process, he may command as many able-bodied inhabitants of his county as he may think proper to assist him in overcoming the resistance, and, if necessary, in seizing, arresting, and confining the persons resisting, their aiders and abettors." See *Posse Comitatus*, Chapter 7, Section 14.

PC 150. Refusal to Aid in Arrest. "Every ablebodied person above 18 years of age who neglects or refuses to join the posse comitatus or power of the county, by neglecting or refusing to aid and assist in taking or arresting any person against whom there may be issued any process, or by neglecting to aid and assist in retaking any person who, after being arrested or confined, may have escaped from such arrest or imprisonment, or by neglecting or refusing to aid and assist in preventing any breach of the peace, or the commission of any criminal offense, being thereto lawfully required by any uniformed peace officer or by any judge, is punishable by fine of not less than fifty dollars ($50) nor more than one thousand dollars ($1,000)."

PC 726. Magistrates and Officers to Command Rioters to Disperse. "Where any number of persons, whether armed or not, are unlawfully or riotously assembled, the sheriff of the county and his deputies, the officials governing the town or city, or the judges of the justice courts and constables thereof, or any of them, must go among the persons assembled, or as near to them as possible, and command them, in the name of the people of the State, immediately to disperse."

PC 727. To Arrest Rioters If They Do Not Disperse. "If the persons assembled do not immediately disperse, such magistrates and officers must arrest them, and to that end may command the aid of all persons present or within the county."

8.6 ROUT AND RIOT DEFINED

PC 406. "Whenever two or more persons, assembled and acting together, make any attempt or advance toward the commission of an act which would be a riot if actually committed, such assembly is a rout."

Discussion

A rout is simply defined as a preparatory stage of a riot. Thus, in every riot, which involves use of force and violence, disturbing the public peace, or a threat to do so, with apparent power available, a rout has necessarily preceded such an offense.

A rout is evidenced by an overt act beyond mere assembly. If an assembly has been lawfully convoked, but suddenly departs from its lawful purpose and proceeds to embark on the execution of an unlawful purpose to be accomplished by force and violence, any act committed toward the consummation of that purpose constitutes a rout. Thus, it has been said that when an unlawful assembly begins to move toward the execution of the common unlawful purpose for which it came together, but before any acts of violence or disorder have occurred, then a rout has been committed.

The legislative intent of PC 406 is to provide law enforcement officers a means by which to control any willful and malicious obstruction of the citizen's free use of a public way (*Rees v. City of Palm Springs, 188 C.A. 2d 339*).

PC 404. Riot. (a) "Any use of force or violence, disturbing public peace, or any threat to use such force or violence, if accompanied by immediate power of execution, by two or more persons acting together, and without authority of law, is a riot.

(b) As used in this section, disturbing the public peace may occur in any place of confinement. Place of confinement means any state prison, county jail, industrial farm, or road camp, or any city jail, industrial farm or road camp."

Discussion (Riot)

To constitute a riot, the object need not be unlawful, provided the acts are done in a manner calculated to inspire terror. Even though the original coming together was lawful and for the carrying out of a lawful purpose, still, if after coming together, the persons proceed to execute either a lawful or an unlawful purpose in such a violent and unlawful manner as to terrorize the populace, it is a riot.

The chief element in riot is the use of force and violence, or threat to use force and violence to disturb the public peace. It is essential to violation of this section that there be a concurrence of at least two persons, acting together, in the use, or threatened use, of force or violence. No previous agreement to use force and violence is necessary as long as there is a common purpose to use force and violence. If the original purpose was a lawful one, but afterwards the

purpose becomes unlawful, i.e., by the use or threatened use of force and violence, the original peaceful purpose is no defense. The power to execute all the threats need not be shown if there is evidence of power to execute some of them.

8.7 INCITING A RIOT

PC 404.6. "Every person who with the intent to cause a riot does an act or engages in conduct which urges a riot, or urges others to commit acts of force and violence, or the burning or destroying of property, and at a time and place and under circumstances which produce a clear and present and immediate danger of acts of force or violence or the burning or destroying of property, is guilty of a misdemeanor."

This section shall not apply to, nor in any way affect, restrain, or interfere with, otherwise lawful activity engaged in, by, or on behalf of a labor organization or organizations or organized by its members, agents, or employees.

Discussion

Under the unlawful assembly, rout, and riot sections of the Penal Code, one of the chief elements is a common purpose by two or more suspects to do an unlawful act. But under this section (PC 404.6), a single suspect, acting alone, can commit the unlawfully prescribed conduct of the section. Greater proof is necessary to arrest for inciting a riot than for evidence necessary to establish unlawful assembly, riot, or rout.

8.8 TRESPASSING

PC 602. Trespasses Upon Lands Enumerated. Every person who willfully commits a trespass by any of the following acts is guilty of a misdemeanor:
a. Cutting down, destroying, or injuring any kind of wood or timber standing or growing upon the lands of another;
b. Carrying away any kind of wood or timber lying on such lands;
c. Maliciously injuring or severing from the freehold of another anything attached thereto, or the produce thereof;
d. Digging, taking, or carrying away from any lot situated within the limits of any incorporated city, without the license of the owner or legal occupant thereof, any earth, soil, or stone;
e. Digging, taking, or carrying away from land in any city or town laid down on the map or plan of

such city, or otherwise recognized or established as a street, alley, avenue, or park, without the license of the proper authorities, any earth, soil, or stone;

f. Maliciously tearing down, damaging, mutilating, or destroying any sign, signboard or notice placed upon, or affixed to, any property belonging to the State, or to any city, county, city and county, town or village, or upon any property of any person, by the State or by an automobile association, which sign, signboard or notice is intended to indicate or designate a road or roads, or a highway or highways, or is intended to direct travelers from one point to another, or relates to fires, fire control, or any other matter involving the protection of the property, or putting up, affixing, fastening, printing or painting upon any property belonging to the State, or to any city, county, town, or village, or dedicated to the public, or upon any property of any person, without license from the owner, any notice, advertisement, or designation of, or any name for any commodity, whether for sale or otherwise, or any picture, sign or device intended to call attention thereto;

g. Entering upon any lands owned by any other person whereon oysters or other shellfish are planted or growing; or injuring, gathering, or carrying away any oysters or other shellfish planted, growing, or being on any such lands, whether covered by water or not, without the license of the owner or legal occupant thereof; or destroying or removing, or causing to be removed or destroyed, any stakes, marks, fences, or signs intended to designate the boundaries and limits of any such lands;

h. Willfully opening, tearing down, or otherwise destroying any fence on the enclosed land of another, or opening any gate, bar or fence of another and willfully leaving it open without the written permission of the owner, or maliciously tearing down, mutilating, or destroying any sign, signboard, or other notice forbidding shooting on private property.

i. Building fires upon any lands owned by another where signs forbidding trespass are displayed at intervals not greater than one mile along the exterior boundaries and at all roads and trails entering such lands, without first having obtained written permission from the owner of such lands or his agent, or the person in lawful possession thereof.

j. Entering any lands, whether unenclosed or enclosed by fence, for the purpose of injuring any property or property rights or with the intention of interfering with, obstructing, or injuring any lawful business or occupation carried on by the owner of such land, his agent or by the person in lawful possession.

k. Entering any lands under cultivation or enclosed by fence, belonging to, or occupied by, another, or entering upon uncultivated or unenclosed lands where signs forbidding trespass are displayed at intervals not less than three to the mile along all exterior boundaries and at all roads and trails entering such lands without the written permission of the owner of such land, his agent or of the person in lawful possession and

　1. Refusing or failing to leave such lands immediately upon being requested by the owner of such land, his agent or by the person in lawful possession to leave such lands, or

　2. Tearing down, mutilating or destroying any sign, signboard, or notice forbidding trespass or hunting on such lands, or

　3. Removing, injuring, unlocking, or tampering with any lock on any gate on or leading into such lands, or

　4. Discharging any firearm.

l. Entering and occupying real property or structures of any kind without the consent of the owner, his agent, or the person in lawful possession thereof.

m. Driving any vehicle, as defined in Section 670 of the Vehicle Code, upon real property belonging to or lawfully occupied by another and known not to be open to the general public, without the consent of the owner, his agent, or the person in lawful possession thereof.

n. Refusing or failing to leave land, real property, or structures belonging to or lawfully occupied by another and not open to the general public, upon being requested to leave (1) by a peace officer and the owner, his agent, or the person in lawful possession thereof, or (2) the owner, his agent, or the person in lawful possession thereof; provided, however, that clause (2) of this subdivision shall not be applicable to persons engaged in lawful labor union activities which are permitted to be carried out on the property by the California Agricultural Labor Relations Act, Part 3.5 (commencing with Section 1140) of Division 2 of the Labor Code, or by the National Labor Relations Act.

o. Entering upon any lands declared closed to entry as provided in Section 4256 of the Public Resources Code; provided, such closed areas shall have been posted with notices declaring such closure, at intervals not greater than one mile along the exterior boundaries or along roads and trails passing through such lands.

p. Refusing or failing to leave a public building of a public agency during those hours of the day or night when the building is regularly closed to the public upon being requested to do so by a regularly employed guard, a watchman, or custodian of the public agency owning or maintaining the building or property, if the surrounding circumstances are such as to indicate to a reasonable man that such person has no apparent lawful business to pursue.

q. Knowingly skiing in an area or on a ski trail which is closed to the public and which has signs posted indicating such closure.

r. Refusing or failing to leave a hotel or motel, where he or she has obtained accommodations and has refused to pay for those accommodations, upon request of the proprietor or manager, and the occupancy is exempt, pursuant to subdivision (b) of Section 1940 of the Civil Code, from Chapter 2 (commencing with Section 1940) of Title 5 of Part 4 of Division 3 of the Civil Code.

Discussion

Demonstrators often temporarily block entrances to public buildings. If the inconvenience to others is slight, little action need be taken. But when a building is intentionally blocked so that passage in and out is willfully impaired for an unreasonable length of time (e.g., "sit-ins" on the steps of the Hall of Justice, etc.), officers can invoke PC 602(j), unlawful assembly, and possibly PC 602(k), trespassing. No one has the right to willfully and intentionally block the right of citizens to enter and move through public buildings under the circumstances outlined, and they are subject to arrest for failing to disperse after a proper order is given.

Under PC 602(p), which relates to a refusal to leave a public building during closing hours, persons such as demonstrators, etc., should be warned by the person in charge of the building. If the persons fail to heed this order, police may be called, whereupon they too should give a dispersal command and if the parties still refuse to leave, they may be arrested for violating this statute.

Demonstrators who refuse to leave a college or university building upon being commanded to do so, and after ample warning, are also subject to arrest under this section.

In a case involving students of the University of California, Berkeley, the court held that students who gathered in a university building to express to the administration their grievances with university rules for content of student speech, assembly, and petition on the campus and who remained when the building was closed for the day and after they were advised that those who remained would be guilty of unlawful assembly, committed conduct clearly encompassed within the proscription of Penal Code, Section 602, sub. (p) (*In re Bacon, 240 Cal. App. 2d 34*).

The court further stated in the same case that "A reasonable interpretation of Penal Code, Section 602 (p) making it a misdemeanor for a person to willfully trespass by refusing or failing to leave a public building of a public agency during the hours the building is regularly closed after a request to leave, does not require that each person inside the building be personally requested to leave. A blanket request over a public address system suffices, particularly where all trespassers hear the request to leave at once (*In re Bacon, supra*).

Under Penal Code, Section 602 (p), making it a misdemeanor to refuse or fail to leave a public building or a public agency during the hours the building is regularly closed after the public agency's custodian requests a departure, the term "custodian" means the one in charge of the building at the time. A request by a university's chancellor and a police officer that students leave a university building constituted substantial compliance with the statute (*In re Bacon, supra.*).

PC 626.6 Nonstudents. In any case in which a person, who is not a student or officer or employee of a state college or a state university, and who is not required by his employment to be on the campus or any other facility owned, operated, or controlled by the governing board on any such state college or state university, enters such campus, or facility, in an effort to interfere with peaceful conduct thereon, he may be ordered off the campus and failure to comply with the order is a misdemeanor (briefed).

PC 602.10 Willfully Obstructing a Student's or Teacher's Access to Classes. Every person who, by physical force and with the intent to prevent attendance or instruction, willfully obstructs or attempts to obstruct any student or teacher seeking to attend or instruct classes at any of the campuses or facilities owned, controlled, or administered by the Regents of the University of California, the Trustees of the California State Colleges, or the governing board of a junior college district or school district maintaining a junior college, shall be punished by a fine not exceeding five hundred dollars ($500), by imprisonment in a county jail for a period of not exceeding one year, or by both such fine and imprisonment.

As used in this section, "physical force" includes, but is not limited to, use of one's person, individually or in concert with others, to impede access to or movement within or otherwise to obstruct the students and teachers of the classes to which the premises are devoted.

PC 647c. Willful or Malicious Obstruction of Street or Sidewalk.
Every person who willfully and maliciously obstructs the free movement of any person on any street, sidewalk, or other public place or on or in any place open to the public is guilty of a misdemeanor.

Nothing in this section affects the power of a county or a city to regulate conduct upon a street, sidewalk, or other public place or on or in a place open to the public.

8.9   DISTURBING PUBLIC MEETINGS

PC 403. Every person, who without authority of law, willfully disturbs or breaks up any assembly or meeting, not unlawful in its character, other than such as is mentioned in Section 302 of the Penal Code and Section 29440 of the Election Code, is guilty of a misdemeanor.

Discussion

Not every interruption of a speaker is a disturbance. The meeting itself must be thrown into such disorder that the business under discussion cannot effectively continue. Thus, the character and nature of the meeting are relevant in determining whether the disturbance is violative of this section. For example, an extemporaneous "soapbox" speaker should expect to be interrupted from time to time. Free speech cannot be used as an excuse to justify converting an orderly meeting into bedlam, but some assemblies can be expected to be somewhat disorderly, e.g., political conventions.

8.10   DISTURBING RELIGIOUS MEETINGS

PC 302. "Every person who willfully disturbs or disquiets any assemblage of people met for religious worship, by profane disturbance, rude or indecent behavior, or by any unnecessary noise, either within

the place where such meeting is held, or so near it as to disturb the order and solemnity of the meeting, is guilty of a misdemeanor."

Discussion

This statute prohibits any interruption of the solemnity of a religious meeting and requires less evidence than the preceding section relative to political meetings. The concluding phrase of the statute prohibits noise inside as well as outside the building, and the disturbance must be willful and intentional.

8.11   LYNCHING

PC 405a. "The taking by means of a riot of any person from the lawful custody of any peace officer is a lynching."

PC 405b. "Any person who participates in any lynching is punishable by imprisonment in the state prison for not more than twenty years."

Discussion

There is a requirement here that the person in custody of an officer must be in "lawful" custody, otherwise there would be no crime. The offense of lynching is seldom committed except during riot or insurrection and there is little case law in this regard. However, as the statute indicates, whenever two or more persons act together (requisites of both a riot and a violation of this section) and take a legally arrested person, or other person in the lawful custody of an officer, they are in violation of this section.

8.12   FORCIBLE ENTRY AND DETAINER

PC 418. "Every person using or procuring, encouraging, or assisting another to use any force or violence in entering upon or detaining any lands or other possessions of another, except in cases and in the manner allowed by law, is guilty of a misdemeanor."

Discussion

Forcible entry occurs where a person violently enters upon real property occupied by another, with menaces, force and arms and without the authority of law. Forcible detainer is detention of the possession of the property by the use of force and violence and may occur where the original entry was forcible or where it was peaceable.

In order that there may be a forcible entry, it must appear that the peaceable possession of someone has been interfered with. It is not necessary that the person in possession should have been actually present at the time of the entry, however, if at that time he had control and authority of the premises.

PC 602.5 Entry Without Consent. "Every person other than a public officer or employee acting within the course and scope of his employment in performance of a duty imposed by law, who enters or remains in any noncommercial dwelling house, apartment, or other such place without consent of the owner, this agent, or the person in lawful possession thereof, is guilty of a misdemeanor.

PC 603. Unlawful Entry. "Every person other than a peace officer engaged in the performance of his duties as such who forcibly and without the consent of the owner, representative of the owner, lessee or representative of the lessee thereof, enters a dwelling house, cabin, or other building occupied or constructed for occupation by humans, and who damages, injures, or destroys any property of value in, around or appertaining to such dwelling house, cabin, or other building, is guilty of a misdemeanor."

8.13   SCHOOL DISTURBANCE LAWS

Due to the nature and extent of a variety of disturbances in California schools, the legislature enacted urgent legislation in an effort to prevent the recurrence of such activity on the campuses of public supported educational institutions. As a result of this legislation, five statutes were added to the Penal Code. Following is a breakdown of the elements of each law.

PC 415.5—Elements

1. Any person who unlawfully fights
2. within the building or upon the grounds
3. of any community college, state college, or state university, or
4. challenges another person within such buildings or upon such grounds to fight, or
5. maliciously and willfully disturbs another person within any such buildings or upon such grounds
6. by loud and unreasonable noise or
7. uses offensive words within any such building or upon such grounds
8. which are inherently likely to produce a violent reaction

9. is guilty of a misdemeanor and shall be punished upon first conviction by a fine not exceeding two hundred dollars ($200) or by imprisonment in the county jail for a period not more than 90 days, or by both such fine and imprisonment (briefed).

Subsequent conviction of a violation of *PC 415* or *PC 626* can result in penalties up to six months in county jail and a fine of $500 or both.

Discussion

This statute does not apply to *all* schools, but only community colleges, state colleges, or state universities. It is *not* applicable to private teaching institutions of higher learning.

This law, as well as the other added legislation provides for escalated punishments where the defendant has a prior conviction for Penal Code, Section 415.5, or for Penal Code, Section 626.2, 626.4, 626.6 and 626.8.

PC 626.2—Elements

1. Every student or employee
2. who *after a hearing*
3. has been suspended or dismissed from a community college, state college or university or school
4. for disrupting the orderly operation of the campus or facility of such institution
5. *and* as a condition has been denied access to the campus or facility, or both, of the institution for a period of the suspension or in the case of dismissal for a period not to exceed one year;
6. who has been served by registered or certified mail.... with a written notice of such suspension or dismissal and condition; and
7. who willfully and knowingly enters upon the campus or facility to which he has been denied access, without the express written permission of the chief administrative officer of the campus or facility,
8. is guilty of a misdemeanor.

Note that the element of *knowledge* shall be presumed if notice has been given as prescribed in this section.

This section makes it a misdemeanor to willfully and knowingly enter the campus or facility of a junior college, state college, or state university after being denied access to such school as a condition of suspension or dismissal. Therefore, the likelihood of enforcement of this section by a police entity appears minimal.

PC 626.4—Elements (briefed)

a.
1. The chief administrative offical of a campus or other facility of a junior college, state college, or state university, or an officer or employee designated by him to maintain order on such campus or facility,
2. may notify a person that consent to remain on the campus or other facility under control of the chief administrative official has been withdrawn
3. whenever there is reasonable cause to believe that such person has willfully disrupted the orderly operation of such school.

b. When such consent is withdrawn by one other than the chief administrative official, such person must make a written report to the chief administrative official of the withdrawal of consent and if, other review by the chief administrative official, it is determined that there was reasonable cause for the withdrawal of consent, the chief administrative official may make written confirmation. If no action is taken by the chief administrative official within twenty-four hours, the withdrawal of consent is deemed void.

c. Consent shall be reinstated by the chief administrative official whenever he has reason to believe that the presence of the person from whom consent was withdrawn will not contribute a threat to the orderly operation of the campus. Consent shall not be withdrawn for more than fourteen days. (Provisions for a hearing are also included.)

d. Any person:
1. who has been notified by the chief administrative official of a campus or other facility of a junior college, state college, or state university, or his designee
2. that consent to remain has been withdrawn pursuant to subdivision (a);
3. who has not had such consent reinstated;
4. and who willfully and knowingly enters or remains upon such campus or facility during the period for which consent has been withdrawn,
5. is guilty of a misdemeanor.

This section requires several acts on the part of school officials before a person may be arrested for violation of this section. Applicability of this section to members of a law enforcement agency would depend upon its personnel being informed by a school official that the necessary conditions, i.e., withdrawal of consent, written report, etc., have been met. This section then applies to *any* person.

PC 626.6—Elements

In any case in which a person:
1. who is not a student or officer or employee of a junior college, state college, or state university; and
2. who is not required by his employment to be on the campus or facility owned, operated, or controlled by the governing board of any such junior college, state college, or state university
3. enters such campus or facility, and it reasonably appears to the chief administrative official or his designee that such person is committing any act likely to interfere with the peaceful conduct of the activities of such campus or facility, *or*
4. has entered such campus or facility for the purpose of committing any such act,
5. the chief administrative official or his designee may direct the person to leave such campus or facility, and
6. if such person fails to do so, or if such person willfully and knowingly re-enters upon such campus or facility within seventy-two hours after being directed to leave,
7. he is guilty of a misdemeanor.

This section makes it a misdemeanor for a person to remain or re-enter a campus or facility of a junior college, state college, or state university after being asked to leave by the chief administrative official or his designee of such campus or facility. Further, the person when asked to leave by the chief administrative official or his designee, may not re-enter such campus or facility for seventy-two hours. Again, this is a section which requires an act by a school official before the section may be enforced.

PC 626.8—Disruptions—Sex Offenders

a. Any person who comes into any school building or upon any school ground or street, sidewalk, or public way adjacent thereto, without lawful business thereon,

b. *and* whose presence or acts interfere with the peaceful conduct of the activities of such school or disrupt the school or its pupils or school activities,

c. or any specified sex offender (one required to register under PC 290) who comes into any school building or upon any school ground or public way adjacent thereto, unless such person is a parent or guardian of a child attending that school or is a student at the school or has prior written permission for the entry from the chief administrator of that school, is guilty of a misdemeanor if he or she:

1. Remains there after being asked to leave by the chief administrator of the school or his designee, or by a school security officer, or a city police officer, deputy sheriff or California Highway Patrol officer;
2. Reenters or comes upon such place within 72 hours of being asked to leave by a person named in (1), above; or
3. Has otherwise established a continued pattern of unauthorized entry (*section briefed*).

Discussion:

The crime is in the failure to leave or the re-entering of the areas described within seventy-two hours after being asked to leave by the chief administrative official or his qualified designee, plus conduct or activities which interfere with the peaceful conduct of the school.

Punishment for a first conviction of this section is a fine not exceeding $500 or six months in the county jail, or both. The penalty is increased for second and subsequent convictions of this and related code sections. Note: "School" under this section means any preschool or school having any grades from kindergarten through twelve (12).

PC 71. Crimes Against Public and School Officials. Every person who, with intent to cause, attempts to cause, or causes, any officer or employee of any public or private educational institution or any public officer or employee to do, or refrain from doing, any act in the performance of his duties, by means of a threat, directly communicated to such person, to inflict an unlawful injury upon any person or property, where it reasonably appears to the recipient of the threat that such threat could be carried out, is guilty of a public offense punishable as follows:

1. Upon a first conviction, such a person is punishable by a fine not exceeding five thousand dollars ($5,000), or by imprisonment in the state prison not exceeding one year or in a county jail not exceeding one year, or by both such fine and imprisonment.
2. If such person has been previously convicted of a violation of this section, such previous conviction shall be charged in the accusatory pleading, and if such previous conviction is found to be true by the jury upon a jury trial, or by the court upon a court trial, or is admitted by the defendant, he is punishable by imprisonment in the state prison.

As used in this section, "directly communicated" includes, but is not limited to, a communication to the recipient of the threat by telephone, telegraph, or letter. (*Added, Stats. 1969, Chap. 1207*).

8.14 DISORDERLY CONDUCT

PC 647. "Every person who commits any of the following acts shall be guilty of disorderly conduct, a misdemeanor:

(a) Who solicits anyone to engage in or who engages in lewd or dissolute conduct in any public place or in any place open to the public or exposed to public view.
(b) Who solicits or who engages in any act of prostitution. As used in this subdivision, 'prostitution' includes any lewd act between persons for money or other consideration.
(c) Who accosts other persons in any public place or any place open to the public for the purpose of begging or soliciting alms.
(d) Who, for the purpose of engaging in or soliciting any lewd or lascivious or any unlawful act, loiters in or about any toilet open to the public.
(e) Who loiters or wanders upon the streets or from place to place without apparent reason or business and who refuses to identify himself and to account for his presence when requested by any peace officer so to do, if the surrounding circumstances are such as to indicate to a reasonable person that the public safety demands such identification. **Important Note:** PC 647(e) was declared unconstitutional by the United States Supreme Court on May 1, 1983. Additional details are given under "Discussion—PC 647(e)," which follows on page 110.
(f) Who is found in any public place under the influence of intoxicating liquor, any drug, toluene, any substance defined as poison in Schedule D of Section 4160 of the Business and Professions Code, or any combination of any intoxicating liquor, drug, toluene, or any such poison in such a condition that he is unable to exercise care for his own safety or the safety of others, or by reason of his being under the influence of intoxicating liquor, any drug, toluene, any substance defined as a poison in Schedule D of Section 4160 of the Business and Professions Code, or any combination of any intoxicating liquor, drug, toluene, or any such poison, interferes with or obstructs or prevents the free use of any street, sidewalk, or other public way.
(ff) When a person has violated subdivision (f) of this section, a peace officer, if he is reasonably able to do so, shall place the person, or cause him to be placed, in civil protective custody. Such

person shall be taken to a facility designated pursuant to Section 5170 of the Welfare and Institutional Code, for the 72-hour treatment and evaluation of inebriates. A peace officer may place a person in civil protective custody with that kind and degree of force which would be lawful were he effecting an arrest for a misdemeanor without a warrant. No person who has been placed in civil protective custody shall thereafter be subject to any criminal prosecution or juvenile court proceeding based on the facts giving rise to such placement. This subdivision shall not apply to the following persons:

(1.) Any person who is under the influence of any drug, or under the combined influence of intoxicating liquor and any drug.

(2.) Any person who a peace officer has probable cause to believe has committed any felony, or who has committed any misdemeanor in addition to subdivision (f) of this section.

(3.) Any person who a peace officer in good faith believes will attempt escape or will be unreasonably difficult for medical personnel to control.

(g) Who loiters, prowls, or wanders upon the private property of another, in the nighttime, without visible or lawful business with the owner or occupant thereof.

(h) Who, while loitering, prowling, or wandering upon the private property of another, in the nighttime, peeks in the door or window of any inhabited building or structure located thereon without visible or lawful business with the owner or occupant thereof."

(i) Who lodges in any building, structure or place, whether public or private, without the permission of the owner or person entitled to the possession or in control thereof.

In any accusatory pleading charging a violation of subdivision (b) of this section, if the defendant has been once previously convicted of a violation of the subdivision, the previous conviction shall be charged in the accusatory pleading, and, if the previous conviction is found to be true by the jury, upon a jury trial, or by the court, upon a court trial, or is admitted by the defendant, the defendant shall be imprisoned in the county jail for a period of not less than 45 days and shall not be eligible for release upon completion of sentence, on parole, or on any other basis until he has served a period of not less than 45 days in the county jail. In no such case shall the trial court grant probation or suspend the execution of sentence imposed upon the defendant.

In any accusatory pleading charging a violation of subdivision (b) of this section, if the defendant has been previously convicted two or more times of a violation of the subdivision, each such previous conviction shall be charged in the accusatory pleading, and, if two or more of such previous convictions are found to be true by the jury, upon a jury trial, or by the court, upon a court trial, or are admitted by the defendant, the defendant shall be imprisoned in the county jail for a period of not less than 90 days and shall not be eligible for release upon completion of sentence, on parole, or on any other basis until he has served a period of not less than 90 days in the county jail. In no such case shall the trial court grant probation or suspend the execution of sentence imposed upon the defendant."

Discussion

PC 647(a). The California State Supreme Court recently rendered a decision that made significant changes in this disorderly conduct section. In *Pryor v. Municipal Court, 25 C. 3d 238*, the court in effect interpreted *PC 647(a)*, so that cases which traditionally have been violations of the law are no longer crimes.

The defendant, Pryor, attacked the statute by contending that the terms "lewd and dissolute conduct" were too vague and general to be meaningful. In addition, it was contended that California law now makes it legal for consenting adults to engage in various sexual conduct (sodomy, for example) in private. How then, the defendant contended, can the state forbid requesting someone to do that which is now legal?

The California Supreme Court held that the language was indeed unconstitutional and in effect set out to "rewrite" the statute. The following elements were thus established under the new interpretation:

1. A "solicitation" of (tempting, seeking to induce, or trying to obtain) or commission of,

2. Lewd criminal conduct (the touching of the genitals, buttocks, or female breast for the purpose of sexual arousal, gratification, annoyance, or offense)

3. To occur or is occurring in a public place, a place open to the public or a place exposed to public view,

4. When the suspect knows or should know of the presence of persons who may be offended by the conduct.

Under the old *PC 647(a)*, it was an offense to solicit an undercover officer to "come home and make love to me." Such is no longer illegal. Also, under the old law, all lewd acts occurring in a public place (such as a restroom, massage parlor, or public park) were automatically violations. Now, it must also be shown that there may be other persons present who might be offended by the conduct.

On the other hand, many of the illegal acts that were prosecuted before can still be prosecuted under this new interpretation. Such acts as masturbation in public, groping of the genitals, and solicitation of acts to occur in public, will still be offenses as long as there are others present who could be offended by them. The court also indicates that solicitations to commit lewd acts to occur in private might still be punishable if the solicitation was so phrased as to be "fighting words" under *PC 415*.

Maintaining a massage parlor for the purpose of keeping a house of ill fame and for soliciting or engaging in lewd or dissolute conduct in a public place is a violation of this section (*Hora v. City and County of San Francisco, 233 C.A. 2d 375*).

PC 647(b). This subsection pertains to soliciting or engaging in any act of prostitution and replaces prior legislation relative to common prostitutes.

Special Note. In view of the legislature's repeal of certain laws which previously made certain sex acts a crime, some legal scholars feel that prostitution may also no longer be a crime. They submit that if the performance of certain sex acts by male and/or female consenting adults in private is no longer a crime, prostitution (which is performed by consenting adults in private) may also be a noncriminal act. At this writing the matter has not been adjudicated and only time will tell. It appears, however, that the legislature did not intend to exempt prostitution, and, in any case, it is likely that *public* solicitation for an act of prostitution will still be a public offense.

Relative to PC 647(b), it might also be noted that an Alameda County (Oakland) Superior Court judge recently declared soliciting for prostitution to be unconstitutional. The judge issued a writ of prohibition enjoining the Municipal Court from hearing 250 cases involving 179 women arrested for prostitution. Two grounds were given for the decision: (1) that the term "soliciting" is unconstitutionally vague and provides no fixed standard on which police can base arrests and (2) that law enforcement policy discriminates against women in its enforcement.

The facts indicate that during the past two years, the police department arrested 1,448 women, but only 59 men, for violation of PC 647(b). Most cases involved the use of decoys and the court maintained that police used many more male decoys to apprehend women than they did women decoys to apprehend men for soliciting.

The court also held that several different definitions of exactly what acts and words constitute soliciting were used, and in some cases the street officers' definitions differed from those of superiors. The Alameda County District Attorney has filed an appeal to keep the decision from taking effect immediately. This Superior Court decision will not affect other jurisdictions, or even Alameda County, unless and until it is reviewed and affirmed by the appellate courts.

This case is reported here for three reasons. One, to alert the reader to the possibility (however slight it might be) of a change in PC 647(b). Two, to illustrate how courts initiate change and interpretations of the statutes; and three, the importance of and need for highly definitive terms in the criminal statutes.

Prostitution is defined as (1) "The act or practice of a woman who permits any man who will pay her price to have sexual intercourse with her," and (2) "The act or practice of a female of prostituting or offering her body to an indiscriminate intercourse with men for money or its equivalent." By statutory definition a male may also be guilty of prostitution.

The legislature has occupied the field with respect to the crime of prostitution (*Spitcauer v. Los Angeles County, 227 C.A. 2d 376*).

A city ordinance attempting to make sexual intercourse between persons not married to each other criminal, conflicted with state law and is void. The legislature has adopted a general scheme for regulating the subject of sexual activity, and neither simple fornication, adultery, or living in a state of cohabitation are crimes in this state (*In re Lane, 58 Cal. 2d 99*).

Discussion

PC 647(c). This subsection punishes those who accost others in a public place for the purpose of begging. The crime is complete at the moment the solicitor makes his request, whether it be verbally or by other means, such as a card identifying him as a mute or otherwise physically handicapped. It is not necessary that the solicited person answer or otherwise acknowledge the solicitor, nor is it necessary to show the transference of property from one to the other.

PC 647(d). This subsection was enacted to preclude persons from loitering about public toilet facilities for the purpose of soliciting lewd conduct. The legislative intent of the section is to prevent innocent persons from being accosted by homosexuals and also to prevent consenting homosexuals from soliciting each other in such locations.

The term "lascivious" is defined as tending to excite lustful, lewd, indecent, obscene, sexual impurity; tending to depress the morals in respect to sexual relations; lewd and lustful and tending to produce voluptuous or lewd emotions.

PC 647(e). The constitutionality of this section was tested in 1977 in the United States District Court for the Southern District of California (*In re Lawson v. Kolender, et al*). The constitutionality of *PC 647(e)*, was raised in connection with a claim for damages against various police agencies involved in the arrest of the plaintiff, Lawson, for violation of this section.

The District Court held *PC 647(e)* **unconstitutional** and the decision was appealed to the United State Supreme Court by the California Attorney General's office. The constitutionality of *PC 647(e)* was last upheld by the United States Supreme Court in *People v. Weger, 251 C.A. 3d 663.*

On May 2, 1983, the United States Supreme Court in a 7–2 decision declared PC 647(e) **unconstitutional** as being "too vague." The decision, however, stopped short of saying that any such law demanding identification of persons found under circumstances suggesting a need for police inquiry would be invalid.

The court's majority, led by Justice Sandra Day O'Conner, said that a more specifically worded law might be acceptable. O'Conner said the current law, in effect, leaves it to "the whim of any police officer" to decide who may walk the public streets because the law "as presently drafted and construed by the state courts, contains no standard for determining what a suspect has to do in order to satisfy the requirement to provide 'credible and reliable' identification."

The essential value of PC 647(e), has been that it provided legal authority for the police to stop and question and, in effect, temporarily detain or even arrest a person found loitering or wandering on the public streets without apparent reason and who refused to identify himself when requested to do so by a peace officer. A major legal issue is what constitutes "proper and reliable identification?" Many joggers, for example, carry no identification.

The case stems from a suit brought by Edward Lawson, who has been described by his lawyer as a "black man of unconventional appearance." Lawson was stopped on the streets in the San Diego area by police at least 15 times between 1975 and mid-1977 in predominantly white areas.

Lawson was convicted of PC 647(e) once. The Supreme Court's ruling, which upheld the 9th U.S. Circuit Court of Appeals, clears the way for a jury trial on the suit brought by Lawson against the police for damages.

While PC 647(e) is not now enforceable, it is possible the Legislature will attempt to rewrite or amend this section to make it more specific in order to meet the court's objections.

PC 647(f). This subsection is applicable to a person who appears in public under the influence of intoxicating liquor, any drug, or the combined influence of intoxicants and is unable to exercise care for his own safety or the safety of others.

Definitions. Applicable to Disorderly Conduct (Black's Law Dictionary). Under the influence of intoxicating liquor means "any abnormal mental or physical condition which is the result of indulging in any degree in intoxicating liquors, and which tends to deprive one of that clearness of intellect and control of himself which he would otherwise possess."

A distinction between "under the influence of intoxicating liquor" and "drunkenness" is necessarily made. A person is "drunk" when he is so far under the influence of liquor that his passions are visibly excited or his judgment impaired, or when his brain is so far affected by liquor that his intelligence, sense perceptions, judgment, continuity of thought or of ideas, speech and coordination of volition with muscular action (or some of these processes) are impaired or not under normal control.

Good police practice and departmental policy provide that a drunk should not be charged with resisting arrest (PC 148) except in aggravated cases. Usually the District Attorney's office or city Attorney's office is reluctant to issue a resisting complaint in drunk cases as drunks are normally considered not able to form the willful (specific) intent required for a resisting charge.

A barber shop was a "public place" for the purpose of this section, embodying a general scheme for regulation of the criminal aspects of being intoxicated in a public place (*Ex parte Zorn, 59 Cal. 2d 650*).

The state, in its regulation of intoxication, has not confined itself exclusively to public intoxication, but has entered into some private areas as well, and, therefore, municipal ordinances prohibiting intoxication in a private house to the annoyance of others are invalid as an invasion of a field of law pre-empted by the state (*People v. DeYoung, 228 C.A. 2d 331*).

Defendant was convicted for violation of Penal Code, Section 647f. After his conviction he appealed, contending that he was not arrested in a "public place" as required by the statute, since he had been arrested in his auto, which was parked illegally at the time. The court held that presence in an automobile parked in a street, under the conditions specified in PC 647f, is presence in a public place and constitutes a violation of that section. They further held that the parking strip comprising the portion of a paved city street and adjacent to the curb is a part of the street. Said the court, "The language of Section 647f clearly indicates that its purpose is to protect the offender himself from the results of his own folly, as well as to protect the general public from the dangers and evils attendant upon the presence of such persons upon the streets and highways and in other public places. We think that a reasonable and commonsense view of the evil at which the statute is directed and the protection which it is designed to afford compels the conclusion that a person in an automobile parked on a public street is in a 'public place' as contemplated by Section 647f." (*People v. Belanger, 243 Cal. App. 2d 819*).

Under cases previously decided by the courts, arrests for intoxication can only be made under the state statute and not for violation of a local ordinance. As a result, arrests under PC 657f (the state statute) may only be made of those who are under the influence of intoxicating liquor in a public place; arrests cannot be made in places exposed to public view. Thus, "intoxication in a place which is not a public place but is exposed to public view should not be criminal." (*In re Koehne, 59 Cal. 2d 646*).

Since an arrest for violation of PC 647f in a "public place" could be made other than in streets, the court in *Belanger* suggests a definition: "A public place has been defined to be a place where the public has a right to go and be, and includes public streets, roads, highways, and sidewalks." One definition of "public" given by Webster is "open to common or general use, participation, enjoyment, etc.; specifically, open to the free and unrestricted use of the public."

As arrests can only be made for a violation of PC 647f in public places, the clear implication is that no arrests can be made for drunkenness on obviously private premises, as homes or apartments (*People v. De Young, 228 C.A. 2d 334*).

The aforementioned cases do not specifically discuss the right of police to request people to alight from a car if they are found asleep at the wheel in a parked car on the street. If there is an official report that some person is drunk in an auto, courts have generally agreed that police have the authority to investigate and, if necessary, and make an arrest. Whether a report of intoxication has been made or not, officers may request people in parked cars who are apparently asleep to alight when it reasonably appears that such a course of conduct is necessary to determine whether a driver can safely care for himself and that he will not endanger the welfare of others. Even in the absence of evidence that the person asleep has been drinking, police are probably justified in attempting to discover the cause of the driver's sleeping in a car parked on a public street. It may be that the unconscious person is in need of assistance. An entry into the car under such circumstances to determine the condition of the driver would most probably be approved by the courts.

PC 647(g). This subsection covers prowling or loitering on private property by one who has no lawful business and without consent of the owner. Note that nighttime is an essential element, as is peeking into the door or window of any *inhabited* building or structure. For purposes of this section, inhabited means "a building which is customarily used as a dwelling house and temporary absence of its occupants, as on a vaction does not change the status of the building."

PC 647(h). This subsection deals with "window peeking" while on private property by one who has no visible or lawful business with the owner or occupant. This subsection, as does (g), requires that the peeking be done at night and that the building be inhabited. It is not necessary that anyone be home at the time, and the peeking may be via a door as well as a window.

PC 647(i). This subsection covers problems arising as a result of persons who: "...lodge in any building, structure or place, whether public or private, without the permission of the owner or person entitled to the possession or in control thereof."

TERMINOLOGY DEFINED—CHAPTER 8

See Terminology Quiz at the end of this chapter.
1. Dissolute: loose of morals and conduct.
2. Double jeopardy: tried a second time for charge previously adjudicated.
3. *Duces tecum:* (Latin: "bring with you"), a type of subpoena for papers, etc.
4. Duress: Coercion on a person to do something against his will.
5. Emancipation: free from another's custody, age of majority from parents.
6. Execution: carrying out orders of court, e.g., warrants, death penalty, etc.
7. Extortion: "blackmail," taking property via illegal threats.

8. Extradition: legal process of returning an accused from another jurisdiction.
9. False pretense: deceit used to unlawfully gain property from another.
10. *Habeas corpus:* (Latin for "have body"), order to bring person to court.
11. Hearsay: evidence not personally known, but heard from another.
12. Homicide: killing of one human being by another, may be legal or illegal.
13. Inquest: inquiry into cause of violent or unusual death.
14. Judgment: official declaration of results of a lawsuit or court ruling.
15. Lascivious: lustful, lewd, indecent, obscene.
16. Lynching: taking a person from custody of police by riot, also illegal hanging.
17. *Posse comitatus:* (Latin, "power of the County"), legal right of police to require assistance.
18. Pre-empt: supersede, take precedence over, prior jurisdiction.
19. Rout: preparatory stages of a riot.
20. Tumultuous: boisterous, disorderly, disturbing.

TRUE-FALSE QUIZ—CHAPTER 8

1. The courts do not recognize the existence of "fighting words" as a basis for disturbing the peace.
2. The use of offensive words other than in a public place do not constitute disturbing the peace.
3. If two or more persons assemble together and advance toward the commission of an act which would be a riot if committed, such is legally an unlawful assembly.
4. It is a crime to remain at the scene of a riot after having been warned to disperse, even if one is only an observer.
5. A rout is simply defined as the preparatory stage of a riot.
6. To constitute a riot, the object of the assembly need not necessarily be unlawful.
7. Taking soil from another's vacant lot without permission constitutes the crime of trespass.
8. Tearing down a "no hunting" sign on another's property constitutes the crime of trespass.
9. The taking by means of riot of any person from the lawful custody of an officer constitutes a crime of rout.
10. One who engages in lewd or dissolute conduct in a public place is guilty of disorderly conduct.
11. Loitering around a public toilet for the purpose of engaging in *any* unlawful act is in violation of

PC 647, disorderly conduct.
12. Begging money in a public place is no longer a crime in California.
13. The State has pre-empted the field of prostitution legislation, making most city and county ordinances in the field void.
14. One can be guilty of window-peeking only if the act was done at night under PC 647.
15. If no one is home at the time, a subject cannot be guilty of window-peeking under PC 647.
16. A "public place" is any place such as an office building, movie house, department store, etc., generally open to the public but which can forbid entry at various appropriate times.
17. One who solicits or engages in any act of prostitution is guilty of disorderly conduct under the penal code.
18. PC 647 authorizes an officer to place one who is found drunk in a public place in civil protective custody.
19. The Penal Code prescribes a mandatory jail sentence for a second conviction of prostitution.
20. An "inhabited building" is one which is customarily used as a dwelling house even if the resident is temporarily absent.

ESSAY-DISCUSSION QUESTIONS— CHAPTER 8

1. What are the three different types of illegal activity which constitute disturbing the peace under PC 415?
2. List the elements of "Failure to Disperse" as defined under PC 416.
3. What are the two elements of unlawful assembly as defined under PC 407?
4. Under what circumstances, if any, is it unlawful to be present at the scene of any rout or riot?
5. Briefly describe the difference between rout and riot.
6. What type of activity or element constitutes violation of PC 404.6, Inciting a Riot?
7. What constitutes a (1) public place and (2) a place open to the public under PC 647?
8. List five of the nine acts or activities which constitute a violation of PC 647, Disorderly Conduct.
9. To what extent must a meeting be disrupted to constitute a violation of PC 403, Disturbing a Public Meeting?
10. List the elements of PC 647 (g) and (h), Prowling and Window Peeking.

TERMINOLOGY QUIZ—CHAPTER 8

Match terms and definitions by placing the correct number in the parentheses. Answers may be written on a separate sheet for submission to the instructor at the instructor's direction.

1. Dissolute
2. Double jeopardy
3. *Duces tecum*
4. Duress
5. Emancipation
6. Execution
7. Extortion
8. Extradition
9. False pretense
10. *Habeas corpus*
11. Hearsay
12. Homicide
13. Inquest
14. Judgment
15. Lascivious
16. Lynching
17. *Posse comitatus*
18. Pre-empt
19. Rout
20. Tumultous

( ) boisterous, disorderly, disturbing
( ) court order to bring "body" to court
( ) loose of morals and conduct
( ) preparatory stages of a riot
( ) deceit used to gain property of another
( ) process for returning accused from another jurisdiction
( ) a subpoena requiring papers, etc., be brought to court
( ) coercing a person to do something against his will
( ) supersede, take precedence over, prior jurisdiction
( ) taking a person from police custody by riot
( ) free from another's legal custody
( ) lustful, lewd, indecent, obscene
( ) blackmail, taking property by illegal threats
( ) carrying out court orders
( ) inquiry into cause of violent or unusual death

CHAPTER 9

Dangerous Weapons Control Laws

9.1 MANUFACTURE, SALE, POSSESSION OF CERTAIN WEAPONS PROHIBITED (PC 12020)

This section makes it a *felony*, punishable by imprisonment in the county jail or the state prison, to (1) possess, (2) manufacture, sell, import, lend, etc., or (3) carry concealed on the person certain deadly or dangerous weapons, items or materials.

1. **Mere possession** of any of the following (other than the exceptions noted) is a felony. It is also a *felony* to:

2. Manufacture, cause to be manufactured, import into the state, keep for sale, offer or expose for sale, give or lend any of the following (other than the exceptions noted):

Blackjack. A blackjack is a small leather-covered club or billy weighted at one end and having an elastic shaft.

A large number of steel washers strung on a rawhide thong was held to be a blackjack or slungshot within the meaning of this act (*People v. Mulherin, 140 C.A. 212*). In another case, a flat steel wrench with a leather thong attached was also held to be a blackjack or slungshot (*People v. Williams, 100 C.A. 149*).

Slungshot. A slungshot is defined as a small mass of metal or stone fixed on a flexible handle, strap, or other similar contrivance. There are relatively few case decisions which reflect the use of a slungshot; however, any object such as a mace, which is suspended by rope, wire, chain, etc., and which can be swung about will generally fit within the purview of this section.

Billy. A billy is defined as a club or a bludgeon. A bludgeon is a short clublike weapon with one end usually loaded and thicker than the other end. A club is a heavy staff of wood, usually tapered at one end.

The courts have included certain articles, such as loaded pool cues, tire irons, police batons, pieces of pipe, etc., to fall within the terms of this section (*People v. Grubb, 63 C. 2d 614*).

Sandbag or Sandclub. These articles may be simply defined as "a bag full of sand." They need not be commercially designed or manufactured, such as stage curtain weights, as long as they substantially fit the description herein.

Sawed-off Shortgun, Altered Rifle or Revolver. As used in this section, a sawed-off shotgun means any firearm (including any revolver) manufactured, designed, or converted to fire shotgun ammunition having a barrel (or barrels) of *less* than 18 inches in length, or a rifle having a barrel *less* than 16 inches in length, or any weapon made from a rifle or shotgun (whether altered, modified, or otherwise) if the weapon has an overall length of less than 26 inches.

Thus a rifle or shotgun would be illegal if its overall length is less than 26 inches, regardless of the length of the barrel. It could also be illegal if its barrel length is less than 18 inches (in the case of a shotgun) or 16 inches (in the case of a rifle) regardless of its overall length.

Exception. The manufacture or possession of sawed-off shotguns for use with blank cartridges solely as props for motion picture or television program production when authorized by the Department of Justice (see PC 12095) is not a violation of law.

Nunchaku. A nunchaku is an instrument consisting of two or more sticks, clubs, bars or rods to be used as handles, connected by rope, cord, wire, or chain, in the design of a weapon used in connection with the practice of a system of self-defense such as karate.

Exception. It is not a crime to manufacture nunchakus for the purpose of selling them to a school which holds a regulatory license and teaches the arts of self-defense. It is also not a violation to possess a nunchaku *on the premises* of a self-defense school providing the school holds a proper business license.

Throwing Stars. This is an instrument, without handles, consisting of a metal plate having three or more radiating points with one or more sharp edges and designed in the shape of a polygon, trefoil, cross, star, diamond, or other geometric shape for use as a weapon for throwing.

Metal Knuckles. This device is variously defined as a metal weapon fitting over the front of the doubled fist. It is likened to four large rings welded together and is often referred to as a "knuckle duster." The courts have held that the use of alternate strips of lead and friction tape, fashioned into a bracelet to fit over four knuckles, is within the term "metal knuckles." (*People v. Quinones, 140 C.A. 609*).

Cane Gun. A cane gun means any firearm mounted or enclosed in a stick, rod, crutch, or similar device, designed to be or capable of being used as an aid in walking, if such firearm may be fired while mounted or enclosed therein.

Wallet Gun. A wallet gun means any firearm mounted or enclosed in a case, resembling a wallet, designed to be or capable of being carried in a pocket or purse, if such firearm may be fired while mounted or enclosed in such case.

Disguised Firearms. This includes any firearm or firearm-type device which is not immediately recognizable as such. Possession is a felony.

Special Ammunition. This includes any ammunition which contains or consists of any flechette dart, or any bullet containing or carrying an explosive agent. Possession is a felony.

Flechette Dart Defined. As used in this section, a "flechette dart" means a dart, capable of being fired from a firearm, which measures approximately one inch in length, with tail fins which take up five-sixteenths inch of the body. Possession is a felony.

Miscellaneous Exceptions. It is not against the law to possess any of the following:
1. **Antique Firearms.** For purposes of this section, the term "antique firearm" means any firearm not designed or redesigned for using rim fire or conventional center fire fixed ammunition and manufactured in or before 1898. This also includes matchlock, flintlock or similar type firearms whether manufactured in or before 1898.
2. **Tracer Ammunition.** Tracer ammunition manufactured for shotguns is also exempt from the provisions of PC 12020(a) and possession of such is not a crime in California.
3. **Relics and Curios.** Any firearm or ammunition which is a curio or relic, as defined in Section 178.11 of the Code of Federal Regulations, is exempt from the provisions of PC 12020(a) and possession of such is not a crime in California.

Possession. The law recognizes two kinds of possession: (1) actual possession and (2) constructive possession. A person who knowingly has direct physical control over a thing is then in *actual* possession of it. A person who, although not in actual possession, knowingly has the right of control over a thing, either directly or through another person or persons, is then in *constructive* possession of it. The law recognizes that one person may have possession alone, or that two or more persons jointly may share actual or constructive possession.

Carrying Concealed Upon the Person.

It is a felony to carry, concealed on the person, any explosive substance or a dirk or dagger.

Explosive Substance. This includes any substance, with the exception of fixed ammunition, which, as the term implies, is capable of being exploded. Note that such materials must be carried on the person in a concealed manner to constitute a crime.

Dirk or Dagger. A dirk is a long straight-bladed dagger, whereas a dagger is a short weapon for stabbing. Both implements are defined as being fixed-bladed weapons with cutting edges on all sides. Mere possession of a dirk or dagger is no crime; they must be carried, concealed, upon the person, which then constitutes a felony. In one case, the court held that a dirk and dagger are synonymous under the law and consist of any straight stabbing weapon with cutting edges on both sides (*People v. Shah, 91 C.A. 2d 176*).

Concealed Weapons. Except as otherwise provided in this chapter, any person who carries concealed within any vehicle which is under his control or direction, any pistol, revolver or other firearm capable of being concealed (barrel less than 12 inches in length) without having a license to carry such firearm is guilty of a *misdemeanor.*

Any person who carries concealed upon his or her person any pistol, revolver or other firearm capable of being concealed upon the person without having a license to carry such firearm, is guilty of a *misdemeanor* (PC 12025, *briefed*). For additional details see Section 9.8 of your text.

Discussion.

No specific intent is necessary to violate this section; general intent will suffice. The mere manufacturing, importation, sale, possession, giving or lending, or carrying concealed upon the person of those weapons listed is sufficient to sustain a conviction, regardless of whether the purpose of the accused was good or bad (*People v. Patterson, 102 C.A. 2d 675*).

Also, a person is said to be in possession of an article when it is under his or her dominion and control. It is absolutely essential that the person have knowledge of the fact that he or she has possession (*People v. Patterson, 102 Cal. App. 2d 675*).

9.2 DEADLY WEAPONS

Certain objects such as blackjacks, sawed-off shotguns, metal knuckles, nunchakus and throwing stars are considered deadly weapons ordinarily associated with criminal activity and therefore the California Legislature has made their possession unlawful (PC 12020). There are other objects and instruments, such as a garden hoe, canes or hatpins, which are not considered weapons when used for the purpose normally intended. However, if two men begin to fist fight and one of them picks up a garden hoe and advances on the other, that garden hoe may very well become a deadly weapon depending on how it is used.

Whenever an object has the capacity for being used to inflict death or great bodily injury, and its possessor intends such a use should the circumstances require it, that object may be considered a deadly weapon. In addition, being armed with a deadly weapon can elevate a simple assault to an assault with a deadly weapon or a burglary or robbery to a first degree offense.

The Test. *In People v. Moran, 33 C.A. 3rd 274,* the defendant was convicted of rape while armed with a deadly weapon. At the time he committed the rape the defendant was armed with a "metal three-pronged instrument." On appeal defendant argued that this object could not be considered a deadly weapon. The court disagreed with the defendant and said:

"When it appears that such an instrument is capable of being used in a dangerous or deadly manner, and it may be fairly inferred from the evidence that its possessor intended on a particular occasion to use it as a weapon should the circumstances require, we believe that its character as a "dangerous or deadly weapon' may thus be established, at least for the purpose of that occasion."

The court in the *Moran* case reiterated the view originally set forth by the court in *People v. Raleigh, 128 C.A. 105* (1932). A defendant may be held to have been armed with a deadly weapon if (1) the object in question was capable of being used to cause death or great bodily injury and, (2) the facts indicate that he intended such a use if the circumstances required it.

In view of this two-pronged approach, i.e., focusing on the object as well as the possessor's intent, such diverse items as a bottle and even a pillow have been considered deadly weapons. However, since almost any object has the potential for causing death (thus meeting the first part of the test) the main focus is most often on the possessor's *intent* at the time of the incident.

In *People v. Gilbert, 188 C.A. 2nd 723,* the defendant was found with a crowbar while committing a burglary. The possession of the crowbar elevated the charge against him to first degree burglary. He appealed the first degree conviction, contending that a crowbar is not a deadly weapon and therefore he did not commit first degree burglary. While the court recognized that a crowbar is capable of being used in a deadly manner, it reduced the conviction to second degree burglary after reviewing the elements of the two-pronged test. The court said:

"Measured by such a test, the evidence in this case fell short of sustaining a finding that the appellant was armed with a deadly weapon because there was no reasonable basis for an inference that he *intended* to use the crowbar as a weapon should the circumstances require. Obviously he intended to use it as a burglar's tool. . . ." (Emphasis added)

High Voltage Electric Dart Guns. In April 1974 Taser Systems Inc., located in Industry, California, patented their Taser F-1 electric dart gun under the title "Weapon for Immobilization and Capture." Since that time, questions have been raised as to its status as a "deadly weapon," under PC 3024 (f), and whether or not it is a "firearm capable of being concealed on the person" under PC 12001.

Discussion

The weapon is composed of a launcher and cartridges. It will accommodate two cartridges which can be rapidly fired. The launcher is nine inches in overall length and is made of plastic. The projectile is powered by six nickel-cadmium batteries. Included in the launcher is a flashlight powered by two similar batteries. The launcher has three white buttons on the top. The one closest to the muzzle activates the flash-light. The middle one is a safety, while the one in the handle is the trigger. On the left side of the launcher is the plug for the battery charger. The muzzle end of the launcher is composed of a flashlight (used for aiming) mounted over two cartridges. The launcher bears the serial number on the inside surface of the handle and on the inside of the flashlight housing. Each cartridge contains two dart-type projectiles. The upper dart in each cartridge is aligned horizontally, while the lower is aligned approximately 30°below horizontal. Each projectile is housed in a barrel, approximately 3.5 centimeters long, contained in the cartridge. Each projectile is attached to a wire 18 feet in length coiled at the side of the projectile. In the back of each projectile is an explosive charge which is composed of a primer and 50 mgs. of smokeless powder. When the trigger is pressed, the primer is electrically detonated. The projectiles are each tipped with a one-quarter inch barb. Upon deployment on the target area, a pulsed low-amperage, high voltage current of 50,000 volts, is carried to the darts by the insulated wires. The current immobilizes the recipient of the barbed darts. The muzzle velocity of the weapon is 200 feet per second.

Attorney General's Opinion No. CR 75/22. On October 30, 1975, the Attorney General, State of California, rendered the following formal opinion in response to a request from the District Attorney of Sacramento County.

1. The Taser TF-1, manufactured by Taser Systems Inc., is a "firearm capable of being concealed upon the person" as that term is used in Penal Code section 12001.

2. The Taser TF-1, manufactured by Taser Systems Inc., is a "deadly weapon" as that term is used in Penal Code section 3024, dubdivision (f).

The mere fact that the Taser TF-1 was designed to be nonlethal to normal healthy people, does not place it outside of the meaning of "deadly weapon" as the term is used in *PC 3024(f)*. Also, the Taser TF-1 is a firearm as used in *PC 12001*.

9.3 PROHIBITED WEAPONS

General Provisions. In California, the field of regulation and licensing of firearms has been pre-empted by the State. A City Ordinance concerning weapons may be upheld as valid, however, insofar as it does *not* duplicate State Law. Finally, the Federal Government has enacted a great deal of weapons regulations under the power granted to Congress in the Commerce Clause.

Policy and Purpose. A major purpose of the regulation of weapons is to outlaw the classic instruments normally used only for criminal purposes. In particular the Legislature has attempted to minimize the danger to public safety arising from the free access to firearms that can be used for crimes of violence. This approach has been upheld as a valid exercise of the "police power" of the State for the protection of the lives and property of citizens (*People v. Billon, 26 C.A. 2nd 537 (1968)*).

Handguns With Altered Numbers. It is a misdemeanor to possess any pistol or revolver that does not bear identification numbers (*PC 12094*). Furthermore, alterations of such numbers is a felony (*PC12090*). There is a rebuttable presumption that one possessing such an altered handgun made the alteration.

Constitutionality. The Second Amendment of the United States Constitution reads: "A well-regulated militia being necessary to the security of a free state, the right of the people to keep and bear arms shall be infringed." This amendment applies, however, only to the exercise of power by the *federal government*. It does *not* provide any restriction against the state government's passing weapons laws. It has been held that the right of the people to keep and bear arms is *not* a right granted by the constitution (*In re Ramirez*, 193 Cal. 633, 651). Furthermore, even where the State Constitution includes the same sort of provision as the Second Amendment, it is interpreted to apply only to the bearing of arms by citizens in defense of a common cause and not to their use in private brawls (*In re Ramirez*). The Supreme Court of the United States has also held, for example, that a shotgun having a barrel less than eighteen inches in length has no reasonable relation to the preservation of a well-regulated militia and is not within the meaning of that provision (*U.S. v. Miller, 307 U.S. 174*).

9.4 CRIME OF POSSESSION

Knowledge. Where the offense is defined as mere possession, the only knowledge required is knowledge of the character of the object possessed. Knowledge that the possession is illegal is unnecessary (*People v. Mendoza 251 C.A. 2nd 835*). It is also not necessary that any illegal use be made of the object (*People v. Odegard, 203 C.A. 2nd 427, 431*).

Possession Alone Sufficient. Proof of possession alone is sufficient to convict in many cases. It is not necessary to prove malicious intent or wrongful use of the instrument (*People v. Odegard*). For example, "Chinese throwing stars" or a sawed-off shotgun are suitable for unlawful purposes because of their concealability and ease of handling (*People v. Stinson, 8 C.A. 3rd 497*). Therefore, under the statute, it is not necessary that the possessor intend to put the instrument to an unlawful use. Possession is illegal *per se* (Id. at 501). It is likewise a felony to possess a machine gun. Knowledge of the fact that the firearm is a machine gun is not an essential element of the offense of possession (*People v. Daniels, 118 C.A. 2nd 340*). Other prohibited firearms and equipment include a shotgun larger then ten gauge, or a shotgun capable of holding more than six cartridges at one time (*Fish and Game Code 2010*). It is unlawful to use or possess any firearm commonly known as a "cane gun" or a gun of similar character (*FG 208*). It is a felony to possess a silencer (*PC 12520*) and a misdemeanor to possess a sniperscope (*PC 468*). It is also a felony to possess a "destructive device" which includes hand grenades, projectiles containing incendiary ammunition, grenade launchers, large rocket type devices and their launchers, and any weapon greater than sixty caliber which fires fixed ammunition (PC 12301 and PC 12303).

General Character of Object. The California Legislature has made it a felony to possess "any instrument or weapon of the kind commonly known as a blackjack, slungshot, billy, nunchaku, sand club, sand bag, sawed-off shotgun, or metal knuckles (PC 12020). The courts note that the instruments are defined "not in specific terms, but as being of a kind commonly known," and therefore will not say a weapon was not the kind prohibited by the statute because of its shape and size (*People v. Canales, 12 C.A. 2nd 215*). The courts believe that "the language of this section should be given liberal construction, so long as no injustice results (*People v. Mulherin, 140 C.A. 2nd 212, 216*). Therefore, while a blackjack is usually covered with leather, it is not necessary for it to be covered at all (*People v. Mulherin*). Likewise, a homemade object of sheet lead and tape was held to be "metal knuckles" even though it was not made entirely of metal (*People v. Quinones, 140 C.A. 609*).

9.5   TEAR GAS POSSESSION

Tear Gas. Effective September 27, 1977 the legislature enacted an urgency statute (PC 12403.7) which now permits citizens to purchase, possess and carry tear gas of th aerosol spray type only. This is subject to the following requirements:

1. Must be at least 18 years of age.
2. Must complete a Department of Justice certified course in the use of tear gas (offered at various Community Colleges.)
3. Has not been convicted of a felony.
4. Is not addicted to any narcotic drug.
5. Has not been convicted of any crime involving assault.
6. Has not been convicted of misuse of tear gas.
7. Has been granted a license as provided by law.

Once the license is issued, it is good for seven years unless revoked for cause. The citizen may then purchase a special "civilian" aerosol spray cannister of a specific size. It must bear the words: "WARNING: The use of this substance or device for any purpose other than self-defense is a felony under California law."

Penalty for Misuse. Any person who has a valid permit, who uses tear gas or tear gas weapons except in self-defense or for authorized training purposes is guilty of a public offense and is punishable by imprisonment in a state prison for sixteen months or two or three years, or in a county jail for a period not to exceed one year, or by fine not to exceed $1,000, or by both such fine and imprisonment (*PC 12403.7*).

9.6   CARRYING CONCEALED KNIVES AND EXPLOSIVES

It is a felony to carry concealed upon the person any dirk or dagger or explosive substance. A dirk is defined as any weapon designed primarily for stabbing (*People v. Forrest, 67 Cal. 2nd, 478, 480*). It does not include an ordinary pocket knife, however. When a knife has many possible uses, some of which are innocent, and it also has a characteristic which limits its effectiveness in stabbing, it cannot be held a weapon primarily designed for stabbing (*People v. Forrest*).

Switchblade Knives. *Carrying* a switchblade knife with a blade length of *over* two inches is a misdemeanor. Mere possession is not an offense. It need not be concealed on a person as with a dagger, however. The definition of switchblade includes a spring blade knife, snap blade, gravity knife, or any similar type knife. The test is that the blade can be released automatically by the flick of a button, pressure on the handle, flip of the wrist, or by the weight of the blade or any type of mechanism at all.

9.7 ILLEGAL FIREARMS USE

The mere pointing of an unloaded firearm at someone, accompanied by a threat to shoot him, but without an attempt to use the gun as a bludgeon, is not considered an assault of any type in California (*People v. Sylva, 143 Cal. 62*). However, the pointing of an unloaded firearm at another in a "rude, angry or threatening manner" may constitute a violation of PC 417, which makes brandishing a firearm in such a manner a misdemeanor (see Chapter 10, Types of Assaults).

The California assault statute (PC 240) requires a showing of "present ability" to do harm, and the courts have held that pointing an unloaded firearm does not imply the present ability to do harm and therefore does not amount to an assault unless the firearm is used as a bludgeon.

Penal Code 12022(a), provides for a penalty enhancement (increase) of one additional consecutive year in prison upon conviction of committing or attempting to commit any felony if one or more of the perpetrators was *armed* with a firearm. The firearm in such cases may be of any type. Whether or not the firearm was concealed or concealable is not an element. The fact that it was not used or even displayed is not important if, in fact, one of the perpetrators was armed.

PC 12022(b) provides that if any person personally *uses* a deadly or dangerous weapon (includes knives, clubs, guns, etc.) during commission of a felony, the one year enhancement applies unless the use of the dangerous or deadly weapon is an element of the crime charged (such as carrying a concealed weapon).

PC 12022.5 provides that any person who uses a *firearm* to commit or attempt to commit a felony, shall be subjected to a two-year consecutive and additional penalty enhancement unless the use of a firearm is an element of the offense charged. Note: The additional term provided by this section may also be imposed in cases of assault with a deadly weapon under PC 245.

The courts have held that even an *unloaded* gun is at least a "dangerous weapon" in its natural state, and has a potential to be used as a club or bludgeon. Penalty enhancements, therefore, would apply in a robbery or burglary committed with an unloaded firearm. It is not necessary to show that the defendant intended to use the gun (*People v. Aranda, 63 C. 2d 518*).

If the defendant was armed with a *loaded* firearm, during the perpetration of a burglary or robbery, penalty enhancements would be proper even if the gun was not drawn or in any way exposed to the victim (Burglary: *People v. Moore, 143 C.A. 2d 333;* Robbery: People v. Hall, 105 C.A. 359).

It is well settled in California that a firearm is a "deadly weapon" even if unloaded and not operable (*People v. Torres, 19 C.A. 724*).

9.8 CONCEALABLE WEAPONS

PC 12001. A larger variety of weapons were recently included within the legal definition of "concealable weapons" under this section by the legislature. The terms (1) "pistol," (2) "revolver," and (3) "firearm capable of being concealed," apply to and include any device designed to be used as a weapon from which a projectile is expelled by force of an explosion, or other form of combustion, and which has a barrel length of *less* than twelve inches. The frame or receiver is to be included for measurement purposes in determining barrel length under this chapter.

Subject to several exceptions, PC 12025 provides that:

"...any person who carries upon his person or concealed within any vehicle which is under his control or direction any pistol, revolver, or other firearm capable of being concealed upon the person without having a license to carry such firearm...is guilty of a misdemeanor..."

Discussion

A firearm "capable of being concealed upon the person" is defined as any device which is designed to be used as a weapon capable of forcefully expelling a projectile by way of combustion and having a barrel of *less* than 12 inches in length (PC 12001). This definition is very narrowly construed by the courts so that a person walking down a public street carrying a firearm with a 12¼ inch barrel hidden under his coat without a license to do so, is not violating PC 12025, because the firearm does not fit within the definition of a concealable firearm (*People v Osterman, 4 CA 3rd 763, 765*). If the ifirearm has been altered so that it comes under the purview of PC 12020, a violation of that section may be present, however.

Addicts and Convicted Felons. Neither addicts nor convicted felons are allowed to possess *concealable* firearms (PC 12021). Furthermore, if the convicted felon used a firearm in the commission of the original felony he is not to possess *any* firearms (PC 12560).

Aliens. The statute barring aliens from possession of concealable firearms has recently been held unconstitutional as having "no reasonable relationship to the threat to public safety which the statute was designed to prevent (*People v. Rappard, 28 C.A. 3rd 302*).

Minors. It is a misdemeanor for a minor to possess a concealable firearm, unless he has either written permission of his parent or guardian or is accompanied by the parent or guardian at the time and place of possession. Selling or otherwise furnishing any firearm, airgun, or gas-operated gun to a minor is restricted (PC 12550, 12551, 12552).

Mental Patients. Mental patients are not allowed to possess *any* firearms. The same restriction applies to people who have been adjudicated by a court to be a danger to others as a result of mental illness.

Exceptions. Peace officers are exempted from most, though not all, of the restrictions applicable to deadly and dangerous weapons control. Certain weapons, to be legally possessed by peace officers must be authorized by their employing agency and in many cases, the officer must possess a certificate showing special training in the use of the weapon, e.g., firearms and tear gas. Also, certain weapons such as metal knuckles cannot be authorized by an employing agency or legally possessed by a peace officer except when being held for evidence.

Inoperable Weapons. The rule is that the prohibition on a weapon remains no matter how disabled it may be if it still retains its efficiency to such an extent that it may in some manner be used as originally intended (*People v. McCloskey, 76 CA 227, 231*). Thus, its essential character is not changed even by dismemberment, if the parts may be easily assembled so as to become effective (*People v. Ekstrand, 28 CA 2nd 1,7*).

Licenses. The prohibitions against carrying concealed firearms do not apply to those who have licenses to carry them. While PC 12050 and PC 12054 detail the way in which a license to carry a concealed weapon may be obtained, it is extremely difficult for most members of the public to qualify for one.

Degree of Concealment. A firearm does not have to be *completely* hidden in order to be held to be concealed for the purposes of PC 12025. In *People v. May, 33 CA 3rd 888*(1973), a police officer observed the defendant walking along an alley in a high-crime area. He noticed a bulge in the defendant's pocket and saw that the top of the object which caused the bulge was silver. While detaining the defendant for questioning, the officer saw that the object in the defendant's pocket was a derringer. The defendant argued that since the gun was partially exposed to

view, it could not be considered concealed. The court disagreed with the defendant's argument since that argument would enable a defendant to "...immunize himself from prosecution on a charge of possessing a concealed weapon merely by intentionally or unintentionally permitting an occasional glimpse of the weapon which would otherwise remain concealed from sight."

Weapons in Vehicles. PC 12025 also make it illegal to carry a concealed firearm "...concealed within any vehicle which is under one's control or direction..." Again, the firearm need not be *completely* hidden in a vehicle in order for it to be deemed concealed. In one case the officer saw a butt of a gun protruding from beneath two pillows on the front seat of defendant's car after stopping him for drunk driving. The gun was considered concealed within the meaning of PC 12025 (*People v. Linden, 185 CA 2nd 752*). It should be noted that PC 12025 does not prohibit the carrying of a concealed firearm in a vehicle so long as the weapon is in plain view. In 38 Opinions Cal. Atty. Gen. 199, 200, the Attorney General has ruled: "It appears quite clear that a concealable firearm carried on the seat of a vehicle is legally carried under PC 12025, so long as the weapon is in plain view. It further appears that a concealable weapon may be carried anywhere else in the vehicle, again provided it remains in plain view."

Possession of Weapons in Vehicles. Suppose officers stop a vehicle in order to issue the driver a traffic citation. During the course of this lawful detention, they spot a concealed firearm under the front seat between the driver and his passenger. The driver tells the officer that the firearm belongs to the passenger. May the driver be arrested for carrying a concealed firearm? May the passenger be arrested for the same charge? The courts have held that in this situation there would be "...circumstantial evidence supportive of a finding of *joint* or constructive possession, custody or control of the firearm by the dirver and sufficient to sustain his conviction." (*People v. Nieto, 247 CA 2nd 364, Certiorari denied, 387 U.S. 911 (1967)*).

The court stated that it is not necessary that the driver have *exclusive* control over a firearm to be guilty of carrying a concealed weapon in his car. The passenger, however, could *not* be convicted of violating PC 12025 *unless* the prosecution could show that he shared "control and direction" of the vehicle. A mere passenger who assumes no share of control or direction over the vehicle cannot be convicted for violating this code section (*People v. Jenkins, 207 CA 2nd 904*).

Exceptions: Concealable Firearms The Penal Code provides that concealable firearms may be kept in one's home or place of business without a license providing the owner is over 18 and not an addict or ex-felon (PC 12026). However, neither the courts nor the Legislature have yet decided on whether a concealable firearm can be *carried concealed* by the owner in his home or place of business. For example, it is not clear whether the owner of a bar is violating the concealed weapons law if he carries a concealable firearm under his shirt while running the bar.

In addition to the above, PC 12025 does not apply to peace officers, members of the armed forces when on duty, licensed hunters when they are hunting or on their way to or from hunting, and certain guards and messengers, among other (PC 12027).

Sale of Concealable Firearms. It is a misdemeanor for anyone, employed in the business of selling firearms, to sell or transfer a concealable firearm without a license to do so (PC 12020 and PC 12071). In addition, there are restrictions on the eligibility of the buyer (must be 18 or over), the time of delivery (must not be delivered within 5 days of the purchase), method of delivery (gun must be unloaded and securely wrapped) and the dealer must register the sale (PC 12072). In the case of a firearm sale between two private parties, where neither party holds a dealer's license, the seller is required to "personally" know the buyer in order to legally make the sale (PC 12072).

9.9 FIREARMS IN PUBLIC PLACES

With certain exceptions, it is a misdemeanor to carry a *loaded* firearm on one's person or in a vehicle while in any public place or street in an incorporated city or in a prohibited area of an unincorporated territory (PC 12031). Exceptions to this prohibition include on-duty members of the military, and those who are licensed to carry concealed firearms, among others (PC 12031(b)).

PC 1203 (c) authorizes officers to examine any firearms carried openly in a public place in order to determine whether or not it is loaded. In fact, refusal to allow a peace officer to inspect a firearm pursuant to the provisions of this section constitutes probable cause for arrest for violation of this section. A firearm will be deemed *loaded* for purposes of this section if there is any unexpended cartridge or shell in or in any way attached to the firearm, including the firing chamber, the magazine or the clip (PC 12031(e)). It is not necessary to prove that the defendant knew the gun was loaded in order for him to be convicted of

violating PC 12031 (*People v. Harrison, 1 CA 3rd 115*). However, this section does not prevent a person from keeping a loaded firearm on his private property or place of business (PC 12031(f)).

Loaded Rifles and Shotguns in Vehicles. It is unlawful to have a loaded rifle or shotgun *in* or *on* any vehicle on a public highway (Fish and Game Code 2006). For purposes of this section, the firearm is considered loaded *only* when there is an unused shell or cartridge in the *chamber*. This section does not apply to peace officers or members of the armed forces while on duty.

Firearms in the State Capitol. PC171c, makes it a felony to carry a loaded firearm into the State Capitol area. This includes the grounds, offices and hearing rooms. It should be noted that in this context a firearm is considered loaded simply whenever the gun and the ammunition are in possession of the same person.

9.10 RELATED CODE SECTIONS

Destruction of Weapons as Nuisances (PC 12028)

This section provides for the destruction of those weapons mentioned in Section 653k, 12020 and 12025. Also included are weapons used in the commission of, or attempt to commit a felony, including those cases where the defendant is found guilty of a lesser included offense or a misdemeanor. Such destruction is to take place between the 1st and 10th days of July each year (briefed).

License to Carry Firearms (PC 12050)

The sheriff of a county, or the chief, or other head of a municipal police department of any city or city and county, upon proof that the person applying is of good moral character, that good cause exists for the issuance, and that the person applying is a resident of the county, may issue to such person a license to carry concealed a pistol, revolver, or other firearm for a period of one yar from the date of license (*Amended, Stats. 1977, Chap. 1188*).

Tampering with Marks on Firearms (PC 12090)

Any person who changes, alters, removes, or obliterates the maker, model, manufacturer's number, or other mark of identification, including any distinguishing number or mark assigned by the State

Bureau of Criminal Identification and Investigation, on any pistol or revolver, without first having secured written permission from the bureau to make such change, alteration, or removal shall be punished by imprisonment in the state prison.

In *People v Wissenfield* evidence sustained a conviction for grand theft and a violation of this section dealing with tampering with identification marks on firearms.

Possession of any pistol or revolver upon which the name of the maker, model, manufacturer's number, or other mark of identification has been changed, altered, removed, or obliterated, shall be presumptive evidence that the possessor has changed, altered, removed, or obliterated the same.

"Machine Gun" Defined (PC 12200)

The term "machine gun" as used in this chapter means any weapon which shoots, or is designed to shoot, automatically, more than one shot, without manual reloading, by a single function of the trigger, and includes any frame or receiver which can only be used with such weapon. The term shall also include any combination of parts designed and intended for use in converting a weapon into a machine gun (*Amended, Stats. 1969; Chap. 1003*).

This section exempts law enforcement officers and the military from any provisions prohibiting private citizens from any transporting or possessing machine guns (briefed).

Transporting or Possession of Machine Gun Unlawful (PC 12220)

Any person, firm, or corporation who within this state sells, offers for sale, possesses, or knowingly transports any firearm of the kind commonly known as a machine gun, except as provided by this chapter, is guilty of a public offense and upon conviction herof shall be punished by imprisonment in the state prison or by a fine not to exceed five thousand dollars ($5,000) or by both such fine and imprisonment.

Tear Gas Weapons—Shell, Chartridge or Bomb (PC 12400)

Sections 12401 through 12458 pertain to tear gas equipment and tear gas, which is defined as a liquid, gaseous, or solid substance intended to produce temporary physical discomfort or permanent injury through being vaporized or otherwise dispersed in the air (briefed).

PC 12403.7 provides that no person shall possess or use any tear gas or tear gas weapon if such person has not completed a certified course in defensive use of tear gas (Mace) and has not been issued a permit as required by law. The illegal possession or use of tear gas is punishable by imprisonment in a state prison for 16 months or two or three years, or in a county jail not to exceed one year, or by fine of $1,000, or by both such fine and imprisonment. (See Tear Gas Possession, Section 9.5.)

Firearms Silencers (PC 12500)

Sections 12500 through 12529 pertain to the definition, illegality, and unlawful possession of any instrument designed to silence the report of any firearm. Such offense is a felony, punishable by imprisonment in state prison or by a fine not to exceed five thousand dollars ($5,000), or by both such fine and imprisonment (briefed).

Unmarked Pistol: Purchase, Sale or Possession (PC 12094)

Any person who knowingly buys, receives, disposes of, sells, offers for sale, or has in his possession any pistol or revolver which does not bear the manufacturer's number or other mark of identification in its original condition or as restored, or a distinguishing number or mark assigned to it by the State Bureau of Criminal Identification and Investigation is guilty of a misdemeanor.

Sale of Firearms to a Minor (Ages 16 to 18) (PC 12550)

No person shall sell any firearm to any minor who is at least sixteen years of age but not over the age of eighteen years without the written consent of a parent or legal guardian of the minor. Violation of this section is a misdemeanor.

Sale of Firearms to Minor (Under Age 18) (PC 12551)

Every person who sells to a minor under the age of eighteen years any firearm, airgun, or gas-operated gun, designed to fire a bullet, pellet, or metal projectile is guilty of a misdemeanor.

Furnishing Weapon to Minor Without Consent of Parent or Guardian (PC 12552)

Every person who furnishes any firearm, airgun, or gas-operated gun, designed to fire a bullet, pellet, or metal projectile, to any minor under the age of eighteen years, without the express or implied permission

DEADLY WEAPONS CONTROL LAW CHART

WEAPONS	MERE POSSESSION	CONCEALED ON PERSON OR IN VEHICLE	CARRIED OPENLY OR VISIBLY
Blackjack, slungshot, billy, sandbag, metal knuckles, nunchaku, throwing stars, cane gun, explosive ammo, wallet gun	Felony to possess, offer for sale or keep for sale. (12020 P.C.)	Mere possession a felony. (12020 P.C.)	Mere possession a felony. (12020 P.C.)
Machine guns	Felony or misdemeanor to possess. (12020 P.C.)	Mere possession a felony or misdemeanor. (12220 P.C.)	Mere possession a felony or misdemeanor. (12220 P.C.)
Firearm silencers	Felony to possess (12520 P.C.)	Felony to possess. Does not have to be concealed (12520 P.C.)	Mere possession a felony. (12520 P.C.)
Handguns (concealable weapons)	Felony or misdemeanor if person has previously been convicted of a felony or is addicted to narcotic drugs. (12021 P.C.) Misdemeanor if possessed by minor not accompanied by parent or guardian or without written permission of parent or guardian. (12021.5 P.C.)	Misdemeanor to carry concealed on the person or concealed in any vehicle under person's direction or control without license or permit to carry concealed (12025 P.C.)* *See exceptions to 12025 P.C. in 12027 P.C.	Misdemeanor to carry loaded on person or in vehicle while in public place, public street within incorporated city, or public place or public street in an unincorporated area where it would be unlawful to discharge a weapon. Defines a "loaded" firearm for purposes of enforcement as that which has an unexpended cartridge or shell in, or attached in any manner to the firearm, including, but not limited to, the firing chamber, magazine or clip thereof attached to the firearm. (12031 P.C.)* Felony to carry loaded on person or in vehicle within the state capitol and other legislative offices, or upon the grounds of or within any residence of the governor or any state legislator, or upon the grounds of or within any public school. Defines a firearm as being "loaded" for purposes of enforcement whenever both the firearm and unexpended ammunition are in the possession of the same person. (171c, 171d and 171c P.C.)* Peace Officers are authorized to examine any such weapon for the purpose of determining if a violation exists. Refusal to allow such examination constitutes probable cause to arrest. *See exceptions in this chapter.
Rifles	Felony to possess only if barrel is less than 16″ in length or if overall length is less than 26″. (12020 P.C.)	Misdemeanor if cartridge is in chamber when the rifle is in a vehicle on any public highway or other way open to the public (2006 Fish and Game Code)	
Shotguns	Felony to possess only if barrel is less than 18″ in length or overall length is less than 26″. (12020 P.C.)	Misdemeanor if cartridge is in chamber when the shotgun is in a vehicle on any public highway or other way open to the public. (2006 Fish and Game Code)	

of the parent or legal guardian of the minor is guilty of a misdemeanor.

Possession of Firearms by Convicted Felon (PC 12560)

This section relates to possession of any firearm by a person previously convicted of a felony who used a firearm in the commission of such felony, and provides that the possession, custody, or control of any firearm (irrespective of whether it is concealable) by a person convicted of a felony who used a firearm in the commission of such prior felony, constitutes a felony, punishable by imprisonment in state prison, or in a county jail not exceeding one year, or by a fine not exceeding five hundred dollars ($500), or by both such term of imprisonment and such fine (briefed).

Possession of Firearms by a Person Previously a Mental Patient (5153 Welfare and Institutions Code)

This section prohibits any person who was involuntarily committed after October 1, 1955, to any mental hospital or sanitarium for a period of thirty days or more from having in his possession, custody, or control any firearm, unless such person has been issued a certificate as set forth in that section, and unless such person has not, subsequent to the issuance of such certificate, again been involuntarily committed for a period of thirty days or more in any such hospital or sanitarium. A violation of this section constitutes a misdemeanor (briefed).

Sales or Possession of Switchblade Knives (PC 653k)

Every person who carries upon his person, and every person who sells, offers for sale, exposes for sale, loans, transfers, or gives to any other person a switchblade knife having a blade over two inches in length is guilty of a misdemeanor.

For the purposes of this section a "switchblade knife" is a knife having the appearance of a pocketknife, and shall include a springblade knife, snapblade knife, gravity knife, or any other similar type knife, the blade or blades of which are two or more inches long and which can be released automatically by a flick of a button, pressure on the handle, flick of the wrist or other mechanical device, or is released by the weight of the blade or by any type of mechanism whatsoever.

TERMINOLOGY DEFINED—CHAPTER 9

See the Terminology Quiz at the end of this chapter.

1. Asphyxiate: to smother, unable to breathe.
2. Blackjack: small, leather-covered, flexible-handled club.
5. Dirk: a straight blade dagger sharpened on both edges.
6. Evidence: means by which facts are established in court.
7. False imprisonment: any unlawful restraint of one's liberty.
8. Hung jury: one unable to reach unanimous verdict.
9. Lethal: capable of causing death, deadly.
10. Penologist: an authority on prisons or rehabilitation.
11. Possession: under one's control or custody.
12. *Post mortem:* scientific examination to determine cause of death.
13. Presumptive evidence: assumed true until contrary is proved.
14. Recidivist: repeat offender, habitual criminal.
15. *Res gestae:* acts and words just before and after a crime.
16. Restitution: payment for loss or damage, repayment.
17. Summons: a writ requiring an answer in a civil suit.
18. Verdict: the decision in a jury or court trial.
19. *Versus:* Latin meaning "against," e.g., *People v. Jones;* abbreviated "*v.*"
20. Warrant: a court order commanding an arrest or a search.

TRUE-FALSE QUIZ—CHAPTER 9

1. Other than for peace officers, mere possession of a blackjack is a crime.
2. A sawed-off shotgun is one having a barrel less than 18 inches long.
3. Possession of a rifle with a barrel less than 16 inches long is a crime.
4. Possession of a shotgun or rifle with an overall length of 28 inches is a crime.
5. Peace officers are legally permitted to carry "metal knuckles" as part of their regular equipment.
6. A "nunchaku" is an instrument with handles and sharp points used for throwing.
7. To be guilty of possession of an illegal weapon it must be proven the defendant knew he had same under his custody and control.
8. Whether or not an item is a dangerous weapon depends on its nature and its intended use.
9. In California, the field of firearms licensing and regulation has been pre-empted by the State.

10. The Second Amendment of the U.S. Constitution restricts the State from passing gun control laws, allocating this power to the Federal Government.
11. The Constitutional phrase "right of the people to keep and bear arms" has been held to apply to an individual's right to own a gun.
12. If one knows he is in possession of "brass knuckles" not knowing that the possession is illegal, he has a good defense to the crime.
13. Unauthorized possession of tear gas by a person for his own personal defense is not a crime.
14. It is a misdemeanor to possess a pistol or revolver which does not bear identification numbers.
15. Mere possession of a dirk or dagger is a crime.
16. Mere possession of a switchblade knife with a blade length of over two inches is a crime.
17. A "concealable firearm" is one having a barrel length of *less* than 12 inches.
18. If a defendant was armed with a loaded weapon during a robbery, the penalty would be more severe even if he never drew the gun or exposed it to the victim.
19. Aliens may *not* legally possess concealable firearms in California.
20. Other than peace officers and on-duty military personnel, it is a misdemeanor to carry a loaded firearm on one's person in a public place or in a vehicle on the public streets without a permit.

ESSAY-DISCUSSION QUESTIONS— CHAPTER 9

1. What is the legal definition of a concealable firearm?
2. Is the possession of a dirk or dagger a crime under the provisions of PC 12020? Explain.
3. Is a .22-caliber rifle, previously 33 inches in overall length but modified and cut down to a 26-inch overall length, still a legal firearm? Explain.
4. What type of intent is necessary to violate the provisions of the Deadly Weapons Control Law?
5. When is a person said to be in possession of an illegal weapon? Need he be the owner to be guilty of illegal possession?
6. Under what circumstances may a minor be sold a firearm?
7. Is a previously convicted felon in violation of the law if he possesses a shotgun for hunting purposes? Explain.
8. Who issues permits (city and county) to carry a concealed weapon? Where and for what length of time are these permits valid?
9. Is a person who possesses a concealable firearm, the serial number of which is missing, removed or altered, guilty of any crime?
10. What loaded firearms are illegal to possess in a vehicle? Define the term "loaded" within the meaning of the statute.

TERMINOLOGY QUIZ—CHAPTER 9

Match terms and definitions by placing the correct number in the parentheses. Answers may be written on a separate sheet for submission to the instructor at the instructor's direction.

1. Asphyxiate
2. Blackjack
3. Criminology
4. Deadly weapon
5. Dirk
6. Evidence
7. False imprisonment
8. Hung jury
9. Lethal
10. Penologist
11. Possession
12. *Post mortem*
13. Presumptive evidence
14. Recidivist
15. *Res gestae*
16. Restitution
17. Summons
18. Verdict
19. *Versus*
20. Warrant

( ) writ requiring answer to a civil suit
( ) payment for loss or damage
( ) capable of causing death, deadly
( ) a repeat offender, habitual criminal
( ) to smother, unable to breathe
( ) a dagger sharpened on both edges
( ) court order commanding an arrest or search
( ) means by which facts are established in court
( ) the decision in a jury or court trial
( ) Latin meaning "against"
( ) examination to determine cause of death
( ) acts and words just before and after a crime
( ) under one's custody and control
( ) small, leather-covered, flexible-handled club
( ) an unlawful restraint of one's liberty

CHAPTER 10

Types of Assault

10.1 SIMPLE ASSAULT (PC 240)

Assault Defined. An assault is an unlawful attempt, coupled with a present ability, to commit a violent injury on the person of another (PC 240).

Elements of Assault

1. An *unlawful attempt* (to commit a battery)
2. Coupled with a *present ability*
3. To commit a *violent injury* (on the person of another).

"Unlawful" Defined. Not all "assaults" are unlawful. Self defense against an assailant, for example, is legal. The necessary force used in making a lawful arrest is also legal. The force used in various athletic events such as in a boxing match or a football game are examples of "legal assaults."

"Attempt" Defined. It is important to realize that an assault is basically an attempt to commit a battery (PC 242) in most cases. To be guilty of assault, it is not necessary that the force or injury intended need actually be inflicted. There need be no contact with the victim and the victim need not be injured for the crime of assault to be complete (such as throwing a rock which misses).

The same rules apply to an assault as for other attempts. There must be more than mere intention and/or preparation or words or threats. While no actual touching is necessary , if such does occur, the crime of battery (PC 242) is committed.

Present Ability Defined. Present ability means that the act attempted is physically capable of being carried out by the assailant. It means that so far as the assailant is personally concerned, the methods he intends to use and the manner in which he or she threatens or intends to use them, will, in fact, inflict the injury intended.

Such "present ability" relates solely to the ability of the person attempting the unlawful injury. It does not refer to the fact that by some reason or some condition not controlled by the assailant, the intended injury cannot be inflicted (see "Discussion," below).

Violent Injury. The words "violent injury" as used in defining the crime of assault do *not* import that the injury attempted must be a severe one or cause great physical pain, but merely mean the unlawful application of physical force upon the person of another.

Terms "violence" and "force" are synonymous when used in relation to assault and include any application of force even though it entails no pain or bodily harm and leaves no mark (*People v. James, 9 C.A. 2d 162*).

Punishment for Assault. The penalty for assaults against private persons is a fine not exceeding $500, or by imprisonment in the county jail not exceeding six months, or by both such fine and imprisonment (PC 241).

When an assault is committed against a peace officer, firefighter, emergency medical technician, paramedic, doctor or nurse (outside a hospital) while engaged in the performance of their duties, and the assailant knows or reasonably should know that the person being assaulted is one of the above, the penalty is a fine not exceeding $1,000, or by imprisonment in the county jail not exceeding one year, or by both such fine and imprisonment (PC 241).

Term "Simple Assault" Defined. The term "simple assault" has become, by common usage, to mean a violation of PC 240, assault. The term is frequently used to differentiate from the more serious Assault With a Deadly Weapon (ADW), a violation of PC 245.

Assault Against Peace Officers, Firefighters, Other Special Classes. Over the last few years, the Legislature has made it a more serious offense to assault certain classes of persons while such persons are engaged in the performance of their duties. These laws, undoubtedly, were passed in response to a perceived increase in public and group violence and riot-like activities used as a problem-solving or attention-getting technique by some groups.

Elements. The elements of assault against these certain classes of persons is the same as for any other assault, except for the addition of three elements as follows:

1. The person assaulted must be a peace officer, firefighter, paramedic, school teacher, administrator, or security officer, bus driver, etc., as defined below.
2. The person assaulted must be engaged in the performance of his or her duties at the time of the assault.
3. The assailant knows, or reasonably should know, that the victim is one of the classes of persons named (such as a peace officer).

The Penal Code defines these special classes of persons against whom the penalty for assault is generally a fine of $1,000, or six months in the county jail, or both. In the case of custodial officers (jailors) and school district peace officers, the crime is a felony ("wobbler") punishable be either one year in the county jail or by imprisonment in the state prison. These special classes are as follows:

1. Peace officer, firefighter, emergency medical technician, mobile intensive care paramedic, physician or nurse (engaged in rendering emergency care outside of a hospital) (PC 241).
2. Custodial officer (jailor), a felony (PC 241.1).
3. Teacher, school administrator or security officer (PC 241.2).
4. Bus or cab driver, streetcar operator, etc. (PC 241.3).
5. School district peace officer, a felony (PC 241.4).

Discussion

Where the unlawful attempt to injure another has been made, the fact that the assailant failed in his attempt, or was prevented or desisted from actually inflicting the injury he was attempting, does not affect his guilt.

The attempt to injure in many cases of assault is usually very evident, especially when actual injury results, and in other cases may be inferred from the circumstances. Where the assailant threatened to kill the victim and seized an axe and started toward her and she fled and escaped, his act was held to be an assault.

The attempt need not be apparent to the victim. Victim may be unconscious, as where powder to which is attached a burning fuse may be left near the person to be assaulted, although the person intended to be injured is ignorant of such attempt.

An assailant need not have been in striking distance to inflict the blow he threatened; it is enough if he comes sufficiently near to the person threatened to warrant the belief that the blow will be instantly struck unless the intended victim defends or flees.

Since an assault is an attempt, the rules generally applicable to the law of attempts apply to both misdemeanor and felony assaults. To constitute an assault there must be more than intention or preparation or words of threat; there must be an overt act from which the inference can be drawn that violent injury to the person of another was intended. It is not necessary that the injury be intended or any injury at all shall have been inflicted. The *attempt,* coupled with the *present ability* to inflict an *unlawful injury,* constitutes the essential elements of the offense (*People v. Roder, 24 CA 477*). The term "violent injury" merely means the application of physical force on the person of another. The kind of physical force is immaterial; it may consist of taking indecent liberties with a woman or taking hold of her and kissing her against her will (*People v. Whalen, 124 CA 2d 713; People v. Bradbury, 151 C. 675*).

There is no such offense as attempted assault in California because assault is itself an attempt (*In Re James M. 9 C. 3d 517*).

Examples. Firing at a person through a door at the place where the assailant believed the potential victim to be, even though he moved and was not hit, is an assault. Where an assailant pointed an unloaded gun and attempted to fire at the victim, there was no assault because "present ability" did not exist. Note: had the assailant then thrown the gun at the victim who was nearby, an assault would have been complete. Also, had the gun been an automatic with bullets in the clip (even though no shell was in the firing chamber) the crime would have been complete because putting a shell into the chamber (present ability) would have been fast and simple (*People v. Bennett, 37 C.A. 646*). In cases where heavy objects are thrown, whether or not it is an assault depends largely on whether the victim was close enough to have been hit.

10.2   BATTERY (PC 242)

A battery is any willful and unlawful use of force or violence upon the person of another.

Battery includes and implies an assault, for there can be no battery without an assault, but there can be assault without a battery.

Battery is a completed assault and the offense of simple assault is a necessarily included offense where battery is charged.

Elements of Battery

1. Willful and unlawful.
2. Use of force or violence.
3. On the person of another.

Willful and Unlawful. Refers to the intent, and general or constructive intent will suffice to sustain a conviction. Proof of willingness to do the unlawful act is proof of the intent to commit the battery.

Gross negligence constituting a reckless disregard for other persons is sufficent. One who is grossly and wantonly negligent or reckless in exposing others to danger is presumed to have intended the natural consequences of his negligence.

Force or Violence Defined. The amount of force applied is immaterial because the gist of the offense is its unlawfulness. It need not cause any pain.

Every touching or laying hold of another, or his clothing, in an angry, revengeful, rude, insolent, or hostile manner, is a battery.

Discussion

Battery is any willful and unlawful use of force or violence upon the person of another. Battery includes an assault, but there can be an assault without a battery. Therefore, battery is a consummated assault and is a necessarily included offense where battery is charged.

It is not necessary that an assailant *directly* apply the force in battery. It would be battery to strike or frigthten a horse, causing it to bolt with its rider, or to drive a car against a person, or for one automobile driver to force another off the road, or to set a dog on a person if the dog actually bites or touches him, if the act is willful and unlawful.

Force and violence are synonymous and mean any wrongful application of physical force against the person of another, even though it causes no pain or bodily harm or leaves no mark, and even though only the feelings of such person are injured by the act. The slightest unlawful touching, if done in an insolent, rude, or angry manner, is sufficent (*People v. Flummerfelt, 153 Cal. App. 2d 104*).

Examples of Battery. To help differentiate between simple assault and battery, it has often been said that if one takes a swing at another and misses, he's committed assault. If he connects with the other person's nose, it's battery. Other examples are spitting on another, running into them with a bicycle, squirting them with water, slapping someone's face, shoveing another off a sidewalk, etc. Note that the amount of force used is not too important, except that causing very serious injury or using dangerous or deadly force can result in increased punishment or a more serious charge.

Battery—Punishment. Battery is in general punishable by a fine not exceeding $1,000, or by imprisonment in the county jail not exceeding six months or by both fine and imprisonment (PC 243(a).

Battery With Special Conditions. When a battery is committed by an assailant:
1. Who knows or reasonably should know
2. The special professional class of any of the following:
   a. Uniformed peace officer
   b. Custodial officer (jailor)
   c. Firefighter
   d. Emergency medical technician
   e. Paramedic
   f. Physician or nurse (away from hospital)
3. Which results in an "injury" (defined below)
4. While any of the above are engaged in the performance of their duty (whether officially on or off duty),

the penalty is imprisonment in the county jail for a period of not more than one year, or by a fine of not more than $1,000, or by imprisonment in the state prison for two, three, or four years (felony "wobbler") PC 243(c).

Injury Defined. "Injury" means any physical injury which requires professional medical treatment PC243(e)(1).

Battery Resulting in Serious Injury. When a battery is committed against *any person* and serious bodily injury (defined below) is inflicted on the person, the battery is punishable by imprisonment in the county jail for a period not to exceed one year or imprisonment in the state prison for two, three, or four years (felony "wobbler") PC 243(d).

Serious Bodily Injury Defined. Serious bodily injury means a serious impairment of physical condition, including, but not limited to the following:
1. Loss of consciousness;
2. Concussion;
3. Bone fracture;

4. Protracted loss or impairment of any bodily member or organ;
5. A wound requiring extensive suturing;
6. Serious disfigurement (PC 243 (d) (5).

Sexual Battery. Any person who touches an intimate part of another person while that person is unlawfully restrained by the accused or an accomplice, and if the touching is against the will of the person touched and is for the purpose of sexual arousal, gratification, or abuse, is guilty of sexual battery.

Such act is punishable by either imprisonment in the county jail for not more than one year or in the state prison for two, three, or four years (PC 243.4).

Intimate Part Defined. As used in this section, "intimate part" means the sexual organ, anus, groin, or buttocks of any person, and the breast of a female. Sexual battery does not include the crime of rape (PC 261 and PC 289). As used in this section, "touches" means physical contact with the skin of another person.

Lawful Resistance (PC 692). Lawful resistance to the commission of a public offense may be made:
1. By the party about to be injured;
2. By other parties.

Where an attack is sudden and personal danger is imminent, a person may stand his ground and slay his attacker even though it be proven that he might have more easily gained safety by flight (*People v. Dawson, 88 C.A. 2d 85*).

Resistance sufficient to prevent the offense may be made by the party about to be injured (PC 693):
1. To prevent an offense against his person, his family, or some member thereof.
2. To prevent an illegal attempt by force to take or injure property in his possession.

The owner of property is justified in using force or a deadly weapon to eject a trespasser only when it is manifest to one, as a reasonable person, that physical injury is contemplated. The owner is then entitled to use only such force as is reasonably necessary to repel attack or to protect property. (*People v. Miller, 72 C.A. 2d 602*).

Any other person, in aid or defense of the person about to be injured, may make resistance sufficient to prevent the offense (PC 694).

A person cannot set up his own standards of reasonableness or belief of injury, or of the amount of force necessary. He is limited to that which the ordinary reasonable and prudent person, placed in the same position, would be warrented in considering reasonable and necessary under the circumstances.

10.3   DRAWING OR EXHIBITING A DEADLY WEAPON (PC 417)

Except in self-defense, every person who draws, or exhibits any firearm, whether loaded or unloaded, or any other deadly weapon in a rude, angry, or threatening manner, or who uses such a weapon in a fight or quarrel, is guilty of a misdemeanor. PC417 (a) (1) and (2) *(Briefed)*.

Elements

1. Drawing or exhibiting.
2. Firearm (loaded or unloaded) or other deadly weapon.
3. Rude, angry, threatening manner.
4. Or using a firearm during a fight or quarrel.

PC 417(b) provides that any person who in the immediate presence of a peace officer, draws or exhibits any firearm, whether loaded or unloaded, in a rude, angry, or threatening manner, and who knows or reasonably should know that such victim is a peace officer engaged in the performance of his duties, and such peace officer is in fact engaged in the performance of his duties, is guilty of a felony punishable by imprisonment in the county jail for a term of not less than six months and not to exceed one year in the state prison.

As used in this section "peace officer" refers to any person designated as a peace officer by PC 830.1, subdivisions (a) to (e) and PC 830.2 and 830.5.

Possession of Deadly Weapon with Intent to Assault (PC 467). Every person having upon him any deadly weapon with intent to assault another, is guilty of a misdemeanor.

Elements

1. Possession, on the person.
2. Deadly weapon.
3. Intent (specific) to assault.

A "deadly weapon" within statutes prohibiting the carrying of deadly weapons does not cease to be such by becoming temporarily inefficient, and its essential character is not changed even by dismemberment if the parts may be easily assembled so as to become effective (*People v. Ekstrand, 28 C.A. 2d I*).

10.4   ASSAULT WITH A DEADLY WEAPON (PC 245)

Every person who commits an assault upon the person of another with a deadly weapon or instrument or by any means of force likely to produce great bodily injury is punishable by imprisonment in the state prison for two, three or four years, or in a county jail not exceeding 6 months or one year, or by fine not exceeding five thousand dollars ($5,000), or by both such fine and imprisonment. (*Briefed*)

Elements

1. Deadly weapon or instrument.
2. Force likely to produce great bodily harm or injury.

Discussion: Assault With a Deadly Weapon or Instrument

Where no direct evidence as to the nature of the weapon used is known it may be established by circumstantial evidence. Thus, where the victim suffered a severe wound such as might have been caused by a sharp instrument the jury is warranted in concluding that a deadly weapon was used (*People v. Stevens, 15 C.A. 293; People v. Lee, 23 C.A. 2d 168*).

Whether or not a particular object or instrument is a deadly weapon depends not upon the use for which it was originally suited or intended but upon whether it was used in a manner likely to produce death or great bodily injury (*People v. Robertson, 217 C. 671; People v. Lee, 23 C.A. 2d 168*).

Where defendant intentionally accelerated his automobile and steered directly at the victim, striking the latter on the legs, a conviction of assault was sustained (*People v. Flummerfelt, 153 C.A. 2d 104*).

In a case in which defendant drove his automobile at night without lights on a public highway and struck a pedestrian it was held that the jury was warranted in finding that the defendant, by such conduct on his part, intended the natural and probable consequence of his acts (*People v. Vasquez, 85 C.A. 575*).

Presenting a loaded gun in a threatening manner, pointed at the back of another, and lowering it when the latter's wife screamed is, regardless of the defendant's reason for not firing, an assault with a deadly weapon (*People v. Dodini, 51 C.A. 179; People v. Bennet, 37 C.A. 324*).

Firing a rifle to frighten decedent and another without aiming at them and without intending to kill or injure anyone, though unlawful, (see PC 417) would not amount to a felony and would fall short of the offense of ADW or even simple assault (*People v. Carmen, 36 C. 2d 768*).

Discussion: Assault by Any Means Likely to Produce Bodily Injury

To commit this form of felonious assault it is not necessary that the defendant shall have used a weapon or other instrument as the means of the assault as it is the violence and likelihood of the assault to produce great bodily injury that is the gist of this offense (*People v. Tallman, 27 C. 2d 209; People v. Yancy, 171 C.A. 2d 371*).

Convictions of this offense have been sustained where the means used were the hands and knees (*People v. Kimmrle, 90 C.A. 186*).

Throwing a person out of a window (*People v. Emmons, 61 C. 487*); knocking a person down and kicking him (*People v. Blake, 129 C.A. 196*); choking the victim (*People v. Blumbaugh, 48 C.A. 2d 791*); vicious assaults with the fists alone; pushing victim so his head hits the parking meter (*People v. Conley, 110 C.A. 2d 731*) are examples of this offense.

Where, after being stopped for questioning by officers, defendant fled in his car and, in departing from the scene, his left front fender struck one of the officers standing in the street, throwing him against another car and inflicting minor injuries, the conviction was sustained.

Intent. The requisite intent for the commission of an assault with a deadly weapon is the intent to commit a battery. Reckless conduct alone does *not* constitute a sufficient basis for assault or for battery even if the assault results in an injury to another. However, when an act inherently dangerous to others is committed with a conscious disregard of human life and safety, the act transcends recklessness, and the intent to commit a battery is presumed (*People v. Lathus, 35 Cal. App 3d 466; 10 Cal. Rptr. 921*).

ADW Against Peace Officers and Firemen. Every person who commits an assault with a deadly weapon or instrument, other than a firearm, or by any means likely to produce great bodily injury, upon a policeman (as defined in PC 830.1, 830.2 and 830.5) or a fireman, and who knows or should reasonably know that such victim is a peace officer or fireman, while the policeman or fireman is performing his duty, shall be punished by imprisonment in the state prison for three, four, or five years (PC 245(b) (*briefed*).

10.5 ASSAULT WITH CAUSTIC CHEMICALS (PC 244)

Every person who willfully and maliciously places or throws, or causes to be placed or thrown, upon the person of another, any vitriol, corrosive acid, or caustic chemical of any nature, with the intent to injure the flesh or disfigure the body of such person, is punishable by imprisonment in state prison for two, three or four years.

Elements

1. Willfully and maliciously.
2. Places or throws; causes to be placed or thrown.
3. Upon the person of another.
4. Vitriol, corrosive acid, or caustic chemical.
5. With intent (specific) to injure the flesh or disfigure.

Specific intent to either injure the flesh or disfigure the body must be proven as an independent factor.

If such intent is absent or the act is done with another intent, the offense is not committed.

The offense is complete if any quantity of substance described, however small in quantity or however weak in strength and however incapable of producing great bodily harm, is thrown or placed upon the person of another, if done willfully and maliciously with intent to injure the flesh or to disfigure to the slightest extent the body of another. If the substance described in this section is thrown toward an intended victim but misses, it is not a violation of this section but could be prosecuted under Section 245.

The crime of assault by means of force likely to produce great bodily injury is not an offense necessarily included within the offense of assault with caustic chemicals (*People v. Warren, 233 C.A. 2d 798*).

10.6 POISONING FOOD, DRINK, WATER, MEDICINE (PC 347)

Poisoning Food, Drink. Any person who willfully mingles any poison with any food, drink or medicine with intent that the same shall be taken by any human being to his injury, and every person who willfully poisons any spring, well or reservoir of water is punishable by a term in state prison of two, three or four years (PC 347).

Poisoning Alcoholic Beverages (PC 347b). It is unlawful for any person, firm, or corporation to manufacture, sell, furnish, or give away, or offer to do so, any alcoholic solution of a potable nature containing any deleterious or posionous substance. Violation is punishable by fine up to twenty-five hundred dollars ($2,500) and/or one year in county jail.

10.7 THROWING OBJECTS OR SHOOTING AT VEHICLES, DWELLINGS, AIRCRAFT

Throwing Substance at Vehicle (CVC 23110). (a): Any person who throws any substance at a vehicle or any occupant thereof on a highway is guilty of a misdemeanor.

(b): Any person, who with intent to do great bodily injury, maliciously and willfully throws or projects any rock, brick, bottle, metal or other missile, or projects any other substance capable of doing serious bodily harm, is guilty of a felony.

Shooting at Aircraft. Any person who willfully and maliciously discharges a firearm at an aircraft, whether parked, in motion, or in flight, and whether occupied or unoccupied is guilty of a felony (PC 247).

Throwing Missiles at Common Carriers (PC 219.1). This includes the throwing, hurling, and projecting of any type of missile at any common carrier vehicle or any other unlawful act done with the intent of wrecking such vehicle or injuring any person. Where a wreck does occur and bodily harm occurs, it is a felony and punishable in state prison for two, four, or six years.

Shooting at Common Carriers (PC 219.2). Includes willfully throwing, hurling, or projecting any hard substance, or shooting at any common carrier. Punishable by a fine of one thousand ($1,000) dollars, and/or one year in jail or in state prison.

Shooting at Inhabited Dwelling House, Occupied Building, Inhabited House, Car or Camper. Any person who shall maliciously and willfully discharge a firearm at an inhabited dwelling house, occupied building, occupied motor vehicle, inhabited housecar (VC 362) or inhabited camper (VC 243) is guilty of a felony and upon conviction shall be punished by imprisonment in the state prison for two, three, or four years or by imprisonment in the county jail for a term of not less than six months and not exceeding one year.

Building Defined. A "building" is a structure that is regularly occupied, wholly or partially, as a habitation by human beings and includes any store, church, schoolhouse, railway station, or other place of assembly (Health & Safety Code 12171). "Building," also means any apartment house, hotel, or dwelling, either singly or in combination (Health & Safety Code 15006).

Inhabited Defined. As used in this section "inhabited" means currently being used for dwelling purposes, whether occupied or not (PC 246).

10.8 DUELS AND CHALLENGES

A duel is any combat with deadly weapons, fought between two or more persons, by previous agreement or upon a previous quarrel (PC 225).

Elements

1. Mutual combat with deadly weapons.
2. Two or more persons.
3. Agreement or understanding.

Punishment for Duel With Death Resulting (PC 226). Every person guilty of fighting a duel, from which death ensues within a year and a day, is punishable by imprisonment in state prison for two, three or four years.

Punishment; Fighting; Sending or Accepting Challenge (PC 227). Every person who fights a duel, or who sends or accepts a challenge to fight a duel, is punishable by imprisonment in state prison or county jail not to exceed one year.

Civil Code 3347: If any person slays or permanently disables another in a duel in this state, the slayer must provide for the maintenance of the widow or wife of the person slain or permanently disabled, and for the minor children, in such a manner and at such cost, either by aggregate compensation in damages to each, or by a monthly, quarterly, or annual allowance to be determined by the court.

Civil Code 3348: If any person slays or permanently disables another in a duel in this state, the slayer is liable for and must pay all debts of the person slain or permanently disabled.

Officers' Duty to Prevent Duel (PC 230). Every judge, sheriff, or other officer bound to preserve the public peace, who had knowledge of the intention on the part of any person to fight a duel, and who does not exert his official authority to arrest the party and prevent the duel, is punishable by fine not exceeding one thousand dollars ($1,000).

10.9 ASSAULT WITH INTENT TO COMMIT CERTAIN FELONIES (PC 220)

Every person who assaults another with intent to commit mayhem, rape, sodomy, oral copulation, or any violation of Section 264.1, 288 or 289, is punishable by imprisonment in the state prison for two, four or six years.

Elements

1. Direct, ineffectual act.
2. Specific intent.
3. To commit mayhem, rape, sodomy, oral copulation or any violation of PC 264.1 (aiding in forcible rape), PC 288 (lewd act on child under 14), or PC 289 (forcible penetration of genital or anal opening by foreign object).

Discussion

There must exist in the mind of the assailant the intent to so act that, if he carried his intent to completion he would have committed one of the crimes specified.

An "assault with intent to commit a crime" necessarily embraces an "attempt" but does not necessarily include an "assault" (*People v. Akin, 25 C.A. 373, 1914*).

Assault With Intent to Commit Rape. The crime is complete if at any moment during the assault the accused intends to have sex with the victim against her will and to use for that purpose whatever force may be required.

When evidence showed that the defendant had attacked the victim on a street at a place where there were no lights, had thrown her down, put his hands under her clothes, torn her underclothing, struck her when she screamed and left when people approached, a conviction was sustained.

Where defendant grabbed a woman who had gone up a hill to look at a view, and threatened to cut her throat if she screamed, and struck her several blows across the face and head when she did scream, and did not ask for any money and, where when the woman fell to the ground, defendant ran away, desisting when in the struggle he cut his thumb, a conviction was sustained.

When a strange man entered the bedroom of a woman, covered her mouth with his hand, grasped her wrist while she screamed and kicked, released her when she bit his hand, and made no effort to take any property, it was reasonable to infer the he intended to commit rape, particularly when such intent was shown by his attempt to rape another woman under similar circumstances in the same month (*People v. Nye, 38 C. 2d 34*).

There may be an assault with intent to commit rape where an assault is committed upon a female under the age of eighteen years with the intent to accomplish an act of sexual intercourse with her even though there be no intent to accomplish that act by force or against her will.

Assault to Commit Sodomy. The offense is complete when the assault has been committed with specific intent to commit the act attempted.

On evidence that the defendant placed his penis between a boy's thighs for several minutes and made movements indicating an attempt to accomplish penetration, a conviction was sustained even though both the defendant and the boy testified that no penetration occurred.

Where accused was interrupted by the sudden and unexpected intrusion of a third person, and his attempt ot commit a sodomy aborted, it did not prevent his conviction of an assault with intent to commit the crime (*People v. Dong Pok Yip, 164 C. 143*).

Assault With Intent to Commit Mayhem, Oral Copulation. PC 220, in effect, makes it a crime to assault another with intent to commit any of the crimes specified. This section, therefore, describes a type of *attempt* to commit the crimes enumerated. In many instances the perpetrator could be charged with either PC 220 or an attempt to commit the crime intended. PC 220 is usually charged, however, because it may be easier to prove and carries a greater penalty than an attempt. Attempts are punishable with one–half the sentence that would have been imposed if the crime was completed.

One can be found guilty of PC 220 even if the crime intended during the assault was *not* completed. To be guilty of assault to commit mayhem, for example, it is not necessary that the victim be disfigured (as described in PC 203) or even seriously injured. If, however, the purpose or intent of the assault is actually accomplished, the perpetrator could be charged with committing the specific crime actually completed.

10.10   ADMINISTERING STUPEFYING DRUGS (PC 222)

Every person guilty of administering to another any chloroform, ether, laudanum, or other narcotic, anesthetic, or intoxicating agent, with intent thereby to enable or assist himself or any other person to commit a felony, is guilty of a felony.

Elements

1. Specific intent to commit a felony.

2. Narcotic, anesthetic, or intoxicating substance.

Discussion

The term "intoxicating agent" includes any drug, substance or compound which, when introduced into the human system, produces a serious disturbance of the physical and mental equilibrium by causing sleep, stupor, unconsciousness, or semi–unconsciousness together with impairment of the power of self–control.

10.11   TRAIN WRECKING (PC 218)

Every person who unlawfully throws out a switch, removes a rail, or places any obstruction or explosive material on any railroad with the intention of derailing any passenger, freight, or other train, car, or engine is guilty of a felony punishable by life imprisonment (briefed).

Elements

1. Specific intent to derail.
2. By throwing switch, removal of rail, or placing obstruction.
3. Uses an explosive substance.

Discussion

This section also includes the following: use of dynamite or other explosive material; use of any other obstruction upon or near the track of any railroad with intention of blowing up or derailing such train, car or engine; or unlawfully setting fire to any railroad bridge or trestle, over which such train, car, or engine must pass with the intention of wrecking such train, car, or engine.

PC 219 is worded the same as Section 218 with the exception that it requires a train, or a portion thereof, be blown up or derailed. Penalties in such cases are more severe.

10.12   MAYHEM (PC 203)

Every person who unlawfully and maliciously deprives a human being of a member of his body, or disables, disfigures, or renders it useless, or cuts or disables the tongue, or puts out an eye, or slits the nose, ear, or lip, is guilty of mayhem. Mayhem is punishable by imprisonment in the state prison for two, four, or six years (*PC 204*).

Elements

1. General intent.

2. To disable, disfigure or render useless.
3. Tongue, eye, nose, ear or lip.
4. By permanent disability.

Discussion

Assault is a lesser and included offense to mayhem (*People v. DeFoor, 100 Cal. 150*).

It is not necessary to show a deliberate or premeditated intent to commit mayhem; the act committed must be done unlawfully and in a malicious state of mind.

It is sufficient to prove only the commission of the act from which the law will presume that it was done unlawfully and maliciously, unless done under circumstances of self–defense, within reason.

If a person unlawfully strikes another and the blow results in the loss or disfigurement of a member of the victim's body or putting out of an eye, the crime is mayhem.

However, evidence disclosing that defendant struck victim several times with a steel pipe resulting in laceration of the lip and nose did not support premise that defendant specifically intended to maim victim (*People v. Sears, 62 C.A. 783*).

10.13 ABANDONMENT OF ASSAULT

Where the acts of a person have proceeded to the extent of amounting in law to an assault, the abandonment by the perpetrator of his purpose before he has accomplished the object for which the assault was committed does not free him from the consequences of his acts.

A defendant is guilty of the assault whether he voluntarily ceases his attack, whether he desisted because of the resistance of his intended victim, or because of the approach of other parties permitting his victim to escape (*People v. Jones, 112 Cal. App. 68*).

Discussion

The fact that defendant voluntarily abandoned his attempt to have sexual intercourse did not indicate that intent to commit rape was not present (*People v. House, 157 C.A. 2d 151*).

Where there is intent to commit a crime, coupled with an overt act, the abandonment of the criminal purpose is no defense to a charge of attempt to commit the crime, in view of PC 664 (*People v. Carter, 70 C.A. 495*).

The fact that a man desisted from attempt to have intercourse with a fourteen–year–old girl when told by her that he was hurting her does not purge him of the crime of attempt to commit rape by assault (*People v. Esposti, 82 C.A. 2d 76*).

If assault with intent to commit rape is made, it is no less a crime, though aggressor should abandon his intentions before consummation of the act (*People v. Bradley, 71 C.A. 2d 114*).

10.14 ASSAULTS—JUSTIFICATION AND EXCUSE

If the use of force, even though it involves an intent to commit physical injuries upon another, is lawful there is no assault.

Consent to an Assault. A person may consent to an assault and battery providing:
1. It is voluntary.
2. It does not disturb the public peace.

Justification for an Assault. The law allows a person to commit certain acts which would ordinarily be considered unlawful, but under certain conditions are not considered unlawful, either because of the law or public policy.

The use of force necessary to accomplish a lawful arrest, corporal punishment (within lawful limits) of a child, etc., would not constitute assault, unless the application of force become unlawful.

Physical injuries inflicted by accident and misfortune in the doing of a lawful act by lawful means and without negligence or criminal intent could not be the basis of a charge of assault.

In action for assault and battery, based on defendant's acts in grabbing a twelve–year–old boy, whom he accused of exploding a firecracker in the vicinity of his home, advising the boy that he was taking him to his parents, shaking the boy when the boy directed filthy language toward him, and in hitting the boy when, on the boy's breaking away, his open hand came in contact with the boy's face, the court chose to believe defendant's testimony that the act was unintentional.

10.15 BATTERY AGAINST COHABITING PERSONS

PC 273.5. Infliction of Corporal Injury Upon Person of Opposite Sex With Whom Cohabiting. (a) Any person who willfully inflicts upon his or her spouse or any person who willfully inflicts upon any person of the opposite sex with whom he or she is cohabiting (living with), corporal injury resulting in a traumatic condition (any injury except the most minor), is guilty of a felony and upon conviction thereof shall be punished by imprisonment in the state prison for two, three, or four years, or in the county jail for not more than one year.

(b) Holding oneself out to be the husband or wife of the person with whom one is cohabiting is not necessary to constitute cohabitation as the term is used in this section.

Willful Cruelty, Unjustified Punishment, Endangering Life or Health of Child.

1. Any person who, under circumstances or conditions likely to produce great bodily harm or death, willfully causes or permits any child to suffer, or inflicts thereon unjustifiable physical pain or mental suffering, or having the care or custody of any child, willfully causes or permits the person or health of such child to be injured, or willfully causes or permits such child to be placed in such situation that its person or health is endangered, is punishable by imprisonment in the county jail not exceeding one year, or in the state prison for 2, 3, or 4 years.
2. Any person who, under circumstances or conditions *other* than those likely to produce great bodily harm or death, willfully causes or permits any child to suffer, or inflicts thereon unjustifiable physical pain or mental suffering, or willfully causes or permits the person or health of such child to be injured, or willfully causes or permits such child to be placed in such situation that its person or health may be endangered, is guilty of a misdemeanor (PC 273a).

PC 273d. Cruel or Inhuman Punishment of a Child.
Any person who willfully inflicts upon any child any cruel or inhuman corporal punishment or injury resulting in a traumatic condition is guilty of a felony, and upon conviction thereof shall be punished by imprisonment in the state prison for 2, 3, or 4 years, or in the county jail for not more than one year.

Discussion

A parent or other person standing in *loco parentis,* chastising his child, does not commit a criminal assault and battery if the punishment administered is reasonable. On the other hand, if a parent uses an instrument likely to cause serious injury, or inflicts punishment to an immoderate extent, either of which would indicate an intent to injure rather than to correct, such person is liable to prosecution for a criminal offense.

Formerly a husband could punish his wife under the common law upon the theory that wives were amenable to the discipline of their husbands rather than the king's officers. Gradually, however, this privilege of husbands was withdrawn and, as indicated in the statute, contemporary legislation punishes such acts as felony offenses.

The *corpus delicti* of the offense of inflicting corporal injury upon a child was established when it was shown that such injury had been inflicted upon a child by the defendant, and circumstances and injuries to the child demonstrated that such injuries had been deliberately and intentionally inflicted upon her, and these facts, having been established independently of the defendant's statement that he had hit the child, were admissible (*People v. Lawrence, 141 C.A. 2d 630*).

10.16   VICTIMS OF VIOLENT CRIME STATUTE

For many years the State of California has had a statute addressed to the aid of victims of violent crimes. However, less than one percent of victims have availed themselves of financial relief through the statute. For this reason the State Legislature enacted Government Code Section 13959 which became effective July 1, 1974.

Section 13968 (c) of the Government Code provides as follows:

It shall be the duty of every local law enforcement agency to inform victims of violent crimes of the provisions of this chapter and to provide application forms to victims who desire to seek assistance pursuant to this article. The State Board of Control shall provide application forms and all other documents which local law enforcement agencies may require to comply with this section. The Attorney General shall set standards to be followed by local law enforcement agencies for this purpose and may require them to file with him a description of the procedures adopted by each agency to comply.

Police Requirements. The above law requires law enforcement officers to provide victims or their families a sheet describing the victim program and where to obtain application forms. Because the field officer or investigator has other pressures on him at the time of contact with victims, the California State Department of Justice has provided an alternative method of complying with this law.

Alternative Procedures. The Records, Detective, or Service Bureaus may, as a normal part of the processing of reports for file, mail a copy of the application form to each victim who is qualified to file a claim with the State of California and will affix a rubber stamped notation on the Record Bureau copy of the report which states: "Victim(s) notification of Government Code 13968 mailed date _____."

This procedure will remove the officer's responsibility of providing the forms to the victims, but the field officer in contact with such victims must be aware of the program and some of its basics. There will be occasions when victims will ask officers about the program.

Victim's Responsibility. The reverse side of the application (Board of Control Form 1-D) provides the essential information about the program. It is the responsibility of the victim to satisfy the Board of Control of need for indemnification. The claimant will be contacted following receipt by the Board of Control of need for indemnification. The claimant will be contacted following receipt by the Board of Control of the application form. The Board provides a questionnaire which requests details, supporting documents, and data on the victim's assets, obligations, losses, and reimbursements. The claimant must also at that time sign an authorization permitting the Attorney General's representatives to obtain and examine all medical and family records related to the victim's injuries and financial status.

Victim Must Cooperate. If a victim refuses to cooperate with the criminal justice system, this information must be available to the Board of Control. The best manner to assure that this is done is to write a supplement indentifying the problem. A copy of the report must be sent to the Board of Control, Sacramento.

Public Hearings. The State Board of Control holds informal public hearings. Claimants are notified at least five days prior to the hearing. One meeting per month is held in Los Angeles and two per month in Sacramento. No meetings are held at other locations. The victim may request that the hearing be set or continued to the location most convenient for appearance, either Los Angeles or Sacramento. The victim may appear personally, be represented by counsel, or may waive appearance at the hearing. The application will be considered in any event.

Required Information. When the Board convenes it will consider the following factors: Whether the victim was a resident of the State of California at the time of the incident; whether a financial loss was incurred which caused serious financial hardship; whether the victim substantially contributed by his or her actions to the injuries (if the incident was an automobile accident, this code does not apply except in hit and run or when caused by a person driving under the influence of alcohol or drugs); whether the victim has cooperated in promptly supplying all requested information and documents; and last, and most important is, whether the victim cooperated with law enforcement agencies.

Attorney General Investigation. An investigation is required by the Attorney General for all applications to be heard by the Board of Control. A report is submitted by the AG to the Board, together with any evidence which may have been obtained, as a result of the investigation.

Who May File. Either the victim or a person dependent upon the victim for support, may file. If the victim is deceased anyone who legally or voluntarily assumed the burial or medical expenses may file. The application must be presented to the Board of Control within one year after the date of the crime, unless an extension is granted by the Board.

Maximum Damages. The maximum amounts the Board may approve are $10,000 for medical or hospital expenses, $10,000 for loss of wages or support, and $3,000 for job retraining or rehabilitation services. These are the maximum amounts authorized under the existing legislation which became effective July 1, 1974. Claimants for crimes which took place prior to July 1 of 1974 can be reimbursed to a total of $5,000.

Legal Fees and Personal Property Loss. The Board may award funds for legal services rendered to the applicant which shall not exceed 10 percent of the amount of the award or $500, whichever is less.

Damage to or loss of personal property, as a result of a crime, will not be indemnified under this code. In all cases the amount of the reimbursement will be reduced by the amount of indemnification to the victim from any other source.

Intent of the Law. The intent of this code is to assist in reducing the financial pressure brought upon the victim as a result of the crime, and in no case is it intended that an improved financial situation shall result for the victim above that which existed prior to becoming a victim.

Implementation. Funding and responsibility for the performance of the Victims of Violent Crime Statute rests at the State level but requires participation at the local level for its success.

TERMINOLOGY DEFINED—CHAPTER 10

See the Terminology Quiz at the end of this chapter.

1. Caustic: corrosive, irritating, capable of burning such as acid.
2. Corporal injury: injury to the body, usually by striking, etc.
3. Enjoin: to prohibit, to command, to require (see Injunction).
4. Injunction: court order prohibiting or requiring some act.
5. *Loco parentis*: Latin meaning "in place of parents."
6. Mayhem: crime of severing another's finger, ear, eye, etc.
7. *Modus operandi*: Latin meaning "method of operation."
8. Moulage: casting used to preserve tire track, footprint, etc.
9. *Nolo contendere*: Latin for "no contest," a type of plea.
10. *Non compos mentis*: Latin meaning "not of sound mind," insane.
11. Parole: conditional release of felon from prison.
12. Peace Officer: persons defined as having police powers in PC 832.
13. Plaintiff: one who is bringing a court action, civil or criminal.
14. Plea: accused's answer to charges against him in court.
15. Police power: State's authority to restrict private rights for public welfare.
16. Present ability: actual immediate possibility of accomplishment.
17. *Quasi*: Latin meaning "similar to," e.g. quasimilitary.
18. Simple assault: usually refers to misdemeanor assault.
19. Traumatic: injury, normally caused by violence.
20. Violent injury: in assault, any unlawful application of force on another.

6. Pointing an unloaded gun at another in an angry, rude or threatening manner constitutes assault.
7. Battery is the willful and unlawful use of force or violence on the person of another.
8. Unlawfully spitting on another constitutes battery.
9. There can be no assault without also committing battery.
10. To be guilty of ADW, some instrument or weapon must be involved.
11. In ADW, where no direct evidence as to the nature of the weapon is known, it may be established by circumstantial evidence.
12. Specific intent to injure the flesh or cause disfigurement is necessary in assault with caustic chemicals.
13. Any person who throws any substance at a vehicle or any occupant thereof on a highway is guilty of a felony.
14. Assault with intent to commit rape is a general intent crime.
15. Assault is a lesser and included offense of mayhem.
16. Accidently cutting off a person's ear during an assault without specifically intending to do so constitutes the crime of mayhem.
17. PC 273d, felony wife beating, is applicable if the couple are in fact living together as husband and wife even though not legally married.
18. Only parents and persons standing in *loco parentis* are subject to PC 273(d), inflicting cruel corporal punishment on a child.
19. Government Code 13968(c) requires the police to provide victims of violent crimes or their families with information as to their rights to financial aid.
20. Financial aid is available to victims of drunk drivers and hit and run crimes where injury is involved under Gov. Code 13968(c).

TRUE-FALSE QUIZ—CHAPTER 10

1. An assault is an unlawful attempt, coupled with a present ability to commit a violent injury on the person of another.
2. No actual touching of another is necessary to constitute assault.
3. In the absence of "present ability" there can be no assault.
4. The words "violent injury" as used in assault import a serious injury.
5. Assaults against on-duty police officers and firemen is a felony.

ESSAY-DISCUSSION QUESTIONS—CHAPTER 10

1. What are the three elements of simple assault? Are certain assaults ever lawful?
2. Define battery and discuss the difference between simple assault and battery.
3. What are the elements of PC 417? Must the weapon be a firearm? If so, must it be loaded?
4. Discuss the elements of ADW (P.C. 245). Must actual injury be inflicted? Must injury be intended?

5. What are the five elements of P.C. 244, assault with caustic chemicals? What is the intent required?
6. What are the elements of P.C. 220, assault with intent to commit certain felonies? Discuss the type of intent required and how proven.
7. In P.C. 222, administering stupefying drugs, what specific intent must be proven? Is administering of alcohol covered?
8. What are the elements of P.C. 203, mayhem? What is the intent which must be proven?
9. What are the current police requirements relative to advising victims of violent crimes of their rights under Gov. Code 13968(c)?

TERMINOLOGY QUIZ—CHAPTER 10

Match terms and definitions by placing the correct number in the parentheses. Answers may be written on a separate sheet for submission to the instructor at the instructor's direction.

1. Caustic
2. Corporal injury
3. Enjoin
4. Injunction
5. *Loco parentis*
6. Mayhem
7. *Modus operandi*
8. Moulage
9. *Nolo contendere*
10. *Non compos mentis*
11. Parole
12. Peace officer
13. Plaintiff
14. Plea
15. Police power
16. Present ability
17. *Quasi*
18. Simple assault
19. Traumatic
20. Violent injury

( ) conditional release of felon from prison
( ) "no contest," a type of plea
( ) crime of severing another's finger, ear, etc.
( ) in assault, any use of unlawful force on another
( ) "similar to," somewhat like
( ) an injury normally caused by violence
( ) corrosive, irritating, capable of burning
( ) one who brings a court action
( ) "in place of parents"
( ) "not of sound mind"
( ) actual immediate possibility of accomplishment
( ) accused's answer to charges against him in court
( ) court order prohibiting or requiring some act
( ) "method of operation"
( ) persons defined in PC 832

CHAPTER 11

Homicides

11.1 HOMICIDE DEFINED

Homicide is the killing of a human being by another human being and may be either justifiable or excusable, in which case it is *not* unlawful; or it may be *felonious*, in which event it is a crime and therefore punishable. The word "homicide" is used to describe *all* taking of human life by human act or agency whether lawfully or unlawfully (PC 187-199).

The Killing. In order that one may commit homicide the first requirement is that he caused the death of the deceased. The death may be the result of a person committing or omitting an act which proximately (directly) causes death in an unlawful manner.

Corpus Delicti. *Corpus delicti* means "the body of the crime" or the essential elements of an offense, and does not necessarily refer to the body of a deceased person in a homicide case. This is especially true in California, since the existence of a dead body in a homicide case is not an essential element of the crime of murder or manslaughter (*People v. Scott, 176 C.A. 2d 458*).

The *corpus delicti* of *felonious* (criminal) homicide consists of two basic elements: (1) death of a human being, and (2) an unlawful act or criminal agency causing such death (*People v. Miller, 37 Cal. 2d 801*). It is not necessary that there be direct evidence as to the means used to accomplish the killing in attempting to prove the *corpus delicti* of homicide; such may, as previously indicated, be proven by circumstantial evidence (*People v. Wetzel, 198 C.A. 2d 541*).

Proximate Cause. If there is an intervening cause which is not the result of the defendant's act so that death is not connected therewith in a regular chain of causes and consequences, the defendant is not responsible. If a mortal wound was inflicted by an assailant and someone else inflicts another mortal wound, the assailant is not relieved of his responsibility for the death of the victim. The same is true should a victim develop blood poisoning as a result of a wound which ordinarily would not be fatal but becomes so due to the intervening illness.

One who commits euthanasia (mercy killing) bears no ill toward his victim and believes his act is morally justified, but he nonetheless acts with malice if he is able to comprehend that society prohibits his act regardless of his personal beliefs (*People v. Conley, 64 A.C. 321*).

The crime may be murder although the person killed is not the one whom the accused intended to kill (*People v. McAuliffe, 154 A.C. 2d 332*).

Proof of Death. Since in California both death and the criminal agency (act causing death) may be proven by circumstantial evidence, a physical body need not be produced. Evidence may be based on eye witnesses, parts of the body, or otherwise circumstantially. The fact that a person is merely missing is not sufficient evidence to support a *prima facie* case of homicide. It should also be noted that one cannot be convicted on his confession alone. However, confessions in this case would be admissible and may be sufficient if corroborated by other circumstances and additional evidence.

Circumstantial evidence supported a first-degree murder conviction of a wife whose husband died as a result of chronic, sub-acute, and acute arsenic poisoning over a four-month period (*People v. Helwinkel, 199 C.A. 2d 207*). In the prosecution of a homicide case, circumstantial evidence can be sufficient to supply proof of guilt so convincing as to preclude every hypothesis of innocence (*People v. Scott, 176 C.A. 2d 458*).

Time of Death

PC 194. Death Must Occur Within Three Years and a Day. To make the killing either murder or manslaughter, it is requisite that the party die within three years and a day after the stroke received or the cause of death administered. In the computation of such time, the whole of the day on which the act was done shall be reckoned the first. (*Amended, Stats. 1969, Chap. 593.*)

11.2 MURDER DEFINED (PC 187)

a. Murder is the unlawful killing of a human being, or a fetus, with malice aforethought.
b. This section shall not apply to any person who commits an act which results in the death of a fetus if any of the following apply:
   1. The act complied with the Therapeutic Abortion Act, Chapter II (commencing with Section 25950) of Division 20 of the Health and Safety Code.
   2. The act was committed by a holder of a physician's and surgeon's certificate, as defined in the Business and Professions Code, in a case where, to a medical certainty, the result of childbirth would be death from childbirth, although not medically certain, would be substantially certain or more likely than not.
   3. The act was solicited, aided, abetted, or consented to by the mother of the fetus.
c. Subdivision (b) shall not be construed to prohibit the prosecution of any person under any provision of law.

PC 1105. "Upon a trial for murder, the commission of the homicide by the defendant being proven, the burden of proving circumstances of mitigation, or that justify or excuse it, devolves upon him, unless the proof on the part of the prosecution tends to show that the crime committed only amounts to manslaughter, or that the defendant was justifiable or excusable."

Malice. PC 188. Such malice may be express or implied. It is express when there is manifested a deliberate intention unlawfully to take away the life of a fellow creature. It is implied when no considerable provocation appears, or when the circumstances attending the killing show an abandoned or malignant heart.

When it is shown that the killing resulted from the intentional doing of an act with express or implied malice as defined above, no other mental state need be shown to establish the mental state of malice aforethought. Neither an awareness of the obligation to act within the general body of laws regulating society nor acting despite such awareness is included within the definition of malice."

Malice aforethought does not necessarily mean an actual intention to kill the deceased, nor does it necessarily imply deliberation; rather, it denotes purpose and design as contrasted with accident or mischance or misfortune. It is present when there is an intention to cause death or grievous bodily harm, or knowledge that one's acts will probably so result, when committed in the commission of a felony or other act which proves inherently dangerous to others.

Malice does not necessarily mean hatred or personal ill will toward the person killed, nor an actual intent to take his life, or anyone's life for that matter. Thus, if the killing was for the purpose of robbery, without any hatred or ill will against the person killed, it would be homicide, in this case, the crime of first-degree murder. The killing may be unintentional, or committed in the commission of another crime, or merely by doing a reckless and dangerous act, yet the law deems that malice aforethought must be present in murder, whether it be in the first or second degree.

Express Malice. Express malice is always present in first-degree murder and is considered to be present where the evidence shows a deliberate intention unlawfully to take the life of another human being; where one kills another with a sedate, deliberate mind and formed design.

Although malice aforethought is an essential element of murder of the second as well as first degree, such malice is not synonymous with the elements of deliberation and premeditation (*People v. Lewie, 174 C.A. 2d 177*).

Where homicide is committed by means of torture, the means used are conclusive evidence of express malice (*People v. Butler, 205 C.A. 2d 437*).

Requisite malice required for murder in the first degree is demonstrated when the evidence shows a deliberate intention to take the life of another human being (*People v. Keeling, 152 C.A. 2d 4*).

Implied Malice. Implied malice has been defined as that which arises or may be inferred from the intentional doing of an unlawful or wrongful act with a wrongful purpose. Implied malice exists where the killing was done suddenly, without justification or excuse, and without provocation, or without provocation sufficient to reduce the homicide to manslaughter.

Malice may be implied when no considerable provocation appears, or when the circumstances attending the killing show an abandoned and malignant heart (*People v. Dugger, 179 C.A. 2d 714*).

Malice as an element of murder is implied where the defendant with antisocial motives and with utter disregard for human life engages in conduct involving high probability of resultant death (*Brooks v. Superior Court, Los Angeles County, 239 A.C.A. 593*).

Evidence of a lack of considerable provocation for a killing, and where the circumstances attending the killing showed an abandoned and malignant heart, malice for such killing may be implied (*People v. Calderon, 195 C.A. 2d 576* and *People v. Hudgins, 236 C.A. 2d 578*).

An act which involves natural consequences inherently dangerous to life and is performed by one who knows that his conduct endangers the life of another need not be unlawful to make the killing proximately resulting from the act second-degree murder, which requires implied malice (*People v. Phillips, 64 A.C. 629*).

11.3 DEGREES OF MURDER (PC 189)

All murder which is perpetrated by means of a destructive device, explosive, knowing use of ammunition designed primarily to penetrate metal or armor, poison, lying in wait, torture, or by any other kind of willful, deliberate, and premeditated killing, or which is committed in the perpetration of, or attempts to perpetrate, arson, rape, robbery, burglary, mayhem or any act punishable under Section 288, is murder in the first degree, and all other kinds of murder are of the second degree.

As used in this section, "destructive device" shall mean any destructive device as defined in Section 12301 and "explosive" shall mean any explosive as defined in Section 12000 of the Health and Safety Code.

First Degree Murder

Armor Piercing Ammunition. As stated above, the knowing use of armor piercing or metal piercing ammunition in a murder makes it first degree. This provision was added by the legislature shortly after the police and many corporate executives began wearing bullet-proof vests.

Except for police and military use, it is a felony to manufacture, import or possess metal or armor piercing ammunition (PC 12320, PC 12311 and PC 12322).

Destructive Device Defined. Murder becomes first degree if either a destructive device or an explosive is used to cause death. A "destructive device" is defined

as any of the following (PC 12301):
1. Any projectile containing an explosive.
2. Any bomb, grenade or explosive missile.
3. Any weapon or fixed ammunition of a caliber greater than .60.
4. Any rocket or rocket propelled projectile.
5. Any breakable container of flammable liquid.

Explosive Defined. An explosive is any highly volatile chemical, nitroglycerine, dynamite, gunpowder as described in Health & Safety Code 12000.

Poison. The word poison includes any substance which, when applied to the human body externally or in any way introduced into the human system without acting mechanically, is capable of destroying life. Thus the introduction of poison into a person's system over a period of time which proximately results in the person's death is first-degree murder.

Lying in Wait. The gist of lying in wait is that the perpetrator places himself in a position where he is waiting and watching with the intention of inflicting bodily injury likely to cause the death of another. Lying in wait, which does not require the perpetrator to be in a prone or reclining position, may be likened to an "ambush" in certain situations, especially in those cases involving a love triangle.

Lying in wait is simply evidence which, if unexplained and unqualified by other evidence, would ordinarily establish that the perpetrator was guilty of willful, deliberate, and premeditated killing (*People v. Wolff, 61 Cal. 2d 795*).

Lying in wait is sufficiently shown in murder prosecution by proof of concealment and watchful waiting (*People v. Harrison, 59 Cal. 2d 622*). Murder committed by lying in wait is murder in the first degree, and a finding that the crime was so committed obviates the necessity for finding of deliberation and premeditation (*People v. Harrison, supra*).

Where defendant went to a cabin to await the arrival of the victim and subsequently fell asleep with a loaded rifle in his hands, and was later awakened by the presence of the victim, who at first fled but later returned and was shot and killed, the court held the defendant's actions to be within the scope of lying in wait (*People v. Tuthill, 31 Cal. 2d 92*).

When the killing is perpetrated by lying in wait, it is murder in the first degree even if the defendant fell asleep while he was lying in wait (*People v. Gibson, 92 C.A. 2d 95*).

Torture. Any murder that was committed by means of torture is murder of the first degree. Such a murder is not, however, necessarily a killing by torture merely because the means used caused severe pain and discomfort to the victim before death.

However, kicking a helpless victim to death for a period of fifteen minutes before death actually resulted was held to be torture and thus first-degree murder, especially in view of the fact that the victim's eye was displaced which would also amount to mayhem, which would also place the offense within the purview of the first-degree murder statute (*People v. Gilliam, 39 Cal. 2d 235*).

Where evidence disclosed that the victim was killed in the perpetration of robbery and in an effort to extort from the victim the combination to his safe, and that he was tortured with specific intent that he suffer, evidence of this nature sustained a conviction for first-degree murder on both theories, (1) perpetration of murder during a robbery and (2) torturous murder (*People v. Turville, 51 Cal. 2d 620*).

Murder by torture requires separate or additional proof of malice or premeditation, such elements being supplied by the fact that it is a murder by torture (*People v. Cooley, 211 C.A. 2d 173*).

Deliberation and Premeditation. To constitute first-degree murder other than by poison, lying in wait or torture, the unlawful killing must be accompanied by a deliberate and premeditated intent to take human life. The intent to kill must be proximately resultant of the deliberate premeditation by the perpetrator during the commission of the crime.

The term "deliberate" means formed, arrived at, or determined upon as a result of careful thought and weighing of considerations. The term "premeditate" means to think on and resolve in the mind beforehand (*People v. Morris, 174 C.A. 2d 93*). No set rule can be laid down as to the amount or type of deliberation necessary in every case of first-degree murder, but evidence must be sufficient to enable the jury to reasonably conclude that the defendant's action in connection with the homicide was actually premeditated (*People v. Nye, 63 Cal. 2d 166*).

Where a husband went to the home of his estranged wife and sought her out, and thereafter fired several shots into her body, evidence was sufficient to support an implied finding of the jury that the husband had a deliberate, thoughtful, and preconceived intent to kill his wife (*People v. Dement, 48 Cal. 2d 600*).

In a murder prosecution, testimony as to statements made by the defendant on the evening of the shooting that he might get in serious trouble, together with subsequent admissions of the killing allegedly made to keep the victim from telling the police something which would "cause the defendant to serve time," established premeditation (*People v. Jennings, 158 C.A. 2d 159*).

In the killing of a police officer during the perpetration of a burglary, wherein the crime of forgery was incident to the burglary, there was adequate evidence to sustain a first-degree murder conviction of the defendant either on the ground that the killing was deliberate and premeditated or that it occurred during the perpetration of a burglary (*People v. Smith, 63 Cal. 2d 779*).

To establish the crime of first-degree murder, deliberation and premeditation may be inferred from proof of facts and circumstances and direct evidence of a deliberate and premeditated purpose to kill is not required (*People v. Cartier, 54 Cal. 2d 300*).

Killing in the Perpetration of a Felony. Where the killing is done in the perpetration or attempt to perpetrate arson, rape, robbery, burglary or mayhem or any act punishable under PC 288 (child molesting), the murder is, as a matter of law, murder in the first degree and this is the law whether the killing was intentional or unintentional or even accidental.

Killing During Burglary. A killing, intentional or otherwise, committed during the course of a burglary constitutes first degree murder (*People v. Pollard, 194 C.A. 2d 830*).

Entering with intent to assault with a deadly weapon, even though this felony was an integral ingredient of the homicide, is a killing during the perpetration of burglary and is thus murder in the first degree (*People v. Hamilton, 55 Cal. 2d 881*).

Where in the perpetration of burglary or attempted rape, the defendant inflicts injuries upon his victim which ultimately causes her death, he is guilty of first-degree murder even if he inflicts such injuries unintentionally. It is immaterial whether he used only his hands or something more inherently dangerous (*People v. Cheary, 48 Cal. 2d 301*).

Where victim was inadvertently killed during a struggle with a shotgun which he was using in an attempt to thwart a burglary, such a killing is considered to have been done during the commission of a burglary and the crime is first-degree murder (*People v. Delaney, 185 C.A. 2d 261*).

Killing During Arson. The word "arson" within this section includes offenses of the type described in PC 451 and 452.

A fatal fire and explosion deliberately caused by a defendant, wherein several persons lost their lives as a result, constitutes killing during the perpetration of arson (*People v. Chavez, 50 Cal. 2d 778*).

Where two persons conspire to set fire to a cafe and one of the principals is accidently killed by the fire, the remaining co-conspirator is guilty of first-degree murder as the result of a killing during the perpetration of arson (*People v. Woodruff, 237 C.A. 2d 749*).

Killing During Rape. The majority of rape-murders must be proven by circumstantial evidence. Thus, where the woman was found beaten to death and physical evidence tended to show forced sexual intercourse shortly before death, a conviction of first degree murder in the perpetration of rape was sustained (*People v. Quicke, 61 Cal. 2d 155*).

In proving a homicide which was perpetrated during the commission of rape, it is not necessary that it be shown that the rape itself had been completed. The fact that there is no gross disturbance of the sexual parts of the victim does not indicate that there was not some attempt to commit the offense, since the perpetrator could have abandoned his purpose before consummation (*People v. Subia, 239 C.A. 262*).

Where a victim's hands are tied behind her back, a gag stuffed in her mouth, and her blouse is pulled down around the shoulders exposing her breasts, and the crotch portion of her jeans are ripped open exposing torn undergarments and the victim's private parts, and where the body of such a victim is lying with legs spread outwardly, there is sufficient evidence to show a murder in the course of rape or an attempt to rape (*People v. Hillery, 62 Cal. 2d 273*).

Killing During Robbery. A murder that is committed during the perpetration or attempt to perpetrate robbery is first degree and continues to be so even after the robbery is consummated. Thus where a store was robbed and one of the employees attempted to follow the robbery suspects and was thereafter shot and killed by one of them, this was held to be first-degree murder on the felony murder theory.

A killing, intentional or otherwise, committed during the perpetration of a robbery, whether it occurs during the process of robbing or immediately thereafter and during flight from the crime scene, is murder in the first degree. Thus, one who commits robbery of a store and thereafter flees in a car which subsequently hits and kills a pedestrian is guilty of first-degree murder since the homicide resulted during flight from the robbery (*People v. Ketchel, 59 Cal. 2d 503*).

Where robbery suspects shot and killed a police officer who had stopped the suspect vehicle within an hour of the robbery, this was held to be within the felony murder rule (*People v. Kendrick, 56 Cal. 2d 71*).

Where a killing occurs during the course of a robbery, a conspirator and abettor stands in the same position as the actual doer and the killing is his act and amounts to first-degree murder *only* if the prosecution can prove that such co-conspirator or abettor actually intended the murder to occur. A principal in the robbery resulting in homicide may be found guilty of murder in the first degree notwithstanding the fact that his co-defendant fired the fatal shot *only* if the prosecution can prove that the co-principal who did *not* fire the shot actually intended the murder to occur (*Enmunds v. Florida, 42 CCH, Supreme Court Bulletin, Pg. B5024*). See your text Section 5.5, "Non-triggerman Murder," regarding guilt of a co-principal.

The requisite intent in first-degree murder is not merely to commit the act of discharging a firearm, but includes the intent to kill a human being as the objective or result of such act (*People v. Gorshen, 51 Cal. 2d 716*). In this connection, statistics reveal that the majority of robberies which are perpetrated by persons armed with a dangerous or deadly weapon usually bludgeon their victims; thus a death which results from such a beating would necessarily be first-degree robbery.

Killing During Mayhem. All murder which is committed in the perpetration of mayhem is murder of the first degree. Thus, the injury caused by the depriving a person of a member of his body or usual uses of a severed organ is mayhem (*People v. Cartier, 54 Cal. 2d 300*).

The manner in which a victim is killed and the circumstances attending the killing may indicate the presence of the malice aforethought required for establishing murder (*People v. Torres, 214 C.A. 2d 734*).

Killing During Child Molestation. Any killing which occurs during the perpetration of acts denounced by PC 288 (crimes against children) is murder in the first degree. Since in the case of child molesting, the majority of victims are killed after having been molested or otherwise sexually violated, it makes no difference whether the homicide precedes or follows acts of molestation, for as previously mentioned, the killing is all part of one continuous transaction which results in murder, a killing which occurs during the process of molesting a child or acts of sex perversion which was unintentional or accidental, and which was inadvertently committed while restraining the victim, or during the course of a perverse act, is nonetheless murder in the first degree.

11.4 PENALTY FOR MURDER (PC 190)

PC 190. First Degree. Every person guilty of murder in the first degree shall suffer death, confinement in state prison for life without possibility of parole, or confinement in state prison for a term of 25 years to life. The penalty to be applied shall be determined as provided in Section 190.1, 190.2, 190.3, 190.4 and 190.5.

Second Degree. Every person guilty of murder in the second degree is punishable in the state prison for a term of 15 years to life [1980].

PC 190.1. This section provides that guilt or innocence must be determined before a finding as to the penalty. PC 190.1 also provides for:

1. A hearing as to sanity if the defendant pleads not guilty by reason of insanity.
2. A special hearing or proceeding if charged with any of the special circumstances enumerated in PC 190.2.

Additionally, PC 190.1 sets forth procedures as to whether the court or a jury must hear certain aspects of the case and make certain findings involving the death penalty (see PC 190.2).

PC 190.2. First Degree Penalty, Special Circumstance. The penalty for a defendant found guilty of murder in the first degree shall be death or confinement in the state prison for life without possibility of parole in any case in which one or more of the following special circumstances have been charged and specially found, in a proceeding under PC 190.4, to be true:

1. The murder was intentional and carried out for financial gain.
2. The defendant was previously convicted of murder in the first degree or second degree. For the purpose of this paragraph an offense committed in another jurisdiction, which if committed in California would be punishable as first- or second-degree murder shall be deemed murder in the first or second degree.
3. The defendant has in this proceeding been convicted of more than one offense of murder in the first or second degree.
4. The murder was committed by means of a destructive device, bomb, or explosive planted, hidden or concealed in any place, area, dwelling, building, or structure, and the defendant knew or reasonably should have known that his act or acts would create a great risk of death to a human being or human beings.
5. The murder was committed for the purpose of avoiding or preventing a lawful arrest or to perfect, or attempt to perfect an escape from lawful custody.
6. The murder was committed by means of a destructive device, bomb, or explosive that the defendant mailed or delivered, attempted to mail or deliver, or cause to be mailed or delivered and the defendant knew or reasonably should have known that his act or acts would create a great risk of death to a human being or human beings.
7. The victim was a peace officer as defined in Section 830.1, 830.2, 830.31, 830.35, 830.36, 830.4, 830.5, 830.5a, 830.6, 830.10, 830.11 or 830.12, who, while engaged in the course of the performance of his duties was intentionally killed, and such defendant knew or reasonably should have known that such victim was a peace officer engaged in the performance of his duties; or the victim was peace officer as defined in the above enumerated sections of the Penal Code, or a former peace officer under any of such sections, and was intentionally killed in retaliation for the performance of his official duties.
8. The victim was a federal law enforcement officer or agent, who, while engaged in the course of the performance of his duties was intentionally killed, and such defendant knew or reasonably should have known that such victim was a federal law enforcement officer or agent, engaged in the performance of his duties; or the victim was a federal law enforcement officer or agent, and was intentionally killed in retaliation for the performance of his official duties.
9. The victim was a fireman as defined in Section 245.1, who while engaged in the course of the performance of his duties was intentionally killed, and such defendant knew or reasonably should have known that such victim was a fireman engaged in the performance of his duties.
10. The victim was a witness to a crime who was intentionally killed for the purpose of preventing his testimony in any criminal proceeding, and the killing was not committed during the commission, or attempted commission of the crime to which he was a witness; or the victim was a witness to a crime and was intentionally killed in retaliation for his testimony in any criminal proceeding.
11. The victim was prosecutor or assistant prosecutor or a former prosecutor or assistant prosecutor of any local or state prosecutor's office in this state or any other state, or a federal prosecutor's

office and the murder was carried out in retaliation for or to prevent the performance of the victim's official duties.

12. The victim was a judge or former judge of any court of record in the local, state or federal system in the State of California or in any other state of the United States and the murder was carried out in retaliation for or to prevent the performance of the victim's official duties.

13. The victim was an elected or appointed official or former official of the Federal Government, a local or State government of California, or of any local or state government of any other state in the United States and the killing was intentionally carried out in retaliation for or to prevent the performance of the victim's official duties.

14. The murder was especially heinous, atrocious, or cruel, manifesting exceptional depravity. As utilized in this section, the phrase especially heinous, atrocious or cruel manifesting exceptional depravity means a conscienceless, or pitiless crime which is unnecessarily torturous to the victim. (Note: This section is no longer applicable, having been struck down by the California Supreme Court. The Legislature has not yet changed the wording of the statute.)

15. The defendant intentionally killed the victim while lying in wait.

16. The victim was intentionally killed because of his race, color, religion, nationality or country of origin.

17. The murder was committed while the defendant was engaged in or was an accomplice in the commission of, attempted commission of, or the immediate flight after committing or attempting to commit the following felonies:

    Note: The law has changed regarding section (17) and (19b), below, due to two recent court decisions. One is *Enmunds v. Florida*, as of this writing cited only as 42 CCH, Supreme Court Bulletin, Page B5024. The court held that the death penalty may not be imposed in a felony-murder situation upon the aider and abettor who did not actually take human life, unless the prosecution can prove that the aider and abettor actually intended the murder to occur.

    In another California Court of Appeal case (*People v. Sims*, published October 25, 1982 and cited as 2d Criminal, No. 40314), the court held that before "special circumstances" can be imposed upon an aider and abettor of a felony-murder, it must be proven that such person actually intended the murder

to occur. This case may still be appealed by the Attorney General. The wording of the statute has not been changed. (Also see your text Section 5.5.)

   i. Robbery in violation of Section 211.

   ii. Kidnapping in violation of Sections 207 and 209.

   iii. Rape in violation of Section 261.

   iv. Sodomy in violation of Section 286.

   v. The performance of a lewd or lascivious act upon person of a child under the age of 14 in violation of Section 288.

   vi. Oral copulation in violation of Section 288a.

   vii. Burglary in the first or second degree in violation of Section 460.

   viii. Arson in violation of Section 451.

   ix. Train wrecking in violation of Section 219.

18. The murder was intentional and involved the infliction of torture. For the purpose of this section torture requires proof of the infliction of extreme physical pain no matter how long its duration.

19. The defendant intentionally killed the victim by the administration of poison.

b. Every person whether or not the actual killer found guilty of intentionally aiding, abetting, counseling, commanding, inducing, soliciting, requesting, or assisting any actor in the commission of murder in the first degree shall suffer death or confinement in state prison for a term of life without the possibility of parole, in any case in which one or more of the special circumstances enumerated in paragraphs (1), (3), (4), (5), (6), (7), (8), (9), (10), (11), (12), (13), (14), (15), (16), (17), (18), or (19) of subdivision (a) of this section has been charged and specially found under Section 190.4 to be true. (Law no longer applicable. See note under (17), above. Wording of the statute has not yet been changed by the legislature.)

The penalty shall be determined as provided in Sections 190.1, 190.2, 190.3, 190.4, and 190.5. [Initiative adopted November 7, 1978.]

PC 190.5. Death Penalty for Persons Under 18 Prohibited. Notwithstanding any other provision of law, the death penalty shall not be imposed upon any person who was under the age of 18 years at the time of the commission of the crime. The burden of proof as to the age of such person shall be upon the defendant.

Second Degree Murder. Murder of the second degree may be simply defined as the unlawful killing of a human being with malice aforethought, but which is not done in any manner as previously described in the crime of first-degree murder.

The real difference between first- and second-degree murder is the element of "malice." Both first- and second-degree murder require malice—*express* malice in first-degree murder and *implied* malice in second-degree murder. Thus, second-degree murder consists of an unlawful killing with malice aforethought but without premeditation or deliberation. The implication in second-degree murder is that the intent on the part of the perpetrator is implied from the unlawful killing as contrasted with first-degree murder where there must be a deliberate intent to kill.

In second-degree murder there is no preconceived design to kill, yet, as previously mentioned, the element of malice is present and implied, under the existing circumstances. Thus, where one kills another as a result of a severe beating, an illegal abortion, during the course of stealing an automobile, or during the course of perpetrating any felony other than those defined in first-degree murder, or during the perpetration of a misdemeanor which is inherently dangerous to human life, the crime is murder in the second degree.

Examples of Second Degree Murder. An actual intent to kill is not a necessary element of second-degree murder; malice may be implied from the assault with a dangerous weapon (*People v. Goodman, 8 Cal. App. 3d 705*).

An act which involves natural consequences dangerous to life and which is performed by one who knows that his conduct endangers the life of another need not be unlawful to make the killing proximately resulting from the act second-degree murder (*People v. Phillips, 64 C. 2d 574*).

Homicide that is the direct causal result of the commission of a felonious assault is murder in the second degree (*People v. Montgomery, 235 C.A. 2d 582*); and a homicide that is directly resultant from the commission of a felony which is inherently dangerous to human life is second-degree murder (*People v. Nichols, 3 C. 3d 150*).

Death which results from the commission of a felony involving the administration of a narcotic substance as denounced by the Health and Safety Code constitutes murder in the second degree (*People v. Taylor, 11 Cal. App. 3d 57*).

Where one assaults another with a deadly weapon which ultimately results in death to the victim of the assault, and such assault is not provoked, nor perpetrated in a heat of passion or in self-defense, the crime is murder in the second degree (*People v. McAuliffe, 154 C.A. 2d 332*).

Where evidence is insufficient to show that a killing was done with premeditation, deliberation, or willfulness, or in the commission of burglary, arson, rape, robbery or mayhem, or by using poison, or lying in wait, or by torturing the victim, the crime will be murder in the second degree (*People v. Granados, 49 Cal. 2d 490; People v. Cooley, 211 C.A. 2d 173*).

11.5   PROXIMATE CAUSE—FELONY MURDER RULE

The felony murder rule and proximate cause were discussed extensively in previous chapters; however, some reiteration of the subject may be necessary in the discussion of homicide. As previously indicated, the felony murder rule now only applies in cases where the defendant commits a homicide in furtherance of one common purpose, intent or design. In the case of *People v. Washington, 62 Cal. 2d 777*, the court decided that a defendant cannot be convicted of the murder of a co-defendant, or anyone else for that matter, where the killing is done by the victim in an attempt to resist the commission of a felony. However, if the defendant or his accomplice initiates resistance by injuring or attempting to injure a victim or a police officer during the course of perpetrating a felony, then in any death that should subsequently occur, whether it be to an innocent party, the victim, a police officer, or even an accomplice in the crime, the defendant will assume the entire responsibility for the resultant death whether the homicide is caused indirectly or by his own hand.

In the Washington case, the court emphasized that the purpose of the felony murder rule is to deter felons from killing negligently by holding them strictly responsible for killings they commit and not to punish them for killings committed by their victims.

11.6   MANSLAUGHTER (PC 192)

PC 192. Manslaughter Defined. Voluntary and Involuntary Manslaughter. Manslaughter is the unlawful killing of a human being, without malice. It is of three kinds:

1. Voluntary—upon a sudden quarrel or heat of passion.
2. Involuntary—in the commission of an unlawful act, not amounting to a felony, or in the commission of a lawful act which might produce death in

an unlawful manner, or without due caution and circumspection; provided that this subdivision shall not apply to acts committed in the driving of a vehicle.

3. In the driving of a vehicle—

a. In the commission of an unlawful act, not amounting to felony, *with gross negligence*; or in the commission of a lawful act which might produce death, in an unlawful manner, and with gross negligence.

b. In the commission of an unlawful act, not amounting to felony, *without gross negligence*; or in the commisssion of a lawful act which might produce death, in an unlawful manner, but without gross negligence.

This section shall not be construed as making any homicide in the driving of a vehicle punishable which is not a proximate result of the commission of an unlawful act, not amounting to felony, or of the commission of a lawful act which might produce death, in an unlawful manner.

Murder and Manslaughter Distinguished. The distinction between murder and manslaughter is that murder requires malice and manslaughter does not.

When the act causing the death, though unlawful, in the heat of passion or is excited by a sudden quarrel such as amounts to adequate provocation, the offense is manslaughter. In such a case, even if an intent to kill exists, the law is that malice, which is an essential element of murder, is absent.

To establish that a killing is murder and not manslaughter, the burden is on the state to prove beyond a reasonable doubt each of the elements of murder and that the act which caused the death was not done in the heat of passion or upon a sudden quarrel.

11.7   VOLUNTARY MANSLAUGHTER

Voluntary manslaughter is committed upon a sudden quarrel or heat of passion. It is an intentional killing of one human being by another without justification or excuse, but without malice; and the crime differs from murder primarily due to the lack of malice on the part of the perpetrator. In order to determine whether malice was present or not in a homicide, it is necessary to determine whether the killing was done in mutual combat upon a sudden quarrel, or whether the accused was subjected to such provocation by the deceased as to cause sudden hot blood or passion which obscured the reason and judgment of the perpetrator.

Heat of passion and provocation must have been sufficient to the extent that passion or hot blood must

have not only been great, but that it was operating at the time of the killing. Thus the actual killing must have been done under and because of the existing passion of the perpetrator, and not after a lapse of time or "cooling period" wherein the defendant could regain a sense of reason and judgment.

Heat of Passion—"Hot Blood." Although the passion of manslaughter is frequently referred to as a passion of anger it may be any of the other emotional outbursts which are referred to as passion, e.g., sudden resentment, fear or terror, etc. In order that it may be said to actually be the cause of the homicide, the killing must have been done in the heat of passion, or "hot blood." However, the heat of passion, or hot blood, need not be so great as to make the accused unconscious that he was about to kill; the actual intent to kill is still present.

To be sufficient to reduce a killing to manslaughter, heat of passion must be such as would naturally be aroused in the minds of ordinary, reasonable persons under given facts and circumstances, or in the mind of a person of ordinary self-control (*People v. Lopez, 205 C.A. 2d 807*).

A homicide is voluntary manslaughter if the defendant's reason was, at the time of his act, disturbed or obscured by some passion. This passion need not necessarily be fear, but must be such as would lead an ordinary man of average disposition to act rashly or without due deliberation (*People v. Dugger, 179 C.A. 2d 714*).

Where a man is so overcome with heat of passion in seeing his wife with another man, and such a relationship continued over a long period of time with the wife continuing to refuse to dissolve the relationship with the other man, defendant, a man of integrity and excellent character, was said to be mentally and emotionally exhausted upon unexpectedly seeing the deceased in the home of his mother-in-law, and the subsequent shooting of the deceased by the defendant was said to be done in such a heat of passion as to render him guilty of voluntary manslaughter and not second-degree murder (*People v. Bridghouse, 47 Cal. 2d 406*).

Provocation. Whether provocation is adequate to reduce the killing of a human being to manslaughter must be determined by considering whether the provocation would have created the passion offered in mitigation in the ordinary man under the same circumstances. If so, then it is adequate and will reduce the offense to manslaughter; if not, it is inadequate even though the degree of passion was indeed great.

In order to reduce murder to manslaughter, the exciting cause of the homicide, whether it be fear or some other incitement, must be such as would naturally tend to arouse the passion of an ordinarily reasonable man (*People v. Webb, 143 C.A. 2d 402*). There must be such adequate provocation as will serve as the basis for a sudden quarrel or heat of passion to the extent that it will reduce the offense of murder to manslaughter (*People v. Haley, 234 C.A. 2d 444*).

Cooling Time. If provocation was originally sufficient to cause hot blood, and did in fact cause such a state, it is no defense if the blood had in fact cooled to a point previous to the homicide, and the crime would then be murder. The test is: "Was there time between the provocation and the killing for the ordinarily reasonable man under the circumstances to have cooled?" Whether there was a sufficient length of time between the provocation and the fatal stroke for the blood of a reasonable man under the circumstances to have cooled is, in the majority of cases, a question of fact which must be resolved by the court or a jury.

Before homicide may be classified as voluntary manslaughter, it must appear that there was no "cooling period" between provocation and the fatal blow to the decedent (*People v. Taylor, 197 C.A. 2d 372*).

"Cooling time," in respect to the crime of manslaughter, is not the time it would take an ideal man to cool, but rather it is the time it would take the reasonable person, under like circumstances, to cool and collect his senses (*People v. Golsh, 63 C.A. 609*).

11.8   INVOLUNTARY MANSLAUGHTER

Involuntary manslaughter is the unlawful killing of a human being without malice. This crime exists in two situations: (1) In the commission of an "unlawful" act, not amounting to a felony; (2) In the commission of a "lawful" act which might produce death in an unlawful manner or without due caution and circumspection (PC 192).

Manslaughter in the Commission of an Unlawful Act, Not Amounting to a Felony. The legislative intent of this section is to punish persons who violate laws designated to prevent injury to others. For example, where one violates a statute enacted under a police power provision, such as the reckless operation of a motor vehicle, or unintentionally killing a victim as the result of simple assault and battery, the crime is involuntary manslaughter. Similarly, where one exhibits a loaded gun in a rude, angry, or threatening

manner (a misdemeanor under PC 417), and the gun discharges accidently, the crime is involuntary manslaughter. The important thing to remember about involuntary manslaughter is that it is a homicide unintentionally caused, and without malice, resulting from the commission of an unlawful act not amounting to a felony.

Involuntary manslaughter is the unlawful killing of a human being without malice, and which results in an act done in the commission of an unlawful act not amounting to a felony, or in the commission of a lawful act which might produce death in an unlawful manner or without due caution or circumspection (*People v. Tophia, 167 C.A. 2d 39*).

A defendant discharging a pistol with intent only to frighten and not to shoot the deceased is guilty of involuntary manslaughter should the victim die from such an act (*People v. McGee, 31 Cal. 2d 229*).

Thus, the intent of the perpetrator is immaterial in such a case (*People v. Barnett, 77 C.A. 2d 299*).

Attempted Involuntary Manslaughter. There is no such crime as an attempted involuntary manslaughter (*People v. Van Brousard, 76 Cal. App. 3d 193*).

Manslaughter in the Commission of a "Lawful" Act Which Might Produce Death (PC 192). If a person, in doing a lawful act which might produce death or serious bodily harm if done without due caution and circumspection, neglects to take such precautions as a reasonable man would take to prevent injury, he is guilty of involuntary manslaughter should the victim die. This may involve the failue to perform a legal duty (see Chapter 6, "Negligence"). If the law requires a person to do an act which he has a legal duty to perform, and thereafter disregards this duty which proximately causes death by virtue of his negligence, misconduct, or refusal to act, he is guilty of involuntary manslaughter. By contradistinction, a person who is under no legal duty to render care and attention to another, regardless of a possible moral duty, is not guilty of manslaughter if death is the result of his neglect.

The doing of an act ordinarily lawful, which results in the death of a human being, may be manslaughter where the act, being one which might cause death, is performed in an unlawful manner or without due caution or circumspection.

Thus, where one is legally licensed to hunt, but does so on posted private property and kills another in the process, the crime is involuntary manslaughter. Also, where a licensed pharmacist fills a prescription inaccurately, and while under the influence of a narcotic or intoxicant, and a death occurs as the result of such negligence and lack of due caution and circumspection, the defendant is guilty of involuntary manslaughter.

An act is criminally negligent when a man of ordinary prudence would foresee that the act would cause a high degree of risk of death or great bodily harm (*People v. Villalobos, 208 C.A. 2d 321*).

To be an "unlawful act" within the meaning of this section, the act must be dangerous to human life or safety to the extent that it satisfies the requirements of every crime, i.e., a union or joint operation of act and intent or criminal negligence as defined by PC 20 (*People v. Villalobos, supra*).

Willful failure of a person to perform a legal duty, whereby the death of another is caused, is murder; however, when such omission to act was not willful, but the result of gross or culpable negligence, it is involuntary manslaughter (*People v. Montecina, 66 C.A. 2d 85*).

11.9   MANSLAUGHTER IN THE DRIVING OF A VEHICLE

This offense involves the commission of an unlawful act, not amounting to a felony, with gross negligence; or in the commission of a lawful act which might produce death, in an unlawful manner, and with gross negligence.

When a motorist fails to yield the right of way to a pedestrian crossing a street at an intersection, which proximately results in death, the crime is involuntary manslaughter in the driving of a motor vehicle with gross negligence (*People v. Leitgeb, 77 C.A. 2d 764*).

Driving at an excessive speed and hitting a person standing by the roadway near a parked car is manslaughter in the driving of a motor vehicle with gross negligence if death occurs (*People v. Markham, 153 C.A. 2d 260*).

Failure to stop at a traffic signal, all conditions being normal, which results in a collision with another vehicle wherein death is caused to the other driver was sufficient to sustain a conviction for manslaughter arising out of the grossly negligent operation of an automobile (*People v. Pfeffer, 224 C.A. 2d 578*).

Death which results in a driver being blinded by approaching lights of another vehicle and where the driver, as a result of his visibility being impaired, strikes and kills a pedestrian in a crosswalk is manslaughter in the driving of a vehicle without gross negligence (*People v. Lett, 77 C.A. 2d 917*).

In a motor vehicle case, where there has been such lack of care as to constitute gross negligence is a question of fact for determination of the trier of fact (*People v. Markham, 153 C.A. 2d 260*).

Punishment for Manslaughter: Voluntary and Involuntary (PC 193).
a. Voluntary manslaughter is punishable by imprisonment in the state prison for two, four or six years.
b. Involuntary manslaughter is punishable by imprisonment in the state prison for two, three or four years.
c. A violation of subsection 3 of PC 192 (vehicle manslaughter) is punishable as follows:

In the case of a violation of subsection (a) of said subsection 3, the punishment shall be either imprisonment in the county jail for not more than one year or in the state prison.

In the case of a violation of subdivision (b) of said subsection 3, the punishment shall be by imprisonment in the county jail for not more than one year.

11.10   EXCUSABLE HOMICIDE (PC 195)

PC 195. "Homicide is excusable in the following cases:
1. When committed by accident and misfortune, in lawfully correcting a child or servant, or in doing any other lawful act by lawful means, with usual and ordinary caution, and without any unlawful intent.
2. When committed by accident and misfortune, in the heat of passion, upon any sudden and sufficient provocation, or upon a sudden combat, when no undue advantage is taken, nor any dangerous weapon used, and when the killing is not done in a cruel or unusual manner."

To excuse a homicide on the grounds of accident and misfortune, the accused must have been engaged in a lawful act and he must have been performing it with due care. If he was engaged in an unlawful act, or if the accident was the result of culpable negligence, he is criminally liable for the consequence of his act.

The so-called "unwritten law" of avenging a wrong done to a female member of one's family has no application in California and any homicide that results is criminal homicide (*People v. Young, 70 C.A. 2d 28*).

Where a parent administers justifiable corporal punishment to a child who thereafter falls to the floor and dies of a skull fracture, there is no crime and the homicide is committed by accident and misfortune.

11.11 JUSTIFIABLE HOMICIDE BY PUBLIC OFFICERS (PC 196)

PC 196. "Homicide is justifiable when committed by public officers and those acting by their command in their aid and assistance, either:

1. In obedience to any judgment of a competent court; or
2. When necessarily committed in overcoming actual resistance to the execution of some legal process, or in the discharge of any other legal duty; or
3. When necessarily committed in retaking felons who have been rescued or have escaped, or when necessarily committed in arresting persons charged with felony, and who are fleeing from justice or resisting such arrest."

Examples of Justifiable Homicide. (1) "In obedience to any judgment of a competent court." The best example of this is the execution of persons in the state prison for crimes of which they have been found guilty in a competent court and have been sentenced to death. This is a homicide. (2) "When *necessarily* committed in overcoming actual resistance to the execution of some legal process, or in the discharge of any other legal duty." An example in this case would be when a police officer has in his possession a warrant of arrest charging a person with robbery. When trying to serve the warrant, the defendant turns on the officer with a loaded gun in his hand, forcing the officer to shoot him in order to protect his own life. (3) "When necessarily committed in retaking *felons* who have been rescued or who have escaped, or when necessarily committed in arresting persons charged with felony, and who are fleeing from justice or resisting such arrest." A typical example of the first case mentioned is when the officer arrests or attempts to arrest a person suspected of committing a felony, and friends of the suspect, using guns, attempt to rescue the suspect. Another example would be the case where the officer has taken a felon into custody, and the felon draws a knife and stabs the officer. The officer is then forced to shoot the defendant in order to prevent an escape.

Another example of justifiable homicide which would be covered under (3) above would apply to the arrest of fugitives from justice who are avoiding arrest. A felon posted on an FBI Bulletin who attempts to resist or flee from arrest is considered a fugitive.

The characteristic of a justifiable homicide, is that while the officer may have the *intent to kill*, and the action he takes is likely to result in death, the occasion is such that the law justifies the killing as a means of protecting and enforcing the rights of an individual, the community or the State.

To be considered a justifiable homicide, the killing in the overcoming of resistance to a legal process or in the discharge of any other legal duty must have been *actually necessary* or have *reasonably appeared to be necessary*. If the duty could have been reasonably performed without the killing, it will not be a justifiable homicide.

The use of lethal force for the prevention of crime or to effect an arrest, is limited to cases of felonies and is not permissible in cases of misdemeanors (*People v. Hughes, 240 Cal. App. 2d 681*).

Justifiable Homicide in Effecting an Arrest. The Penal Code is very specific as to the amount of force that can be used in making an arrest. It limits the use of force by a peace officer in making an arrest to what is reasonable to effect the arrest, prevent escape, or overcome resistance. However, the officer does not lose the right of self-defense by the use of such reasonable force (PC 835a).

An officer is justified when making an arrest for a felony in using as much force to compel the submission to arrest as appears reasonably necessary to accomplish the arrest with safety to himself (*People v. Brite, 9 Cal. 2d 666*).

The Penal Code further distinguishes the amount of force that can be used when arresting or retaking a felon and that which can be used if the person is a misdemeanant. For example, PC 196(3) refers only to felons in justifying killing by public offices in arresting or retaking persons who are fleeing or resisting arrest; and, therefore, if the person is a misdemeanant, his death would not be justifiable homicide.

As previously indicated, a police officer acting lawfully has at all times the right to self-defense, and if attacked by the person he is arresting, he has the same rights as any citizen to defend himself. In such a situation the law of self-defense (PC 197) will apply rather than the laws governing arrests and recaptures of persons fleeing from, or resisting arrest. However, to justify a killing in self-defense, it must appear necessary to the officer (or private person), as a reasonable man, that he believes that he is in danger of receiving great bodily harm and he must also believe, as a reasonable man, that it is necessary for him to use in his own defense such force and means as might cause the death of his adversary to avoid this great bodily harm.

Homicide necessarily and inadvertently committed by a public officer, or one acting under his authority, while in the exercise of his authority or duty, is generally justifiable or excusable (*People v. Mason, 72 C.A. 2d 699*).

While a peace officer, when attempting an arrest, may use all necessary force to effect it, or may take the life of the supposed offender if necessary, to save his own life, there must be a real or apparent necessity to justify resorting to such a measure for the officer's own safety or protection (*People v. Newsome, 51 C.A. 42*).

Justifiable Homicide in Preventing Escape and in Recapturing Escaped Persons. In general, the same rules of law apply as in making arrests. Only that force which is necessary and reasonable is allowed. Force that is likely to cause death can only be used if necessary to prevent serious injury to the officer or another person in preventing the escape or to effect the recapture of a felon. However, it should be noted here that in accordance with the recently decided case, *People v. Redmond, 55 Cal. Rptr., 195*, neither a felon nor a misdemeanant who flees the physical custody of an officer is violating any statutory authority or provisions relative to the crime of escape.

It is the general policy of the law to allow a misdemeanant to escape or avoid recapture rather than to kill him; but a police officer at all times retains the right of self-defense and if attacked, he may use reasonable force to defend himself and kill, if necessary, to prevent great bodily harm to himself.

11.12   JUSTIFIABLE HOMICIDE BY ANY PERSON (PC 197)

PC 197 justifies killings by private persons in self-defense or in the defense of others or in the defense of habitation. A police officer has, when acting lawfully, the right of self-defense and the right to protect the lives and property of others. Thus, these laws will apply to the police officer while on duty as well as while acting as a private person outside the political subdivision for which he is employed.

Homicide is justifiable when committed by any person:

1. "When resisting any attempt to murder any person, or to commit a felony, or to do some great bodily injury upon any person. . ."

Under this subsection a killing must be reasonably necessary and justified on the basis that there is reason to believe that a felony will be, or is being committed, and a homicide must be committed as a means to prevent the felony, there being no other immediate means of thwarting the act. Obviously an attempt to commit a felony involving no immediate injury to life or property, such as in forgery cases,

etc., would not justify homicide. The necessity of the killing need not be actual; apparent necessity will suffice, but it must appear necessary to any reasonable person.

2. "When committed in defense of habitation, property, or person, against one who manifestly intends or endeavors, by violence or surprise, to commit a felony, or against one who manifestly intends and endeavors, in a violent, riotous, or tumultuous manner, to enter the habitation of another for the purpose of offering violence to any person therein. . ."

Under this provision, defense of property alone will not justify killing. Defense of property against one who evidences an intention to commit a felony justifies a killing, and a person may use force to remove an intruder who refuses to leave. In using such force, the person may not intentionally kill another solely in defense of habitation.

3. "When committed in the lawful defense of such person, or of a wife or husband, parent, child, master, mistress, or servant of such person, when there is reasonable ground to apprehend a design to commit a felony or to do some great bodily injury, and imminent danger of such design being accomplished; but such person or the person in whose behalf the defense was made, if he was the assailant or engaged in mutual combat, must really and in good faith have endeavored to decline any further struggle before the homicide was committed. . ."

Under this section there must be a reasonable ground to apprehend a design to commit a felony or to do some great bodily injury, and real or apparent imminent danger of such design must exist at the time of the killing. Where the killing is actually justified under these circumstances, a third person who furnishes the killer the fatal weapon used is also justified in his actions (*People v. Ortiz, 63 C.A. 662*).

4. "When necessarily committed in attempting, by lawful ways and means, to apprehend any person for any felony committed, or in lawfully suppressing any riot, or in lawfully keeping and preserving the peace."

Again, one may use only that amount of force necessary to accomplish a lawful purpose. Generally, deadly force may be used only to prevent death or serious injury to the person (and others) who are acting lawfully to accomplish the purposes listed in subsection 4.

Self-Defense. In considering the law justifying self-defense, the necessity for committing homicide must be founded upon a reasonableness that not only is there an existence of grave apprehension, but that there is imminent danger of receiving great bodily harm, and that the ordinarily reasonable man, placed in the position of the slayer, and under the existing circumstances, would believe that it was necessary for him to use in his own defense such force and means as might cause the death of his adversary in order to avoid actual or threatened bodily injury (*People v. Scroggins, 37 Cal. 675*).

A bare fear by the slayer's own standards is not sufficient. Such a person must act as a reasonable and prudent individual would act under similar circumstances. The degree of resistance must be proportionate to the injury threatened; one cannot kill a person who threatens to commit a simple assault or battery. However, a person can act on appearance, i.e., if the deceased threatens to kill the slayer and reaches for his pocket, and it reasonably appears that he is reaching for a deadly weapon, the slayer can act, even if the deceased was merely bluffing.

If a person initiates a quarrel, and gets more than he bargains for, he must "honestly endeavor to retreat"; and only thereafter can he stand his ground. If, on the other hand, a person actually starts a fight, indicating that deadly counterattack is necessary, he must decline further combat and notify his assailant that he abandons the contest. The person need not go out of his way to avoid an attack, however, even though the attack is anticipated. The same rule applies here if the fight is by mutual agreement.

TERMINOLOGY DEFINED—CHAPTER 11

See the Terminology Quiz at the end of this chapter.
1. Arson: an intentional unlawful setting on fire.
2. Dying declaration: dying person's statement on cause of death.
3. Excusable homicide: unintentional killing by accident or misfortune.
4. Express malice: deliberate malicious intention to unlawfully take a life.
5. Euthanasia: "mercy killing," putting one to death painlessly who is incurably ill.
6. Gross negligence: great negligence, extremely careless of consequences.
7. Heat of passion: in anger, under emotional stress.
8. Implied malice: malice inferred from intentionally doing a wrongful act.
9. Judicial notice: court's acknowledgment of fact unnecessary to prove.
10. Justifiable homicide: legally necessary killing although intentional.
11. Legal insanity: inability to tell right from wrong.

12. Manslaughter: unlawful killing without malice through negligence or anger.
13. Murder: unlawful killing of a human being with malice aforethought.
14. Mutual provocation: joint consent such as agreement to fight.
15. Nighttime: legally hours between sunset and sunrise.
16. Prosecution: court proceedings for convicting a criminal.
17. Psychotic: a person having serious mental disorders.
18. Real evidence: physical things as opposed to verbal testimony.
19. Relevant: pertinent, related to case at hand.
20. Remand: to send back into custody, to commit to jail.

TRUE-FALSE QUIZ—CHAPTER 11

1. The term "homicide" refers to the killing of a human being which may not necessarily constitute a crime.
2. To convict one of murder in California a physical body need not necessarily be produced or even found.
3. The way someone is killed may be proven entirely by circumstantial evidence even if a weapon is used.
4. To convict someone of murder, the victim's death must occur within one year and a day from the date injury is inflicted.
5. Generally one who commits euthanasia is not guilty of criminal homicide.
6. One can be guilty of felonious homicide by omitting an act which proximately causes the victim's death.
7. Manslaughter is the unlawful killing of a human being or fetus with malice aforethought.
8. Malice in murder may be either expressed or implied.
9. Malice aforethought does not necessarily mean actual intention to kill the deceased.
10. Malice aforethought is a necessary element of both first and second degree murder.
11. Murder which is committed in the perpetration of any felony is murder of the first degree.
12. Any murder which is not willful, deliberate, and premeditated is of the second degree.
13. Any unintentional killing during a robbery would be murder of the second degree.
14. Under the felony murder theory, the killing of a witness who attempted to follow the suspect

after a robbery was committed is still first degree.

15. Every person who commits first degree murder is subject to the death penalty in all cases as a matter of law.

16. Under no circumstances may the death penalty be imposed upon any person who was under 18 when he committed the crime.

17. If a jury finds the defendant guilty of "murder for hire" the mandatory death penalty is applicable.

18. Express malice must be proven to constitute first degree murder.

19. Voluntary manslaughter is the intentional killing of another in heat of passion but without justification and without malice.

20. Motive is a legally required element of any first degree murder.

ESSAY-DISCUSSION QUESTIONS—CHAPTER 11

1. Briefly define the term "homicide."
2. Within what period of time must the victim die to constitute either murder or manslaughter?
3. What is the definition of murder as given in PC 187?
4. What is the difference between express malice and implied malice?
5. A killing committed during the perpetration of what crimes is first degree murder?
6. Under what four circumstances is a homicide by private persons justifiable under PC 197?
7. Under what two circumstances is a homicide excusable under PC 195?
8. Define manslaughter and list the three kinds described in PC 192.
9. Under what three circumstances is a homicide by public officers justified under PC 196?
10. Briefly define "proximate cause" and describe its importance in a homicide case.

TERMINOLOGY QUIZ—CHAPTER 11

Match terms and definitions by placing the correct number in the parentheses. Answers may be written on a separate sheet for submission to the instructor at the instructor's direction.

1. Arson
2. Dying declaration
3. Excusable homicide
4. Euthanasia
5. Express malice
6. Gross negligence
7. Heat of passion
8. Implied malice
9. Judicial notice
10. Justifiable homicide
11. Legal insanity
12. Manslaughter
13. Murder
14. Mutual provocation
15. Nighttime
16. Prosecution
17. Psychotic
18. Real evidence
19. Relevant
20. Remand

( ) unintentional killing by accident or misfortune
( ) to commit to jail
( ) inability to tell right from wrong
( ) killing without malice through negligence or anger
( ) pertinent, related to case at hand
( ) physical things as opposed to testimony
( ) deliberate malicious intent to unlawfully take a life
( ) mercy killing
( ) in anger, under emotional stress
( ) a person having serious mental disorders
( ) malice inferred from intentionally doing wrongful act
( ) court proceedings for convicting a criminal
( ) court's acknowledgment of fact without proof
( ) legally necessary killing although intentional
( ) unlawfully killing a human being without malice aforethought

HOMICIDE CHART
(Not a Crime Itself—Descriptive of Several Acts)

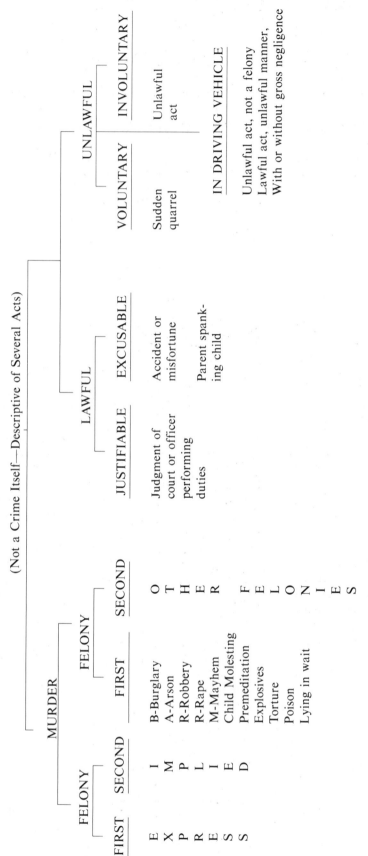

MURDER

FELONY

FIRST	SECOND
E	I
X	M
P	P
R	L
E	I
S	E
S	D

FELONY

FIRST	SECOND
B-Burglary	O
A- Arson	T
R-Robbery	H
R-Rape	E
M-Mayhem	R
Child Molesting	F
Premeditation	E
Explosives	L
Torture	O
Poison	N
Lying in wait	I
	E
	S

LAWFUL

JUSTIFIABLE	EXCUSABLE
Judgment of court or officer performing duties	Accident or misfortune
	Parent spanking child

UNLAWFUL

VOLUNTARY	INVOLUNTARY
Sudden quarrel	Unlawful act

IN DRIVING VEHICLE

Unlawful act, not a felony
Lawful act, unlawful manner,
With or without gross negligence

Definition of Malice: Two types—express and implied (P.C. 188)

Express: Manifested by a deliberate intent to take the life of another willfully.

Implied: Exists where no considerable provocation appears or when the circumstances attending the killing show an abandoned and malignant heart.

The difference between first- and second-degree murder is the malice—express is first and implied is second.

Premeditation must be proven to establish murder. Premeditation means to think of the act beforehand. Premeditation may take only seconds. Deliberation is simply prolonged meditation.

CHAPTER 12

KIDNAPPING—SEXUAL ASSAULT—
CRIMES OF RESTRAINT

12.1 KIDNAPPING DEFINED

PC 207

a. Every person who forcibly steals, takes, or arrests any person in this state, and carries the person into another country, state, or county, or into another part of the same county, is guilty of kidnapping.

b. Every person, who for the purpose of committing any act defined in Section 288 (child molesting), hires, persuades, entices, decoys, or seduces by false promises, misrepresentations, or the like, any child under the age of 14 to go out of this country, state, or county, or into another part of the same county, is guilty of kidnapping.

c. Every person who forcibly takes or arrests any person, with a design to take the person out of this state, without having established a claim, according to the laws of the United States, or of this state, or who hires, persuades, entices, decoys, or seduces by false promises, misrepresentations, or the like, any person to go out of this state or to be taken or removed therefrom, for the purpose and with the intent to sell such person into slavery or involuntary servitude, or otherwise to employ such person for his or her own use, or to the use of another, without the free will and consent of such persuaded person, is guilty of kidnapping.

d. Every person who, being out of this state, abducts or takes by force or fraud any person contrary to the law of the place where such act is committed, and brings, sends, or conveys such person within the limits of this state, and is afterwards found within the limits thereof, is guilty of kidnapping.

Discussion

Penal Code, Section 207, defines "kidnapping" as the act of one who "forcibly steals, takes, or arrests any person in this state and carries him into another country, state, or county, or into another part of the same county."

Kidnapping at common law amounted to the forcible abduction of a person from his own country and sending him to another. Contemporary criminal statutes refer to the crime as a false imprisonment aggravated by the conveying of a person imprisoned to another place in the country, or to another country.

In analyzing the first part of this section, the crime of kidnapping is complete when the victim has been taken to another part of the county, as long as the taking or carrying is forcible. Compelling a driver to convey one to a certain location is kidnapping.

This section is also designed to cover those instances where a police officer from another state, in fresh pursuit of a felon from that state, takes the suspect into custody in this state but fails to arraign him before the nearest magistrate, taking him instead back to the other state. Such an act is kidnapping in California.

Additional acts punishable under this section include the enticing or seducing of one by false promises, misrepresentation, etc., to exploit the person for various reasons or purposes. Such acts may include, but are not limited to, prostitution, selling magazine subscriptions, or becoming involved in other activity which the victim did not contemplate at the time due to the pretense or artifice on the part of the defendant. In order to satisfy or establish the elements of kidnapping in this case, the victim must be taken out of the state and must have relied upon the misrepresentations made by the defendant.

The final portion of PC 207 pertains to the bringing into this state of a person from another state, by force or fraud, or in any other manner contrary to the law of the other state. Under these circumstances, the crime is consummated in this state and is punishable under this section.

In order to constitute a kidnapping, the taking is forcible within the meaning of the statute if it is accomplished through the giving of orders which the victim feels compelled to obey because he fears harm or injury from the defendant, and the victim's apprehension is not unreasonable under such circumstances (*People v. Dagampat, 167 C.A. 2d 492*).

Where a victim of a kidnapping has at first willingly accompanied the accused, a subsequent restraining of the victim's liberties by force and the compelling of the victim to accompany the accused is sufficient to constitute the crime of kidnapping under this section (*People v Gallagher, 164 C.A. 2d 414*).

On is guilty of simple kidnapping if he forcibly steals or arrests any person and carries him out of the county or to any other part of the county (*People v. O'Farrell, 161 C.A. 2d 13*).

Where defendant took a child from its room, walked a short distance to a rear door, and was then observed outside the home by the father of the child, the court held that the distance involved, slight as it was, constituted a carrying into another part of the same county within the kidnapping statute. (*People v. Phillips, 173 C.A. 2d 412*).

Multiple Offenses. Where a victim was dragged into a truck by two individuals, who therafter stopped to purchase some beer, and then drove for some twenty minutes before raping the victim, the codefendants were convicted of both simple kidnapping and of the crime of rape (*People v. Fields, 190 C.A. 2d 515*). However, where kidnappings, though complete before the crime of rape was committed , were incidental to and a means of accomplishing the rape, a defendant, under the multiple punishment rule of PC 654 can be punished only for the most serious crime, that of rape in this case (*People v. Nelson, 233 C.A. 2d 440*).

Kidnapping, forcible rape, and robbery were divisible offenses under the circumstances of this case, and the defendants were properly sentenced for each crime and were not entitled to have a single sentence imposed under the provisions of PC 654 precluding double punsihment (*People v. Mistretta, 221 C.A. 2d 42*).

Punishment for Kidnappings. Kidnapping is punishable by imprisonment in the state prison for three, five, or seven years (*PC 208*).

12.2   KIDNAPPING FOR RANSOM, EXTORTION OR ROBBERY

PC 209

a. Every person who seizes, confines, inveigles, entices, decoys, abducts, conceals, kidnaps, or carries away any individual by any means whatsoever, with intent to hold or detain, or who holds or detains such individual for ransom, reward, or to commit extortion or to exact from another person any money or valuable thing, or any person who aids or abets any such act is guilty of a felony and upon conviction thereof shall be punished by imprisonment in the state prison for life *without* possibility of parole in cases in which any person subjected to any such act suffers death or bodily harm, or is intentionally confined in a manner which exposes such person to a substantial likelihood of death, or shall be punished by imprisonment in the state prison for life *with* possibility of parole in cases where no such person suffers death or bodily harm.

b. Any person who kidnaps or carries away any individual to commit robbery shall be punished by imprisonment in the state prison for life *with* possibility of parole.

Elements: Kidnapping for Robbery. In order to prove the commission of the crime of kidnapping to commit robbery, each of the following elements must be proved:

1. That a person was moved by the use of physical force.
2. That a person unlawfully was compelled to move because of a reasonable apprehension of harm.
3. That the movement of such person was caused with the specific intent to rob him, and that the person causing such movement had such specific intent to rob when the movement commenced.
4. That the movement of such person was against his or her will and without his or her consent.
5. That the movement of such person was for a substantial distance, that is, a distance more than slight or trivial.
6. That such movement substantially increased the risk of significant physical injuries to such person over and above those to which such person normally would have been exposed in the commission of the crime of robbery itself.

Discussion

The "risk of harm" refers to an increase in the risk that the victim may suffer significant physical injuries over and above those to which a victim of a robbery is normally exposed (*People v. Timmons, 4 C. 3d 411*).

The "risk of harm" test is satisfied when a person is forced to travel over five miles under a threat of imminent injury by a deadly weapon (*People v. Sanford, 63 Cal. App. 3d 952*).

Movement by car of 10 to 13 blocks is substantial and not merely incidental to the commission of the robbery (*In re Earley, 14 C. 3d 122*).

The courts have *previously*interpreted the phrase, "kidnaps or carries away," to mean the act of forcibly moving the victim any distance whatever, no matter how short or for what purpose, declaring that, "It is the fact, not the distance of forcible removal, which constitutes kidnapping in this state."

Landmark Decision. In People v. Daniels, 71 C. 2d 1165, the California Supreme Court repudiated its former rule regarding the *fact* of forcible removal rather than *distance* as constituting kidnapping. In the *Daniels* case, the evidence showed that the defendants, in the course of robbing and raping three women in their homes, forced them to move about their rooms for distances of eighteen feet, six feet, and thirty feet respectively. Under the former interpretation of the phrase, "any person who kidnaps or carries away any individual to commit robbery," appearing in PC 209, defendants were properly convicted of kidnapping in violation of PC 209.

Current Court Ruling. The court's current position is that PC 209 is no longer applicable to robberies in which the movements of the victim are merely incidental to the commission of the robbery and do not substantially increase the risk of harm over and above that neccessarily present in the crime of robbery itself. The court said: ". . .when in the course of a robbery a defendant does no more than move his victim around inside the premises in which he finds him—whether it be a residence. . .or a place of business or other enclosure—his conduct generally will not be deemed to constitute the offense proscribed by Section 209. Movement across a room or from one room to another, in short, cannot reasonably be found to be asportation into another part of the same county."

Applying this interpretation, the court reversed the convictions of the defendants for the offense of kidnapping for the purpose of robbery. Because the death penalty can be imposed upon a defendant who has committed such an offense where the victim suffers bodily harm, it can be clearly seen that the court's new rule limits the number of cases where the

death penalty could be imposed. "Standstill" robberies will no longer come under the purview of PC 209 (*People v. Brown, 29 C. 2d 555*).

Discussion

Under this section the robbery and kidnapping need not relate to the same person as long as the defendant's purpose was that of accomplishing a robbery. Thus, where one robs a store and thereafter commandeers the driver of a vehicle to effect an escape, the crime is kidnapping for the purpose of robbery, extortion, ransom, or reward. It is sufficient if any of this activity takes place during the course of the kidnapping.

Defendant who kidnapped a person and thereafter robbed him was found guilty of the offense of kidnapping for the purpose of robbery, but not for the lesser offense of robbery (*In re Ward, Cal. App. 2d 672*).

Defendant could be convicted for kidnapping for the purpose of robbery, but not for robbery itself, where no specific intent and objective of the defendant was directed toward any other purpose than the robbery itself (*People v. Burks, 204 C.A. 2d 494*).

Where defendant, after robbing a man and his female companion, later forced the woman to submit to an act of sex perversion some distance from where the robbery took place both acts were held to be within the scope of this statute (*People v. Chessman, 38 Cal. 2d 494*).

Bodily Harm. Trivial injuries sustained by the victims held by a robbery suspect in the course of escape were not sufficient to constitute "bodily harm" within the purview of this section (*People v. Gilbert, 63 Cal. 2d 690*).

"Bodily harm" within the meaning of PC 209 was not intended to include as aggravation the self-inflicted injuries sustained by the victim in effecting an escape or release from custody (*People v. Baker, 231 C.A. 2d 301*). However, in a case where a female victim jumped from a moving car being driven by her kidnapper, when he threatened to rape her, the court held such to constitute "bodily harm" under PC 209 (*People v. Monk, 56 C. 2d 288*).

Attempted rape and compelling one to submit to oral copulation, are "bodily harm" within the meaning of this section, prescribing the punishment if such a victim is kidnapped (*People v. Chessman, 38 Cal. 2d 166*).

PC 209. Punishment. Where a kidnap victim suffers bodily harm, the penalty is death or life imprisonment without possibility of parole in the discretion of the jury, or, if the trial be without a jury, or upon a plea of guilty, the discretion is that of the judge.

If the victim does *not* suffer bodily harm, the penalty is life imprisonment *with* the possibility of parole.

12.3   EXTORTION BY POSING AS KIDNAPPER

PC 210. Every person who for the purpose of obtaining any ransom or reward, or to extort or exact from any person any money or thing of value, poses as, or in any manner represents himself to be a person who has seized, confined, inveigled, enticed, decoyed, abducted, concealed, kidnapped or carried away any person, or who poses as, or in any manner represents himself to be a person who holds or detains such person, or who poses as, or in any manner represents himself to be a person who has aided or abetted any such act, or who poses as or in any manner represents himself to be a person who has the influence, power, or ability to obtain the release of such person so seized, confined, inveigled, enticed, decoyed, abducted, concealed, kidnapped, or carried away, is guilty of a felony and upon conviction thereof shall be punished by imprisonment for two, three or four years.

Discussion

Nothing in this section prohibits any person who in good faith believes that he can rescue any person who has been seized, confined, inveigled, enticed, abducted, concealed, kidnapped, or carried away, and who has had no part in, or connection with such confinement, inveigling, decoying, abducting, concealing, kidnapping or carrying away, from offering to rescue or obtain the release of such person for a monetary consideration or other thing of value.

This statute is applicable to those who pose as the real kidnappers in a case, and indicate the ability to obtain release of the victim for some consideration, usually financial. Otherwise, any person who, though not connected with the actual kidnapping, makes some false pretense that he in fact was connected with the crime and, as such, has the ability to release the kidnapped person for some consideration is punishable under this section.

12.4   CHILD STEALING

PC 278

a. "Every person, not having a right to custody, who maliciously takes, entices away, detains, or

conceals any minor child with intent to detain or conceal such child from a parent or guardian, or other person having lawful charge of such child shall be punished by imprisonment in the state prison for two, threee, or four years, a fine of not more than ten thousand dollars ($10,000), or both or imprisonment in a county jail for a period of not more than one year, a fine of not more than one thousand dollars ($1,000), or both."

b. Any child who has been detained or concealed in violation of subdivision (a) shall be returned to the person having lawful charge of the child. Any expenses incurred in returning the child shall be reimbursed as provided in Section 4605 of the Civil Code. Such costs shall be assessed against any defendant convicted of a violation of this section.

Discussion

The legislative intent of this section is to protect parents against worry and grief which necessarily follow decoying away and retaining of their children. The essence of the offense of child stealing consists of the taking and enticing away of a minor child with the intent both to detain and to conceal such child from the person having legal charge of it (*People v. Black, 147 Cal. 426*).

The crime of child stealing is complete the moment that one transports a child from the environs of his own home with the intent to detain and conceal him from his parents (*People v. Wisecarver, 67 C.A. 2d 203*).

While this section does not include "concealment" or "detention," it does contain as an essential element the "intent to detain and conceal" (*People v. Simmons, 12 C.A. 2d 329*).

PC 280. Willfully Causing or Permitting Removal or Concealment of Child Pursuant to Adoption Proceeding. Every person who willfully causes or permits the removal or concealment of any child in violation of Section 226.10 of the Civil Code (adoption procedures) is punishable by (a) imprisonment in the county jail for not more than one year if the child is concealed in the county in which the adoption proceeding is pending or removed from the county in question and concealed elsewhere in the state, or (b) by imprisonment in the state prison or by imprisonment in the county jail for not more than one year if the child is removed from the county to a place outside the state.

Discussion

This section makes it a misdemeanor if a child who is being adopted is concealed within the state and a felony if the child is taken out of the state. Cases of this type usually occur as a result of disputes between the Welfare Department and foster parents or amongst relatives. Children of unwed mothers are frequently subject to the purview of this Penal Code section.

12.5 FALSE IMPRISONMENT

PC 236. False imprisonment is the unlawful violation of the personal liberty of another.

Punishment. False imprisonment is punishable by fine not exceeding five hundred dollars ($500), or by imprisonment in the county jail not more than one year, or by both. If such false imprisonment be effected by violence, menace, fraud, or deceit, it shall be punishable by imprisonment in the state prison. (PC 237).

Discussion

False imprisonment is any unlawful restraint of a person's liberty and is committed whenever a person detains the body of another, by force, actual or constructive, and without his consent and without legal cause. Two essential elements are necessary to the consummation of this crime: (1) There must be an imprisonment, and (2) the imprisonment must be unlawful.

A bare false imprisonment constitutes a misdemeanor; however, if it is accompanied by the use of any violence or menace or fraud or deceit, it is a felony. Significant problems could arise in the area of law enforcement should one falsely imprison another as a result of an illegal arrest. The taking of a person into custody without probable cause amounts to a violation of PC 236 or 237.

There is a difference between false imprisonment and malicious prosecution. The former is the unlawful violation of the personal liberty of another while malicious prosecution is procuring the arrest or prosecution of another under lawful process, but for malicious motives and without probable cause (*Singleton v. Perry, 48 Cal. 2d 489*).

The courts do not distinguish clearly between a "false arrest" and "false imprisonment" because an unlawful arrest is regarded as a wrongful confinement on which an action for false imprisonment may be based; (*Wilson v Lousatalot, 193 P2d 127*). In order to bring an action against an officer for false imprisonment, it is only necessary to allege sufficient facts to show a confinement or restraint resulting from an arrest without a warrant (*Monk v. Ehret, 219 P. 2d 452*). It then becomes the responsibility of the officer to show some legal privilege that will justify the restraint upon the individual (Penal Code Section 836).

Restraint. False imprisonment requires direct restraint of the person for some length of time, however short, compelling him to stay or go somewhere against his will. Merely preventing a person from going to a particular place is not false imprisonment. A false arrest is one way to commit false imprisonment; i.e., since the arrest involves detention or restraint, it always involves imprisonment. False arrest and false imprisonment are therefore not separate wrongs.

Confinement. The confinement necessary to constitute the imprisonment may consist of any kind of confinement, in the broadest sense of that term; e.g., detention of an individual in a room, building, street or vehicle; or compelling by force, or threat of force, to go from one place to another (*People v. Agnew, 107 P. 2d 601*). Any exercise of force, or express or implied threat of force, by which in fact the other person is deprived of his liberty or is compelled to remain where he does not wish to remain, or to go where he does not wish to go, is an imprisonment. The wrong may be committed by acts, words, or both, and by merely operating upon the will of the individual, or by personal violence, or both (*People v. Agnew, supra*).

The physical force used to secure the confinement may be slight, however actual physical force is not essential; the restraint may be by apprehension of force resulting from words, gestures, or acts. The restraint is sufficient where an individual voluntarily submits to a show of authority by an officer threatening an arrest (*Gibson v. Penney, 331 P. 2d 1057*).

Private Person Arrests. Officers are completely protected against false arrest and imprisonment charges by PC 847(c) when they aid in a private persons arrest. The rationale is that PC 142 makes it a felony for an officer to refuse to accept a person arrested by the private person; therefore he does not appear to have a true choice whether to accept the prisoner of a "questionable" arrest. However, it is perfectly legal for the officer to immediately release the prisoner on his or her written promise to appear (citation) where appropriate.

A private person who assists in the making of an arrest pursuant to request or persuasion of an officer is not liable for false imprisonment; (*Peterson v. Robinson, 277 P.2d 19*). However, an officer who persuades a private person to make an unlawful arrest may be held liable for the false imprisonment.

Note: For an additional discussion of the laws of arrest and false arrest, see Chapter 7.

12.6   CRIMES OF RESTRAINT

PC 265. Abduction for Defilement. Every person who takes any woman unlawfully, against her will, and by force, menace, or duress, and compels her to marry him, or to marry any other person, or to be defiled, is punishable by imprisonment in the state prison.

Discussion

This section requires that the female be abducted against her will, but also be forced to marry someone whom she does not want to marry, or to be "defiled." Defiled, as used here, refers to sex acts of any type to which she does not consent willingly and without duress.

PC 266. Enticing Unmarried Female. Every person who inveigles or entices any unmarried female, of previous chaste character, under the age of 18 years, into any house of ill fame for the purpose of prostitution or to have illicit carnal connection (sex acts) with any man; and every person who aids or assists in the enticement; and every person who by false pretenses, or any fraudulent means procures any female to have illicit carnal connection with any man, is punishable by imprisonment in the state prison, or by imprisonment in the county jail not exceeding one year or by a fine not exceeding $1,000, or by both such fine and imprisonment (*briefed*).

Discussion

The primary purpose of this section is to prosecute those who take advantage of young women, such as run-a-ways, etc. It should be noted the female must be under the age of 18 and of previous "chaste" character. It is not necessary in all cases that the female be enticed into a house of prostitution, only that she have "illicit carnal connection" (sex relations) with any man.

PC 266a. Abduction for Prostitution. Every person who, within this state, takes any person against his or her will and without his or her consent, or with his or her consent procured by fraudulent inducement or misrepresentation, for the purpose of prostitution, as

defined in PC 647, is punishable by imprisonment in the state prison, and a fine not exceeding $1,000.

Discussion

This is a so-called "White Slavery" law for the purpose of preventing young men and women from being taken for purposes of prostitution against their will or by false representations (offer of a job, modeling career, movie contract, etc.). Note that the law is equally applicable to male and female victims. Note, also, the law does not refer to age or previous moral character of the victim.

PC 266b. Abduction for Cohabitation. Every person who takes any other person unlawfully, and against his or her will, and by force, menace or duress, compels him or her to live with such person in an illicit relation, against his or her consent, or to so live with any other person, is punishable by imprisonment in the state prison.

Discussion

This section is similar to PC 266a, except that the question or element of prostitution (sex for money) is not involved. As in the previous section, the victim's sex is not a factor. This section would punish anyone who kept another prisoner for purposes of illicit sex.

PC 266g. Placing Wife in House of Prostitution. This section makes it a felony punishable by imprisonment in the state prison for two, three, or four years to force, intimidate, persuade or by any means place one's wife in a house of prostitution or consent to or permit her to remain there. In such cases, a wife is a competent witness against her husband.

PC 267. Abduction of Juvenile For Prostitution. Any person who takes away any other person under the age of 18 years from the father, mother, guardian, or other person having the legal charge of the other person, without their consent, for the purpose of prostitution, is punishable by imprisonment in the state prison and a fine not exceeding $1,000.

Discussion

Under this section, the victim must be under the age of 18. It does not matter if the abduction is with or without the consent of the victim and the law is equally applicable to males and females. The "taking away" must be without the consent of the parents, etc., and for the purpose of prostitution.

PC 280. Concealing Child. Every person who willfully causes or permits the removal or concealment of any child in violation of Section 226.10 of the Civil Code (adoption proceedings) is punishable by either county jail or state prison depending on whether the child is concealed in or out of the state (*briefed*).

VC 22516. Occupied Locked Vehicles. No person shall leave standing a locked vehicle in which there is any person who cannot readily escape therefrom.

Discussion

This section is applicable to thoughtless or careless parents or any other person who might leave a helpless child in a locked vehicle. It would also be applicable if the person left locked in the car was very elderly or incapacitated mentally or physically to the point they could not readily escape. The obvious intent of this legislation is to prevent injury and death in the case of emergency or overheating of the interior of the car.

PC 784. Jurisdiction for Kidnapping, Abduction, Child Stealing. A defendant can be charged in any competent court within the jurisdictional area in which the offense was committed, or in the jurisdiction from which the victim was taken, or in the jurisdiction in which any act was done by the defendant in instigating, or in abetting any parties involved in the act.

12.7 RAPE AND UNLAWFUL SEXUAL INTERCOURSE

PC 261. Rape is an act of sexual intercourse, accomplished with a person not the spouse of the perpetrator under any of the following circumstances:
1. Where a person is incapable, through lunacy or other unsoundness of mind, whether temporary or permanent, of giving legal consent;
2. Where it is accomplished against a person's will by means of force or fear of immediate and unlawful bodily injury to the person or another;
3. Where the person is prevented from resisting by any intoxicating narcotic, or anesthetic substance, administered by or with the privity of the accused;
4. Where a person is at the time unconscious of the nature of the act, and this is known to the accused;
5. Where a person submits under the belief that the person committing the act is the victim's spouse,

and this belief is induced by any artifice, pretense, or concealment practiced by the accused, with intent to induce such belief.
6. Where the act is accomplished against the victim's will by threatening to retaliate in the future against the victim or any other person, and there is a reasonable possibility that the perpetrator will execute the threat. As used in this paragraph "threatening to retaliate" means a threat to kidnap or falsely imprison, or to inflict extreme pain, serious bodily injury, or death.

Discussion

Many think of rape as a "sex crime," primarily. It is, only to a very minor degree. Rape is much more aptly described as a hostile personal assault against a female by an assailant who is giving vent to deep-seated hostility and hatred of women. Many rapes have few aspects having anything to do with sexual attraction. Many female victims are extremely elderly and physically infirm; offering little in the way of "sex appeal" as we normally think of the term. Other victims are so very young and undeveloped physically, the same could be said of them relative to mature sex appeal.

In many cases, the assailant beats, mutilates, abuses and even murders the victim. None of these acts have any relationship to sex, *per se*. It is not uncommon to read of rapes where the victim is the assailant's mother, again demonstrating what current psychologists tell us: that rape is not a crime involving sexual satisfaction on the part of the male in the traditional sense. Interviews with convicted rapists further substantiate the fact that they did not experience sexual gratification or satisfaction in any traditional sense. A domination and demeaning of the victim for the purpose of releasing latent deep-seated feelings of hatred of and hostility toward women is the real purpose of attack in forcible rape crimes.

Rape is actually an act of having unlawful "carnal knowledge" of a person by force and against their will, except in cases of unlawful sexual intercourse, which will be discussed at some length later. The force used in rape may be actual or constructive, as where acquiescence is secured by fear or intimidation, or in some cases by fraud or some other artifice. Absence of consent may be constructive, as where the person is legally incapable of giving consent, by reason of insanity, imbecility, or infancy. The act of rape is consummated where the slightest penetration takes place, and it is not now necessary, as it was at common law, that emission must occur. (Also see *PC 262*, Rape of Spouse, following.)

PC 261 (1): Victim of Unsound Mind. This subdivision provides that the act of intercourse is rape where the person is incapable of consenting by reason of unsoundness of mind. Even though the victim submits or assents to the act, but is unable to comprehend its true meaning, or the moral significance and probable consequences of the acts (*People v. Perry, 26 C.A. 143*).

Unsound Mind. It makes no difference whether the perpetrator had knowledge of the victim's unsoundness of mind. All that is required is that the sexual act be perpetrated upon one who has not sufficient intellect to know the nature of the act and who does not yield to satisfy their own lust (*People v. Griffin, 117 Cal. 583*).

Where a twenty-two-year-old female with the mentality of one twelve years of age gave a childish explanation for consenting to an act of sexual relations with the defendant, his conviction under this section was upheld (*People v. Boggs, 107 C.A. 492*).

In a prosecution for committing an act of sexual intercourse upon a mental defective, evidence was sufficient to show that the victim was incapable, through lunacy or other unsoundness of mind, of giving legal consent to the act of sexual intercourse in which she became involved with the defendant (*People v. Stilwell, 165 C.A. 2d 786*).

PC 261 (2): Forcible Rape. This is probably the most frequently committed form of rape. Known as "forcible rape," the provision here is that the victim's resistance be overcome by the perpetrator. The California courts no longer follow the rule that the victim must resist to the utmost as was the common law case. It is now sufficient merely to show nonconsent to the sexual act.

Force or Fear. Many of the provisions relative to force, violence, or threats, and the element of resistance in connection with rape have practically all been eliminated under PC 261, subdivision 2. Under current law, a victim who "freezes" in fear (induced by the perpetrator) of being raped and then submits to intercourse against their will, could still charge the assailant with rape under this section. For example, if the victim has reasonable cause to fear immediate and unlawful bodily injury to themselves *or* to the perosn of another, they need not physically resist their attacker for the crime of rape to be committed. The act must, of course, be against their will.

Where the defendant held a knife at the victim's throat and threatened to kill her if she did not submit and at the time told her of others he had killed it was not unreasonable for the prosecutrix to believe that the means of effecting great and immediate bodily harm were within the defendant's reach and to be afraid to resist or scream for help (*People v. Adkins, 165 C.A. 2d 29*).

The crime of forcible rape is accomplished if at any moment during the struggle the accused intends to use such force as may be necessary to gratify his sexual desires against the will of his victim (*People v. Newlan, 173 C.A. 2d 579*).

The force necessary to accomplish the crime of forcible rape does not necessarily mean bodily harm, but rather a physical power required to overcome resistance by the victim, and the crime is committed if at any moment during the ensuing struggle the accused intends to use such force as may be necessary to gratify his lustful passions (*People v. Peckham, 232 C.A. 2d 163*).

Threats of Bodily Harm. Threats made to the victim in an effort to cause the victim to submit to an act of sexual intercourse need not be accompanied by the use of a weapon, but must be such as would indicate to the victim the immediate possibility of making good the threats made. Otherwise, the threats made must be accompanied by an apparent power of execution. On the other hand, such threats need not be made orally by the perpetrator, and the entire act may take place through the exhibition of a dangerous or deadly weapon. Further, such threats need not be limited to the victim but may be made to others present, such as the victim's small child, spouse, or companion.

A conviction for rape by threat was sustained where the defendant held a knife to the victim's throat and threatened to kill her child, and where the victim offered no resistance and was given permission to use a contraceptive to avoid possible pregnancy (*People v. Blankenship, 171 C.A. 2d 66*).

Consent to intercourse induced by fear is no consent at all and when a victim reasonably determines that they cannot resist without peril to her life, or the safety of others, no further resistance is demanded by the law (*People v. Hinton, 166 C.A. 846* and *People v. Nazworth, 152 C.A. 2d 790*).

Resistance. In a charge of PC 261, subdivision 2, forcible rape, there may be some showing of resistance on the part of the victim. However, the extent to which the victim must resist is a determination for the victim to make under the existing circumstances, and one is required to go no further than is necessary to make manifest their unwillingness to yield to the perpetrator (*People v. Peckham, supra*).

The importance of a victim's resistance to a rapist inheres in the perpetrator's intent to use force, and victim's nonconsent, but the crime of forcible rape does not hinge upon resisting to the utmost, as was the case at common law (*People v. Newlan, 173 C.A. 2d 579*).

PC 261 (3): Rape by Threat or Drugs. This section of PC 261 is divided into two parts: (1) the use of threats of great and immediate bodily harm to accomplish an act of intercourse, and (2) the administering of an intoxicating narcotic or anesthetic substance by or with the privity of the accused. The term "privity" as used in this section means "without privacy or joint knowledge," or "without the cognizance of one of the parties."

In both of the above situations, proof of actual resistance is not an essential element, since the threat of injury or use of an overpowering drug creates a situation which is deemed by law as one in which resistance of the victim is thus overcome.

Use of Drugs. Where a victim is rendered wholly insensible so as to be incapable of consenting to an act of sexual intercourse, the crime of rape is committed. Any victim in a state of utter stupefication, whether caused by drunkenness, drugs, or some other anesthetic substance, administered without his or her knowledge, would be unprotected from personal dishonor. Thus, one who administers a chloral hydrate (Mickey Finn) and thereafter rapes the victim while the victim is unconscious, would be guilty under this section. Similarly, one who, using a cloth saturated with chloroform, renders his victim unconscious and commits the crime of rape is guilty under this section. In other instances, the administration of any narcotic substance, intoxicants, sleeping pills, etc., after which rape is committed, will result in a violation of this section.

Evidence was sufficient to sustain a conviction of rape by use of drugs given by defendant during a medical examination (*People v. Wojahn, 169 C.A. 2d 135*).

PC 261 (4): Victim Unconscious of the Nature of the Act. This section punishes one who takes advantage of a person under certain circumstances where, the person although physically conscious, is not fully aware that the offense is being consummated, or is about to take place. Such cases in California are extremely rare but may be likened somewhat to subdivision 2 (victim of unsound mind), in that no consent can be given by the victim because his or her state of mind does not possess the power to consent. Thus where one is undergoing medical treatment and is not truly aware of the act being perpetrated upon the victim, the act being sexual intercourse, such an act is punishable under this section.

In a recent California case, a physician fraudulently induced a female patient to believe that sexual intercourse was essential to a course of medical treatment. Submission of the female under these circumstances did not amount to consent.

In a case in which a doctor was convicted of rape for sexual penetration perpetrated upon a woman by surprise during a medical examination, the evidence disclosed that the prosecutrix, because of embarrassment, closed her eyes, and covered them with her arms, and did not see what the appellant was doing, and he accomplished penetration before she became fully cognizant of the act, and would not have realized the significance of the act except for reliance on her marital experience.

PC 261 (5): Rape by Fraud. The leading case in California relative to this section is *People v. McCoy, 58 C.A. 534*. In this case, the parties became involved in a "mock marriage" arranged by the male and entered into in good faith by the female. All subsequent acts of sexual relations would constitute a violation of this section up to a three-year period, which is the statute of limitations on rape. Thus, this section provides that under a set of circumstances where a fraud is perpetrated, such a fraud precludes the existence of consent as a matter of law.

It is well settled that if a young female, as a result of embarrassment, closes her eyes against the sight of a man making an intimate examination of her person, and such man thereafter pretends to treat the victim with medical or surgical instruments but instead has unlawful intercourse with the victim, the crime is rape.

PC 261 (6): Threatened Retaliation. This subdivision is similar to PC 261(2), except that much of the "force and violence" may be threatened as a future consequence to befall the victim if she does not cooperate. Many of the comments relative to "force or fear," discussed under forcible rape, are also applicable here, because PC 261(6) is also forcible rape. Consent to sexual relations induced by threats to retaliate for resisting is not legal consent in any sense of the word.

As stated in the law, "threatening to retaliate means a threat by the assailant to either kidnap the victim, falsely imprison her, or to inflict extreme pain, serious bodily injury or death to the victim if she does not give in to her assailant's demands no matter how demeaning or repulsive they might be to the victim."

Consent Defined. In prosecutions under PC 261, 286, 288a, or 289, in which consent is at issue, "consent" shall be defined to mean positive cooperation in act or attitude pursuant to an exercise of free will. The person must act freely and voluntarily and have knowledge of the nature of the act or transaction involved (PC 261.6).

PC 261.5 Unlawful Sexual Intercourse. Unlawful sexual intercourse is an act of sexual intercourse accomplished with a female not the wife of the perpetrator, where the female is under the age of eighteen years.

PC 261.5 defines what is sometimes known as "statutory rape" and is distinguished from other forms of rape in that the consent of the female is neither an excuse nor a defense. The law makes it a legal impossibility for a female under eighteen years of age to consent to an act of sexual intercourse, except with her husband if she is married.

Apparent Age. Contrary to past legal provisions relative to unlawful sexual intercourse, ignorance of age of the prosecutrix may now be a defense in a case where good faith belief that the female was eighteen years of age or over was apparent from the standpoint of dress, and obvious physical maturity, coupled with the fact that the female lied about her age (*People v. Hernandez, 61 Cal. 2d 537*).

In *Hernandez* it was held reversible error to refuse to permit a defendant in a PC 261.5 case to present evidence showing that he had a good faith belief that the prosecutrix was over eighteen years of age. The case overruled the long-standing rule of law that the reasonable belief of the defendant was not a valid defense.

Unchastity of the female in an unlawful sexual intercourse case is no defense. Proof that the female was not of previous chaste character or had had acts of sexual intercourse with other men would not affect the guilt of the accused (*People v. Derbert, 138 Cal 467*).

A lack of outcry or complaint is immaterial in this crime, since a failure to do so has no significance in this case, the essential element being that the crime is perpetrated against one who cannot legally consent. Whether the act is by mutual consent of both parties involved, as is most often the case, or whether the act is forced makes little difference, as the crime of unlawful sexual intercourse is committed in either case when the female is under eighteen years of age.

If a jury finds that the defendant in a "statutory rape" case did not really believe that the consenting girl was over the statutory age of consent or that if he believed that she was over eighteen years, he was not acting as a reasonable person in view of the circumstances, he may be convicted of statutory rape (*People v. Winters, 242 C.A. 880*).

One of the requisites of all rape (in violation of PC 261) is that the female victim must not be the wife of the perpetrator; however, sexual intercourse with a female who was under age eighteen and who was not the defendant's wife, constituted the crime of rape even though the female was a married woman (*People v. Courtney, 180 C.A. 2d 61*). (See PC 262, rape of spouse, following.)

The fact that a previously married female under eighteen years of age may consent to a second marriage without parental consent does not mean that she can consent to an illicit act of sexual intercourse, and she is a legitimate victim of "statutory rape" (*People v. Courtney, supra*).

Willful participation by a mother in applying for a Mexican marriage license for her thirteen-year-old daughter, in which the daughter's age was falsified with the full knowledge of the mother, and in which case the mother knew that no legal marriage actually existed supported a conviction of the mother for "statutory rape" on the theory of aiding and abetting its commission (*People v. Smith, 204 C.A. 2d 797*).

PC 263. Penetration Sufficient to Complete the Crime. The essential guilt of rape consists in the outrage to the person and feelings of the victim. Any sexual penetration, however slight, is sufficient to complete the crime (*People v. Ray, 187 C.A. 2d 182*).

To establish the element of sexual intercourse at the preliminary hearing upon a charge of forcible rape, there must be proof of penetration (*Smith v. Superior Court, 140 C.A. 2d 862*).

Marital Status. *Formerly* a wife could not be raped by her husband, nor could a man be the victim of rape. With the addition of PC 262 (rape of spouse) and the rewording of PC 261 (rape of a person) neither is any longer the case. Either a male or female may be the victim of rape and the crime can be committed by either spouse against the other or any other person [1980].

Fornication and Other Sex Acts. Fornication is sexual intercourse between an unmarried male and female, both of whom are 18 years of age or over. There is no statute (law) in California which makes fornication, as described, a crime. The same is true of any other sex act, providing both parties are 18 or over and both knowingly consent to the act. As soon as the element of fraud, force, or any of the factors given in PC 261 are present, the act becomes a crime. (Also, see "Incest," at 13.6 of your text.)

No Corroboration Required—Rape Cases. A conviction for rape may be had upon the uncorroborated testimony of the victim. PC 1111, which requires corroboration of an accomplice's testimony, does not apply in rape cases since the person attacked is not an accomplice but a victim. PC 1108 also does not apply since that section has to do with corroborating victim's testimony in cases of abortion and seduction for purposes of prostitution (*Peo. v. Frye, 117 Cal App 2d 101*).

PC 262.   Rape of Spouse

a. Rape of a person who is the spouse of a perpetrator is an act of sexual intercourse accomplished against the will of the spouse by means of force or fear of immediate and unlawful bodily injury on the spouse or another, or where the act is accomplished against the victim's will by threatening to retaliate in the future against the victim or any other person, and there is a reasonable possibility that the perpetrator will execute the threat.

As used in this section, "threatening to retaliate" means a threat to kidnap or falsely imprison, or to inflict extreme pain, serious bodily injury, or death.

b. The provisions of PC 800 (statute of limitations in felony cases) shall apply to this section; however, there shall be no arrest or prosecution under this section unless the violation of this section is reported to a peace officer having the power to arrest for a violation of this section or to the district attorney of the county in which the violation occurred, within 30 days after the day of the violation (*PC 262*).

Punishment for Rape. Rape, as defined in PC 261, is punishable by imprisonment in the state prison for three, six, or eight years.

Rape as defined in PC 262, is punishable either by imprisonment in the county jail for not more than one year or in the state prison for three, six, or eight years.

Unlawful sexual intercourse, as defined in PC 261.5, is punishable either by imprisonment in the county jail for not more than one year or in the state prison, and in such cases the jury shall recommend by their verdict whether punishment shall be by imprisonment in the county jail or in the state prison (*PC 264*).

Rape—Using Foreign Objects—Acting in Concert. The provisions of PC 264 (punishment for rape) notwithstanding, in any case in which the defendant, voluntarily acting in concert with another person, by force or violence and against the will of the victim, committed an act described in PC 261 (rape) or PC 289 (penetration of genital or anal opening by foreign object), either personally or by aiding and abetting the other person, that fact shall be charged in the indictment or information and if found to be true by the court, upon a court trial, or if found to be true by the jury, upon a jury trial, or if admitted by the defendant, the defendant shall suffer confinement in the state prison for five, seven, or nine years (*PC 264.1*).

TERMINOLOGY DEFINED—CHAPTER 12

See the Terminology Quiz at the end of this chapter.

1. Abduct: to kidnap, to wrongfully carry away.
2. Accost: to approach, to solicit, to confront or attack.
3. Artifice: a ruse, deception, trickery.
4. Carnal knowledge: sexual intercourse, sexual contact with female.
5. Carry away: kidnapping, moving victim any distance whatever.
6. Castration: removal of testicles.
7. Coroner: official with duty to determine cause of unusual deaths.
8. Grand Jury: body sworn to inquire into crime and irregularities in county.
9. Indictment: formal accusation of crime by Grand Jury.
10. Kidnapping: carrying away a person unlawfully; usually for ransom.
11. Libel: malicious publication injurious to reputation.
12. Maiming: to mutilate, cripple, to render imperfect.
13. Personal property: money, goods, animals, clothing, vehicles, etc.
14. Privileged communication: conversation with spouse, attorney, priest, etc.
15. Probation: conditional release from jail sentence.
16. Repudiate: refuse to accept, to deny or reject.
17. Robbery: felonious taking of personal property by force or fear.
18. Shanghaiing: slang for type of kidnapping, usually for servitude.
19. Trespass: entry upon another's land without permission.
20. Surreptitious: secretive, clandestine, stealth.

TRUE—FALSE QUIZ—CHAPTER 12

1. The crime of kidnapping is applicable to both persons and property.

2. Premeditation is a necessary element which must be proven in kidnapping.
3. A police officer who is in "fresh pursuit" of a felon from another state is guilty of kidnapping if he catches the suspect in California and returns him without first arraigning him in California.
4. Not all movement of a victim from one place to another constitutes kidnapping.
5. The taking or imprisonment of the victim must be against the victim's will to constitute child stealing under PC 278.
6. Kidnapping at common law amounted to the forcible abduction of a person from his own country and sending him to another.
7. Compelling a cab driver against his will to take someone to another part of town legally constitutes kidnapping.
8. Enticing one by false promises for purposes of keeping for prostitution or involuntary servitude constitutes kidnapping.
9. The crime of kidnapping is complete where one willingly accompanied the accused but was subsequently restrained from leaving by force.
10. It is the fact of movement, not the distance of forcible removal, which constitutes kidnapping under the *People v. Daniels* rule.
11. Kidnapping is no longer applicable to robberies in which the movement of the victim is merely incidental to the robbery.
12. If the victim does not suffer bodily harm, the penalty for kidnapping is life imprisonment without possibility of parole.
13. False imprisonment is the unlawful violation of the personal liberty of another.
14. PC 847(c) protects an officer against false arrest and imprisonment charges when the officer aids in a private person arrest.
15. Generally, a man cannot be found guilty of committing rape on his own wife.
16. The element of force or fear is required in the crime of unlawful sexual intercourse.
17. Legally, both men and women can be raped.
18. It is legally possible for one female to be found guilty of the rape of another female.
19. The degree of resistance which a rape victim must make to convict the accused depends on the circumstances at the time.
20. A conviction for rape may legally be had on the uncorroborated testimony of the prosecutrix.

ESSAY-DISCUSSION QUESTIONS— CHAPTER 12

1. Does kidnapping (PC 207) require general or specific intent? Must the victim be moved? If so, how far?
2. What activities come under the purview of PC 210 (posing as kidnapper)? Is the crime a felony or misdemeanor?
3. What are the elements of child stealing (PC 278)? What effect does consent of the child have?
4. What is the difference, element-wise, between felony and misdemeanor false imprisonment under PC 236-237?
5. Briefly explain the minimum restraint and confinement necessary to constitute false imprisonment?
6. What is "constructive force" as it applies in rape cases?
7. Discuss the legal effect in "statutory rape" cases when the suspect believes the victim is eighteen or over even though she is not.
8. What degree of force is necessary to constitute "forcible rape" under PC 261, subdivision 3? What degree of resistance is required of the female?
9. Discuss whether or not a subject can be guilty of raping a woman by use of alcoholic beverages. Must these be given to her involuntarily? Must the victim be passed out to constitute a crime?
10. Under what circumstances, if any, may a female be found guilty of rape?

TERMINOLOGY QUIZ—CHAPTER 12

Match terms and definitions by placing the correct number in the parentheses. Answers may be written on a separate sheet for submission to the instructor at the instructor's direction.

 1. Abduct
 2. Accost
 3. Artifice
 4. Carnal knowledge
 5. Carry away
 6. Castration
 7. Coroner
 8. Grand Jury
 9. Indictment
10. Kidnapping
11. Libel
12. Maiming
13. Personal property
14. Privileged communication
15. Probation
16. Repudiate
17. Robbery
18. Shanghaiing
19. Trespass
20. Surreptitious

( ) formal accusation of crime by Grand Jury
( ) mutilate, cripple, to render imperfect
( ) conditional release from jail sentence
( ) unlawfully stealing a person, usually for ransom
( ) to kidnap, to wrongfully carry away
( ) entry upon another's lands without permission
( ) malicious publication injurious to reputation
( ) to approach, to solicit, to confront
( ) refuse to accept, to deny or reject
( ) a ruse, deception or trickery
( ) sexual intercourse with female
( ) slang for type of kidnapping
( ) felonious taking personal property by force or fear
( ) secretive, clandestine, stealth
( ) money, goods, animals, clothing, vehicles, etc.

CHAPTER 13

Public Safety and Morals

13.1 OBSCENE MATTER

Definitions: PC 311. "As used in this chapter:

a. 'Obscene matter' means matter, taken as a whole, the predominant appeal of which to the average person, applying contemporary standards, is to the purient (lewd) interest, i.e., a shameful or morbid interest in nudity, sex, or excretion; and is matter which, taken as a whole, goes substantially beyond customary limits of candor in description or representation of such matters; and is matter which taken as a whole is utterly without redeeming social importance.

1. The predominant appeal to prurient interest of the matter is judged with reference to average adults unless it appears from the nature of the matter of the circumstances of its dissemination, distribution, or exhibition, that it is designed for clearly defined deviant sexual groups, in which case the predominant appeal of the matter shall be judged with reference to its intended recipient group.

2. In prosecutions under this chapter, where circumstances of production, presentation, sale, dissemination, distribution, or publicity indicate that matter is being commercially exploited by the defendant for the sake of its prurient appeal, such evidence is probative with respect to the nature of the matter and can justify the conclusion that the matter is utterly without redeeming social importance.

3. In determining whether the matter taken as a whole goes substantially beyond customary limits of candor or in description or representation of such matters, the fact that the defendant knew that the matter depicts persons under the age of 16 years engaged in sexual conduct, as defined in subdivision

(c) of Section 311.4, is a factor which can be considered in making such a determination.

b. 'Matter' means any book, magazine, newspaper, or other printed or written material or any picture, drawing, photograph, motion picture, or other pictorial representation or any statue or other figure, or any recording transcription or mechanical, chemical, or electrical reproduction or any other articles, equipment, machines, or materials.

c. 'Person' means any individual, partnership, firm, association, corporation, or other legal entity.

d. 'Distribute' means to transfer possession of, whether with or without consideration.

e. 'Knowingly' means being aware of the character of the matter.

f. 'Exhibit' means to show.

g. 'Obscene live conduct' means any physical human body activity, whether performed or engaged in alone or with other persons, including but not limited to singing, speaking, dancing, acting, simulating, or pantomiming, where, taken as a whole, the predominant appeal of such conduct to the average person, applying contemporary standards is to prurient interest, i.e., a shameful or morbid interest in nudity, sex, or excretion; and is conduct which taken as a whole goes substantially beyond customary limits of candor in description or representation of such matters; and is conduct which taken as a whole is utterly without redeeming social importance.

1. The predominant appeal to prurient interest of the conduct is judged with reference to average adults unless it appears from the nature of the conduct or the circumstances of its production, presentation or exhibition, that it is designed for clearly defined deviant sexual groups, in which case the predominant appeal of the conduct shall be

judged with reference to its intended recipient group.

2. In prosecutions under this chapter, where circumstances of production, presentation, advertising, or exhibition indicate that live conduct is being commercially exploited by the defendant for the sake of its prurient appeal, such evidence is probative with respect to the nature of the conduct and can justify the conclusion that the conduct is utterly without redeeming social importance.

3. In determining whether the live conduct taken as a whole goes substantially beyond customary limits of candor in description or presentation of such matters the fact that the defendant knew the live conduct depicts persons under the age of 16 years engaged in sexual conduct, as defined in PC 311.4(c), is a factor which can be considered in making such determination.

Discussion

"Obscene matter" means that which when judged by the average person, and applying current standards, appeals predominantly to a shameful or morbid (abnormal) interest in sex, nudity, or body excrement. It is also matter which goes considerably beyond our customary limits of candor and frankness. Obscene matter must be judged on the whole and must be utterly without redeeming social importance or purpose. It must also portray sexual conduct in an offensive way, as judged by the average person applying contemporary standards of the community.

NOTE: PC 311, as now written, meets the requirements for constitutional validity as established by the U.S. Supreme Court and is therefore enforceable.

Sale or Distribution, etc., of Obscene Matter: Penalty. PC 311.2.

"a. Every person who knowingly sends or causes to be sent, or brings or causes to be brought, into this state for sale or distribution, or in this state possesses, prepares, publishes, or prints, with intent to distribute or to exhibit to others, or who offers to distribute, distributes, or exhibits to others, any obscene matter is guilty of a misdemeanor.

b. Every person who knowingly sends or causes to be sent, or brings or causes to be brought, into this state for sale or distribution, or in this state possesses, prepares, publishes, or prints, with intent to distribute or to exhibit to others for commercial consideration, or who offers to distribute, distributes, or exhibits to others for commercial consideration, any obscene matter, knowing that such matter depicts a person under the age of 18 years personally engaging in or personally simulating sexual intercourse, masturbation, sodomy, bestiality, or oral copulation is guilty of a felony and shall be punished by imprisonment in state prison for two, three, or four years, or by a fine not exceeding fifty thousand dollars ($50,000), in the absence of a finding that the defendant would be incapable of paying such a fine, or by both such fine and imprisonment.

c. The provisions of this section with respect to the exhibition of, or the possession with intent to exhibit, any obscene matter shall not apply to a motion picture operator or projectionist who is employed by a person licensed by any city or county and who is acting within the scope of his employment, provided that such operator or projectionist has no financial interest in the place wherein he is so employed."

Discussion

One who knowingly brings obscene matter into California for the purpose of resale is guilty of a misdemeanor. Generally, the provisions of PC 311.2 do not apply to a person who is employed by a licensed business who is acting within the scope of his or her employment, provided that such employee does not have any financial interest or control directly or indirectly over the exhibition of the obscene matter.

Employing Minor under 16 to Engage in Acts Described in 311.2: Penalty.

"a. Every person who, with knowledge that a person is a minor, or who, while in possession of such facts that he should reasonably know that such a person is a minor, hires, employs, or uses such minor to do or assist in doing any of the acts described in Section 311.2, is guilty of a misdemeanor."

b. Every person who, with knowledge that a person is a minor under the age of 16 years, or who, while in possession of such facts that he should reasonably know that such person is a minor under the age of 16 years, knowingly promotes, employs, uses, persuades, induces, or coerces a minor under the age of 16 years, or any parent or guardian of a minor under the age of 16 years under his or her control who knowingly permits such minor, to engage in or assist others to engage in either posing or modeling alone or with others for purposes of preparing a film, photograph, negative, slide, or live performance involving sexual conduct by a minor under the age of 16 years alone or with other persons or animals, for commercial purposes, is guilty of a felony and shall be punished by imprisonment in the state prison for three, four, or five years.

c. Every person who, with knowledge that a person is a minor under the age of 14 years, or who reasonably should know that the person is a minor under the age of 14 years, knowingly promotes, employs, uses, persuades, induces or coerces a minor under the age of 14 years, or any parent or guardian of a minor under the age of 14 years under his or her control who knowingly permits the minor to engage in or assist others to engage in either posing or modeling alone or with others for the purpose of preparing a film, photograph, negative, slide, or live performance involving sexual conduct by a minor under the age of 14 years alone or with other persons or animals for commercial purposes, is guilty of a felony and shall be punished by imprisonment in the state prison for three, six, or eight years.

d. As used in subdivision (b) and (c), sexual conduct means any of the following, whether actual or simulated: sexual intercourse, oral copulation, anal intercourse, anal oral copulation, masturbation, bestiality, sexual sadism, sexual masochism, any lewd or lascivious sexual activity, or excretory functions performed in a lewd or lascivious manner, whether or not any of the above conduct is performed alone or between members of the same or opposite sex or between humans and animals. An act is simulated when it gives the appearance of being sexual conduct" (PC 311.4).

Advertisement, Promotion of Sale, etc., of Matter Represented to be Obscene: Penalty. PC 311.5. "Every person who writes, creates, or solicits the publication or distribution of advertising or other promotional material, or who in any manner promotes the sale, distribution, or exhibition of matter represented or held out by him to be obscene, is guilty of a misdemeanor."

Obscene Live Conduct in Public Prohibited, Misdemeanor. PC 311.6. Every person who knowingly engages or participates in, manages, produces, sponsors, presents, or exhibits obscene live conduct to or before an assembly or audience consisting of at least one person or spectator in any public place or in any place exposed to public view, or in any place open to the public or to a segment thereof, whether or not an admission fee is charged, or whether or not attendance is conditioned upon the presentation of a membership card or other token, is guilty of a misdemeanor.

Requiring Purchaser or Consignee to Receive Obscene Matter as Condition to Sale, etc.: Penalty. PC 311.7. "Every person who, knowingly, as a condition to a sale, allocation, consignment, or delivery for resale of any paper, magazine, book, periodical, publication, or other merchandise, required that the purchaser or consignee receive any obscene matter or who denies or threatens to deny a franchise, revokes or threatens to revoke, or imposes any penalty, financial or otherwise, by reason of the failure of any person to accept obscene matter, or by reason of the return of such obscene matter, is guilty of a misdemeanor."

Defense. PC 311.8. "It shall be a defense in any prosecution for a violation of this chapter that the act charged was commited in aid of legitimate scientific or educational purposes."

Punishment. PC 311.9.

"a. Every person who violates Section 311.2 or 311.5 is punishable by fine of not more than one thousand dollars ($1,000) plus five dollars ($5) for each additional unit of material coming within the provisions of this chapter, which is involved in the offense, not to exceed ten thousand dollars ($10,000), or by imprisonment in the county jail for not more than six months plus one day for each additional unit of material coming within the provisions of this chapter, and which is involved in the offense, such basic maximum and additional days not to exceed 360 days in the county jail, or by both such fine and imprisonment. If such person has previously been convicted of any offense in this chapter, or of a violation of Section 313.1, a violation of Section 311.2 or 311.5 is punishable as a felony.

b. Every person who violates Section 311.4 is punishable by a fine of not more than two thousand dollars ($2,000) or by imprisonment in the county jail for not more than six months, or by both such fine and imprisonment. If such person has been previously convicted of a violation of former Section 311.3 or 311.4, he is punishable by imprisonment in the state prison.

c. Every person who violates PC 311.7, is punishable by a fine of not more than one thousand dollars ($1,000) or by imprisonment in the county jail for not more than six months, or by both such fine and imprisonment. For a second and subsequent offense he shall be punished by a fine of not more than two thousand dollars ($2,000) or by imprisonment in the county jail for not more than one year or by both such fine and imprisonment. If such person has twice been convicted of a violation of this chapter, a violation of PC 311.7 is punishable as a felony." (PC 311.9)

13.2   HARMFUL MATTER. PC 313

Definitions. "As used in this chapter:

a. 'Harmful matter' means matter, taken as a whole, the predominant appeal of which to the average person, applying contemporary standards, is to prurient interest, i.e., a shameful or morbid interest in nudity, sex, or excretion, and is matter which, taken as a whole, goes substantially beyond customary limits of candor in description or representation of such matters; and is matter which taken as a whole is utterly without redeeming social importance for minors.

   1. When it appears from the nature of the matter or the circumstances of its dissemination, distribution, or exhibition that it is designed for clearly defined deviant sexual groups, the predominant appeal of the matter shall be judged with reference to its intended recipient group.

   2. In prosecutions under this chapter, where circumstances of production, presentation, sale, dissemination, distribution, or publicity indicate that matter is being commercially exploited by the defendant for the sake of its prurient appeal, such evidence is probative with respect to the nature of the matter and can justify the conclusion that the matter is utterly without redeeming social importance for minors.

b. 'Matter' means any book, magazine, newspaper, or other printed or written material or any picture, drawing, photograph, motion picture, or other pictorial representation or any statue or other figure, or any recording, transcription, or mechanical, chemical, or electrical reproduction or any other articles, equipment, machines, or materials.

c. 'Person' means any individual, partnership, firm, association, corporation, or other legal entity.

d. 'Distribute' means to transfer possession of, whether with or without consideration.

e. 'Knowingly' means being aware of the character of the matter.

f. 'Exhibit' means to show.

g. 'Minor' means any natural person under eighteen years of age."

Failure to Ascertain Age of Minor, Misrepresentation as Parent or Guardian. PC 313.1.

a. Every person who, with knowledge that a person is a minor, or who fails to exercise reasonable care in ascertaining the true age of a minor, knowingly distributes, sends, causes to be sent, exhibits, or offers to distribute or exhibit any harmful matter to the minor is guilty of a misdemeanor.

b. Every person who misrepresents himself to be the parent or guardian of a minor and thereby causes the minor to be admitted to an exhibition of any harmful matter is guilty of a misdemeanor.

c. Any person who, within 500 meters of any elementary school, junior high school, high school, or public playground, knowingly sells in any vending machine which is located on a public sidewalk, any harmful matter displaying pictures of the commission of the following acts is guilty of a misdemeanor: sodomy, oral copulation, sexual intercourse, masturbation, bestiality or a photograph of an erect penis (briefed).

Destruction of Matter or Advertisement Upon Conviction of Accused. Upon the conviction of the accused, the court may, when the conviction becomes final, order any matter or advertisement in respect whereof the accused stands convicted, and which remains in the possession or under the control of the district attorney or any law enforcement agency, to be destroyed, and the court may cause to be destroyed any such material in its possession or under its control. (PC 312.)

Evidence in Prosecution: Nonrequirement as to Expert Testimony. In any prosecution for violation of the provisions of this chapter or of PC Chapter 7.6 (commencing with Section PC 313), neither the prosecution nor the defense shall be required to introduce expert witness testimony concerning the obscene or harmful character of the matter which is the subject of any such prosecution. Any evidence which tends to establish contemporary community standards of appeal to prurient interest or of customary limits of candor in the description or representation of nudity, sex, or excretion, or which bears upon the question of redeeming social importance, shall, subject to the provisions of the Evidence Code, be admissible when offered by either the prosecution or by the defense (PC 312.1).

Exemption of Parent or Guardian.

a. Nothing in this chapter shall prohibit any parent or guardian from distributing any harmful matter to his child or ward or permitting his child or ward to attend an exhibiton of any harmful matter if the child or ward is accompanied by him.

b. Nothing in this chapter shall prohibit any person from exhibiting harmful matter to any of the following:

   1. A minor who is accompanied by his parent or guardian.

   2. A minor who is accompanied by an adult who represents himself to be the parent or guardian of the minor and whom the person, by the exercise of reasonable care, does not have reason to know is not the parent or guardian of the minor (PC 313.2).

Scientific or Educational Purposes as Defense. "It shall be a defense in any prosecution for a violation of this chapter that the act charged was committed in aid of legitimate scientific or educational purposes." (PC 313.3.)

Penalty. Every person who violates Section 313.1 is punishable by a fine of not more than two thousand dollars ($2,000) or by imprisonment in the county jail for not more than one year, or by both such fine and imprisonment. If such person has been previously convicted of a violation of Section 313.1 or any section of Chapter 7.5 (commencing with Section 311) of Title 9 of Part I of this code, he is punishable by imprisonment in the state prison (PC 313.4).

13.3 CONTRIBUTING TO THE DELINQUENCY OF MINORS

PC 272. "Every person who commits any act or omits the performance of any duty, which act or omission causes or tends to cause or encourage any person under the age of 18 years to come within the provisions of Sections 600, 601, or 602 of the Welfare and Institutions Code or which act or omission, contributes thereto, or any person who, by any act or omission, or by threats, commands, or persuasion, induces or endeavors to induce any person under the age of 18 years or any ward or dependent child of the juvenile court to fail or refuse to conform to a lawful order of the juvenile court, or to do or to perform any act or to follow any course of conduct or to so live as would cause, or manifestly tend to cause, any such person to become or to remain a person within the provisions of Sections 600, 601, or 602 of the Welfare and Institutions Code, is guilty of a misdemeanor and upon conviction thereof shall be punished by a fine

not exceeding two thousand five hundred dollars ($2,500), or by imprisonment in a county jail for not more than one year, or by both such fine and imprisonment in a county jail, or may be released on probation for a period not exceeding five years. The district attorney shall prosecute all violations charged under this section."

13.4 CRIMES AGAINST CHILDREN

PC 288.

a. Any person who shall willfully and lewdly commit any lewd or lascivious act including any of the acts constituting other crimes provided for in Part 1 of this code upon or with the body, or any part or member thereof, of a child under the age of 14 years, with the intent of arousing, appealing to, or gratifying the lust or passions or sexual desires of such person or of such child, shall be guilty of a felony and shall be imprisoned in the state prison for a term of three, six, or eight years.

b. Any person who commits an act described in subdivision (a), by use of force, violence, duress, menace, or threat of great bodily harm, shall be guilty of a felony and shall be imprisoned in the state prison for a term of three, six or eight years.

c. In any arrest or prosecution under this section, the peace officer, the district attorney, and the court shall consider the needs of the child victim and shall do whatever is necessary and constitutionally permissible to prevent psychological harm to the child victim."

Immoral Practices

PC 273g. Any person who in the presence of any child indulges in any degrading, lewd, immoral or vicious habits or practices, or who is habitually drunk in the presence of any child in his care, custody or control, is guilty of a misdemeanor.

PC 288.1. Suspension of Sentence. Any person convicted of committing any lewd or lascivious act with or upon the body of a child under the age of fourteen years, shall not have his sentence suspended until the court obtains proof from a reputable psychiatrist as to the mental condition of such person.

Discussion

This offense, often referred to as "child molesting," consists of committing lewd and lascivious acts upon any part of the body of a child under fourteen years with the intent of arousing, appealing to or gratifying the lust or passions or sexual desires of either the victim or the perpetrator. In analyzing the statute, it is well to remember three things: (1) the sex of the child is immaterial as long as it is *under* fourteen years (not to be misinterpreted as fourteen years or under); (2) That portion of the statute which refers to "upon or with the body" indicates that some physical touching is necessary but such touching is not restricted to the private parts; and (3) The intent is specific, i.e., to arouse, appeal to, etc., either the victim or the suspect; however, it is not necessary that either actually be aroused as long as the intent is present.

The crime of child molesting may be proven by either direct or circumstantial evidence. The child's testimony is not necessary especially when causing a psychological trauma. Thus, where the physical condition of the child is such as to indicate an obvious physical trauma to the genitals, the *corpus delicti* is sufficiently established (*People v. Smith, 100 C.A. 2d 166*).

In crimes against children, punishable under this section, the child is a victim, not an accomplice, since the offense can only be perpetrated against one under the age of fourteen years (*People v. Wilder, 151 C.A. 2d 698*).

A violation of PC 288 requires specific intent and such may be inferred from the circumstances of the case (*People v. Mansell, 227 C.A. 2d 842*): and the child's willing consent to such an act is immaterial (*People v. Piccionelli, 175 C.A. 2d 39*).

Proof of the commission of the crime of child molestation may be made circumstantially, and it is not necessary to show that there was any actual arousal of either the passions of the accused or the victim (*People v. Piccionelli, supra*).

Corroboration of victim's testimony is not necessary in proving acts of a lewd and lascivious nature with a child under the age of fourteen years (*People v. Pilgram, 215 C.A. 2d 374*).

13.5   SODOMY AND ORAL COPULATION

Sodomy. PC 286.

a. Sodomy is sexual contact consisting of contact between the penis of one person and the anus of another person.

b. 1. Except as provided in PC 288, any person who participates in an act of sodomy with another person who is under 18 years of age shall be punished by imprisonment in the state prison or in a county jail for a period of not more than one year.

   2. Except as provided in PC 288, any person over the age of 21 who participates in an act of sodomy with another person who is under 16 years of age shall be guilty of a felony.

c. Any person who participates in an act of sodomy with another person who is under 14 years of age and more than 10 years younger than he, or when the act is accomplished against the victim's will by means of force, violence, duress, menace, or threat of great bodily injury on the victim or another person, shall be punished by imprisonment in the state prison for three, six or eight years.

d. Any person who, while voluntarily acting in concert with another person, either personally or by aiding and abetting such other person, commits an act of sodomy when the act is accomplished against the victim's will by means of force or fear of immediate and unlawful bodily injury on the victim or another person, shall be punished by imprisonment in the state prison for five, seven, or nine years.

e. Any person who participates in an act of sodomy with any person of any age while confined in any state prison, as defined in Section 4504, or in any local detention facility, as defined in Section 6031.4, shall be punished by imprisonment in the state prison, or in a county jail for a period of not more than one year.

f. Any person who commits an act of sodomy and whose victim is at the time unconscious of the nature of the act, and this is known to the person committing the act, shall be punished by imprisonment in the state prison, or in a county jail for a period of not more than one year.

g. Any person who commits an act of sodomy and the victim is at the time incapable, through lunacy or other unsoundness of mind, whether temporary or permanent, of giving legal consent, and this is known or reasonably should be known to the person committing the act, shall be punished by imprisonment in the state prison or in a county jail for a period of not more than one year.

Oral Copulation. PC 288a.

a. Oral copulation is the act of copulating the mouth of one person with the sexual organ of another person.

b. 1. Any person who participates in an act of oral copulation with another person who is under 18 years of age shall be punished by imprisonment in the state prison, or in a county jail for a period of not more than one year.

2. Except as provided in PC 288, any person over the age of 21 years who participates in an act of oral copulation with another person who is under 16 years of age shall be guilty of felony.

3. Any person who participates in an act of oral copulation with another person who is under 14 years of age and more than 10 years younger than he, or when the act is accomplished against the victim's will by means of force, violence, duress, menace, or threat of great bodily injury on the victim or another person, shall be punished by imprisonment in the state prison for three, six, or eight years.

d. Any person who, while voluntarily acting in concert with another person, either personally or by aiding and abetting such other person commits an act of oral copulation when the act is accomplished against the victim's will by means of force or fear of immediate and unlawful bodily injury on the victim or another person, shall be punished by imprisonment in the state prison for five, seven or nine years.

e. Any person who participates in an act of oral copulation while confined in any state prison, as defined in Section 4504, or in any local detention facility, as defined in Section 6031.4, shall be punished by imprisonment in the state prison, or in a county jail for a period of not more than one year.

f. Any person who commits an act of oral copulation and whose victim is at the time unconscious of the nature of the act, and this is known to the person committing the act, shall be punished by imprisonment in the state prison, or in a county jail for a period of not more than one year.

g. Any person who commits an act of oral copulation, and the victim is at the time incapable, through lunacy or other unsoundness of mind, whether temporary or permanent, of giving legal consent and this is known or reasonably should be known to the person committing the act, shall be punished by imprisonment in the state prison, or in a county jail for a period of not more than one year.

Genital or Anal Penetration by Foreign Object. PC 289.

a. Any person who causes the penetration, however slight, of the genital or anal opening of another by any foreign object, substance, instrument, or device when the act is accomplished against the victim's will by means of force, violence, duress,

menace, or fear of immediate and unlawful bodily injury on the victim or another person for the purpose of sexual arousal, gratification, or abuse, shall be punished by imprisonment in the state prison for three, six, or eight years.

b. This subsection of PC 289 is similar to the above except that it covers instances in which the victim is at the time incapable, through lunacy or other unsoundness of mind, whether temporary or permanent, of giving legal consent. This fact must be known to the person committing the act. The penalty is imprisonment in the state prison, or in a county jail for a period of not more than one year.

c. As used in this section, "foreign object, substance, instrument or device" shall include any part of the body except a sexual organ.

Discussion

Effective January, 1976, criminal sanctions (punishment) were removed for the act of sodomy and oral copulation except:

1. when the sodomy or oral copulation is committed with a minor or by force, violence, duress, menace, or threat of great bodily harm; and

2. except where the participants are confined in state prison or detention facilities as specified above.

Sexual acts with an animal has been made a misdemeanor (PC 286.5). The previous crime of voluntary participation in the act of sodomy (PC 286.1) and voluntary participation in the act of oral copulation (PC 288b), whether with persons of the same or opposite sex, has been repealed, thus is no longer a crime. Participants must, however, be 18 years of age or older.

13.6 INCEST

PC 285. "Persons being within the degrees of consanguinity within which marriages are declared by law to be incestuous and void, who intermarry with each other, or who commit fornication or adultery with each other, are punishable by imprisonment in the state prison."

Discussion

Incest was not a common law crime, but is generally so declared by statute today. It is simply defined as illicit sexual intercourse between persons who are related within the degrees of consanguinity or affinity wherein marriage is prohibited by law. Prior to

1650, incest was an offense punished by the ecclesiastical courts. In that year it was made a capital offense.

In California, the crime of incest is punished as a felony whenever sexual intercourse is had by a man and a woman who are so nearly related that the law prohibits them from marrying, as in the case of father and daughter, mother and son, or brother and sister. One act of intercourse is enough to constitute the crime.

Section 59 of the Civil Code declares incestuous and void all marriages between parent and child, ancestors and descendants, brothers and sisters of the half or whole blood, uncles and nieces and aunts and nephews, whether the relationship is legitimate or illegitimate. First cousins, therefore, may legally marry in the state of California.

Although the act need not be consummated by virtue of both parties consenting, if there is mutual consent, then both parties are guilty and may be prosecuted.

No distinction is made by the law in the crime of incest between relatives of half blood or whole blood. A man who has sexual intercourse with the daughter of his half-sister is guilty of incest (*People v. Womack, 167 C.A. 2d 130*).

13.7   INDECENT EXPOSURE

PC 314. "Every person who willfully and lewdly, either:

1. Exposes his person, or the private parts thereof in any public place, or in any place where there are present other persons to be offended or annoyed thereby; or,
2. Procures, counsels, or assists any person so to expose himself or take any part in any model artist exhibition, or to make any other exhibition of himself to public view, or the view of any number of persons, such as is offensive to decency, or is adapted to excite to vicious or lewd thoughts, or acts, is guilty of a misdemeanor.

Every person who violates subdivision 1 of PC 314 (above) after having entered, without consent, an inhabited dwelling house or trailer coach as defined in VC 635, or the inhabited portion of any other building, is punishable by imprisonment in the state prison, or in the county jail not exceeding one year.

Upon the second and each subsequent conviction under subdivision 1 of this section, or upon a first conviction under subdivision 1 of this section after previous conviction under Section 288 of this code,

every person so convicted is guilty of a felony and is punishable by imprisonment in the state prison."

Discussion

A conviction of PC 314(1), requires proof beyond a reasonable doubt that the actor not only meant to expose himself, but intended by such conduct to direct public attention to his genitals for the purposes of sexual arousal, gratification, or affront (*In re Smith, 7 Cal. 3d 362 and In re Birch, 10 Cal. 3d 314*).

Indecent exposure is a nuisance type of offense which is punishable as a misdemeanor except with a prior conviction, or prior conviction of PC 288, crimes against children. Both willfulness and lewdness are requisites of this offense although no movement or manipulation of the body parts or parts thereof are necessary to the establishment of a *prima facie* case, though the private parts must be exposed at the time.

Education Code, Section 13207, requires a mandatory revocation of a teaching credential for cases involving convictions under PC 647(a) and (d), PC 272, and this section (*39 Ops. Atty. Gen. 304*).

The state legislature has seen fit to pre-empt the field of sexual activity as it relates to criminal conduct, and therefore local ordinances relating to certain acts of exposure and exhibition are invalid (*Ex parte Moss, 58 Cal. 2d 117*).

In January, 1970, the California Supreme Court ruled that live theatrical performances are exempt from the law against lewd conduct. This decision granted a writ restraining the Los Angeles Superior Court from trying actors in the controversial play, *The Beard*. The drama, littered with four-letter words, depicted an imaginary meeting between Billy the Kid and the late screen siren, Jean Harlow. The meeting ends in a simulated sex act. The four to three decision had the effect of dismissing obscenity charges against cast members, the producer, and the director.

13.8   ANNOYING OR MOLESTING CHILDREN

PC 647a. "Every person who annoys or molests any child under the age of eighteen is a vagrant and is punishable by a fine of not exceeding five hundred dollars ($500) or by imprisonment in the county jail for not exceeding six months or by both such fine and imprisonment.

Every person who violates this section after having entered, without consent, an inhabited dwelling, house, or trailer coach as defined in VC 635, or the inhabited portion of any other building, is punishable by imprisonment in the state prison, or in the county jail not exceeding one year.

Every person who violates this section is punishable upon the second and each subsequent conviction or upon the first conviction after a previous conviction under PC 288, by imprisonment in the state prison."

Discussion

While at first glance this section appears somewhat ambiguous, the legislative intent is interpreted to preclude abnormal sex motivation and conduct on the part of the perpetrator. Some interpretation of the terminology used in the section is necessary, however, as the courts are seemingly not all in agreement with the words "annoy" and "molest." The term "annoy" as used here means to disturb or irritate, and implies a continued or repeated activity. The term "molest" is generally synonymous with "annoy" and has reference to injury, injustice, inconvenience, damage, or some other physical hurt. Although there is no indication that physical contact is necessary to sustain a conviction for this offense, such acts as *frottage* or *toucherism,* or other acts of physical molesting wherein sexual gratification is apparent, would be conducive to *prima facie* case.

This section providing that every person who annoys or molests any child is a vagrant does not require a physical act as contrasted to an utterance (*People v. Carskaddon, 170 C.A. 2d 45*).In order to justify a conviction of this section, it is not necessary to show that the defendant touched the body of the child (*People v. Thompson, 167 C.A. 2d 727*).

The words "annoy" and "molest" as used within this section have an abnormal and sexual connotation (*People v. Moore, 137 C.A. 2d 197*).

The child (victim) in cases prosecuted under this section is a victim and not an accomplice, and thus her testimony need not be corroborated. In a prosecution for such a crime, the trial court properly ruled that a five-year-old girl, who was exceptionally bright and intelligent for her age, was a competent witness (*People v. Thompson, 167 C.A. 2d 727*).

It is the objectional acts of the accused and not the state of mind of the child that constitutes this offense, and such acts as characterized as being so lewd or obscene that the normal person would unhesitantly be irritated by them (*People v. Hernandex, 196 C.A. 2d 265*).

Mistake in Age. An honest, justified and reasonable mistaken belief as to the age of a child is a defense to

annoying or molesting a child under age 18, under PC 647a (*People v. Atcheson, 22 C. 3d 181*).

13.9 LOITERING

PC 653g. Every person who loiters about any school or public place at or near which children attend or normally congregate, *and* who remains at any school or public place at or near which children so attend or congregate *or* who reenters or returns to such place within 72 hours, after having been asked to leave by the chief administrative official (or his designee) of that school, or by a member of the security patrol of the school district, or any peace officer, is a vagrant, and is punishable by a fine not exceeding five hundred dollars ($500) or by imprisonment in the county jail for not exceeding six months, or by both such fine and imprisonment (briefed).

Discussion

As used in this section, "loiter" means to delay, to linger, or to idle about any such school or public place without any lawful purpose or lawful business for being present. The words "and who remains," as used above, means not leaving when *requested* to do so. Note, also, that it is a violation of this section to return to such school or place where children congregate within 72 hours after having been asked to leave by an appropriate official or peace officer.

The constitutionality of this section may be questionable in that the Appellate Court recently stated that the term "loiter" as used in PC 653g is extremely vague. In this case, the respondents had been arrested for violating the section which precludes loitering about any school or public place at or near which children attend or normally congregate. Their main contention was that the statute was unconstitutional because of being too vague and indefinite, contending that the word "loiter" has both an innocent general meaning, and a restricted sinister meaning. The court, in their opinion, stated that persons who merely sit on park benches, loll on park benches, pause in the vicinity of schools, or linger in the many public areas frequented by children cannot be reasonably considered as loitering within the compass of the statute. It is only when the loitering is of such a nature that from the totality of the person's actions, and in the light of prevailing circumstances, it may be reasonably concluded that it is being engaged in "for the purpose of committing a crime as opportunity may be discovered" that such conduct falls within the statute. (*People v. Huddleson, 229 C.A. 2d 618*).

Loitering within the meaning of this section prohibiting loitering near schools, etc., refers to lingering and idling engaged in for evil or sinister purposes as when it is apparent from the totality of a person's actions and under circumstances that it may be reasonably concluded that it is engaged in for the purpose of committing a crime when an opportunity presents itself. Thus, the section was not so vague and indefinite as to offend the constitutional guarantees, did not invade, deny, or abridge personal rights and liberties, and possessed required uniformity of operation (*In Huddleston, supra*).

13.10   SEX REGISTRATION ACT

PC 290. Any person who, since the first day of July, 1944, has been or is hereafter convicted in the State of California of the offense of assault with intent to commit rape, the infamous crime against nature, or sodomy under Section 220, or of any offense defined in Section 266, 267, 268, 285, 286, 288, 288a, 289, subdivision 1 of Section 647a, subdivision 2 or 3 of Section 261, subdivision (a) or (d) of Section 647, or subdivision 1 or 2 of Section 314, or of any offense involving lewd and lascivious conduct under Section 272; or any person who since such date has been or is hereafter convicted of the attempt to commit any of the above-mentioned offenses; or any person who since such date or at any time hereafter is discharged or paroled from a penal institution where he was confined because of the commission or attempt to commit one of the above- mentioned offenses; or any person who since such date or at any time hereafter is determined to be a mentally disordered sex offender under the provisions of Article 1 (commencing with Section 6300) of Chapter 2 of Part 2 of Division 6 of the Welfare and Institutions Code; or any person who has been since such date or is hereafter convicted in any other state of any offense which, if committed or attempted in this state, would have been punishable as one or more of the above-mentioned offenses shall within 30 days after the effective date of this section or within 30 days of his coming into any county or city, or city and county in which he resides or is temporarily domiciled for such length of time register with the chief of police of the city in which he resides or the sheriff of the county if he resides in an unincorporated area.

Notice of Duty to Register. Any person who, after the first day of August, 1950, is discharged or paroled from a jail, prison, school, road camp, or other institution where he was confined because of the commission or attempt to commit one of the above-mentioned offenses or is released from a state hospital to which he was committed as a mentally disordered sex offender under the provisions of Article 1 (commencing with Section 6300) of Chapter 2 or Part 2 of Division 6 of the Welfare and Institutions Code shall, prior to such discharge, parole, or release, be informed of his duty to register under this section by the official in charge of the place of confinement or hospital and the official shall requrie the person to read and sign such form as may be required by the Department of Justice, stating that the duty of the person to register under this section has been explained to him. The official in charge of the place of confinement or hospital shall obtain the address where the person expects to reside upon his discharge, parole, or release and shall report such address to the Department of Justice. The official in charge of the place of confinement or hospital shall give one copy of the form to the person, and shall send four copies to the Department of Justice, which, in turn, shall forward one copy to the appropriate law enforcement agency having local jurisdiction where the person expects to reside upon his discharge, parole, or release (briefed).

Notice of Duty—Probationer. Any person who after the first day of August, 1950, is convicted in the State of California of the commission or attempt to commit any of the above-mentioned offenses and who is released on probation or discharged upon payment of a fine shall, prior to such release or discharge, be informed of his duty to register under this section by the court in which he has been convicted and the court shall require the person to read and sign such form as may be required by the Department of Justice, stating that the duty of the person to register under this section has been explained to him. The court shall obtain the address where the person expects to reside upon his release or discharge and shall report within three days such address to the Department of Justice. The court shall give one copy of the form to the person, and shall send two copies to the Department of Justice, which, in turn, shall forward one copy to the appropriate law enforcement agency having local jurisdiction where the person expects to reside upon his discharge, parole, or release.

Content of Registration. Such registration shall consist of (a) a statement in writing signed by such person, giving such information as may be required by the Department of Justice, and (b) the fingerprints and photograph of such person. Within three days thereafter the registering law enforcement agency shall forward such statement, fingerprints and photograph to the Department of Justice.

Change of Address. If any person required to register hereunder changes his residence address he shall inform, in writing within 10 days, the law enforcement agency with whom he last registered of his new address. The law enforcement agency shall, within three days after receipt of such information, forward it to the Department of Justice. The Department of Justice shall forward appropriate registration data to the law enforcement agency having local jurisdiction of the new place of residence.

Violation. Any person required to register under the provisions of this section who shall violate any of the provisions thereof is guilty of a misdemeanor.

The statement, photographs and fingerprints herein required shall not be open to inspection by the public or by any person other than a regularly employed peace or other law enforcement officer.

Restoration of Rights; Certification of Rehabilitation. "A person required to register under Section 290 may initiate a proceeding under Chapter 3.5 (commencing with Section 4852.01) of Title 6 of Part 3 of this code, and upon obtaining a certificate of rehabilitation, shall be relieved of any further duty to register under Section 290. Such certificate shall not relieve petitioner of the duty to register under Section 290 for any offense subject to that section of which he is convicted in the future" (PC 290.5).

Notice of Arrest of Any School Employee. "Every sheriff or chief of police upon the arrest for any of the offenses enumerated in Section 290 or in subdivision 1 or Section 261 of any school employee, shall do either of the following:
1. If such school employee is a teacher in any of the public schools of this state, he shall immediately notify by telephone the superintendent of schools of the school district employing such teacher and shall immediately give written notice of the arrest to the State Department of Education and to the superintendent of schools in the county wherein such person is employed. Upon receipt of such notice, the county superintendent of schools shall immediately notify the governing board of the school district employing such person.
2. If such school employee is a nonteacher in any of the public schools of this state, he shall immediately notify by telephone the superintendent of schools of the school district employing such non-teacher and shall immediately give written notice of the arrest to the governing board of the

school district employing such person." (PC 291.)

Private School Employees. "Every sheriff or chief of police, upon the arrest for any of the offenses enumerated in Section 290 or any person who is employed as a teacher in any private school of this state, shall immediately give written notice of the arrest to the private school authorities employing the teacher. The sheriff or chief of police shall immediately notify by telephone the private school authorities employing such teacher" (PC 291.1).

13.11 ABORTION

The 1967 Legislature added Chapter 11 (commencing with Section 25950) to Division 20 of the Health and Safety Code which amended 2377 of the Business and Professions Code and Sections 274, 275, and 276 of the Penal Code relating to Therapeutic Abortion.

Health and Safety Code 25951. "A holder of the physician's and surgeon's certificate, as defined in the Business and Profession's Code, is authorized to perform an abortion, or aid or assist or attempt an abortion, only if each of the following requirements is met:
a. The abortion takes place in a hospital which is accredited by the Joint Commission on Accreditation of Hospitals.
b. The abortion is approved in advance by a committee of the medical staff of the hospital, which committee is established and maintained in accordance with standards promulgated by the Joint Commission on Accreditation of Hospitals. In any case in which the committee of the medical staff consists of no more than three licensed physicians and surgeons, the unanimous consent of all committee members shall be required in order to approve the abortion.
c. The Committee of the Medical Staff finds that one or more of the following conditions exist:
   1. There is substantial risk that continuance of the pregnancy would gravely impair the physical or mental health of the mother.
   2. The pregnancy resulted from rape or incest."

PC 274. "Every person who provides, supplies, or administers to any woman, or procures any woman to take any medicine, drug, or substance, or uses or employs any instrument or other means whatever, with intent thereby to procure the miscarriage of such woman, except as provided in the Therapeutic

Abortion Act, Chapter 11 (commencing with Section 25950) of Division 20 of the Health and Safety Code, is punishable by imprisonment in the state prison.

PC 275. "Every woman who solicits of any person any medicine, drug, or substance whatever, and takes the same, or who submits to any operation, or to the use of any means whatever, with intent thereby to procure a miscarriage, except as provided in the Therapeutic Abortion Act, Chapter 11 (commencing with Section 25950) of Division 20 of the Health and Safety Code, is punishable by imprisonment in the state prison.

PC 276. "Every person who solicits any woman to submit to any operation, or to the use of any means whatever, to procure a miscarriage, except as provided in the Therapeutic Abortion Act, Chapter 11 (commencing with Section 25950) of Division 20 of the Health and Safety Code, is punishable by imprisonment in the county jail not longer than one year or in the state prison or by fine of not more than five thousand dollars ($5,000). Such offense must be proven by the testimony of two witnesses, or of one witness and corroborating circumstances."

TERMINOLOGY DEFINED—CHAPTER 13

See the Terminology Quiz at the end of this chapter.

1. Bestiality: sexual intercourse with animals.
2. Brothel: house of prostitution.
3. Buggery: common term for anal intercourse, sodomy.
4. Consanguinity: related by blood.
5. Cunnilingus: oral copulation of the clitoris or vulva.
6. Ecclesiastical law: religious doctrine, canon law.
7. Fellatio: oral stimulation of the penis.
8. Fetus: unborn or less than full-term human child.
9. Fornication: sexual intercourse between unmarried persons.
10. Indecent exposure: public exposure of one's private parts.
11. Lottery: distribution of prizes by chance drawing.
12. Miscarriage: premature delivery of a fetus.
13. Nuisance: a health or safety hazard, interference with property rights.
14. Obscene: appealing primarily to prurient interest.
15. Panderer: one who derives income from pimping.
16. Pimping: common term for selling services of prostitute.

17. Prurient: lewd, lustful, impure, shameful, morbid.
18. Seduction: unlawful sexual intercourse induced by promise of marriage.
19. Slander: spoken word injurious to another's reputation.
20. Sodomy: anal sexual intercourse with humans or animals.

TRUE-FALSE QUIZ—CHAPTER 13

1. Obscene matter, as defined in PC 311, means any matter which offends the individual.
2. It is a misdemeanor to bring obscene matter into California for personal use.
3. Providing entry is by membership card only, a show involving live sex acts is legal.
4. It is a defense to PC 311 that the act charged was committed in aid of legitimate scientific or educational purposes.
5. Under present law, even if convicted, all obscene material must be returned to the defendant as his personal property at the end of the trial.
6. "Harmful matter," as defined under PC 313, is that which appeals primarily to prurient interest and is without redeeming social importance for minors.
7. There is nothing in the law to prohibit a parent or guardian from providing a minor child with pornographic material.
8. To be guilty of selling hard core pornographic material it must be proven the defendant was aware of the character of the material.
9. It is not against the law for one to possess pornographic movies for private showing in his own home.
10. Encouraging a minor to leave home against the parent's wishes constitutes "contributing" under PC 272.
11. To constitute "child molesting" under PC 288, the defendant must have touched the child's private parts.
12. To constitute a violation of PC 288, the victim must be the opposite sex of the defendant.
13. Voluntary oral copulation between persons of the opposite sex is not a crime if both are 18.
14. Voluntary oral copulation between adults of the same sex is a misdemeanor.
15. It is a crime for the one who is more than 10 years older to praticipate in a voluntary act of sodomy with an 18-year-old.
16. Sodomy and oral copulation are felonies if one of the participants uses duress or if the other person

is 14 years of age and 10 years younger than the defendant.

17. A marriage or sexual relations between first cousins is incestuous and unlawful in California.

18. Other persons must be present in a public place before exposing one's private parts constitutes indecent exposure under PC 314.

19. Under PC 653g, to be guilty of loitering about a school, a suspect need only be found lingering about the school even if he has no evil intentions.

20. Except as provided in the Therapeutic Abortion Act, it is a crime to provide a woman with any device or medication whatever for the purpose of procuring a miscarriage.

ESSAY-DISCUSSION QUESTIONS— CHAPTER 13

1. What is the legal definition of the word "obscene" for the purpose of PC 311 (obscene matter)?

2. What is meant by "distribute" as the word is used in obscene matter, PC 311?

3. What is the age limit given in PC 272 (contributing) and what results must the suspect's acts cause or tend to cause in the victim or the accused?

4. What are the elements of PC 273g (immoral acts in the presence of children)?

5. List by name any three of the several crimes which come under PC 290 (Sex Registration Act).

6. List the instances or circumstances wherein sodomy and oral copulation are crimes.

7. May an uncle and his niece who commit fornication be guilty of incest? What would be the legal effect if they should marry each other?

8. May a person commit indecent exposure, PC 314, in his own home? If so, under what circumstances to make it a crime?

9. Briefly, what is the difference between PC 288, crimes against children, and PC 647a, annoying or molesting children?

10. What are the elements of "loitering" under PC 653g (loitering about schools)?

TERMINOLOGY QUIZ—CHAPTER 13

1. Bestiality
2. Brothel
3. Buggery
4. Consanguinity
5. Cunnilingus
6. Ecclesiastical law
7. Fellatio
8. Fetus
9. Fornication
10. Indecent exposure
11. Lottery
12. Miscarriage
13. Nuisance
14. Obscene
15. Panderer
16. Pimping
17. *Post mortem*
18. Presumptive evidence
19. Prurient
20. Slander

( ) anal intercourse, sodomy
( ) lewd, lustful, impure, shameful, morbid
( ) unborn child, less than full term
( ) sexual intercourse between unmarried persons
( ) sexual relations with animals
( ) house of prostitution
( ) unlawful sexual intercourse induced by marriage promise
( ) anal sexual intercourse with humans or animals
( ) related by blood, rather than marriage
( ) distribution of prizes by chance drawing
( ) oral copulation of the clitoris or vulva
( ) church or religious doctrine
( ) one who derives income from pimping
( ) oral stimulation of the penis
( ) appealing primarily to prurient interest

CHAPTER 14

Burglary

14.1 BURGLARY DEFINED

PC 459. "Every person who enters any house, room, apartment, tenement, shop, warehouse, store, mill, barn, stable, outhouse or other building, tent, vessel, railroad car, trailer coach as defined in Section 635 of the Vehicle Code, any house car as defined in Section 362 of the Vehicle Code, inhabited camper as defined in Section 243 of the Vehicle Code, vehicle as defined by the Vehicle Code when the doors of such vehicle are locked, aircraft as defined by the Harbors and Navigation Code, mine, or any underground portion thereof, with intent to commit grand or petit larceny or any felony is guilty of burglary. As used in this section, 'inhabited' means currently being used for dwelling purposes, whether occupied or not."

Elements

1. Entry (actual or constructive).
2. Of a building or structure (as defined in PC 459).
   a. Or a locked vehicle, trailer coach, house car or inhabited camper (as defined in the Vehicle Code).
3. With *specific* intent to commit
   a. Grand or petty theft or
   b. Any felony.

Discussion

At common law, burglary is a felony and was formerly punishable by death. The crime at the time consisted of breaking, either actually or constructively, and entering the dwelling house of another in the nighttime; both the breaking and the subsequent entry being for the purpose of committing a felony therein.

Statutory Provisions. As indicated in the penal statute, California law requires only entry, without the necessity of a breaking, as long as the perpetrator has the requisite intent to enter one of the numerous structures listed, i.e., to commit grand or petty theft, or any felony. It is not necessary that the crime of burglary be committed at nighttime, as was the provision at common law; however, when such occurs, the degree of the offense becomes more serious and the penalty more severe. See degrees of burglary, *PC 460*.

Burglary, being a crime of stealth, is seldom witnessed, and it is therefore necessary to establish proof of the crime by purely circumstantial evidence in the majority of cases. Identity of the perpetrator is not part of the *corpus delicti*. Thus, where evidence exists which clearly shows entry of a structure as listed in the statute for the purpose of stealing or committing a felony, the prosecution is said to have a *prima facie* case. However, should the sole purpose of entry be made for the purpose of causing malicious damage to the property, it would be difficult to sustain a conviction for burglary under such circumstances.

14.2 THE ACT OF ENTRY IN BURGLARY

As previously indicated, in order to constitute a burglary, there must be an entry, no matter how slight, of one of the various structures listed in the statute. While at common law the entry had to be accomplished by a "breaking and entering," in California no particular degree of breaking is necessary and the entry itself need not, in some cases, amount to a trespass. For example, the entry may be lawful where a person enters a store which is open to the public, during normal business hours, but if he enters with the intent to steal goods therein, it would be a burglary. From a practical standpoint, most of these cases are prosecuted as petty theft "shoplifting" inasmuch as it is difficult to prove that the perpetrator had the requisite intent to steal or commit a felony prior to entering the structure.

Examples of Lawful Entry. If a person enters a store with the intention of stealing goods therein, it would be a burglary even though he or she enters the building during the day with a crowd of customers (*People v. Ferns, 27 C.A. 285*).

Entering a public store through the public entrance during business hours, with the intent to commit larceny (theft), completes the crime of burglary (*People v. Barry, 94 Cal. 481*).

Under PC 459, no breaking or use of force is required, and the entry need not constitute a trespass. One who enters a room or building with intent to commit a theft is guilty of burglary even though permission to enter has been extended to him personally or as a member of the public (*People v. Talbot, 64 Cal. 2d*). Thus it may be seen that a person invited to a party, and who subsequently steals property or commits a felony within the structure where the party is being held, may be guilty of burglary if it can be shown he entered with the intent to steal or commit a felony.

A person who enters a laundromat with the intent to commit a theft therein commits a crime of burglary, even though the laundromat was a public place and the entrance was made during business hours (*People v. Hildreth, 202 C.A. 2d 468*).

One who enters a room or building with intent to commit a felony is guilty of burglary even though permission to enter has been extended to him personally or as a member of the public, and entry need not constitute a trespass (*People v. Sears, 62 Cal. 2d 737*).

The act necessary to the completion of the crime of burglary need not amount to the taking, or asportation (moving) of an article of value, nor is it necessary that some felony actually be consummated within one of the designated structures. The offense is complete the moment that entry is made, even though after the entry the burglar abandons his purpose (*People v. Steward, 113 C.A. 2d 687*). Thus if a man walks into his own home, armed with a loaded gun, and bent on killing his wife, but later desists in this effort after entry has been made, he may be said to have burglarized his own residence.

Where one has an agreement with a salesman in a retail store to obtain merchandise at below wholesale price, the salesman pocketing the money given him by the knowing buyer, the offense is burglary on the part of the buyer on the theory that he knowingly entered the store (a structure as defined by the burglary statute) and participated in a theft. Though it is apparent that the salesman in this case was guilty of embezzlement, the court held him guilty of the more serious offense of burglary, since he was a principal to the crime thereof (*People v. Sparks, 44 C.A. 2d 748*).

In essence, any person who enters a structure with the felonious intent to commit theft or any felony would be guilty of the crime of burglary, assuming that the essential element of intent could be proven.

Constructive Entry. Entry of a structure for the purpose of burglary need not be made by the physical person of the defendant. Entry may be made by another person on the defendant's behalf, or by means of an animal or instrument under the defendant's control. It is totally reasonable that a structure could be burglarized by a trained monkey or dog, or some other animal; however, in such cases the liability for the illegal act committed by the animal is imputed to the person having control over such agency. Similarly, one might enter a building by using a hook which is thrust through a broken window to retrieve articles within a structure.

14.3 THE INTENT IN BURGLARY

In all cases of burglary, there must be a *specific intent* to commit a theft, either grand or petty, or a felony within the structure burglarized. No other intent, however strong it may be, will suffice. The intent may be interferred, in most cases necessarily, from the facts and circumstances surrounding the commission of the crime. Thus, an entry into a structure with the intent to commit an act denounced by PC 288a (copulation) constitutes the crime of burglary if it can be inferred that the defendant's conduct was such as to enter with the specific intent to consummate this sex act (*People v. Bias, 170 C.A. 2d 502*). Similarly, a *prima facie* case of burglary is established when a defendant enters a dwelling in the nighttime and seizes a female who is asleep and then runs away after the victim screams. In this case it may be inferred from the facts and circumstances present that the accused entered with the intent to commit rape (*People v. Nanez, 84 C.A. 2d 778*). Although the burden is on the prosecution to prove a specific intent to commit a felony within a structure, in the above two cases such intent might reasonably be inferred from the unlawful entry alone.

Since the gist of the offense of burglary is the defendant's intent to commit theft or a felony at the time he or she enters the building, the proof of the intent at the time of the burglary does not depend on the subsequent commission of a felony or theft, or even an attempt to commit such acts (*People v. Robles, 207 C.A. 2d 891*).

A burglarious intent can reasonably be inferred from the unlawful entry alone of a structure, even if no crime was committed after entry. Thus, where one goes into a store to "boost" articles within the store, by using any number of contrivances to accomplish this purpose (booster box, large coat with inside pockets, shopping bag, bloomers, etc.), the crime is complete the moment that the perpetrator enters the structure. No overt act need be made toward the commission of theft; the acquiring of dominion over articles of property within the store is not necessary, nor is the element of asportation, which is requisite to the crime of theft. It is enough that entry is made with the intent to commit grand or petty theft, or any felony.

When a person enters a store, removes an article, and thereafter takes the article to a sales person stating that he lost his receipt and would like a refund, not only is he perpetrating a fraud (theft), but the crime is burglary if, prior to entering the store, his purpose (specific intent) was to accomplish this act. Moreover, such activity may usually be shown by checking the perpetrator's identity and background. *Modus operandi* will not prove a *corpus delicti*, but it certainly helps in these cases. The requisite proof of specific intent to commit a theft at the time of entering a building may be established inferentially by the facts and circumstances surrounding a burglary (*People v. Huber, 225 C.A. 2d 536*).

Consummation of Intent. The specific intent necessary to the commission of burglary need not be consummated. Thus, the breaking and entering with the intent to commit rape constitutes burglary even though the rape is not committed (*People v. Shaber, 32 Cal. 36*).

Also, where the accused pursued a woman and attempted to enter a house with the intention of killing her, the crime was held to be attempted burglary (*People v. Miller, 121 Cal. 343*). When the intent is carried out, the accomplishment is, so far as the charge of burglary is concerned, merely an evidence of intent (*People v. Hall, 94 Cal. 545*).

Existence of Intent. The *specific intent* to commit burglary must exist at the time of entry. If a person enters a structure without either the intent to steal or to commit a felony, but, after the entry has been made, decides to steal or commit a felony, his intent is said to have been formed within the building and thus the crime of burglary is not committed (*People v. Lowen, 109 Cal. 381*). Again, it is the facts and circumstances surrounding the case on which a basis for proof of the crime is founded. As indicated in the cases cited relative to entry and intent, it will be noted

that a *prima facie* case may be established by such things as articles used to make entry, *modus operandi*, constructive entry, and implements with which to commit theft or felony, to name but a few facts from which inferences may be drawn.

14.4   STRUCTURES SUBJECT TO BURGLARY

Vessel. The word "vessel" includes ships of all kinds, steamboats, canal boats, barges and every structure adapted to be navigated from place to place for the transportation of merchandise or persons (PC 7).

Trailer Coach. A "trailer coach" is a vehicle, other than a motor vehicle, designed for human habitation, or human occupancy for industrial, professional, or commercial purposes, for carrying property on its own structure, and for being drawn by a motor vehicle (VC 635).

Vehicle. A "vehicle" is a device by which any person or property may be propelled, moved, or drawn upon a highway, excepting a device moved by human power or used exclusively on stationary rails or tracks (VC 670).

Aircraft. An "aircraft" includes any contrivance used or designed for flying except a parachute or other device used primarily for safety (Harbors and Navigation Code 1940).

House Car. A "house car" (motor home) is a motor vehicle originally designed or permanently altered, and equipped for human habitation, or to which a camper has been permanently attached (VC 362).

Camper. A "camper" is a structure designed to be mounted upon a motor vehicle and to provide facilities for human habitation or camping purposes (VC 243).

Discussion.

A necessary and essential element of the crime of burglary is the entry of a house, room, apartment, tenement, shop, warehouse, etc., as enumerated in the burglary statute. Occasionally a structure will be entered which, in itself, is not descriptive of one of those listed in the statute. In such instances, one may look to *stare decisis* for the answer. The leading case in California as to the definition of a structure within the purview of the burglary statute is *People v. Stickman, 34 Cal. 242*. In this case, the court held that a building which may be the subject of a burglary, notwithstanding the legal definitions of a mine, vehicle, trailer house, or aircraft, is a structure which has *walls on all sides and is covered with a roof*.

In a more recent (1970) case, the California Appellate Court held (in *People v. Nunez, 86 Cal. Rptr. 707 and 7 Cal. App. 3d 655*) that a telephone booth with three walls, a door, roof, and floor was a "building" within the meaning of *PC 459*. As such a telephone booth could be the subject of a burglary and anyone who enters same with intent to steal (even if there is no forced entry) could be found guilty of burglary.

An old passenger bus, stationary on cement blocks and with the wheels removed, and which had a door, windows, and a roof, and which was used as an office by a firm, was a "building" within the meaning of the burglary statute (*People v. McLaughlin, 156 C.A. 291*).

A roofed garage having walls on three sides, the fourth side being a door, is a building within the law of burglary, even though at the time of entry the door was open (*People v. Picaroni, 131 C.A. 2d 612*).

Questions often arise as to the possibility of burglarizing a house or building under construction. The test is usually the *Stickman* case, previously discussed; however, there is little case law in this area. It is assumed that if the structure has a roof and walls on all sides, whether either is permanently covered, a burglary could be committed, especially if the building could be secured. However, a building which consists of only framing, without some covering, insecure and impermanent as it may be, would ordinarily not be the subject of a burglary.

Motor Vehicles. The statute defining burglary specifically states that a vehicle may be the subject of burglary only when it is a vehicle as defined by the Vehicle Code and when the doors are locked. No mention is made in the statute relative to the windows being up, but common sense dictates that the legislature intended that the vehicle be secure in order to be burglarized. Thus, the entry of an unlocked vehicle would only amount to theft, especially where there is no evidence to indicate the locking or securing of the vehicle (*People v. Burns, 114 C.A. 2d 566*).

Entry into a sealed semitrailer, which was a separate enclosed part of the tractor-trailer combination, and which could not be entered from the passenger or cab part of the tractor, is burglary even though the doors on the cab part of the tractor were not locked. The court held the vehicle to be "locked" within the meaning of the burglary statute (*People v. Massie, 241 C.A. 1023*).

Under the provision of this section making it burglary to enter a motor vehicle when the doors of such are locked, with intent to commit theft or a felony, the term "door" in this case included a trunk cover of an automobile when the door of the trunk and all other doors were locked, and entry constituted burglary (*People v. Toomes, 148 C.A. 2d 465*).

Automobile Burglary. In a recent case, the owner of an older model car reported it stolen. The victim stated the doors of the vehicle were locked. The trunk of the car was locked and could only be opened with a screwdriver. The next day the defendant was observed standing near the trunk of the stolen vehicle. He was seen to open the trunk with a screwdriver and remove two tool boxes and the jack. The defendant was apprehended by police officers and convicted of burglary, PC 459.

The defendant appealed his conviction on the theory that the prosecution failed to show the *doors* of the vehicle were locked, and that in order to constitute burglary of an auto trunk, all the doors *and* the trunk had to be locked. The Court of Appeal sustained the conviction, noting:

1. It would be ridiculous to make the existence of burglary turn on the locked or unlocked state of an area *not* involved in the entry. If the entry is made by unlocking the trunk lid, it is immaterial that some other door leading to some other space was unlocked.
2. The entry of a locked trunk of an automobile for the purpose of theft is burglary as defined in PC 459.
3. The corpus delicti of burglary, i.e., the entry by someone into the victim's automobile trunk, when that trunk was locked, with intent to commit theft, was more than amply met (*People v. Blalock, C.A. 2d 435*).

14.5   DEGREES OF BURGLARY

PC 460. Burglary Defined.
1. "Every burglary of an inhabited dwelling house, trailer coach as defined by the Vehicle Code, or inhabited portion of any other building, is burglary of the first degree.
2. *All other kinds of burglary are of the second degree.*
3. This section shall not be construed to supersede or affect Section 464 of the Penal Code," (safe burglary).

Note: For many years, to constitute first-degree burglary of an "inhabited dwelling house, trailer coach," etc., or the "inhabited portion of any other building," the burglary had to occur in the "nighttime" (between sunset and sunrise as defined by PC 643). *Such is no longer the case.*

There is now no distinction between day and night burglaries relative to degree. All burglaries of an "inhabited dwelling," etc., whether committed during the day or at night are first degree. (See text Section 14.6 for first and second degree burglary punishment).

Discussion

Inhabited Dwelling. The word "inhabited" as used in PC 460 includes both a "dwelling house" and a "building." Inhabited means that persons must actually reside in the building, customarily used as a dwelling house, although the occupant may be temporarily absent as long as he or she intends to return.

Any unoccupied dwelling, not scheduled for immediate occupancy, is not considered an inhabited dwelling, and, therefore, is not subject to first-degree burglary (*People v. Valdez, 203 C.A. 2d 559*).

Any Other Building. The building referred to in this section means any inhabited building, such as a hotel or motel lobby, room, or other similar enclosure, a tent or barrack used as a place of habitation, or any similar structure whose primary purpose is used as a dwelling or place of habitation. However, as in the case of residential dwelling, the inhabited building need not be physically occupied at the time of the burglary as long as the occupants intend to return.

PC 463 defines "nighttime" as the period between sunset and sunrise.

Trailer Coach. A "trailer coach" is a vehicle, other than a motor vehicle, without motive power, designed for human habitation, or for human occupancy for industrial, professional or commercial purposes (temporary offices), for carrying property on its own structure, and for being drawn by a motor vehicle (VC 635).

House Car. A "house car" (frequently called a motor home) is a motor vehicle originally designed, or permanently altered, and equipped for human habitation, or to which a camper has been *permanently* attached. A motor vehicle to which a camper has been *temporarily* attached is not a house car, but rather a camper as described in VC 243, below.

A motor vehicle equipped with a camper having an axle that is designed to support a portion of the weight of the camper unit, shall be considered a three-axle house car regardless of the method of attachment or manner of registration (VC 362). This latter type house car usually has the tongue of the trailer sitting well up into and attached to the bed of a pick-up truck.

Camper. A "camper" is a structure designed to be mounted upon a motor vehicle (usually a pick-up truck) and to provide facilities for human habitation or camping purposes. It should be noted here that, to constitute burglary of a camper, the camper must be inhabited. As stated in PC 459, "inhabited" means currently being used for dwelling purposes. Theft from an uninhabited camper would be petty or grand theft depending on the value of the property stolen.

14.6 PUNISHMENT FOR BURGLARY

PC 461. "Burglary is punishable as follows.
1. Burglary in the first degree: by imprisonment in the state prison for two, four or six years.
2. Burglary in the second degree: by imprisonment in the county jail not exceeding one year or in the state prison for 16 months, or two or three years."

Multiple Punishment. Where the intent of the defendant, convicted of burglary, grand theft, and assault with a deadly weapon, had been to enter a premises to commit theft, and the assaults on the occupants were merely incidental to the main objective, separate sentences imposed for each conviction violated PC 654 proscribing multiple punishment of a single act, and thus defendant could only be punished for burglary which was the most serious of all of the offenses committed (*People v. Collins, 220 C.A. 2d 563*).

14.7 BURGLARY WITH EXPLOSIVES OR ACETYLENE TORCH

PC 464. "Any person who, with intent to commit crime, enters, either by day or by night, any building, whether inhabited or not, and opens or attempts to open any vault, safe or other secure place by use of acetylene torch or electric arc, burning bar, thermal lance, oxygen lance, or any other similar device capable of burning through steel, concrete, or any other solid substance, or by use of nitroglycerine, dynamite, gunpowder, or any other explosive, is guilty of a felony and upon conviction shall be punished by imprisonment in the state prison for a term of three, five, or seven years."

In a prosecution resulting in a conviction for burglary, possession of tetratol, and willfully and maliciously placing an explosive in a building, testimony of a police officer as to his findings at the scene of the crime and as to the conduct of the accused were ample to sustain a conviction for this offense (*People v. Robinson, 149 C.A. 2d 342*).

Evidence showing that the defendants entered a safe by the use of an oxy-acetylene torch was sufficient to sustain a conviction under this section (*People v. Wilson, 46 C.A. 2d 218*).

14.8 POSSESSION OF BURGLARS' TOOLS, UNAUTHORIZED KEYS, DEVICES

PC 466. "Every person having upon him or his possession a picklock, crow, keybit, or other instrument or tool with intent feloniously to break or enter into any building, railroad car, aircraft or vessel, trailer coach, or vehicle as defined in the Vehicle Code, or who shall knowingly make or alter, or shall attempt to make or alter, any key or other instrument above named so that the same will fit or open the lock of a building, railroad car, aircraft or vessel, trailer coach, or vehicle as defined in the Vehicle Code, without being requested so to do by some person having the right to open the same, or who shall make, alter, or repair any instrument or thing, knowing or having reason to believe that it is intended to be used in committing a misdemeanor or felony, is guilty of a misdemeanor. Any of the structures mentioned in Section 459 of this code shall be deemed to be a building within the meaning of this section."

Possession of Means to Enter Coin-Operated Machine (PC 466.3).

a. Whoever possesses a key, tool, instrument, explosive, or device, or a drawing, print or mold of a key, tool, instrument, explosive, or device designed to open, break into, tamper with, or damage a coin-operated machine as defined in subdivision (b) with intent to commit a theft from such machine, is punishable by imprisonment in the county jail for not more than one year, or by fine of not more than one thousand dollars ($1,000), or by both.

b. As used in this section, the term "coin-operated machine" shall include any automatic vending machine or any part thereof, parking meter, coin telephone, coin laundry machine, coin dry-cleaning machine, amusement machine, music machine, vending machine dispensing goods or service, or moneychangers (PC 466.3).

Possession or Use of Motor Vehicle Master Key (PC 466.5).

a. Every person who, with the intent to use it in the commission of an unlawful act, possesses a motor vehicle master key is guilty of a misdemeanor.

b. Every person who, with the intent to use it in the commission of an unlawful act, uses a motor vehicle master key to open a lock or operate the ignition switch of any motor vehicle is guilty of a misdemeanor.

c. Every person who knowingly manufactures for sale, advertises for sale, offers for sale, or sells a motor vehicle master key or a motor vehicle wheel master key, except to persons who use such keys in their lawful occupations or businesses, is guilty of a misdemeanor.

d. As used in this section:
  1. "Motor vehicle master key" means a key which will operate all the locks or ignition switches, or both the locks and ignition switches, in a given group of motor vehicle locks or motor vehicle ignition switches, or both motor vehicle ignition switches, each of which can be operated by a key which will not operate one or more of the other locks or ignition switches in such group.
  2. "Motor vehicle wheel lock" means a device attached to a motor vehicle for theft protection purposes which can be removed only by a key unit unique to the wheel lock attached to a particular motor vehicle.
  3. "Motor vehicle wheel lock master key" means a key unit which will operate all the wheel locks in a given group of motor vehicle wheel locks, each of which can be operated by a key unit which will not operate any of the other wheel locks in the group (PC 466.5).

Motor Vehicle Keys: Unlawful Possession (PC 466.7). Every person who, with the intent to use it in the commission of an unlawful act, possesses a motor vehicle key with knowledge that such key was made without the consent of either the registered or legal owner of the motor vehicle or of a person who is in lawful possession of the motor vehicle, is guilty of a misdemeanor (PC 466.7).

Unauthorized Duplication or Possession of Keys. "Any person who knowingly makes duplicates, causes to be duplicated, or uses or attempts to make, duplicates, cause to be duplicated, or used, or has in his possession any key to a building or other area owned, operated or controlled by the State of California, any state agency, board, or commission, a county, city, or any public school or community college district without authorization from the person in charge of such building or area or his designated representative and with knowledge of the lack of such authorization is guilty of a misdemeanor" (PC 469).

14.9 UNLAWFUL FORCED ENTRY

PC 603. Every person other than a peace officer engaged in the performance of his duties as such who *forcibly* and without consent of the owner, representative of the owner, lessee or representative of the lessee thereof, enters a dwelling house, cabin, or other building occupied or constructed for occupation by humans, and who damages, injures, or destroys any property of value in, around or appertaining to such dwelling house, cabin or other building, is guilty of a misdemeanor.

Discussion

PC 603 is an appropriate section to use in "burglaries" where the specific intent of entering to commit theft or a felony is absent or cannot be proved. The building entered must be a *dwelling house* and the entry must be *forced*. One should also note that the culprit must cause some damage to the building or its contents. Generally the damage caused by the forced entry is sufficient to satisfy this element of the offense. Consumption of food in the house would constitute "destruction of property" as used in this section, as would a malicious mischief or defacing of property in the house.

TERMINOLOGY DEFINED—CHAPTER 14

See the Terminology Quiz at the end of this chapter.

1. Abandonment: surrender of property rights, giving up an attempted crime.
2. Abate: to end, nullify, e.g., abatement proceedings.
3. Abscond: to leave secretly, fleeing to avoid legal proceedings.
4. Abstract: a summary of essential points.
5. Boost: slang term for theft, to steal especially with special device.
6. Building: any structure with walls on all sides and a roof.
7. Burglary: entering a building with intent to steal or commit a felony.
8. Burglary tools: picklock, any tool used or designed for unlawful entry.
9. Constructive entry: removing items without personally entering, e.g., via a pole.
10. Dwelling house: a residence, apartment, etc.
11. Entering: any physical intrusion or by reaching in.
12. Forced entry: physically breaking in, prying door, window or lock.
13. Inhabited building: occupied as a residence, even if absent at time.
14. Larcenous intent: with intent to steal, to commit theft.
15. Larceny: theft, to permanently deprive owner of property.
16. Lockpick: a device for opening locks without a key.
17. Master key: one which will open all locks of a given type.
18. Tenant: a renter, one who holds a lease on property, leasee.
19. Trailer coach: house trailer, designed for habitation.
20. True bill: indictment by Grand Jury.

TRUE-FALSE QUIZ—CHAPTER 14

1. In order to constitute burglary, there must be a physical breaking and entering of a building as defined in the Penal Code.
2. One can commit burglary and still not physically enter a building.
3. Burglary is a specific intent crime.
4. A building for purposes of burglary is any structure with walls on all sides and a roof.
5. One may commit burglary by entering a building for the purpose of committing rape.
6. Walking into a super market during business hours for the purpose of stealing a loaf of bread constitutes burglary.
7. One would not be guilty of burglary even though he broke into a building with intent to burglarize it, if he abandoned his purpose once inside and left without taking anything.
8. "Constructive entry" is sufficient to constitute burglary if the other elements are present.
9. Unauthorized breaking into a building for the purpose of retrieving one's own property is not burglary.
10. Asportation is an essential element of burglary.
11. One is guilty of burglary if after he enters a building on legitimate business he subsequently steals something.
12. One cannot be found guilty of burglary unless he enters one of the structures specifically named in PC 459.
13. To constitute burglary of a vehicle it must be defined as such in the Vehicle Code and the doors must be locked.
14. If a building under construction meets the *Stickman* test, it may be the subject of a burglary.

15. One is guilty of first degree burglary if one enters a locked office building in the nighttime.
16. Burglary of an inhabited residence during the afternoon hours is first degree burglary.
17. A burglar who steals a loaded firearm as part of his loot is considered to have armed himself and, therefore, is guilty of first degree burglary.
18. It is a misdemeanor to possess any type of lockpick or altered key for the purpose of unlawfully entering any building or opening any coin-operated machine.
19. Knowing and unauthorized possession of a key to any State, city, county or school building is a misdemeanor.
20. To be guilty of unauthorized forced entry under PC 603, the building entered must be a dwelling.

ESSAY-DISCUSSION QUESTIONS— CHAPTER 14

1. What are the elements of burglary?
2. Discuss and give an example of how a person might "constructively" enter a building in the crime of burglary. How might one lawfully enter a building and still be guilty of burglary?
3. May a person be guilty of burglarizing his own home? If so, how?
4. Define a building as it is used in PC 459 and cite the prevailing case which so defines it.
5. List five types of structure as defined in PC 459 which are not residences which can be burglarized.
6. What are the elements of burglary of a motor vehicle?
7. What are the elements which differentiate first and second degree burglary from one another?
8. Define the term "inhabited dwelling" as it applies to burglary.
9. With what specific intent would one have to possess a "picklock" to be guilty of PC 466 (possession of burglary tools).
10. Discuss whether or not a drunk who broke a window at night of an inhabited dwelling and entered for the purpose of "sleeping it off" would be guilty of burglary, PC 459.

TERMINOLOGY QUIZ—CHAPTER 14

Match terms and definitions by placing the correct number in the parentheses. Answers may be written on a separate sheet for submission to the instructor at the instructor's direction.

1. Abandonment
2. Abate
3. Abscond
4. Abstract
5. Boost
6. Building
7. Burglary
8. Burglary tools
9. Constructive entry
10. Dwelling house
11. Entering
12. Forced entry
13. Inhabited building
14. Larcenous intent
15. Larceny
16. Lockpick
17. Master key
18. Tenant
19. Trailer coach
20. True bill

( ) a residence, apartment, etc.
( ) any physical intrusion or reaching in
( ) house trailer, designed for habitation
( ) indictment by Grand Jury
( ) a device for opening locks without a key
( ) with intent to steal, to commit theft
( ) slang term for theft, to steal
( ) occupied as a residence, even if absent at time
( ) any structure with walls on all sides and a roof
( ) physically breaking in; prying door, lock, etc.
( ) entering a building intending to steal or commit a felony
( ) removing items without personally entering building
( ) any tool designed or used for unlawful entry
( ) to leave secretly, flight to avoid prosecution
( ) to end, nullify, e.g., abatement proceedings

CHAPTER 15

Robbery and Extortion

15.1 ROBBERY DEFINED

PC 211. Robbery is the felonious taking of personal property in the possession of another, from his person or immediate presence, or against his will, accomplished by means of force or fear.

Discussion

At common law, robbery was a felony crime against both the person and the property of another. It amounted to the taking with intent to steal, of the personal property of another, from his person or in his presence, by violence or intimidation, and against his will. Robbery is actually an aggravated theft inasmuch as the property taken must be such as may be the subject of larceny.

The California Penal Code provides that robbery is both a crime against the person and the property. Robbery is distinguished from theft in that theft (larceny) is an offense against property, while in robbery it is necessary that the taking be with force or fear, and from the immediate presence of the victim (*People v. Jones, 53 Cal. 58*).

It is interesting to note that the vast majority of robberies are committed by armed perpetrators between the ages of nineteen and twenty-five years.

15.2 ELEMENTS OF ROBBERY

Robbery includes, as a necessary element, the specific intent to permanently deprive the owner of his property, and the crime must include asportation (*People v. Jones, 53 Cal. 58*); that is, the defendant must have actually taken or acquired dominion over the property of the victim before the crime is complete.

The *corpus delicti* of robbery may be proven by circumstantial evidence. Thus, where the victim is assaulted and rendered unconscious and awakes with his property missing, it may be properly inferred that

the elements of robbery have been established (*People v. Hubler, 102 C.A. 2d 689*).

The essential elements (*corpus delicti*) of robbery include:

1. Taking of personal property in the possession of another (asportation).
2. From the person or immediate presence of the victim.
3. Against his will (without consent).
4. Accomplished by means of force or fear (violence or threatened violence).

Asportation. Taking of personal property (asportation) includes the taking and carrying away of the property of another. This must be accomplished by the use of force or by intimidation, or the "putting in fear" of the victim. Therefore, without asportation the crime is not complete but may amount to an attempt under PC 664.

Robbery may not be completed at the moment the defendant obtains possession of stolen property, but includes the element of asportation which is as important in the commission of the crime as gaining possession (*People v. Anderson, 64 C. 3d 633*). Similarly, the courts have held that forcing the victim to throw a wallet on the ground is asportation even though the defendant failed to pick it up (*People v. Quinn, 77 C.A. 2d 734*).

To support a conviction of robbery there must be a taking of personal property which is in the possession of another from his person or immediate possession, and although some asportation is required, the distance the property is taken may be very short; therefore, the fact that the defendant and his partner returned the wallet taken from the victim did not preclude a finding that the victim had actually been robbed (*People v. Salcido, 186 C.A. 2d 684*).

Person—Immediate Presence. The taking in order to constitute robbery must be either from the owner's person or in his actual presence. It is difficult to draw a line between person or presence; however such is not actually necessary in most cases inasmuch as either is generally sufficient to complete the crime. For example, forcibly binding the owner in one room of a home and extorting information as to money or valuables in another room is considered "from the person." Also, tying an owner of a theater in one room and taking money from a safe in another is accomplishing the act "in the presence" of the victim.

Defendant, after raping victim, removed money from her purse. The court held that the property was taken from her "immediate presence" within the meaning of the robbery statute. The taking further constituted force or fear in that the victim testified that she was "scared" at the time of the robbery, which was an incident of the rape offense (*People v. Fields, 190 C.A. 2d 515*).

Where the robbery is committed within the hearing or perception of the victim who is restrained nearby, the defendant cannot contend that the robbery was not in his victim's "immediate presence" (*People v. Lavender, 137 C.A. 582*).

Against the Victim's Will. The element of consent is lacking in the crime of robbery and thus distinguishes it from the crime of extortion, which is defined as "obtaining property from another with his consent." Generally, in the crime of extortion there is also the element of choice, but such is not the case in robbery (see "Extortion" this chapter).

Fear as a Means of Robbery. The fear mentioned in Section 212 may be either:
1. The fear of an unlawful injury to the person or property of the person robbed, or of any relative of his or member of his family; or
2. The fear of an immediate and unlawful injury to the person or property of any one in the company of the person robbed at the time of the robbery (PC 212).

Force or Fear. Some violence or intimidation must be used in the taking of property by robbing or the crime is merely theft. Thus, while pocket picking and purse snatching is grand theft, it being a theft from the person, such is generally not robbery unless sufficient force or fear is added and can be proven.

Whenever there is a struggle by the owner to keep his property, or if it is detached by force, as, for instance a watch chain broken in snatching a watch, there is generally held to be sufficient force where resistance is offered.

Intimidation, or putting in fear, will supply the requisite fear in the commission of robbery. It must be remembered however, that the crime does not require both force and fear, but force *or* fear; thus one element may operate independently of the other. It has also been held that the threat of violence must be such as to create a reasonable apprehension of danger or it is not sufficient to make the taking robbery. Such fear need not be of a personal nature; it may be instilling fear of burning one's home or office.

A person may be unconscious and devoid of will, as from a blow on the head, accompanied by the actual taking of his property, but in such cases where absence of will is brought on independently by the victim, such as voluntary intoxication, where the victim is being "rolled" and is unconscious therefore of any activity, the crime is not robbery but grand theft.

The fear in robbery may be directed to another person who is present at the time of the commission of the robbery. Thus, where the victim, a relative, or another person in his company is threatened should the victim fail to comply in giving up his property, this is robbery. For example, where "A" and "B" are walking in a park and "R," a robber, attempts to relieve "A" of his property by threatening to shoot "B," this is proper fear, and the crime of robbery is consummated when there is some asportation apparent.

Robbery has been committed if one who has stolen property from the person of another uses force or fear in removing or attempting to remove property from the owner's immediate presence (*People v. Anderson, 64 A.C. 689*).

The crime of robbery is complete when money and property are taken from the person or immediate presence accomplished by force or fear, and the crime does not become incomplete by the intervention of police officers as long as the essential elements of the crime are satisfied (*People v. Johnson, 219 C.A. 2d 631*).

Either force or intimidation is the essence of the crime of robbery (*People v. Calliham, 81 C.A. 2d 928*), and the force or violence necessary to the crime of robbery distinguishes it from the crime of larceny.

The snatching of property from the owner's person or the taking by threats or menaces of great bodily harm creating grave apprehension on the part of the victim is sufficient "force or fear" necessary to the commission of robbery (*People v. Jefferson, 31 C.A. 2d 562*).

Return of Property. Once the act of asportation has occurred the crime is complete and it is no defense that the property was returned, not even if the restitution occurred directly after the taking (*People v. Tipton, 96 C.A. 2d 840*).

Robbery in an Inhabited Dwelling House, Trailer Coach. Every robbery perpetrated in an inhabited dwelling house or trailer coach as defined in the Vehicle Code is punishable by imprisonment in the state prison for three, four or six years (PC 213.5).

15.3   OWNERSHIP AND VALUE OF PROPERTY

In robbery, the amount and value of an item of personal property taken by the perpetrator is immaterial. If all other elements of the crime are present, the offense is complete though the value of the property be slight (*People v. Simmons, 28 Cal. 2d 699; People v. Ferlito, 100 C.A. 355*). However, as in the crime of theft, the property itself must have some legal value.

Where defendants took money from a theater during the manager's absence, the court concluded that when force or fear is instilled in other employees in an effort to obtain the theater property, the crime is robbery (*People v. Dean, 66 C.A. 459*). Thus, a security guard or night watchman could be placed in a similar position since he is in a "quasi-fiduciary" position to the owner of the goods and property which he is guarding. For example, when a Standard Oil Company service station is held up by robbery suspects, though the money or property is taken from, or in the immediate presence of the attendant, the victim in the case is Standard Oil Company. However, should the attendant be relieved of his own personal property, such as a wallet or watch, he becomes a second victim to a single robbery transaction.

15.4   MISCELLANEOUS ASPECTS —INCREASED PENALTY

Effective July 1, 1977, the Legislature eliminated the two (first and second) degrees of robbery. Previously, robbery by a person armed with a dangerous or deadly weapon or robbery perpetrated by torture was first degree and punished more severely. Robbery of drivers of vehicles transporting for hire (previously first-degree) is still punished more severely, but is now listed as a separate type of robbery under PC 211a.

Robbery of Operator of Vehicle For Transportation of Persons For Hire. The robbery of any person who is performing his duties as an operator of any motor vehicle, streetcar, or trackless trolley used for the transportation of persons for hire, is punishable by imprisonment in the state prison for three, four or six years (PC 211a). Section 214 of the Penal Code also makes it a felony to board any railroad train with intention of robbing any person.

Torture. Torture is frequently used in the commission of the crime of robbery, often to compel the victim to disclose the location of money or property. Obviously torture would constitute "force" as used in PC 211.

There are cases, however, where the victim is subjected to severe physical abuse such as choking, kicking, or vicious assault with fists or some instrument, *after* consummation of the robbery. In such instances the suspect is still guilty of robbery. It is apparent, however, the Legislature intended the penalty be substantially increased in such cases by virtue of PC 12022.7.

Great Bodily Injury Inflicted During Commission of a Felony. Added Penalty of Three Years. (PC 12022.7). Any person who, with intent to inflict such injury, personally inflicts great bodily injury on any person other than an accomplice in the commission or attempted commission of a felony shall, in addition and consecutive to the punishment prescribed for the felony or attempted felony of which he has been convicted, be punished by an additional term of three years, unless infliction of great bodily injury is an element of the offense of which he is convicted (such as PC 245, ADW).

As used in PC 12022.7, great bodily injury means a significant or substantial physical injury.

Armed With a Dangerous or Deadly Weapon. Any person who is armed with a *firearm* in the commission or attempted commission of a felony shall, upon conviction of such felony or attempted felony, in addition and consecutive to the punishment prescribed for the felony or attempted felony of which he has been convicted, be punished by an additional term of one year, unless such arming is an element of the offense of which he was convicted. This additional term shall apply to any person who is a principal in the commission or attempted commission of a felony if one or more of the principals is armed with a firearm, whether or not such person is personally armed with a firearm (PC 12022(a)).

Any person who personally used a deadly or *dangerous* weapon in the commission or attempted commission of a felony shall, upon conviction of such felony or attempted felony, in addition and consecutive to the punishment prescribed for the felony or attempted felony of which he has been convicted, be punished by an additional term of one year, unless use of a deadly or dangerous weapon is an element of the offense of which he was convicted (PC 12022(b)).

The terms "dangerous" and "deadly" in reference to weapons as used in the above section are not necessarily equivalent terms. This means that a defendant is subject to the increased penalty for commission of a robbery where he used either.

It is interesting to note in PC 12022(a), above, that if one participant is armed with a firearm, any and all other participants are subject to the increased penalty even though not all were personally armed.

Personal Use of Firearms. A person who personally uses a firearm in the commission or attempted commission of a felony shall, upon conviction of such felony or attempted felony, in addition and consecutive to the punishment prescribed for the felony or attempted felony of which he has been convicted, be punished by an additional term of *two years*, unless use of a firearm is an element of the offense of which he was convicted (PC 12022.5).

The additional term provided by this section may be imposed in cases of assault with a deadly weapon under PC 245 (PC 12022.5).

15.5   PUNISHMENT FOR ROBBERY

Except as provided in PC 211a and PC 213.5, robbery is punishable by imprisonment in the state prison for two, three, or five years. Notwithstanding PC 664 (punishment for attempts), attempted robbery is punishable by imprisonment in the state prison (PC 213).

Robbery of Pharmacy. If the person robbed is someone who at the time is in legal control of narcotics (controlled substances) or the robbery is of a pharmacy, and the purpose of the robbery is to obtain narcotics, the law requires the court to give the longest of the three sentences listed in PC 213.

Discussion

In the case of kidnapping, forcible rape, and robbery, the court stated that the offenses were divisible under the attending circumstances, and the defendants were properly sentenced for each crime and were not entitled to have a single sentence imposed under the statute (PC 654) precluding double punishment (*People v. Mistretta, 221 C.A. 2d 42*).

15.6   EXTORTION DEFINED

PC 518. "Extortion is the obtaining of property from another, *with his consent*, or the obtaining of an official act of a public officer, induced by a wrongful use of force or fear, or under color of official right."

Discussion

The crime of extortion, which is called "blackmail" in several jurisdictions, is closely akin to robbery in many respects. The essence of the offense of extortion is that it results in the unlawful obtainment of something of value; however, it is also an offense against property. The legislative intent of this statute is to occupy that area wherein money or property is obtained from another, with his consent, and with force or fear, and which is not appropriately covered by the robbery statute.

The origin of the term "blackmail," has an interesting history. Rich knights of old wore gilded armor with fancy chain mail. Poor knights wore black armor with plain mail. Any knight knocked off his horse in a tourney lost his horse to his opponent. A few especially crafty jousters donned black armor, unhorsed the richest knights and sold the prize horses back to the knights who lost them. The scam became so common it was given a name only later to mean something else: blackmail.

The differentiation between robbery and extortion is slight and amounts to the element of "consent" on the part of the victim. Robbery, like theft, requires that the property be taken without the consent of the owner, whereas extortion is the taking of property by means of force or fear, or under color of official right, but does not amount to larceny and is with the consent of the victim.

15.7   CONSENT—FORCE—FEAR

The Element of Consent. Consent in extortion is more in the nature of a choice. Thus, while the victim of extortion need not wish to voluntarily part with his property, he generally has the choice to do so or suffer the consequences of being subjected to accusations, unlawful injury, or the exposing of any deformity, whether such is true or not.

Force or Fear. The elements of force or fear requisite to the crime of extortion may be accomplished by a threat to do an unlawful injury to the person or property of the individual threatened or of a third party.

PC 519 states that "Fear, such as will constitute extortion, may be induced by a threat, either:
1. To do an unlawful injury to the person or property of the individual threatened or of a third person.
2. To accuse the individual threatened, or any relative of his or member of his family, of any crime; or

3. To expose, or impute to him or them any deformity or disgrace, or crime; or
4. To expose any secret affecting him or them."

To constitute extortion, the victim must consent unwillingly, and with obvious coercion, to surrender his property, and the wrongful use of force or fear must be the operating or controlling cause compelling such consent by the victim (*People v. Goodman, 159 C.A. 2d 54*).

One who threatens to "blast" his victims in a magazine for a failure to advertise in the defendant's publication is guilty of extortion if the threats made amount to those outlined in PC 519 (*People v. Terantino, 45 Cal. 2d 590*).

Evidence was sufficient to support an implied finding that the defendant attempted to place the owner of a bar in fear of an unlawful injury to his business or person and a conviction for attempted extortion was sustained in this case (*People v. Camodeca, 52 Cal. 2d 142*).

15.8 THREAT OF UNLAWFUL INJURY

A threat to do bodily harm to others, or to inflict property damage is a threat to do an unlawful injury within the meaning of PC 519. Thus, when one threatens to burn down the factory of a wealthy industrialist if money or property is not paid, the crime is extortion if the victim consents to part with his property because of the unlawful threat. By contradistinction, the intimidation in the crime of robbery is so extreme as to overcome the will of the victim and cause him to part with his money or property without consent.

Threat of Exposure. The "badger game" is a type of an extortion trick, usually in the form of enticing a man into a compromising position with a woman whose real or pretended husband comes upon the scene and demands payment under the threat of prosecution or exposure. Such a threat is sufficient under this section to constitute the crime of extortion within the meaning of PC 519.

15.9 ATTEMPTED EXTORTION

PC 524. "Every person who attempts, by means of any threat, such as is specified in Section 519 of this code, to extort money or other property from another is punishable by imprisonment in the county jail not longer than one year or in the state prison, or by fine not exceeding five thousand dollars ($5,000), or by both such fine and imprisonment."

Discussion

One is guilty of the crime of attempted extortion when his acts are ineffectual in bringing about the contemplated results of extorting money or property from his victim. Thus, if a victim feigns the amount of fear necessary to the commission of the crime, leading his extortioner to believe that he will consent to giving up his property, but does so only to detect and prosecute the extortioner, the crime is attempted extortion, on the theory that the requisite element of force or fear was not actual and the crime of extortion itself is, therefore, not consummated.

To commit the offense of attempted extortion, there must be a specific intent to commit the crime and a direct ineffectual act done toward its commission, but the effect produced on the alleged victim is immaterial (*People v. Franquelin, 109 C.A. 525*).

The crime of attempted extortion depends upon the acts, mind, and intent of the person threatening, and not upon the result upon the person to be coerced.

15.10 OBTAINING SIGNATURE BY THREAT

PC 522. "Every person who, by an extortionate means, obtains from another his signature to any paper or instrument, whereby, if such signature were freely given, any property would be transferred, or any debt, demand, charge, or right of action created, is punishable in the same manner as if the actual delivery of such debt, demand, charge, or right of action were obtained."

15.11 SENDING THREATENING LETTERS

PC 523. "Every person who, with intent to extort any money or other property from another, sends or delivers to any person any letter or other writing, whether subscribed or not, expressing or implying, or adapted to imply, any threat such as is specified in Section 519, is punishable in the same manner as if such money or property were actually obtained by means of such threat."

Where the defendant sent a letter to a complainant in which he indicated that he would expose the complainant if the latter did not withdraw an appeal in a civil case, it was held that this was sufficient threat within the purview of PC 523 and PC 519 (*People v. Cadman, 57 Cal. 562*).

Letters sent to a judge by a defendant fined and jailed by the jurist, which demanded return of the fine paid, and also inquired as to whether the judge's windows were insured was held to be not a simple inquiry but rather an implied threat within the purview of PC 523 and PC 519 (*People v. Oppenheimer, 209 C.A. 2d 413*).

PC 650. "Every person who knowingly and willfully sends or delivers to another any letter or writing, whether subscribed or not, threatening to accuse him or another of a crime, or to expose or publish any of his failings or infirmities, is guilty of a misdemeanor."

Discussion

In the various cases in which the sending of a letter is made criminal by this code, the offense is deemed complete from the time when such letter is deposited in any post-office or any other place, or delivered to any person, with intent that it shall be forwarded (PC 660).

15.12 PENALTY FOR EXTORTION

PC 520. "Every person who extorts any money or property from another, under circumstances not amounting to robbery, by means of force, or any threat such as is mentioned in the preceding section is punishable by imprisonment in the state prison for two, three, or four years."

Public Officials: Penalty. Every person who commits any extortion under color of official right, in cases for which a different punishment is not prescribed in this Code, is guilty of a misdemeanor (PC 521).

COMPARISON OF ELEMENTS: ROBBERY AND EXTORTION	
ROBBERY (PC 211)	**EXTORTION (PC 518)**
1. Felonious taking (asportation) 2. Personal property of victim 3. From Victim's person or immediate presence 4. Against victim's will 5. By means of force or fear	1. Obtaining (need not actually take) 2. Personal property of another or an official act by a public officer 3. With victim's consent (Note difference between robbery and extortion) 4. Induced by wrongful use of force or fear

FEAR IN ROBBERY
1. Threat of unlawful injury to:
  a. Victim's person
  b. Victim's property
  c. Victim's relative
2. Immediate and unlawful injury to:
  a. Victim's person
  b. Victim's property
  c. Anyone accompanying victim at time of robbery
	FEAR IN EXTORTION
	1. Threat of unlawful injury to:
	  a. Victim's person
	  b. Victim's property
	  c. Victim's relatives
	  d. Any third person
	2. Fear of accusation or exposure of:
	  a. Any crime (victim or relative)
	  b. Deformity, disgrace or crime
	  c. Any secret

TERMINOLOGY DEFINED—CHAPTER 15

See the Terminology Quiz at the end of this chapter.

1. Against will: absence of voluntary consent.
2. Appurtenant: pertaining or belonging to, an attachment.
3. Asportation: physical control or movement of property.
4. Badger Game: extortion fraud based on accusation of adultery.
5. Blackmail: another term for extortion.
6. Dangerous weapon: article capable of being used as a weapon.
7. Deadly weapon: an article designed to be used as a weapon.
8. Extortion: taking property by illegal threats or fear.
9. Fear: intimidation based on realistic threats.
10. Fence: a receiver of stolen property.
11. Force: physically striking, struggling, abusing.
12. Immediate presence: within hearing or perception range, nearby.
13. Impute: to accuse or attribute, to ascribe.
14. Intimidation: putting one in fear.
15. Market value: reasonable current value of any property.
16. Misprison: to conceal a felony, to inferfere with justice.
17. Nullify: make void, abrogate, enjoin, cancel.
18. *Obiter dictim*: An opinion of a judge, may be informal.
19. Quasi-fiduciary: Latin meaning "similar to position of trust."
20. Torture: intentional infliction of pain or anguish on another.

TRUE-FALSE—CHAPTER 15

1. Robbery is the felonious taking of personal property from another with or without his knowledge or consent.
2. The element of asportation is essential for the crime of robbery to be complete.
3. The *corpus delicti* of robbery may be proven entirely by circumstantial evidence.
4. If all other elements are present, forcing a victim to throw his wallet on the ground constitutes asportation and the robbery is complete even though the suspect does not pick it up.
5. If a victim is bound and gagged in another room, it is still considered "immediate presence" for purposes of robbery.
6. The "fear" mentioned in PC 211 must be fear of unlawful injury to the victim personally.
7. Some violence or intimidation must be used in the taking of property by robbery or the crime is merely theft.
8. Immediate restitution of the stolen property in robbery would nullify the crime by eliminating the element of theft.
9. In robbery, the amount and value of the property taken is immaterial.
10. The taking of property by robbery from one who is not the true owner is merely theft.
11. Robbery from an off-duty bus driver is a misdemeanor.
12. Robbery while "armed" with a toy gun is a felony.
13. Any instrument, depending on how it was used, could make one guilty of using force in robbery.
14. If only one of two suspects is armed with a loaded gun during a robbery, both are guilty of armed robbery.
15. To be guilty of robbery involving a gun, the weapon must have been displayed, if only for a moment.
16. If one uses a loaded gun for the purpose of committing rape, he may be charged with both robbery and rape.
17. The key difference between robbery and extortion is the element of consent.
18. Threatening to have someone arrested for failing to pay a legal debt constitutes extortion.
19. Threatening to publicly accuse a city official of being a homosexual unless he issues a needed permit is extortion even though no money or property is involved.
20. The "Badger Game" is an example of a type of extortion.

ESSAY-DISCUSSION QUESTIONS—
CHAPTER 15

1. What are the elements of extortion (PC 518)? By what common name is the crime sometimes known?
2. Discuss the element of "consent" as it applies to extortion.
3. Discuss force or fear requisite to the crime of extortion. What are the four ways in which fear, such as will constitute extortion, may be induced?
4. What are the elements of PC 523 relative to sending threatening letters? Must this be done for purposes of extortion to constitute a crime under this section?
5. In cases where one sends threatening letters which do not involve extortion, what type of threats or accusations must they contain to constitute a crime under PC 650?
6. Define the elements of robbery and discuss the following factors: (1) asportation, (2) immediate presence, (3) force or fear.
7. What effect does ownership and value of the property taken in robbery have on the *corpus delicti*?
8. How does armed robbery differ in its *corpus delicti* from extortion?
9. Discuss the meaning of "dangerous" or "deadly" weapon as it applies to robbery.
10. What is the punishment for robbery?

TERMINOLOGY QUIZ—CHAPTER 15

Match terms and definitions by placing the correct number in the parentheses. Answers may be written on a separate sheet for submission to the instructor at the instructor's direction.

1. Against will
2. Appurtenant
3. Asportation
4. Badger Game
5. Blackmail
6. Dangerous weapon
7. Deadly weapon
8. Extortion
9. Fear
10. Fence
11. Force
12. Immediate presence
13. Impute
14. Intimidation
15. Market value
16. Misprison
17. Nullify
18. *Obiter dictim*
19. Quasi-fiduciary
20. Torture

( ) an article designed to be used as a weapon
( ) to accuse or attribute to, ascribe to
( ) article capable of being used as a weapon
( ) intimidation based on realistic threats
( ) make void, abrogate, enjoin, cancel
( ) absence of voluntary consent
( ) physical control or movement or property
( ) to conceal a felony, to interfere with justice
( ) extortion based on accusation of adultery
( ) putting one in fear
( ) another term for extortion
( ) a receiver of stolen property
( ) physically striking, struggling, abusing
( ) within hearing or perception, nearby
( ) taking property by illegal threats or fear

CHAPTER 16

Theft and Embezzlement

16.1 THEFT DEFINED (PC 484)

a. Every person who shall feloniously steal, take, carry, lead or drive away the personal property of another, or who shall fraudulently appropriate property which has been entrusted to him, or who shall knowingly and designedly, by any false or fraudulent representation or pretense, defraud any other person of money, labor, or real or personal property, or who causes or procures others to report falsely of his wealth or mercantile character and by thus imposing upon any person, obtains credit and thereby fraudulently gets or obtains the labor or service of another, is guilty of theft. In determining the value of the property obtained, for purposes of this section, the reasonable and fair market value shall be the test, and in determining the value of services received, the contract price shall be the test. If there be no contract price, the reasonable and going wage for the service rendered shall govern. For the purposes of this section, any false or fraudulent representation or pretense made shall be treated as continuing, so as to cover any money, property or service received as a result thereof, and the complaint, information, or indictment may charge that the crime was committed on any date during the particular period in question. The hiring of any additional employee or employees without advising each of them of every labor claim due and unpaid and every judgment that the employer has been unable to meet shall be *prima facie* evidence of intent to defraud.

b. Except as provided in Section 10855 of the Vehicle Code, intent to commit theft by fraud is presumed if one who has leased or rented the personal property of another pursuant to a written contract fails to return the personal property to its owner within twenty days after the owner has made written demand by certified or registered mail following the expiration of the lease or rental agreement for return of the property so leased or rented.

c. Notwithstanding the provisions of subdivision (b), if one presents, with criminal intent, identification which bears a false or fictitious name or address for the purposes of obtaining the lease or rental of the personal property of another, the presumption created herein shall apply upon the failure of the lessee to return the rental property at the expiration of the lease or rental agreement, and no written demand for the return of the leased or rented property shall be required.

d. The presumptions created by subdivision (b) are presumptions affecting the burden of producing evidence.

e. Within thirty days after the lease or rental agreement has expired, the owner shall make written demand for return of the property so leased or rented. Notice addressed and mailed to the lessee or renter at the address given at the time of the making of the lease or rental agreement and to any other known address shall constitute proper demand. Where the owner fails to make such written demand the presumption created by subdivision (b) shall not apply."

Theft Defined

1. Feloniously (unlawfully):
   a. steal, take, carry, lead or drive away
2. Personal property of another.
3. Fraudulently appropriate property:
   a. By person to whom entrusted.
4. Defrauding another:
   a. By false or fraudulent pretense,
   b. Of money, labor, or real or personal property.

5. Causing or procuring another to falsely report wealth:
   a. For purpose of obtaining credit, and
   b. Fraudulently obtains money, property, or services of another.

Diversion of Money Received for Labor or Materials: Punishment: Diversion Constituting Misdemeanor. "Any person who receives money for the purpose of obtaining or paying for services, labor, materials, or equipment and willfully fails to apply such money for such purpose by either willfully failing to complete the improvements for which funds were provided or willfully failing to pay for services, labor, materials or equipment provided incident to such construction, and wrongfully diverts the funds to a use other than that for which the funds were received, shall be guilty of a public offense and punishable by a fine not exceeding five thousand dollars ($5,000), or by imprisonment in the state prison, or in the county jail not exceeding one year, or by both such fine and such imprisonment if the amount diverted is in excess of one thousand dollars ($1,000). If the amount diverted is less than one thousand dollars ($1,000), the person shall be guilty of a misdemeanor (PC 484b).

Discussion

Larceny at common law is the obtaining of possession of personal property, by trespass in the taking and carrying away of the same, from the possession of another, and with the felonious intent to deprive him of his ownership therein.

Prior to 1927 the Penal Code made a technical distinction between larceny (theft), embezzlement, and obtaining money under false pretenses. Due to the difficulty in determining which crime had been committed, Section 490(a) was added, which said "Whenever any law or statute of this state refers to or mentions larceny, embezzlement, or stealing, said law or statute shall hereafter be read and interpreted as if the word 'theft' was substituted therefor."

Value of Property Taken. To determine the value of the property taken, the reasonable and fair market value shall be the test. In determining the value of services received, the contract price shall be the test. If there is no contract price, the reasonable and going wage for the service rendered shall govern.

Property Subject of Theft. In order for property to be capable of being stolen, it must have some legal value, intrinsic or extrinsic as it may be. Thus it has been held that the theft of a lottery ticket, being a contraband item, is not theft; however, the intrinsic

value of the paper on which it is written does have value and would thus constitute a theft (*People v. Gonzales, 62 C.A. 2d 274*).

Real property as well as personal property may be the subject of theft. Thus where a fixture which is part of the reality of a property is severed, such as an act constitutes theft. In addition, dogs are considered personal property under PC 491 and may thus be the subject of theft; however, cats are generally not placed within this category unless some legal value can be established, the theory being that cats are not personal property since no taxes are paid on them.

Certain types of thefts are made crimes by separate statute. Thus, passenger tickets may be stolen (PC 493), as well as water (PC 499) and electricity (PC 499a). Also, if the thing stolen consists of any evidence of debt or other written instrument, the amount of money due thereon, or secured to be paid thereby, and remaining unsatisfied, or which in any contingency might be collected thereon, or the value of the property the title to which is shown thereby, or the sum which might be recovered in the absence thereof, is the value of the thing stolen (PC 492).

16.2 THE ACT IN THEFT (ASPORTATION)

The act in theft consists in taking *and* carrying away the property of another, not taking *or* carrying away. Such a taking and carrying away is called *asportation* and is an essential element to every crime of theft. In addition, the taking requires a violation of another's possession; there must be a trespass. Consequently, if the defendant was in possession of the goods, there could be no taking. Cases illustrating this point include instances in which the defendant had hired the property, or where he is a bailee (for hire or gratuitous), or where possession of an article is given to a servant for his master. In all such cases as these, the defendant had possession and not mere custody of the property.

Where the accused endeavored to steal an overcoat hung on a clothing dummy standing in front of a store and had unbuttoned the coat and removed it from the dummy, but was prevented from carrying it away because of a chain which passed through the sleeve and was fastened to the dummy, there was not sufficient asportation to constitute larceny (*People v. Meyer, 75 Cal. 838*).

To constitute the necessary asportation, the thief must move the property so that in some degree it occupies a different position than it previously occupied and the conditions must be such that the thief secures such dominion over the property as to be able to carry it away. The moving need not of necessity be by the actual seizing of the property, for any act equivalent to such actual seizure would be sufficient asportation (*People v. Wilcoxin, 69 C.A. 267*).

Asportation need not be by hand nor by the use of any personal force. An animal may be stolen by being enticed away by food; or tapping a pipe and taking gas or water therefrom will constitute the necessary asportation to commit the crime of theft.

Elements of Theft. The four elements necessary to constitute theft are:
1. The taking of a thing of value from the owner (or any other person in possession of the property);
2. Without consent of the owner or person then in possession of the property;
3. With intent to *permanently* deprive the owner of the use or title of the property.
4. Asportation (movement) of the property. One cannot commit theft by looking at, longing for, or even wanting to steal property (*People v. Johnson, 136 C.A. 2d 665*).

16.3 THE INTENT IN THEFT

One of the essential elements of the crime of theft is an intent to steal, and such intent must be to specifically deprive the owner therein of his property. The intent to steal must exist in the mind of the perpetrator at the time of the theft, and thus one who takes property with the intent to return it to its lawful owner does not commit a theft.

Since specific intent must exist at the time of the taking of the property of another, the taking of an automobile belonging to another in his absence and without his consent, but without any intention of permanently depriving the owner of his property, while it might constitute a violation of Section 10851 of the Vehicle Code, would not constitute theft under this section (*People v. Tucker, 104 Cal. 440*). Similarly, the taking of property which is rented on a time basis, and failing to return it at a specified time, is not necessarily theft, unless, however, the person renting the property entertained the requisite intent at the time of negotiating the rental. Or, if one in good faith takes the property of another, thinking it to be his own, and assuming that he has a legal right to it, it is not theft due to the absence of a specific intent to deprive the owner of his property. However, where a person takes a car which does not belong to him, and without the owner's consent, and thereafter fills the gas tank of the vehicle to capacity, it has been held that the evidence was sufficient to establish the

required specific intent to consummate the crime (*People v. Cawford, 115 C.A. 2d 838*).

In the prosecution for grand theft of an automobile, it was for the court to determine the intention with which the vehicle was taken by the defendant (*People v. Wallace, 173 C.A. 2d 762*).

Theft is ordinarily the felonious taking of property of another without his consent with the intent to deprive him thereof, and includes larceny, embezzlement, obtaining money by false pretenses, and theft by trick or device (*People v. Goodman, 159 C.A. 2d 54*).

To complete the crime of theft, intent to steal or to take property is necessarily an addition to the actual stealing or taking, and a defendant who is in possession of stolen property has a duty to explain his possession in order to remove the effect of possession as a circumstance, taken with other suspicious facts (*People v. Arriola, 164 C.A. 2d 430; People v. Wells, 187 C.A. 2d 324*).

Possession of Stolen Property. Where the perpetrator of a theft takes the personal property of another and is subsequently found in possession of same, such evidence is admissible for two purposes: (1) It tends to show the identity of the perpetrator, and (2) it tends to connect the defendant with the offense. However, there must be, in addition to proof of the possession of stolen property, other evidence tending to show guilt, such as direct evidence of the commission of the offense by the accused or other conduct indicative of the commission of the offense (See Text Section 16.5).

Where recently stolen property is found in conscious possession of a defendant who, upon being questioned by police, gives an erroneous and false explanation regarding his possession or remains silent under circumstances indicative of guilt, an inference of guilt is permissible and is a question for the jury to resolve (*Rollins v. Superior Court, Los Angeles, 223 C.A. 2d 219*).

A defendant who is in possession of stolen property has a duty to explain his possession in order to remove the effect of possession as a circumstance, taken with other suspicious facts of guilt (*People v. Wells, 187 C.A. 2d 324*).

Possession of stolen goods is not of itself sufficient to justify a conviction of theft, although it is a circumstance to be considered in connection with other proven facts (*People v. Edwards, 159 C.A. 2d 208*).

Evidence of possession of stolen property by the defendant, coupled with his attempt to dispose of the property at far less than its market value, together with inconsistent and misleading statements as to its procurement, justified a finding that the property was stolen and a conviction for grand theft was sustained even though there was no direct testimony or admission of the theft by the accused (*People v. Phelps, 192 C.A. 2d 12*).

16.4   ANALYSIS OF TYPES OF THEFT

There are four general categories of theft: (1) theft in general (larceny), (2) obtaining property by false pretenses, (3) obtaining property by trick or device, and (4) embezzlement. As previously indicated, whenever any law or statute of this state refers to or mentions larceny, embezzlement, or stealing, said law or statute shall hereafter be read and interpreted as if the word "theft" were substituted (PC 490a). Thus the former crimes of larceny, embezzlement, and obtaining property by false pretenses are merged into the one crime of theft. The punishment for the commission of these offenses will either be grand or petit theft, depending on the circumstances of the case and the value of the property.

16.5   THEFT IN GENERAL

Theft in general consists of a wrongful or fraudulent taking and carrying away, by any person, of the personal goods of another, from any place, without any color of right for the act, with the intention to deprive the owner, not temporarily, but permanently of his property. General theft, which simply involves a taking, accompanied by the requisite intent, and coupled with asportation, has already been described in detail.

The intent is to feloniously steal, at the time of the taking, which means to intend to deprive the owner permanently of his property. The intent of the owner is that he never intends that the taker shall take or keep his property, and title remains with the owner at all times. Possession of the property taken remains "constructively" with the owner, while the wrongdoer obtains custody. No corroboration is necessary to prove a general theft, which is simply the stealing of another's property.

16.6   FALSE PRETENSES

The crime of obtaining property by false pretenses is included in PC 484 defining theft, but is more specifically defined in PC 532, which states, "Every person

who knowingly and designedly, by any false or fraudulent representation or pretense, defrauds any other person of money, labor, or property, whether real or personal, or who causes or procures others to report falsely of his wealth or mercantile character, and by thus imposing upon any person obtains credit, and thereby fraudulently gets possession of money or property, or obtains the labor or service of another, is punishable in the same manner and to the same extent as for larceny of the money or property so obtained."

The Act in Theft by False Pretenses consists in the perpetrator gaining control over the property of another in an illegal manner. Such property may be tangible or in the form of credit or services rendered. The intent of the taker is to defraud by making false representations of a present or past existing fact and not opinions, future promises, or so-called puffing of wares.

The owner in this case voluntarily gives his property to the wrongdoer in reliance on the false representations and deceit, without any reservations. Both title and possession of the property pass into the hands of the wrongdoer because the owner intends to part with his property in reliance of the fraud. Corroboration is necessary to sustain a conviction for theft perpetrated under these circumstances (PC 1110).

A conviction of grand theft by false pretenses can rest either on a fraudulent statement of a factual character or on a promise made without intent to perform it (*People v. Carlin, 178 C.A. 2d 705*). And, a promise made without intention to perform is a misrepresentation of a state of mind and hence a misrepresentation of existing facts and is a false pretense within the meaning of this section (*People v. DeCasaus, 194 C.A. 2d 666*). While corroboration is necessary to prove a theft by false pretenses, corroboration is not necessary in proving a theft by trick or device (*People v. Reinschreiber, 141 C.A. 2d 688*).

In a prosecution of a chiropractor for theft in treating of patients with an oscillociast, even if the treatments were reasonably worth the consideration paid, this fact was no defense when patients were induced to submit to treatments by means of false pretenses (*People v. Schmitt, 155 C.A. 2d 87*).

Where a party offers to sell an interest in a business which has not been established and paints a rosy picture of the future based on false statements which the prospect purchaser believes to be true, the fraud is complete (*People v. Carlin, 178 C.A. 2d 705*).

16.7 TRICK OR DEVICE

Obtaining Property by Trick or Device. This type of theft, often referred to as "bunco theft" or the perpetration of a "confidence" game, is similar to theft by false pretenses. The act of this type consists in the perpetrator gaining control over the property of another by some trick, fraud, or false representation. The intent of the taker is to feloniously steal, which means to permanently deprive the owner of his property at the time the possession is acquired.

The intent of the owner in a theft by trick and device is to voluntarily give his property to the wrongdoer on reliance of some scheme, device, trick or artifice, but only for some agreed-upon special use, and generally for a specified period of time. Title of the property taken remains with the owner because the owner never actually intends to give up title. Possession, on the other hand, passes to the wrongdoer, but again, only for a special purpose. Corroboration is unnecessary in sustaining a conviction for this type of theft.

Examples of this type of theft include false and fraudulent spiritual manifestations, obtaining money to bet on an allegedly "fixed" horse race, or buying property for the victim and then "jacking" up the price in an effort to pocket the proceeds therefrom.

Inherent in the crime of larceny (theft) by trick and device is the employment of fraud and trickery in obtaining possession of property by one who has a preconceived design to appropriate it to his own use (*People v. Fulton, 188 C.A. 2d 105*). Thus where one perpetrates a short-change trick, the crime of theft by trick and device is committed and the amount of money taken in the exchange will determine the degree of theft (*People v. Stone, 155 C.A. 2d 259*).

Where the defendant arranged to draw a winning ticket for theater bank night and palmed and pretended to draw from the drum the previously acquired ticket so that the defendant's coconspirator could receive a large sum of money, there was a felonious taking of property of the theater operators by trick and fraudulent representation, constituting a theft under this theory (*People v. Carpenter, 141 C.A. 2d 884*).

The gist of the offense of larceny (theft) by trick and device is the appropriation of property, the possession of which was fraudulently acquired, and if a person, with a preconceived design to appropriate property to his own use, obtains possession of it by means of fraud or trickery, the taking is unquestionably theft (*People v. Robertson, 167 C.A. 2d 571*).

Theft by trick and device and theft by false pretenses are distinguished in that the former is the appropriation of property the possession of which was fraudulently acquired, and requires no corroboration to sustain a conviction, while the latter is the fraudulent or deceitful acquisition of both title and possession, and requires corroboration to sustain a conviction (*People v. Hodges, 153 C.A. 2d 788*).

16.8 EMBEZZLEMENT

Embezzlement is the fraudulent appropriation of property by a person to whom it has been entrusted (Penal Code, Sections 484, and 503 through 508).

The act of embezzlement does not require a distinct act of taking because the gist of the offense is the wrongful use of property entrusted to a servant employee, agent, bailee, trustee, or public servant. The perpetrator is said to enjoy a "ficuciary relationship" with the owner of the property, and he thus comes into possession of the property legally. For example, a store manager gives possession of a specific number of dollars in cash to a clerk at the beginning of a day to make change. If the clerk thereafter appropriates this cash, which he has legal possession of at the time, to his own use, he is then surreptitiously claiming ownership and title of the property which he is not entitled to do, since this aspect of the transaction remains with the store manager.

The intent in embezzlement is to feloniously steal, but only after possession is acquired. This is called "appropriation with fraudulent intent." The intent of the owner is that he never intends to part with title or ownership of the property, but stipulates that the "trustee" shall use the property only for a specified purpose agreed upon. As previously indicated, title remains with the owner at all times, but possession passes to the wrongdoer only for a special purpose of trust. No corroboration is necessary to sustain a conviction for embezzlement.

The property which may be the subject of embezzlement may be money, goods, chattels, things in action, or evidence of debt (*People v. Hart, 28 C.A. 335*).

Possession of property in some kind of fiduciary capacity is an essential element of embezzlement, and therefore one cannot be guilty of embezzling money when he has acquired title to it by contract or sale (*People v. Parker, 235 C.A. 2d 100*).

Where a trustee of a union welfare fund withdrew excessive amounts of money from a fund in the form of a cashier's check which he did not endorse or cash but which check was still outstanding, there was a completed embezzlement, regardless of his alleged intention to return the check to the trust fund (*People v. Williams, 145 C.A. 2d 163*).

There is no settled mode by which the fraudulent appropriation of the property of another, which constitutes embezzlement, must take place, and there are countless methods by which the appropriation might be made as long as the essential elements of the crime are present (*People v. Swanson, 174 C.A. 2d 453*).

Where an official of a union had control of union-owned realty, and he directed the making of a sale thereof, and thereafter appropriated to his own use part of the proceeds of the sale, he was guilty of embezzlement (*People v. Swanson, supra*).

The essential elements of embezzlement are a fiduciary relationship arising where one entrusts property to another, and fraudulent appropriation of that property by the latter (*People v. Darling, 230 C.A. 2d 615*).

16.9   THEFT OF CREDIT CARDS

Definitions. As used in this section and Sections 484e to 484j, inclusive:

1. *"Cardholder"* means any person to whom a credit card is issued or any person who has agreed with the card issuer to pay obligations arising from the issuance of a credit card to another person.
2. *"Credit card"* means any card, plate, coupon book, or other credit device existing for the purpose of being used from time to time upon presentation to obtain money, property, labor, or services on credit.
3. *"Expired credit card"* means a credit card which shows on its face it has elapsed.
4. *"Card issuer"* means any person who issues a credit card or the agent of such person with respect to such card.
5. *"Retailer"* means every person who is authorized by an issuer to furnish goods, money, services or anything else of value upon presentation of a credit card by a cardholder.
6. *A credit card* is "incomplete" if part of the matter other than the signature of the cardholder which an issuer requires to appear on the card before it can be used by a cardholder has not been stamped, embossed, imprinted, or written on it.
7. *"Revoked credit card"* means a credit card which is no longer authorized for use by the issuer, such authorization having been suspended or terminated and written notice thereof having been given the cardholder (PC 484d).

Theft of Credit Card

"1. Every person who acquires a credit card from another without the cardholder's or issuer's consent or who, with knowledge that it has been so acquired, acquires the credit card, with intent to use it or to sell or transfer it to a person other than the issuer or the cardholder, is guilty of petty theft.
2. Every person who acquires a credit card that he knows to have been lost, mislaid, or delivered under a mistake as to the identity or address of the cardholder, and who retains possession with intent to use it or to sell it or to transfer it to a person other than the issuer or the cardholder is guilty of petty theft.
3. Every person who sells, transfers, conveys, or receives a credit card with the intent to defraud is guilty of petty theft.
4. Every person other than the issuer, who within any consecutive twelve-month period, acquires credit cards issued in the names of four or more persons which he has reason to know were taken or retained under circumstances which constitute a violation of subdivisions (1),(2), or (3) of this section is guilty of grand theft." (PC 484e).

Forgery of Credit Card

"1. Every person who, with intent to defraud, makes, alters, or embosses a card purporting to be a credit card or offers for use such a card is guilty of forgery.
2. A person other than the cardholder or a person authorized by him who, with intent to defraud, signs the name of another or of a fictitious person to a credit card, sales slip, sales draft, or instrument for the payment of money which evidences a credit card transaction, is guilty of forgery" (PC 484f).

Use of Forged Credit Card: "Every person, who with intent to defraud, (a) uses for the purpose of obtaining money, goods, services, or anything else of value a credit card obtained or retained in violation of Section 484e or a credit card which he knows is forged, expired, or revoked, or (b) obtains money, goods, services or anything else of value by representing, without the consent of the cardholder, that he is the holder of a credit card or by representing that he is the holder of a credit card and such card has not in fact been issued, is guilty of theft. If the value of all money, goods, services, and other things of value obtained in violation of this section exceeds two hundred dollars ($200) in any consecutive six-month period, then the same shall constitute grand theft" (PC 484g).

Knowingly Furnishing Goods or Services on Forged Credit Card. "Every retailer who, with intent to defraud:

a. Furnishes money, goods, services or anything else of value upon presentation of a credit card obtained or retained in violation of Section 484e hereof or a credit card which he knows is forged, expired, or revoked, and who receives any payment therefore, is guilty of theft. If the payment received by the merchant for all money, goods, services, and other things of value furnished in violation of this section exceeds two hundred dollars ($200) in any consecutive six-month period, then the same shall constitute grand theft.

b. Fails to furnish money, goods, services, or anything else of value which he represents in writing to the issuer or a participating party that he has furnished, and who receives any payment therefore, is guilty of theft. If the difference between the value of all money, goods, services, and anything else of value actually furnished and the payment or payments received by the merchant therefore upon such representation exceeds two hundred dollars ($200) in any consecutive six-month period, then the same shall constitute grand theft" (PC 484h).

Filling in Incomplete and Counterfeit Cards

"a. Every person who possesses an incomplete credit card, with intent to complete it without the consent of the issuer is guilty of a misdemeanor.

b. Every person who with intent to defraud possesses, with knowledge of its character, machinery, plates, or any other contrivance designed for, and made use of in, the reproduction of instruments purporting to be the credit cards of an issuer who has not consented to the preparation of such credit cards, is punishable by imprisonment in the state prison or by imprisonment in the county jail for not more than one year" (PC 484i).

16.10 THEFT OF LOST PROPERTY

PC 485. "One who finds lost property, under circumstances which give him knowledge of or means of inquiry as to the true owner, and who appropriates such property to his own use or to the use of another person not entitled thereto, without first making reasonable and just efforts to find the owner and restore the property to him, is guilty of theft."

Discussion

This section applies only to cases in which the property was first lost and then found by one who took it, not as a thief, but as a finder of lost property. In such a case the finder is not guilty of this offense until having the means of inquiry as to the true owner, he appropriates the property to his own use without making reasonable efforts to find the owner and restore the property to him.

Finder of Lost Property. The Civil Code provides the manner in which one who has found lost property should pursue a legal course of action in attempting to restore such property to its rightful owner.

Duty of Finder: "Any person who finds a thing lost is not bound to take charge of it, but if he does so he is thenceforward a depositary for the owner, with the rights and obligations of a depositary for hire. Any person who finds and takes possession of any money, goods, things of action, or other personal property, or saves any domestic animal from drowning or starvation shall, within a reasonable time, inform the owner, if known, and make restitution without compensation, except a reasonable charge for saving and taking care of the property" (Civil Code, Section 2080).

Unknown Owner

a. If the owner is unknown or has not claimed the property, the person saving or finding the property shall, if such property is of the value of ten dollars ($10) or more, within a reasonable time, turn the property over to the police department of the city, if found therein, or the sheriff's department if found outside the city limits, and make an affidavit stating when and where he found or saved the property, particularly describing it. If the property was saved, he shall state:
   1. From what and how it was saved.
   2. Whether the owner of the property is known to him.
   3. That he has not secreted, withheld, or disposed of any part of the property.

b. The police department or the sheriff's department shall notify the owner, if his identity is reasonably ascertainable, that it possesses the property and where it may be claimed. The police department or sheriff's department may require payment by the owner of a reasonable charge to defray costs of storage and care of the property (Civil Code, Section 2080).

Claiming Property. If the owner appears within ninety days and proves his ownership and pays all reasonable charges, the police department or sheriff's department shall restore the property to him. (Civil Code, Section 2080.2).

Finder Gets Title. If no owner appears within ninety days, the police or sheriff's department shall publish at least once in a newspaper notice of the found or saved property. If after seven days following the notice, no owner appears and proves ownership, then title shall vest in the person who found or saved the property. If the property was found by an employee of any public agency, the property shall be sold at public auction (Civil Code, Section 2080.3).

16.11 DEGREES OF THEFT

PC 486. "Theft is divided into two degrees, the first of which is termed grand theft; the second, petty theft."

PC 487. Grand Theft Defined. "Grand theft is committed in any of the following cases:
1. When the money, labor, or real or personal property taken is of a value *exceeding* four hundred dollars ($400); provided, that when domestic fowls, avocados, olives, citrus or deciduous fruits, nuts and artichokes are taken of a value *exceeding* one hundred dollars ($100); provided, further, that where the money, labor, real or personal property is taken by a servant, agent, or employee from his principal or employer and aggregates (totals) four hundred dollars ($400) or more in any twelve consecutive month period, then the same shall constitute grand theft.
2. When the property is taken from the person of another.
3. When the property taken is an automobile, firearm, horse, mare, gelding, any bovine (cattle) animal, any caprine (goat) animal, mule, jack, jenny, sheep, lamb, hog, sow, boar, gilt, barrow or pig."

PC 487a. Stealing Carcass

a. Every person who shall feloniously steal, take, transport, or carry the carcass of any bovine (cattle), caprine (goat), equine (horse), ovine (sheep), or suine (pig) animal or of any mule, jack, or jenny, which is the personal property of another, or who shall fraudulently appropriate such property which has been entrusted to him, is guilty of grand theft.

b. Every person who shall feloniously steal, take, transport, or carry any portion of the carcass of any bovine, caprine, equine, ovine or suine animal or of any mule, jack or jenny, which has been killed without the consent of the owner thereof, is guilty of grand theft.

PC 487b. Grand Theft of Real Estate. "Every person who converts real estate of the value of one hundred ($100) or more into personal property by severance from the realty of another, and with felonious intent to do so, steals, takes, and carries away such property is guilty of grand theft and is punishable by imprisonment in the state prison."

PC 487c. Petit Theft of Real Estate. "Every person who converts real estate of the value of less than one hundred dollars ($100) into personal property by severance from the realty of another, and with felonious intent to do so, steals, takes, and carries away such property is guilty of petit theft and is punishable by imprisonment in the county jail for not more than one year, or by a fine not exceeding one thousand dollars ($1,000), or by both fine and imprisonment."

PC 487d. Grand Theft at Mine. "Every person who feloniously steals, takes, and carries away, or attempts to take, steal, and carry from any mining claim, tunnel, sluice, undercurrent, riffle box, or sulfurate machine another's gold dust, amalgam, or quicksilver is guilty of grand theft and is punishable by imprisonment in the state prison."

PC 487e. Dog Stealing: Grand Theft. "Every person who feloniously steals, takes, or carries away a dog of another which is of a value *exceeding* four hundred dollars ($400) is guilty of grand theft."

PC 487f. Dog Stealing: Petty Theft. "Every person who feloniously steals, takes, or carries away a dog of another which is of a value *not exceeding* four hundred dollars ($400) is guilty of petty theft."

PC 487g. Dog Stealing for Sale, Medical Research, or Commercial Use: Grand Theft. "Every person who feloniously steals, takes, or carries away a dog of another for purposes of sale, medical research, or other commercial uses, is guilty of grand theft."

PC 488. Petty Theft Defined. "Theft in other cases is petty theft."

Discussion

The requisite intent to commit grand theft and the concerted action between the defendant and an alleged co-principal may be proven solely by circumstantial evidence. Thus, in a prosecution for grand theft of an automobile, tried by the court, it was for the court to determine the intention with which the automobile was obtained by the defendant (*People v. Moore, 234 A.C.A. 30; People v. Wallace, 173 C.A. 2d 762*).

The surreptitious taking of an automobile from a garage which acquired a repairman's lien thereon constituted a surreptitious removal of the vehicle within the meaning of Civil Code, Section 3075, which has reference to removing vehicles subject to lien. The court thus held that the taking of the car by its owner constituted a misdemeanor under the Civil Code section rather than under PC 487, grand theft (*180 C.A. 2d 250*).

The offense of grand theft includes larceny, embezzlement, larceny by trick or device, and obtaining property by false pretenses (*People v. Schwenkner, 191 C.A. 2d 46*). Thus, the offense is complete when the accused takes property not his own with the intent to steal it, and a defendant may be convicted of grand theft upon proof of facts establishing embezzlement, larceny, or obtaining property under false pretenses (*People v. Hunter, 147 C.A. 2d 472*).

The elements of the crime of theft remain the same except that the distinction between grand and petty theft is in the type of articles stolen, the articles were taken from the person of another, and in the value thereof (*Gomez v. Superior Court, Mendocino County, 50 Cal. 2d 640*).

Elements of Grand Theft. The essential elements of grand theft consist of: (1) taking the personal property of another which is subject matter of the crime; (2) without the owner's consent or claim of right; (3) asportation of the subject matter; and (4) intent to deprive the owner of his property wholly and permanently (*People v. Torres, 201 C.A. 2d 290*).

Value of Property Taken. The owner of the property taken in theft, whether generally familiar with fair market value or not, is competent to estimate its worth. The market value which is referred to in the law is that value at the time and at the place where the property was unlawfully taken (*People v. Simpson, 26 C.A. 2d 223*).

Where the evidence shows a specific intent to steal, and the thief takes personal property of a value exceeding two hundred dollars, the prosecution is not required to prove that the defendant knew the value of the stolen property (*People v. Earle, 222 C.A. 2d 476*).

Grand Theft From Person. *Value of Property Stolen.* As was noted in PC 487, Section 2, property taken from the person of another constitutes grand theft. This is true regardless of what is taken as long as it has any value whatever. Theft of an empty wallet by a pickpocket would be grand theft on the theory that the wallet itself would have some value, even if small. Theft of a bus token worth but a few cents, if taken *from the person,* would be grand theft.

From the Person. To constitute taking "from the person," the property must be taken from: (1) a receptacle (purse, etc.) being carried at the time, (2) from the victim's clothing being worn at the time, (3) from his hands while he is carrying the item stolen or (4) attached to his person physically in some way such as a locket hanging around the neck. If the victim lays the property down, even for a moment, at which time it is stolen, the theft is not "from the person."

Property placed under one's pillow while sleeping is *not* considered to be on the person, thus, theft of such property would not automatically constitute grand theft unless the amount stolen exceeded four hundred dollars.

In summary, to constitute theft "from the person," the property must be either held, secured to or "attached" in some way to the victim's physical person at the time it is stolen. Otherwise the theft is petty or grand depending solely on the type of property stolen and its value.

16.12 PUNISHMENT FOR THEFT

PC 489. "Grand theft is punishable by imprisonment in the county jail for not more than one year or in the state prison."

PC 490. "Petty theft is punishable by a fine not exceeding one thousand ($1,000) dollars, or by imprisonment in the county jail not exceeding six months, or both."

PC 514. Theft of Public Funds. "Every person guilty of embezzlement is punishable in the matter prescribed for theft of property of the value or kind embezzled; and where the property embezzled is an evidence of debt or right of action, the sum due upon it or secured to be paid by it must be taken as its value. If the embezzlement or defalcation (default, failure to pay) is of the *public funds* of the United States, or of this state, or any county or municipality within this state, the offense is a felony, and is punishable by imprisonment in the state prison; and the person so convicted is ineligible thereafter to any office of honor, trust, or profit in this state."

THEFT ANALYSIS CHART

Theft Includes	Larceny (Theft)	Obtaining Property By False Pretenses	Obtaining Property By Trick And Device	Embezzlement (Trust Relationship)
The Act	Must be a taking and carrying away of personal property (known as intent to steal). Original taking is a trespass.	Control over the property is illegally obtained. Property may be tangible or is in the form of credit or services rendered.	Control over the property is obtained by some trick, fraud, or false representation. Usually referred to as a "bunco game."	Distinct act of taking is not required because gist of offense is a wrongful use of property entrusted to servant, employee, agent, bailee, trustee or public servant.
The Intent of the Taker	Intent is to "feloniously" steal, at the time of the taking, which means to intend to deprive the owner permanently of his property, not in jest, claim of right, or temporarily.	Intent is to defraud by making false representations of a present or past fact—not opinions, future promises or "puffing" of wares.	Intent to "feloniously" steal, which means to intend to deprive the owner permanently of his property, by false schemes or trickery.	Intent is to "feloniously" steal, but only *after* possession is acquired. This is called "appropriation with fraudulent intent."
The Intent of the Owner	Owner never intends that the taker shall take or keep his property.	Owner voluntarily gives his property to the wrongdoer in reliance on these false representations and deceit, without any reservation.	Owner voluntarily gives his property in reliance on the scheme of the wrongdoer, but only for some agreed special use.	Owner never intends that the "trustee" shall use the property for any purpose other than specified or agreed upon.
Title	Remains with the owner at all times.	Passes to the wrongdoer because the owner so intends.	Remains with the owner because owner never intends to give up title.	Remains with the owner at all times.
Custody or Possession	Remains "constructively" with owner—the wrongdoer obtains custody, unlawfully.	Passes to the wrongdoer with consent of owner because of the fraud.	Passes to wrongdoer but only for a special purpose or use.	Passes to wrongdoer but only for a special purpose of trust.
Proof	Corroboration not necessary.	Corroboration necessary.	Corroboration not necessary.	Corroboration not necessary.

16.13 PETTY THEFT—PRIOR CONVICTIONS

PC 666. Petit Theft. Second Offenses. "Every person who having been convicted of petit theft, grand theft, burglary or robbery and having served a term therefor in any penal institution, or having been imprisoned therein as a condition of probation for such offense, is subsequently convicted of petit theft, then the person convicted of such subsequent offense is punishable by imprisonment in the county jail not exceeding one year, or in the state prison."

PC 668. Foreign Conviction of Former Offense. "Every person who has been convicted in any other state, government, country or jurisdiction of an offense for which, if committed within this state, such person could have been punished under the laws of this state by imprisonment in a state prison, is punishable for any subsequent crime committed within this state in the manner prescribed by law, and to the same extent as if such prior conviction had taken place in a court of this state."

PC 969b. Evidence: Penitentiary Records. "For the purpose of establishing *prima facie* evidence of the fact that a person being tried for a crime or public offense under the laws of this state has been convicted of an act punishable by imprisonment in a state prison, county jail, or city jail of this state, and has served a term therefor in any penal institution, or has been convicted of an act in any other state, which would be punishable as a crime in this state, and has served a term therefor in any state penitentiary, reformatory, county jail, or city jail, or has been convicted of an act declared to be a crime by any act or law of the United States, and has served a term therefor in any penal institution, the records or copies of records of any state penitentiary, reformatory, county jail, city jail, or federal penitentiary in which such person has been imprisoned, when such records or copies thereof have been certified by the official custodian of such records, may be introduced as such evidence.

Discussion

There is no conflict between PC 969(b) (above) and PC 13850 Career Criminal Law) relative to double jeopardy or cruel or unusual punishment, nor do such statutes deprive the defendant of due process of law or equal protection under the law (*People v. McDaniels, 165 C.A. 2d 283; People v. Collins, 172 C.A. 2d 295*).

Defendant's plea of guilty and his admission of a prior conviction supported a judgment finding defendant guilty of petty theft with a prior felony conviction (*People v. Moranda, 222 A.C.A. 473*).

The object in charging prior felony convictions is not necessarily for a determination of the career criminal status of the person charged, but is for the information of the court in determining the punishment to be imposed in case of conviction (*People v. Cole, 148 C.A. 2d 25*).

In order to subject the defendant to an increased penalty on conviction for petty theft because of a prior felony conviction, it was not necessary for the prosecution to allege and prove that the defendant had been imprisoned for the full term of his sentence (*People v. James, 155 C.A. 2d 604*).

It is not necessary that the defendant shall have served the full term of imprisonment for his prior offense; service of a portion thereof is sufficient (*People v. James, supra*).

16.14 SEPARATE AND RELATED ACTS CONSTITUTING THEFT

When the property of several victims is stolen at the same time, and under the same circumstances, they are considered to be but one thing and but one theft, however many victims there may be. For example, if three surfboards are taken from atop a vehicle while the three owners are absent from the vehicle, there is but a single theft committed with three victims of the theft. Assuming that the surf boards are worth $150 each, the offense would be grand theft, a felony. However, where the taking is from different persons at different places and under different circumstances, or where property is taken *from the persons* of different individuals at the same time or from different individuals by the same trick and device, each transaction is a separate theft (*People v. Sichofsky, 58 C.A. 257*).

Where it is the intent of a person to steal an entire lot of merchandise, it makes no difference whether asportation is complete in one time period or is extended over a period of time to facilitate the carrying away of property, as long as there is one common purpose, intent, and design to remove the lot of property. For example, if one intends to steal $450 worth of property which will take three successive nights, he is committing one act of grand theft rather than three separate and distinct acts of petty theft wherein the value of the property taken on each occasion is less than $400. However, the intent of the perpetrator in these cases must be in pursuance of but one intention, one general impulse, and one plan, even though there is a series of transactions (*People v. Bailey, 55 Cal., 2d 514*).

A defendant may be properly convicted upon separate counts charging grand theft from the same person if the evidence shows that the offenses are separate and distinct, and were not committed pursuant to one intention, general impulse, or course of action (*People v. Stanford, 16 Cal. 2d 247*).

Thus where a person embezzles, on various occasions, with but a single purpose on each occasion, and there was no evidence of a common purpose, intent, design, or general impulse in taking the money entrusted to him in a fiduciary capacity, each taking constituted a separate intent and thus resulted in a separate crime of embezzlement (*People v. Hill, 32 C.A. 554*).

A similar situation arises when a clerk, in pursuance of one design and purpose, takes merchandise of his employer and converts it to his own use by selling it to "personal customers" and thereafter pockets the proceeds made on the transaction. This is clearly but one theft (embezzlement), since there was but one general intent on the part of the perpetrator (*People v. Howes, 99 C.A. 2d 808;* also see Chapter 14 "Burglary" for further ramifications of such an act).

16.15 RECEIVING STOLEN PROPERTY

PC 496. Buying, Receiving, or Concealing Stolen Property: Punishment

1. "Every person who buys or receives any property which has been stolen or which has been obtained in any manner constituting theft or extortion, knowing the property to be so stolen or obtained, or who conceals, sells, withholds or aids in concealing or withholding any such property from the owner, knowing the property to be so stolen or obtained, is punishable by imprisonment in a state prison, or in a county jail for not more than one year; provided, that where the district attorney or the grand jury determines that such action would be in the interests of justice, the district attorney or the grand jury, as the case may be, may, if the value of the property does not exceed four hundred dollars ($400), specify in the accusatory pleading (complaint or accusation) that the offense shall be a misdemeanor, punishable only by imprisonment in the county jail not exceeding one year.

2. Every swap meet vendor as defined in Section 21661 of the Business and Professions Code and every person whose principal business is dealing in or collecting used or second-hand merchandise or personal property, and every agent, employee, or representative of such person, who buys or receives any property which has been stolen or obtained in any manner constituting theft or extortion, under such circumstances as should cause such person, agent, employee, or representative to make reasonable inquiry to ascertain that the person from whom such property was bought or received had the legal right to sell or deliver it, without making such reasonable inquiry, shall be presumed to have bought or received such property knowing it to have been so stolen or obtained. This presumption may, however, be rebutted by proof.

3. When in a prosecution under this section it shall appear from the evidence that the defendant was a swap meet vendor or that the defendant's principal business was as set forth in the preceding paragraph, that the defendant bought, received, or otherwise obtained, or concealed, withheld, or aided in concealing or withholding from the owner, any property which had been stolen or obtained in any manner constituting theft or extortion, and that the defendant bought, received, obtained, concealed, or withheld such property under such circumstances as should have caused him to make reasonable inquiry to ascertain that the person from whom he bought, received, or obtained such property had the legal right to sell or deliver it to him, then the burden shall be upon the defendant to show that before so buying, receiving, or otherwise obtaining such property, he made such reasonable inquiry to ascertain that the person so selling or delivering the same to him had the legal right to sell or deliver it.

4. Any person who has been injured by a violation of paragraph one of this section may bring an action for three times the amount of actual damages, if any, sustained by the plaintiff, costs of suit and reasonable attorney's fees."

Discussion

Where it is definitely established that the defendant is the thief, he may not be prosecuted under this section proscribing receipt of stolen property if concealment and withholding of stolen goods have been part of the activities connected with the theft itself (*People v. Marquez, 237 C.A. 2d 627*).

The essence of the offense of receiving stolen property is that purchase or receipt be with the knowledge that the property was stolen (*People v. Salazar, 210 C.A. 2d 89*).

Even though a person is not aware the property is stolen when he first comes into possession of it, if he subsequently learns of its stolen nature and then conceals or withholds it from the true owner, he is guilty of receipt of stolen property (*People v. Scaggs, 153 C.A. 2d 339*).

Elements of Receiving Stolen Property

The elements of receiving stolen property are (1) that property found in possession of defendant was acquired by acts constituting theft or extortion; (2) that defendant received, concealed, or withheld property from the owner; and (3) that the defendant knew that the property was stolen (*People v. Azevedo, 218 C.A. 483*).

To constitute the offense of receiving stolen property, there must be proof that the property found in possession of the accused was acquired by means of theft or extortion, that the accused received, concealed, or withheld such property from its owners, and that the accused knew that the property was stolen (*People v. Candiotto, 183 C.A. 2d 348*).

Possession of stolen property, accompanied by no explanation, or an unsatisfactory explanation of the possession, or by suspicious circumstances, will justify an inference that the goods were received with the knowledge that they had been stolen (*People v. McNeal, 212 CA 2d 731; People v. Barnes, 210 C.A. 2d 740*).

Defendant who received stolen property from two minors, one who appeared to be between fourteen and sixteen years and the other who appeared slightly older, was presumed to have known that the property was stolen (*People v. Arrant, 184 C.A. 2d 532*).

Among the elements from which knowledge as to stolen property may be inferred by the defendant is the fact that the property was obtained from a person of questionable character, and failure of the defendant to satisfactorily explain his possession (*People v. Boinus, 153 C.A. 2d 618*).

PC 789. Receiving Stolen Property in Another State. The jurisdiction for receiving stolen property in another state and bringing it into this state is in any competent court into or through which the property has been brought.

16.16   RELATED THEFTS

PC 496a. Purchase of Wire, etc., by Junk Dealers. This section punishes second-hand dealers who do not use due diligence in ascertaining the right of persons who attempt to sell solder, iron, brass, wire, cable, copper, lead, etc.

PC 496b. Buying or Receiving Stolen Books. This statute relates to book dealers and collectors and prohibits them from buying or receiving books, manuscripts, and other literature bearing a mark indicating ownership by a public library or institution, without ascertaining by diligent inquiry the seller's right to dispose of such property.

PC 496c. Copying Information Relating to Title to Real Property. This section prohibits the surreptitious copying, transcribing, photographing, etc., of a private or unpublished paper, book, record, map, or file containing information relating to the title to real property without the owner's consent.

PC 497. Bringing Stolen Property into This State. A person who receives stolen property in another state or country and brings it into this state may be convicted and punished in this state.

PC 498. Tapping into a Main Illuminating or Fuel Gas Main with the intent to defraud or injure, and with the intent to evade or cause evasion of payment therefore, and the injuring or altering of any gas meter or register is a misdemeanor.

PC 499. Tapping into a Water Main with Any Instrument without the knowledge of the owner thereof, and with intent to evade payment therefor, or with the intent to injure or defraud, and the injuring or altering of any water meter, seal, service valve, or other service connection is a misdemeanor.

PC 499a. Stealing Electricity; Misdemeanor. This section punishes the theft of electricity by one who has the intent to injure or defraud the owner thereof, including the injuring, altering, or tampering with of any electric meter. Violation of this section is a misdemeanor.

PC 499b. Taking Motor Vehicle, Bicycle, Temporarily, a Misdemeanor. "Any person who shall, without the permission of the owner thereof, take any automobile, bicycle, motorcycle, or other vehicle, or motorboat or vessel, for the purpose of temporarily using or operating the same shall be deemed guilty of a misdemeanor, and upon conviction thereof, shall be punished by a fine not exceeding two hundred dollars ($200), or by imprisonment not exceeding three months, or by both such fine and imprisonment."

PC 499d. Taking of Aircraft a Felony. "Any person who operates or takes an aircraft not his own, without the consent of the owner thereof, and with intent to either permanently or temporarily deprive the owner thereof of his title or possession of such vehicle, whether with or without intent to steal the same, or any person who is a party or accessory to or an accomplice in any operation or unauthorized taking or stealing is guilty of a felony and upon conviction thereof shall be punished by imprisonment in the state prison, or in the county jail for not more than one year, or by a fine of not more than five thousand dollars ($5,000), or by both such fine and imprisonment."

Purchasing Scrap From Minors. "Every person who purchases or receives in pledge or by way of mortgage, from any person under the age of sixteen years, any junk, metal, mechanical tools, or implements, is guilty of a misdemeanor.

b. Nothing in this section applies to or affects the sale of recyclable discards by persons under the age of 16 years to a consumer recycling center.

   As used in this subdivision, 'consumer recycling center' means any permanent or mobile facility that accepts for purchase recyclable aluminum, tin, bimetal, glass and paper discards from consumers." (PC 501).

PC 502.7. Obtaining Telephone or Telegraph Services with Intent to Defraud

a. A person who, knowingly, willfully, and with intent to defraud a person providing telephone or telegraph service, avoids or attempts to avoid, or aids, abets, or causes another to avoid the lawful charge, in whole or in part, for telephone or telegraph service by one of the following means is guilty of a misdemeanor:

   1. By charging such service to an existing telephone number or credit card number without the authority of the subscriber thereto or the lawful holder thereof; or

   2. By charging such service to an existing telephone number or credit card number, or to a number associated with telephone service which is suspended or terminated, or to a revoked or canceled (as distinguished from expired) credit card number, notice of such suspension, termination, revocation, or cancellation of such telephone service or credit card having been given to the subscriber thereto or the holder thereof; or

   3. By use of a code, prearranged scheme, or other similar stratagem or device whereby said person, in effect, sends or receives information; or

   4. By rearranging, tampering with, or making connection with telephone or telegraph facilities or equipment whether physically, electrically, acoustically, inductively or otherwise, or by using telephone or telegraph service with knowledge or reason to believe that such rearrangement, tampering, or connection existed at the time of such use; or

   5. By using any other deception, false pretense, trick, scheme, device or means.

b. A person who (1) makes, possesses, sells, gives, or otherwise transfers to another, or offers or advertises an instrument, apparatus, or device with intent to use it or with knowledge or reason to believe it is intended to be used to avoid any lawful telephone or telegraph toll charge or to conceal the existence or place of origin or destination or (2) sells, gives or otherwise transfers to another or offers or advertises plans or instructions for making or assembling an instrument, apparatus, or device described in paragraph (1) of this subdivision with knowledge or reason to believe that they may be used to make or assemble such instrument, apparatus, or device, is guilty of a misdemeanor.

c. Any person who publishes the number or code of an existing, canceled, revoked, expired or nonexistent credit card, or the number or coding which is employed in the issuance of credit cards, with the intent that it be used or with knowledge or reason to believe that it will be used to avoid the payment of any lawful telephone or telegraph toll charge is guilty of a misdemeanor (briefed).

d. Subdivision (a) of this section shall apply when the telephone or telegraph communication involved either originates or terminates, or both originates and terminates, in this state, or when the charges for service would have been billable, in normal course, by a person providing telephone or telegraph service in this state, but for the fact that the charge for service was avoided, or attempted to be avoided by one or more of the means set forth in subdivision (a) of this section.

e. Jurisdiction of an offense under this section is in the territory where the telephone or telegram originates or terminates or to which a bill would otherwise have been sent (briefed).

f. If the total value of all telephone or telegraph services obtained in violation of this section total *over* $200 within 12 consecutive months during the three years immediately prior to the filing of charges, or if the defendant has previously been convicted of a previous similar offense, such offense is punishable by imprisonment in the state prison not exceeding one year and one day, or in the county jail not exceeding one year, or by fine not exceeding $5,000 or by both such fine and imprisonment (briefed).

g. Any instrument or device described in this section may be seized under warrant or incident to arrest and upon conviction of the accused, may be destroyed by the sheriff or turned over to the telephone or telegraph company in the area (briefed).

Discussion

As pointed out in Section 502.7(a), defrauding, or attempting to defraud a telephone or telegraph company is generally a misdemeanor. However, PC 502.7(f) makes it a felony if the total value of all services obtained by any of the fraudulent means mentioned above, amount to over two hundred dollars within any consecutive twelve-month period. Note: This amount is being changed by the legislature to $400. The crime is also a felony if the defendant has been previously convicted under this section in this state or a similar section (or Federal Law) in another state. Felony conviction carries a penalty of one year in state prison, or one year in the county jail, or five thousand dollars ($5,000) fine, or both.

14.17 DISPOSAL OF STOLEN PROPERTY BY OFFICIALS

The following sections pertain to the manner in which stolen or embezzled property shall be disposed of by authorities.

PC 1407. When property, alleged to have been stolen or embezzled, comes into the custody of a peace officer, he must hold it subject to the order of the magistrate authorized by the next section to direct the disposal thereof.

PC 1408. Order for its delivery to owner. This section provides that the magistrate before whom the complaint is laid must order stolen or embezzled property returned to the owner.

PC 1411. If the property is not claimed before six months (three months in the case of bicycles) from the conviction of the thief, the officer must deliver it to the city or county treasurer for sale.

PC 1412. The officer must give a receipt when taking money or property from the defendant and deliver one copy of the receipt to the defendant and keep one copy with the property.

PC 1413. Duties of persons having a charge of property. The police clerk must attach a number to each article and enter the description and number of each article into a suitable book.

16.18 DEFRAUDING AN INNKEEPER

PC 537(a). Any person who obtains any food or accommodations at an hotel, inn, restaurant, boarding house, lodging house, apartment house, bungalow court, motel, or auto camp, ski area, or public or private campground, without paying therefor, with intent to defraud the proprietor or manager thereof, or who obtains credit at an hotel, inn, restaurant, boarding house, lodging house, apartment house, bungalow court, motel, or auto camp or public or private campground, by the use of any false pretense, or who after obtaining credit, food, accommodations, at an hotel, inn, restaurant, boarding house, lodging house, apartment house, bungalow court, motel, or auto camp, or public or private campground, absconds, or surreptitiously, or by force, menace, or threats, removes any part of his baggage therefrom without paying for his food or accommodations is punishable as follows:

1. If the value of the credit, food, or accommodations is four hundred dollars ($400) or *less,* by a fine not exceeding one thousand dollars ($1,000) or by imprisonment in the county jail for a term not exceeding six months or both.

2. If the value of the credit, food, or accommodations is *greater* than four hundred dollars ($400), by imprisonment in the county jail for a term of not more than one year, or in the state prison.

3. Any person who uses or attempts to use ski area facilities for which payment is required without paying as required, or who resells a ski lift ticket to another when the resale is not authorized by the proprietor, is guilty of an infraction.

16.19 POSSESSION OF ARTICLES WITH SERIAL NUMBERS REMOVED, ALTERED

PC 537e. Any person who knowingly buys, sells, receives, disposes of, conceals, or has in his possession a radio, piano, phonograph, sewing machine, washing machine, typewriter, adding machine, comptometer, bicycle, safe or vacuum cleaner, dictaphone, watch, watch movement, watch case, or any mechanical or electrical device, appliance, contrivance, material, piece of apparatus or equipment, or any computer chip, printed circuit, or any computer part, from which the manufacturer's name plate, serial number or any other distinguishing number or identification mark has been removed, defaced, covered, altered or destroyed, is guilty of a misdemeanor (briefed).

Computer Parts: Felony. If the value of any integrated chip from which the nameplate, serial number, or other distinguishing number or identification mark is removed, defaced, covered, altered, or destroyed exceeds four hundred dollars ($400), the offense is a felony punishable by imprisonment in the county jail not to exceed one year or in the state prison.

TERMINOLOGY DEFINED—CHAPTER 16

See the Terminology Quiz at the end of the chapter.
1. Chattels: any personal or real property, possessions.
2. Contingency: an event possible, uncertain or unforeseen.
3. Corroboration: additional proof or substantiation.
4. Diversion: personal use of funds intended for another purpose.
5. Embezzlement: theft by a person entrusted with the property.
6. Fiduciary capacity: position of trust, e.g., employer-employee.
7. Fraud: theft by false pretense or promises.
8. Gaming: gambling with dice, cards or other devices.
9. Intrinsic: inherent, basic, internal, e.g., inherent value.
10. Joy riding: taking car without permission, not a theft.
11. Kleptomaniac: one with abnormal impulse to steal.
12. Misappropriate: misuse, divert from intended purpose.
13. Ownership: legal title or right to possession of property.
14. Possession: under one's care, direction, or control.
15. Presumption: assumed true until proven otherwise.
16. Real value: the fair market value, the going price.
17. Reliance: dependence upon, trusting in, confidence in.
18. Steal: taking with intent to permanently deprive owner of property.
19. Trial: court action to determine guilt or innocence.
20. Trustee: one entrusted with certain duties and obligations.

TRUE-FALSE QUIZ—CHAPTER 16

1. One is not guilty of theft unless he takes something of value intending to permanently deprive the owner of the use or title of the property.
2. The terms "theft" and larceny" are synonymous.
3. To constitute asportation in theft, the thief must move or otherwise attain some dominion over the property stolen.
4. To determine the value of property taken in a theft, the value placed on it by the owner shall be the ultimate test.
5. In order for property to be stolen it must have some real value.
6. Asportation is an essential element of theft.
7. Taking an automobile without the owner's consent, using it for two days, and returning it is not auto theft.
8. Selling parts from a car which was taken without the owner's permission would be evidence of grand theft auto.
9. Possession of stolen property is of itself sufficient to justify a conviction of theft.
10. Once stolen property is sold to an innocent third person, the owner legally loses his title to the property.
11. In theft by false pretenses, PC 532, both title and possession of the property pass to the wrongdoer.
12. The crime of embezzlement requires a distinct act of taking the same as other types of theft.
13. Some kind of fiduciary relationship between the victim and the wrongdoer is essential to the crime of embezzlement.
14. If a trustee diverts funds for some unauthorized purpose, even if he does not personally gain from the diversion, he is still guilty of embezzlement.
15. Theft of a credit card, because it has no intrinsic value, is not a crime until it has been fraudulently used.
16. Theft of $400 from one's employer within a twelve consecutive month period constitutes grand theft.
17. Theft of $100 worth of avocados constitutes grand theft.
18. Theft of money from under a pillow where the victim was sleeping constitutes grand theft from the person.
19. Theft of money from a purse lying immediately next to the owner is grand theft.
20. Theft of any amount by picking a pocket is grand theft.

*ESSAY-DISCUSSION QUESTIONS—
CHAPTER 16*

1. What is the basis or test for determining the value of stolen property?
2. What are the four basic elements of theft?
3. May real property as well as personal property be the subject of theft? Are farm animals considered personal property? What about dogs and cats?
4. What are the four general categories or types of theft?

5. Of what does the "act" in theft consist? What is meant by asportation in theft?
6. Is theft a general or specific intent crime? What is it that makes it one or the other?
7. Is possession of stolen property of itself sufficient to justify conviction of theft? Does the possessor have any *legal* duty to explain his possession?
8. What are the elements of embezzlement?
9. What constitutes "from the person" in theft under PC 487, Section 2? Is this a felony or misdemeanor?
10. What are the three elements of receiving stolen property under PC 496?

TERMINOLOGY QUIZ—CHAPTER 16

Match terms and definitions by placing the correct number in the parentheses. Answers may be written on a separate sheet for submission to the instructor at the instructor's direction.

1. Chattels
2. Contingency
3. Corroboration
4. Diversion
5. Embezzlement
6. Fiduciary capacity
7. Fraud
8. Gaming
9. Intrinsic
10. Joy riding
11. Kleptomaniac
12. Misappropriate
13. Ownership
14. Possession
15. Presumption
16. Real value
17. Reliance
18. Steal
19. Trial
20. Trustee

( ) assumed to be true until proven otherwise
( ) one with abnormal impulse to steal
( ) under one's care, direction, or control
( ) inherent, basic, internal, inherent value
( ) taking with intent to permanently deprive
( ) any personal or real property, possessions
( ) an event possible, uncertain, unforeseen
( ) dependence upon, trusting or confidence in
( ) personal use of funds intended for other purposes
( ) theft by a person entrusted with the property
( ) legal title or right to possession of property
( ) one entrusted with certain duties and obligations
( ) theft by false pretense or promises
( ) position of trust, employer-employee
( ) misuse, divert from intended purpose

CHAPTER 17

Controlled Substances

17.1 DRUG ABUSE AND MISUSE[1]

The Illegal Drug Traffic. Drug misuse or abuse is found in every sector of society. It occurs increasingly in affluent suburbs as well as in slums. It is becoming commonplace in schools, colleges, and also in industry. It is a particular problem among young people. Drug laws are designed to help control the problem; they do not eliminate or prevent it. Education is needed, too.

This chapter defines drugs that are most commonly misused, describes their uses, abuses, and effects, and lists the common symptoms they produce. In these times, it is particularly important that responsible people throughout the community—especially law enforcement officials—know such basic facts about the drug problem so that they can be alert for the signs of possible drug misuse.

Although alcohol is still the most widely used—and misused—of all drugs, the stress in this chapter is directed toward other drugs which are becoming an increasing cause for concern.

17.2 DEFINITIONS

Drug: A substance which by its chemical nature alters the structure or function of the living organism. (For the purpose of this chapter, a drug is any chemical substance that alters mood, perception, or consciousness, and is misused to the apparent injury of the individual or society.)

Tolerance: A state in which the body's tissue cells adjust to the presence of a drug. The term "Tolerance" refers to a state in which the body becomes used to the presence of a drug in given amounts and

eventually fails to respond to ordinarily effective dosages. Hence, increasingly larger doses are necessary to produce desired effects.

Habituation (*psychological dependence*): The result of repeated consumption of a drug which produces psychological but no physical dependence. The psychological dependence produces a desire (not a compulsion) to continue taking drugs for the sense of improved well-being.

Physical Dependence (*addiction*): This occurs when a person cannot function normally without the repeated use of a drug. If the drug is withdrawn, the person has severe physical and psychic disturbance.

Harmful Drugs: Are all drugs harmful? Every drug is harmful when taken in excess, e.g., even aspirin and, of course, alcohol. Some drugs can also be harmful if taken in dangerous combinations or by hypersensitive people in ordinary amounts.

17.3 IDENTIFYING THE DRUG USER

A drug user will do everything possible to conceal his or her habit. So it is important to be able to recognize the outward signs and symptoms of drug misuse. One should be alert to these symptoms, but it is important to realize that the drug problem is so complex that even experts sometimes have difficulty making accurate diagnoses.

It should also be remembered that a person may have a legitimate reason for possessing a syringe and needle (he or she may be a diabetic) or having tablets and capsules (they may be prescribed by a doctor). Having the sniffles and running eyes may be due to a head cold or an allergy. Unusual or odd behavior may not be connected in any way with drug use.

---

1. Section 17.1–17.6 from U.S. Government Printing Office: 1979 O–293–289.

Drugs other than narcotics can become addicting. Some people have acquired an addiction to sedatives and certain tranquilizers. Stimulants in very large doses are addictive.

17.4 COMMON SIGNS OF DRUG MISUSE

Law enforcement officers must be familiar with the following for their own use in the field and for instructing parents and others.

1. Changes in attendance at work or school.
2. Change from normal capabilities (work habits, efficiency, etc.)
3. Poor physical appearance, including inattention to dress and personal hygiene.
4. Wearing sunglasses constantly at inappropriate times (indoors or at night, for instance) not only to hide dilated or constricted pupils but also to compensate for the eye's inability to adjust to sunlight. Marijuana smoking may cause blood shot eyes.
5. Unusual effort made to cover arms in order to hide needle marks.
6. Association with known drug users.
7. Stealing items which can be readily sold for cash (to support a drug habit).

17.5 INDICATIONS OF POSSIBLE MISUSE

1. **DEPRESSANTS e.g., Quaalude, Doriden (Barbiturates)**
   A. Behavior like that of alcohol intoxication, but without the odor of alcohol on breath.
   B. Staggering, stumbling, or apparent drunkenness without odor or use of alcohol.
   C. Falling asleep while at work.
   D. Slurred speech.
   E. Pupils dilated.
   F. Difficulty concentrating.
2. **STIMULANTS (Amphetamines)**
   A. The user may be excessively active, irritable, argumentative, or nervous.
   B. Excitation, euphoria, and talkativeness.
   C. Pupils dilated
   D. Long period without eating or sleeping.
   E. Increased blood pressure or pulse rates.
3. **NARCOTICS**
   A. Scars ("tracks") on the arms or on the backs of hands, caused by injecting drugs.
   B. Pupils constricted and fixed; possibly dilated during withdrawal.
   C. Scratches self frequently.
   D. Loss of appetite. Frequently eats candy, cookies, and drinks sweet liquids.
   E. May have sniffles, red, watering eyes and a cough which disappears when he or she gets a "fix". During withdrawal the addict may be nauseated and vomiting. Flushed skin, frequent yawning, and muscular twitching are common. These symptoms also disappear when the addict get a "fix".
   F. Users often leave syringes, bentspoons, cotton, needles, metal bottle caps, medicine droppers, and glassine bags in locker or desk drawers.
   G. The user is lethargic, drowsy, and may go on the "nod" (i.e., an alternating cycle of dozing and awakening.)
   H. Anyone dissolving tablets for injection runs a great risk and danger of lung impairment due to deposits of talcum (part of the tablet) obstructing or occluding the lung through the blood stream.
4. **MARIJUANA**
   A. In the early stages of marijuana usage, the person may appear animated with rapid, loud talking and bursts of laughter. In later stages, he or she may be sleepy.
   B. Pupils may be dilated and the eyes blood shot.
   C. May have distortions of perception and hallucinations.

   The marijuana user is difficult to recognize unless actually under the influence of the drug, and even then, he or she may be able to work reasonably well. The drug may distort depth and time perception, making driving or the operation of machinery hazardous. Long continued use of marijuana has been associated with mental deterioration.
5. **OTHER HALLUCINOGENS**
   A. Behavior and mood vary widely. The user may sit or recline quietly in a trance-like state or may appear fearful or even terrified.
   B. In some cases, dilated pupils.
   C. Increase in blood pressure, heart rate, and blood sugar.
   D. May experience nausea, chills, flushes, irregular breathing, sweating and trembling of hands.
   E. There may be changes in sense of sight, hearing, touch, smell, and time.

It is unlikely that a person who uses LSD, for instance, would do so at work, since a controlled environment, often involving a friend to provide care and supervision of the user, is generally desired.

17.6   COMMONLY MISUSED DRUGS

1. **NARCOTICS**
   A class of drugs which induces sleep or stupor and relieves pain. This classification includes opiates and their derivatives. (Also see Table of Controlled Substances and Related Health and Safety Code Section, p. 238.)
   A. **OPIUM (Papaver Somniferum)**
      Description: The dried, coagulated milk of an unripe opium poppy.
      Identification: A dark brown, coagulated, plastic-like substance.
      Methods of use: Opium may be smoked through a long-stemmed pipe. it has for the most part been replaced by its more powerful derivatives, morphine and heroin.
      Slang Terms: "Opium", "OP", "Pen Yan", "Hop", "Tar", "Black Stuff". (Also see Text Section 17.8.)
   B. **MORPHINE**
      Description: Medically, the preferred drug for the relief of pain. Morphine is widely used by addicts, particularly when heroin is difficult to obtain. It is derived from crude opium. Tolerance builds rapidly.
      Identification: An odorless, light brown or white crystalline power. Morphine may appear on the market as tablets, capsules, or in power form.
      Methods of use: Morphine is either injected as a liquid, or taken by mouth. It acts on the central nervous system as an analgesic or pain killer. Traces of morphine detectable by laboratory techniques remain in the body for 6-18 hours.
      Signs and symptoms: Much like those of the more commonly misused drug, heroin.
      Slang terms: "White Stuff", "Hard Stuff", "M", "Morpho", "Unkie", "Miss Emma".
   C. **HEROIN (Diacetylmorphine)**
      Description: Heroin is much more potent than morphine and is a derivative of morphine. The intense euphoria or "high" produced by the drug has made heroin the most popular narcotic among addicts. Heroin is similar to all narcotic drugs in that tolerance to its effects rapidly develops. As a result, the user must take larger quantities. An individual may begin with a dose of two to eight milligrams but addicts may use as much as 450 milligrams per day as tolerance is acquired.
      Identification: Most often found as an odorless, white, off-white, or light brown powder.
      Methods of use: The most common administration is intravenous (mainlining). A drug user's "work kit" is used to convert heroin into a solution. The kit generally contains matches, a teaspoon with a bent handle or small metal bottle cap, medicine dropper, hypodermic needle, and a piece of cotton. The powder is put into a spoon, mixed with water and heated to form a solution. The solution is then injected into the blood stream, generally into the arm. The addict may use his belt as a tourniquet to make a vein stand out. Heroin is also taken by mouth. When injected under the skin, the term "skin popping" is used. The effect is slower and less intense.
      Signs and Symptoms: (See Narcotics Section) Detectable in body (urine) within 10 hours.
      Slang terms: "H", "Junk", "Harry", "Joy Powder", "Horse", "White Stuff", "Snow", "Sugar", "Smack".
      (Also see Text Section 17.15.)
   D. **CODEINE (Methylmorphine)**
      Description: A derivative of morphine, it is commonly available in cough preparations. Some of these cough preparations containing codeine have been available without prescription and they have been subject to abuse. Codeine is less addictive than morphine or heroin and less potent in terms of inducing euphoria. Withdrawal symptoms, when they occur, are less severe than with the more potent drugs. Codeine may be used for the maintenance of addition or as a temporary replacement for morphine or heroin.
      Identification: A white crystalline power or tablet added to various liquids (cough syrup).
      Methods of use: Most often taken internally by swallowing the liquid. On occasion, addicts will boil cough syrup to reduce the solution to a higher concentration of codeine.
      Slang term: "School Boy".
2. **STIMULANTS**
   A stimulant is a substance which increases the central nervous system reaction. The most

widely known and used stimulant is caffeine which is found in coffee, tea, cola, and other beverages. Caffeine is, of course, very mild. The amphetamines, synthetic stimulants, and cocaine, a stimulant manufactured from the leaves of the coca bush, are controlled under the Controlled Substances Act of 1970. (Also see Table of Controlled Substances and Related Health and Safety Code Sections, p. 238.)

A. AMPHETAMINES

Description: The stimulant effects of amphetamines are medically used to treat a variety of conditions including obesity, short term control of fatigue, Parkinsonism, depressive syndromes, behavior disorders, and poisoning by central nervous system depressants. Psychological dependence is common to amphetamine misuse. Abuse of stimulant drugs brings about hyperactivity, hallucinations, and a general excitability. Continuous misuse of amphetamines may produce a psychosis resembling paranoid schizophrenia with accompanying delusions and hallucinations. Amphetamine abuse can also produce high blood pressure and abnormal heart rhythm. Types of amphetamines include di-amphetamine (benzedrine), d-amphetamine (dexedrine, dextro-amphetamine).

Amphetamines may be used in a social setting although there are many solitary users. Many combine this stimulant with other drugs, including alcohol, to experiment with the effects obtained from the various combinations. Serious drug abusers most often inject amphetamines intravenously. In fact, the excitability and intense paranoia that result from amphetamine injection suggests a much greater danger of violent outburst than would occur with a heroin addict. Amphetamine users often stay awake for days without food, undergoing hallucinations and bouts of paranoia, then lapsing into long, deep recovery sleeps. Unlike the "drifting off" effect of heroin, injected amphetamine creates a "flash" or "high" and an illusion of heightened mental power.

Methamphetamine (Speed): There has been an alarming increase in the number of "Speed" users, generally among teenagers and young adults. Methamphetamine is the most potent and hence the most dangerous of all the amphetamines. Its effects are similar to those from other drugs in this category but are far more intense.

Identification: Most amphetamines are legitimately manufactured in capsule or tablet form. The commonest form is as white powder in many operations.

Methods of use: Amphetamines are used as tablets, capsules, and in solution for injection. Most amphetamine users begin with low doses or oral amphetamine and slowly increase their dosage to 150 and 250 milligrams daily. When the desired results are not obtained, they change to the intravenous route. The toxic dose of amphetamine varies, depending upon the individual. Increased dosages are continually made in order to obtain the desired effects. Period of detectability in body fluids is 24-36 hours.

Signs and symptoms: Amphetamine users tend to be very talkative and engage in compulsive but purposeless activity such as dismantling and attempting to reassemble machinery that was working properly.

Slang terms: "Bennies", "Pep Pills", "Peaches", "Roses", "Hearts", "Cartwheels", "Dexies", "Oranges", "Football", "Coast to Coast", "L.A. Turnabouts". The slang terms for Methamphetamine include "Speed", "Meth", "Crystal" and "Bombida".

B. COCAINE (Erythroxylon Coca)

Description: Cocaine is an odorless, white fluffy powder. Cocaine is prohibited under the drug abuse laws. Cocaine is a potent central nervous system stimulant and therefore it is in no way similar to heroin or morphine, which are narcotics. It is a stimulant similar to the amphetamines. At one time, cocaine was widely used as a local anesthetic, but it has now been largely replaced by synthetic substitutes such as Procaine or Novocain or Xylocaine. Cocaine is a Schedule II drug under the Comprehensive Drug Abuse Law of 1970 (Public law 91-513).

Identification: On the illegal market, cocaine appears generally as an odorless, white, fluffy powder.

Methods of use: Cocaine is generally sniffed and is absorbed through the mucous membrane of the nose. It can also be injected intravenously, directly into the bloodstream. The result of either method is a strong stimulation of the central nervous system. One well-known method is to combine cocaine with heroin into a powerful injection known as a "speedball." Morphine is also used in combination with cocaine.

Signs and Symptoms: The user will appear to have an euphoric feeling and be energetic. Pupils are dilated and fixed. Tremors may occur. The euphoric sensations are short lived and accompanied by feelings of superiority. These are quickly replaced by feelings of anxiety and depression, sometimes accompanied by hallucinations and paranoid delusions. The user may indicate a feeling of superiority.

Slang terms: "Coke", "Snow", "Happy Dust", "C", "Flake", "Speedballs", "Snowbirds", "Cecil", "Stardust", "Bernice Gold Dust".

3. DEPRESSANTS

Depressants affect the central nervous system. They are used to induce sleep or act as a mild sedative or tranquilizer. Other depressants such as Quaalude and Doriden have the same effect. (Also see Table of Controlled Substances and Related Health and Safety Code Sections, p. 238.)

A. BARBITURATES

Description: A barbiturate is a sedative and a hypnotic and it exerts a powerful depressant or calming action on the central nervous system. The medical uses for barbiturates are varied and extensive: nervous tension (to calm people suffering from anxiety), hypertension (to reduce blood pressure), insomnia (to induce sleep), epilepsy (to prevent convulsions). Barbiturates are also used for a variety of other physical and psychological ailments. Barbiturates, like heroin, create a physical and psychological dependence. The dangers of barbiturates lie in the withdrawal syndromes which include a lack of muscular coordination similar to epileptic seizures. Respiratory failure can also occur with withdrawal. As a result, barbiturate addicts must be withdrawn under close medical supervision. Convulsions can occur up to the 16th day of withdrawal. High doses of barbiturates among chronic users may create a feeling of elation, tranquility and well being.

There are three different classifications of barbiturates. They are:

1. Those where the effect is slow in starting but of long duration, such as phenobarbital.
2. Those where the effect is intermediate in terms of starting time and duration. These include butabarbital and amobarbital.
3. The short acting, fast starters which include secobarbital and pentobarbital.

Identification: Barbiturates are most often manufactured in capsule or tablet form. The slang names for the barbiturates come from the color and shape of the capsule or tablet. Often a shortening of the trade name is used.

Methods of use: Barbiturates can be taken by mouth, intravenously or rectally. Daily doses, over a long period of time, of 0.4 grams have been claimed to produce a significant degree of dependence. Barbiturates depress the individual's mental and physical functions. The abuser is slow in speech, slow in action and very erratic in his judgment. On withdrawal, a long-term barbiturate user experiences similar reactions to the hard core narcotic addict because his body develops a tolerance and suffers severely.

Signs and symptoms: (See "Depressants.")

Slang terms: "Goof Balls", "Goofers", "Barbs".

1. (Pentobarbital sodium)—"Yellow Jackets", "Yellows", "Nimbys".
2. (Amobarbital sodium)—"Blues", "Blue Heaven", "Blue Birds", "Blue Devils".
3. (Secobarbital sodium)—"Reds", "Red Birds", "Red Devils", "Seccy", "Pink".
4. (Amobarbital and Secobarbital)—"Tuinal", "Tuies", "Rainbow", "Double Trouble".
5. Quaalude, Doriden, and others.

B. CHLORAL HYDRATE

Description: Like the barbiturates, alcohol, and various sedative hypnotics, chloral hydrate causes habituation, tolerance and addiction. However, addiction to chloral hydrate is less frequent than addiction to barbiturates due to its irritant effect on the gastrointestinal tract. Chloral hydrate addicts will suffer from extreme stomach disturbances, and drug users tend to find other drugs more attractive.

Identification: Chloral hydrate is usually found in soft gelatin capsules.

Methods of use: Chloral hydrate can be taken orally or rectally. Large doses are required to sustain the dependence, and withdrawal symptoms resemble a form of delirium. When mixed with alcohol, it is called a "Mickey Finn."

Signs and symptoms: Resembles acute barbiturate intoxication. There is gastric irritation and possibly vomiting. Pinpoint pupils. Overdose produces breathing difficulties and dangerously low blood pressure

Slang terms: "Mickey Finn", Mickey", "Peter", "Knockout Drops".

4. HALLUCINOGENS

A. MARIJUANA or Marihuana (Cannabis sativa)

Description: Marijuana is a plant which belongs to the hemp family. It can grow to heights of 12 to 14 feet. The active principle, tetrahydrocannabinol, is obtained from the amber colored resin of the flowering tops and leaves of the plant. At one time marijuana was used to relieve pain and promote sleep, but unpredictable effects led to its abandonment. Marijuana is a hallucinogen possessing both the elements of stimulation and depression.

Identification: Marijuana usually looks like green tobacco and often contains seeds and stems. Because of its coarseness, cigarettes are made with a heavy grade of tobacco paper. These "Joints" are usually hand rolled and closed on both ends because of the loose fill and the dryness of the weed. When burning, marijuana has a distinctive odor similar to burning rope or alfalfa. The odor will hang in the air and for a short time is noticeable on the user's breath and clothing.

Methods of use: The most popular method of abusing marijuana is by smoking it through a cigarette or a pipe. Often, tobacco is mixed with marijuana to act as a binder and to make it burn more slowly. Another method of smoking marijuana is known as "steamboating." The marijuana is smoked through a cardboard tube. One method involves extracting and separating the marijuana resins and taking them orally with tea or mixed in a cookie. The resin can also be extracted by boiling the plant.

The effects of smoking marijuana are often similar in many respects to those of alcohol. The marijuana user will speak freely, daydream, and appear in a state of semi-sedation. However, the overall effect of the drug is predictable largely by the user's personality and the presence of others in the room who are having similar sensations. After five or ten minutes, many users have a feeling of restlessness and anxiety. Speech becomes rapid, time appears to pass slowly, distances

may appear shortened, memory deteriorates, and concentration becomes difficult. Large amounts of marijuana may produce hallucinations after 20 to 25 minutes. The total effects of a marijuana "trip" can last from three to five hours.

The after-effects of marijuana are visually minimal. Physical addiction is absent, but use of marijuana may result in psychological dependence. There appears to be no withdrawal symptoms. The dangers from the use of marijuana have recently been greatly enhanced by the large scale introduction of hashish (a concentrated resin from the marijuana plant).

Signs and Symptoms: (See Marijuana.)

Slang terms: "Pot", "Tea", "Grass", "Weed", "Stuff", "Rope", "Hay", "Joints", "Reefer", "Hemp", "Mary Jane", "Hashish" (a concentrated form of marijuana), "Texas Tea", "Acapulco Gold", "A stick", "Goof Butt", "Jive", "Sweet Lunch", "Stinkweed", "Bhang", "Ganja".

B. LSD (D-lysergic acid diethylamide)

Description: LSD is a powerful synthetic chemical developed in Switzerland in 1938. Its perception-altering properties were accidentally discovered in 1943. LSD is synthesized from substance obtained from ergot, a fungus that grows as a rust on rye. LSD has been used experimentally to treat patients with severe psychosis; however, such use has created many more adverse than beneficial effects. Its medical use is extremely limited and it is not accepted for medical treatment at present. Recent studies have indicated that LSD may cause chronomsomal damage resulting in congenital birth defects.

LSD can produce a feeling of complete detachment from reality and can cause actions that lead to serious injury or even death to users. An LSD user can also become dangerous to others.

Identification: LSD commonly appears as a white power or tablet and also as a clear, colorless, odorless liquid. It is impossible to identify visually and its presence can only be substantiated by qualitative and quantitative analytical tests.

Methods of use: LSD is generally taken by mouth. Practically any substance such as a tablet, sugar cube, cookie, paper, etc., can be a source. When LSD was first introduced into the illicit market it was commonly added to a sugar cube. On rare occasions, LSD is injected directly into the bloodstream. The effect of LSD changes the levels of certain chemicals found in the brain, including serotonin, which produces changes in the brain's electrical activity. This may result in hallucinations, the intensification and distortion of sensory perception, panic, violence, suicide, or a loss of sanity. Hallucinations may recur (with the same intensity) any time up to two years after the original "trip."

Signs and symptoms: (See "Indications of Possible Misuse—Other Hallucinogens.")

Slang terms: "LSD", "Acid", "Cubes", "Sugar", "25", "The Big D", "The Cube", "Lucy in the Sky with Diamonds."

C. MESCALINE
(3, 4, 5-trimethoxphenylethylamine)

Description: Mescaline is obtained from the peyote cactus. Hallucinogenic effects of a full dosage may last up to 12 hours. Peyote is the "button" that grows on the peyote cactus. Peyote has been used by Indians in religious ceremonies. No valid medical use is known.

Identification: The peyote button is dried and ground into a powder, dark brown in color. It is often put into gelatin capsules.

Signs and symptoms: Similar to those of LSD but usually a more intense stimulation of visual sensation.

Methods of use: Mescaline (peyote) is always taken by mouth, although a few cases of injection have been reported. Because of its bitter taste, peyote is usually taken with tea, coffee or soda.

Slang terms: "Peyote", "Plants", "Buttons".

D. "SMASH"
This is a new concoction that is reportedly being sold by narcotic peddlers. Marijuana is cooked with acetone to obtain oil of cannabis. The oil is then added to hashish to form a tarlike material. This is then rolled into small pellets and smoked. It is reported that "smash" is being manufactured in Mexico.

E. THC (delta 1, tetrahydrocannabinol)
A recent discovery which may become popular as an abuse drug. THC is synthetic marijuana and is being used in medical research.

F. METHADONE
This is a synthetic narcotic whose pharmacologic actions are similar to morphine. Methadone has been used in medicine for its antitussive and analgesic properties. It has also been utilized in withdrawal management of heroin addicts and in Methadone Maintenance Programs. It is known to produce cross-tolerance to opiates and when given in lieu of heroin, it is claimed that individuals under this regime do not manifest most of the undesirable anti-social effects. Since methadone is addictive, it is also subject to abuse.

G. (PCP) PHENCYCLIDINE
Phencyclidine, developed in the 1950's, is now legally manufactured as a veterinary anesthetic under the trade name Sernylan. Since 1967 it has also been produced in clandestine laboratories, frequently in dangerously contaminated forms. The prevailing patterns of street-level abuse are by oral ingestion of tablets or capsules, containing the drug in powder form both alone and in combination with other drugs, and by smoking the drug after it has been sprinkled on parsley, marijuana, or some form of tobacco. It is sometimes sold to unsuspecting consumers as LSD, THC, or mescaline.

Reported experiences under the influence of phencyclidine are mainly nondescript or unpleasant. In low doses the experience usually proceeds in three successive stages: changes in body image, sometimes accompanied by feelings of depersonalization; perceptual distortions, infrequently evidenced as visual or auditory hallucinations; and feelings of apathy or estrangement. The experience often includes drowsiness, inability to verbalize, and feelings of emptiness or "nothingness." Reports of difficulty in thinking, poor concentration, and preoccupation with death are common.

Many users have reacted to its use with an acute psychotic episode. Common signs of phencyclidine use include flushing and profuse sweating. Analgesia, involuntary eye movements, muscular incoordination, double vision, dizziness, nausea, and vomiting may also be present.

17.7 OPIATES, HALLUCINOGENICS, STIMULANTS, DEPRESSANTS, SCHEDULES I-V

Controlled Subtstances Schedules. The following schedules (*Health and Safety Code Sections 11054 through 11058),* list substances formerly identified as "Narcotics or Restricted Dangerous Drugs." A careful review of the Table of Controlled Substances and

Related Health and Safety Code Sections (p. 238) of this manual will reveal the following:
1. Substances such as heroin, LSD, and marijuana are now listed under Schedule I.
2. Cocaine and other stimulants are listed under Schedule II.
3. The depressants such as the barbiturates and tranquilizers are listed under Schedules III and IV.
4. Compounds containing narcotic and non-narcotic medicinal ingredients are listed in Schedule V.

SCHEDULE I: SUBSTANCES INCLUDED. (H & S Code 11054)

a. Except for purposes of Chapter 4 (commencing with Section 11150) of this division, the controlled substances listed in this section are included in Schedule I.
b. Any of the following opiates, including their isomers, esters, ethers, salts, and salts of isomers, esters, and ethers, unless specifically excepted, whenever the existence of these isomers, esters, ethers and salts is possible within the specific chemical designation:
   1. Acetylmethadol
   2. Allylprodine
   3. Alphacetylmethadol
   4. Alphameprodine
   5. Alphamethadol
   6. Benzethidine
   7. Betacetylmethadol
   8. Betameprodine
   9. Betamethodol
   10. Betaprodine
   11. Clonitazene
   12. Dextromoramide
   13. Dextrorphan
   14. Diampromide
   15. Diethylthiambutene
   16. Dimenoxadol
   17. Dimepheptanol
   18. Dimethylthiambutene
   19. Dioxaphetyl butyrate
   20. Dipipanone
   21. Ethylmethylthiambutene
   22. Etonitazene
   23. Etoxeridine
   24. Furethidine
   25. Hydroxypethidine
   26. Ketobemidone
   27. Levomoramide
   28. Levophenacylmorphan
   29. Morpheridine
   30. Noracymethadol
   31. Norlevorphanol
   32. Normethadone
   33. Norpipanone
   34. Phenadoxone
   35. Phenampromide
   36. Phenomorphan
   37. Phenoperidine
   38. Piritramide
   39. Proheptazine
   40. Properidine
   41. Propiran
   42. Racemoramide
   43. Trimeperidine
c. Any of the following opium derivatives, their salts, isomers and salts of isomers, unless specifically excepted, whenever the existence of these salts, isomers and salts of isomers is possible within the specific chemical designation:
   1. Acetorphine
   2. Acetyldihydrocodeine
   3. Benzylmorphine
   4. Codeine methylbromide
   5. Codeine-N-oxide
   6. Cyprenorphine
   7. Desomorphine
   8. Dihydromorphine
   9. Etorphine
   10. Heroin
   11. Hydromorphinol
   12. Methyldesorphine
   13. Methyldihydromorphine
   14. Morphine methylbromide
   15. Morphine methylsulfonate
   16. Morphine-N-oxide
   17. Myrophine
   18. Nicocodeine
   19. Nicomorphine
   20. Normorphine
   21. Phoclodine
   22. Thebacon
d. Any material, compound, mixture, or preparation which contains any quantity of the following hallucinogenic substances, their salts, isomers, and salts of isomers, unless specifically excepted, whenever the existences of these salts, isomers, and salts of isomers is possible within the specific chemical designation:
   1. 3, 4-methylenedioxy amphetamine
   2. 5-methoxy-3, 4-methylenedioxy amphetamine
   3. 3, 4, 5-trimethoxy amphetamine
   4. Bufotenine

5. Diethyltryptamine
6. Dimethyltryptamine
7. 4-methyl-2, 5-dimethoxylamphetamine
8. Ibogaine
9. Lysergic acid diethylamide
10. Marijuana
11. Mescaline
12. Peyote
13. N-ethyl-3-piperidyl benzilate
14. N-methyl-3-piperidyl benzilate
15. Psilocybin
16. Psilocyn
17. Tetrahydrocannabinols

SCHEDULE II: SUBSTANCES INCLUDED. (H & S Code 11055)

a. Except for purposes of Chapter 4 (commencing with Section 11150) of this division, the substances listed in this section are included in Schedule II.

b. Any of the following substances, except those narcotic drugs listed in other schedules, whether produced directly or indirectly by extraction from substances of vegetable origin, or independently by means of chemical synthesis, or by combination of extraction and chemical synthesis:

1. Opium and opiate, and any salt, compound, derivative, or preparation of opium or opiate, with the exception of naloxone hydrochloride (N-allyl-14-hydroxy-nordihydromorphinone hydrochloride), but including the following:

    i. Raw opium
    ii. Opium extracts
    iii. Opium fluid extracts
    iv. Powdered opium
    v. Granulated opium
    vi. Tincture of opium
    vii. Apomorphine
    viii. Codeine
    ix. Ethylmorphine
    x. Hydrocodone
    xi. Hydromorphone
    xii. Metopon
    xiii. Morphine
    xiv. Oxycodone
    xv. Oxymorphone
    xvi. Thebaine

2. Any salt, compound, isomer, derivative, or preparation thereof which is chemically equivalent or identical with any of the substances referred to in paragraph (1), but not

including the isoquinoline alkaloids of opium.

3. Opium poppy and poppy straw.

4. Coca leaves and any salt, compound, derivative, or preparation of coca leaves, and any salt, compound, derivative, or preparation thereof which is chemically equivalent or identical with any of these substances, but not including decocainized coca leaves or extractions which do not contain cocaine or ecgonine.

c. Any of the following opiates, including their isomers, esters, ethers, salts, and salts of isomers, whenever the existence of these isomers, esters, ethers and salts is possible within the specific chemical designation:

1. Alphaprodine
2. Anileridine
3. Bezitramide
4. Dihydrocodeine
5. Diphenoxylate
6. Fentanyl
7. Isomethadone
8. Levomethorphon
9. Levorphanol
10. Metazocine
11. Methadone
12. Methadone—intermediate, 4-cyano-2 (N, N-dimethylamino)-4, 4-diphenylbutane
13. Moramide—intermediate, 3-methyl-4-morpholino-2, 2-diphenylbutanoic acid
14. Pethidine
15. Pethidine—intermediate—A, 4-cyano-N-methyl-4-phenylpiperidine
16. Pethidine—intermediate—B, ethyl-4-phenylpiperidine-4-carboxylate
17. Pethidine—intermediate—C, N-methyl-4-phenylpiperidine-4-carboxylic acid
18. Phenazocine
19. Piminodine
20. Racemethorphan
21. Racemorphan

d. Any material, compound, mixture, or preparation which contains any quantity of the following substances having a potential for abuse associated with a stimulant effect on the central nervous system:

1. Amphetamine, its salts, optical isomers, and salts of its optical isomers
2. Phenmetrazine and its salts
3. Any substance which contains any quantity of methamphetamine, including its salts, isomers, and salts of isomers
4. Methylphenidate

e. Any material, compound, mixture, or preparation which contains any quantity of phencyclidine having a potential for abuse associated with a depressant effect on the central nervous system.

Schedule III: SUBSTANCES INCLUDED (H & S Code 11056).

a. Except for purposes of chapter 4 (commencing with Section 11150) of this division, the controlled substances listed in this section are included in Schedule III.

b. Unless listed in another schedule, any material, compound, mixture, or preparation which contains any quantity of the following substances having a potential for abuse associated with a depressant effect on the central nervous system:
  1. Any substance which contains any quantity of a derivative of barbituric acid, or any salt of a derivative of barbituric acid, except those substances which are specifically listed in other schedules.
  2. Chlorhexadol
  3. Glutethimide
  4. Lysergic acid
  5. Lysergic acid amide
  6. Methaqualone and its salts
  7. Methprylon
  8. Sulfondiethylmethane
  9. Sulfonethylmethane
  10. Sulfonmethane

c. Nalorphine

d. Any material, compound, mixture or preparation containing limited quantities of any of the following narcotic drugs, or any salts thereof:
  1. Not more than 1.8 grams of codeine, or any of its salts, per 100 milliliters or not more than 90 milligrams per dosage unit, with an equal or greater quantity of an isoquinoline alkaloid of opium.
  2. Not more than 1.8 grams of codeine, or any of its salts, per 100 milliliters or not more than 90 milligrams per dosage unit, with one or more active, nonnarcotic ingredients in recognized therapeutic amounts.
  3. Not more than 300 milligrams of dihydrocodeinone, or any of its salts, per 100 milliliters or not more than 15 milligrams per dosage unit, with a fourfold or greater quantity of an isoquinoline alkaloid of opium.
  4. Not more than 300 milligrams of dihydrocodeinone, or any of its salts, per 100 milliliters or not more than 15 milligrams per dosage unit with one or more active, nonnarcotic ingredients in recognized therapeutic amounts.
  5. Not more than 1.8 grams of dihydrocodeine, or any of its salts, per 100 milliliters or not more than 90 milligrams per dosage unit, with one or more active, nonnarcotic ingredients in recognized therapeutic amounts.
  6. Not more than 300 milligrams of ethylmorphine, or any of its salts, per 010 milliliters or not more than 15 milligrams per dosage unit, with one or more ingredients in recognized therapeutic amounts.
  7. Not more than 500 milligrams of opium per 100 milliliters or per 100 grams, or not more than 25 milligrams per dosage unit, with one or more active, nonnarcotic ingredients in recognized therapeutic amounts.
  8. Not more than 50 milligrams of morphine, or any of its salts, per 100 milliliters or per 100 grams with one or more active nonnarcotic ingredients in recognized therapeutic amounts.

SCHEDULE IV: SUBSTANCES INCLUDED (H & S Code 11057)

a. Except for the purposes of Chapter 4 (commencing with Section 11105) of this division, the controlled substances listed in this section are included in Schedule IV.

b. Any material, compound, mixture, or preparation which contains any quantity of the following substances having a potential for abuse associated with a depressant effect on the central nervous system:
  1. Barbital
  2. Chloral betaine
  3. Chloral hydrate
  4. Ethchlorvynol
  5. Ethinamate
  6. Methohexital
  7. Meprobamate
  8. Methylphenobarbital
  9. Paraldehyde
  10. Petrichloral
  11. Phenobarbital

SCHEDULE V: SUBSTANCES INCLUDED. (H & S Code 11058)

a. Except for purposes of Chapter 4 (commencing with Section 11150) of this division, the controlled substances listed in this section are included in Schedule V.

b. Any compound, mixture, or preparation containing limited quantities of any of the following narcotic drugs, which also contains one or more nonnarcotic active medicinal ingredients in sufficient proportion to confer upon the compound, mixture, or preparation, valuable medicinal qualities other than those possessed by the narcotic drug alone:

1. Not more than 200 milligrams of codeine, or any of its salts, per 100 milliliters or per 100 grams.
2. Not more than 100 milligrams of dihydrocodeine, or any of its salts per 100 milliliters or per 100 grams.
3. Not more than 100 milligrams of ethylmorphine, or any of its salts, per 100 milliliters or per 100 grams.
4. Not more than 2.5 milligrams of diphenoxylate and not less than 25 micrograms of atrophine sulfate per dosage unit.
5. Not more than 100 milligrams of opium per 100 milliliters or per 100 grams.

17.8 CONTROLLED SUBSTANCE POSSESSION

Controlled Substance Defined (H & S Code 11007). "Controlled substance" means any drug included in Schedules I through V, inclusive. (Controlled Substances were formerly classified as "Restricted Drugs").

Unlawful Possession (H & S Code 11377). This section makes illegal possession of any of the substances listed in Schedule III, IV or V a felony ("wobbler") punishable by imprisonment in the county jail for a period not more than one year or in the state prison.

Possession For Sale (H & S Code 11378). This section makes possession for sale of any of the substances listed in Schedule III, IV or V, a felony punishable by imprisonment in the state prison.

17.9 ELEMENTS OF POSSESSION

Controlled Substance Defined. A "controlled substance" means a drug, substance or compound from which another compound is formed, the chemical names of which are set forth in the California Health and Safety Code.

Elements. In order to prove the commission of the crime of possession under H & S Code, each of the following elements must be proved:

1. That a person unlawfully exercised control over, or had the right to exercise control over a certain controlled substance.
2. That such person had knowledge of the presence of the controlled substance.
3. That such person had knowledge of its nature as a controlled substance.
4. That the substance was in an amount sufficient to be used as a controlled substance.

Two Types of Possession. The law recognized two kinds of possession: actual possession and constructive possession.

1. Actual possession: A person who knowingly has direct physical control over a thing is then in actual possession of it.
2. Constructive possession: A person who, although not in actual possession, knowingly has the right of control over a thing, either directly or through another person or persons, is then in constructive possession of it.

The law recognizes that one person may have possession alone, or that two or more persons jointly may share actual or constructive possession. The following court cases help to illustrate some of the above points.

1. Handling a narcotic for the sole purpose of disposal is not possession (*People v. Mijares, 6 Cal. 3d 415*).
2. Conviction for possession of a restricted dangerous drug (now called "controlled substance") may not be predicated upon possession of an amount so limited in quantity or so altered in form as to be useless as a restricted drug (*People v. Johnson, 5 Cal. App. 3d 844*).
3. While the prosecution has the burden to prove the amount possessed was sufficient for use, it does not have to prove that the contraband possessed had a potential of producing a narcotic effect (*People v. Piper, 19 Cal. App. 3d 248*).

17.10 UNLAWFUL TRANSPORTATION, MANUFACTURE, ETC.

Unlawful Manufacture, Import, Etc. (H & S Code 11379). This section makes it a felony punishable by imprisonment in the state prison for two, three, or four years to: illegally transport, import, sell, manufacture, compound, furnish, administer, give away (or offer to do any of these) any controlled substance listed in Schedule III, IV, or V. (See Text Section 17.7 and Chart, p. 238.)

17.11   PHENCYCLIDINE (PCP)

Unlawful Possession. (See H & S Code 11377, Text Section 17.8, p. 231).

Unlawful Possession for Sale (H & S Code 11378.5). Except as otherwise provided in Article 8 (commencing with Section 4211) of Chapter 9 of Division 2 of the Business and Professions Code, every person who possesses for sale any controlled substance which is specified in subdivision (e) of Section 11055, shall be punished by imprisonment in the state prison for a period of three, four, or five years.

Unlawful Transportation, Sale or Manufacture (H & S Code 11379.5). Except as otherwise provided in Article 8 (commencing with Section 4211) of Chapter 9 of Division 2 of the Business and Professions Code, every person who transports, imports into this state, sells, manufactures, compounds, furnishes, administers, or gives away, or offers to transport, import into this state, sell, manufacture, compound, furnish, administer, or give away, or attempts to import into this state or transport any controlled substance which is specified in subdivision (e) of Section 11055, unless upon the prescription of a physician, dentist, podiatrist, or veterinarian licensed to practice in this state, shall be punished by imprisonment in the state prison for a period of three, four, or five years.

Unlawful Use of Minor by Adult (H & S Code 11380).

a. Every person 18 years of age or over who violates any provision of this chapter involving controlled substances which are (1) classified in Schedule III, IV, or V and which are not narcotic drugs or (2) which are specified in subdivision (d) of Section 11054, except paragraphs (10), (11), (12), and (17) of such subdivision, or specified in subdivision (d) of Section 11055, by the use of a minor as agent, who solicits, induces, encourages, or intimidates any minor with the intent that the minor shall violate any provision of this article involving such controlled substances or who unlawfully furnishes, offers to furnish or attempts to furnish such controlled substances to a minor shall be punished by imprisonment in the state prison for a period of three, four, or five years.

17.12   MARIJUANA (CANNABIS)

Unlawful Possession (H & S Code 11357).

a. Except as authorized by law, every person who possesses any concentrated cannabis shall be punished by imprisonment in the county jail for a period of not more than one year or by a fine of not more than five hundred dollars ($500), or by both such fine and imprisonment, or shall be punished by imprisonment in the state prison.

b. Except as authorized by law, every person who possesses not more than one avoirdupois ounce of marijuana, other than concentrated cannabis is guilty of a misdemeanor and shall be punished by a fine of not more than one hundred dollars ($100). Notwithstanding other provisions of law, if such person has been previously convicted three or more times of an offense described in this subdivision during the two-year period immediately preceding the date of commission of the violation to be charged, the previous convictions shall also be charged in the accusatory pleading and, if found to be true by the jury upon a jury trial or by the court upon a court trial or if admitted by the person, the provisions of Sections 1000.1 and 1000.2 of the Penal Code shall be applicable to him, and the court shall divert and refer him for education, treatment, or rehabilitation, without a court hearing or determination or the concurrence of the district attorney, to an appropriate community program which will accept him. If the person is so diverted and referred he shall not be subject to the fine specified in this subdivision. If no community program will accept him, the person shall be subject to the fine specified in this subdivision.

Release on Citation. In any case in which a person is arrested for a violation of this subdivision and does not demand to be taken before a magistrate, such person shall be released by the arresting officer upon presentation of satisfactory evidence of identity and giving his written promise to appear in court, as provided in Section 853.6 of the Penal Code, and shall not be subjected to booking.

c. Except as authorized by law, every person who possesses more than one avoirdupois ounce of marijuana, other than concentrated cannabis, shall be punished by imprisonment in the county jail for a period of not more than six months or by a fine of not more than five hundred dollars ($500), or by both such fine and imprisonment. **Note:** Effective September 1, 1983, an additional Section (d) will be added to H & S Code 11357 (above). This new section will make it a misdemeanor punishable by a fine of five hundred dollars ($500) or ten (10) days in the county jail or both, for any *adult* to possess marijuana on any school grounds, grades K-12, during school hours or during school related programs.

The same offense, if committed by a minor, will result in a two hundred fifty dollar ($250) fine for the first offense and the same penalty as for an adult on a second and all subsequent offenses.

Unlawful Planting, Processing (H & S Code 11358). Every person who plants, cultivates, harvests, dries, or processes any marijuana or any part thereof, except as otherwise provided by law, shall be punished by imprisonment in the state prison.

Unlawful Possession for Sale (H & S Code 11359). Every person who possesses for sale any marijuana, except as otherwise provided by law, shall be punished by imprisonment in the state prison.

Unlawful Transportation, Sale (H & S Code 11360).

a. Except as otherwise provided by this section or as authorized by law, every person who transports, imports into this state, sells, furnishes, administers, or gives away, or offers to transport, import into this state, sell, furnish, administer, or give away, or attempts to import into this state or transport any marijuana shall be punished by imprisonment in the state prison for a period of two, three, or four years.

b. Except as authorized by law, every person who gives away, offers to give away, transports, offers to transport, or attempts to transport not more than one avoirdupois ounce of marijuana, other than concentrated cannabis, is guilty of a misdemeanor and shall be punished by a fine of not more than one hundred dollars ($100).

Release on Citation. In any case in which a person is arrested for a violation of this subdivision and does not demand to be taken before a magistrate, such person shall be released by the arresting officer upon presentation of satisfactory evidence of identity and giving his written promise to appear in court, as provided in Section 853.6 of the Penal Code, and shall not be subjected to booking.

17.13   ELEMENTS OF MARIJUANA POSSESSION

Marijuana and Cannabis Defined. "Marijuana" means all parts of the plant *cannabis sativa L.,* whether growing or not; the seeds thereof; the resin extracted from any part of the plant; and every compound, manufacture, salt, derivative, mixture, or preparation of the plant, its seeds, or its resin.

It does not include the mature stalks of the plant, fiber produced from the stalks, oil or cake made from the seeds of the plant, any other compounds, manufacture, salt, derivative, mixture, or preparation of the mature stalks (except the resin extracted therefrom), fiber, oil or cake, or the sterilized seed of the plant, which is incapable of germination. "Concentrated cannabis" means the separated resin, whether crude or purified, obtained from marijuana.

Elements of Possession. To constitute illegal possession of marijuana, it must be established:

1. That the defendant exercised control or had the right to exercise control over the marijuana.
2. That the defendant had knowledge of its presence.
3. That the defendant had knowledge that the substance was marijuana.
4. That the substance was in an amount sufficient to be used as marijuana.

Proof that any marijuana possessed was in an amount sufficient to be used may be established by:

1. Expert testimony.
2. Evidence that the amount possessed was sufficient to be used in any manner customarily employed by users of the substance.

17.14   HEROIN, COCAINE, OPIATES, OTHER CONTROLLED SUBSTANCES

Offenses Involving Controlled Substances Formerly Classified as Narcotics. Unlawful Possession (H & S Code 11350). Except as otherwise provided in this division, every person who possesses (1) any controlled substance specified in subdivision (b) or (c) of Section 11054, specified in paragraph (11), (12), or (17) of subdivision (d) of Section 11054, or specified in subdivision (b) or (c) of Section 11055, or (2) any controlled substance classified in Schedule III, IV, or V which is a narcotic drug, unless upon the written prescription of a physician, dentist, podiatrist, or veterinarian licensed to practice in this state, shall be punished by imprisonment in the state prison.

Unlawful Possession for Sale (H & S Code 11351). Except as otherwise provided in this division, every person who possesses for sale (1) any controlled substance specified in subdivision (b) or (c) of Section 11054, specified in paragraph (11), (12), or (17) of subdivision (d) of Section 11054, or specified in subdivision (b) or (c) of Section 11055, or (2) any controlled substance classified in Schedule III, IV, or V which is a narcotic drug, shall be punished by imprisonment in the state prison for two, three, or four years.

Unlawful Transportation, Sale Administration (H & S Code 11352). Except as otherwise provided in this division, every person who transports, imports into this state, sells, furnishes, administers, or gives away, or offers to transport, import into this state, sell, furnish, administer, or give away, or attempts to import into this state or transport (1) any controlled substance specified in subdivision (b) or (c) of Section 11054, specified in paragraph (11), (12), or (17) of subdivision (d) of Section 11054, or specified in subdivision (b) or (c) of Section 11055, or (2) any controlled substance classified in Schedule III, IV, or V which is a narcotic drug, unless upon the written prescription of a physician, dentist, podiatrist, or veterinarian licensed to practice in this state, shall be punished by imprisonment in the state prison for three, four, or five years.

Elements: Possession for Sale. In order to prove the commission of the offense "possession for sale" of a controlled substance, each of the following elements must be proved:

1. That a person unlawfully exercised control or had the right to exercise control over a certain controlled substance.
2. That such person had knowledge of its presence.
3. That such person had knowledge of its nature as a controlled substance.
4. That the substance was in an amount sufficient to be used for sale or consumption as a controlled substance.
5. That such person possessed the controlled substance with the specific intent to sell same.

Convictions Not Subject to Probation or Suspended Sentence. (P.C. 1203.07) Notwithstanding the provision of PC 1203, probation shall not be granted to, nor shall the sentence be suspended for any person who is convicted of Health and Safety code Sections:

1. H & S 11351, for *possessing* for sale one-half ounce or more of a substance containing heroin.
2. H & S 11352, for *selling* or offering to sell one-half ounce or more of a substance containing heroin.
3. H & S 11351 or 11352, with one or more prior convictions of these sections.
4. H & S 11378.5, for possessing for sale one-half ounce or more of any salt or solution of any controlled substance specified in H & S 11055(e), phencyclidine (see Text, Schedule II).

5. H & S 11379.5 or 11380.5, for transporting, administering phencyclidine, or importing same for sale or using, inducing, encouraging or intimidating a minor for this purpose.
6. H & S 11378.5, 11379.5 or 11380.5 for use of a minor as an agent.
7. H & S 11383(b), for possessing piperdine and cyclohexanone with intent to manufacture.

17.15 UNDER THE INFLUENCE

Under the Influence of Controlled Substance (H & S Code 11550). No person shall use, or be under the influence of any controlled substance which is (1) specified in subdivision (b) or (c) of Section 11054, specified in paragraph (11), (12), or (17) of subdivision (d) of Section 11054, or specified in subdivision (b) or (c) of Section 11055; or (2) which is a narcotic drug classified in Schedule III, IV, or V, excepting when administered by or under the direction of a person licensed by the state to dispense, prescribe, or administer controlled substances. It shall be the burden of the defense to show that it comes within the exception. Any person convicted of violating any provision of this section is guilty of a misdemeanor and shall be sentenced to serve a term of not less than 90 days nor more than one year in the county jail. The court may place a person convicted hereunder on probation for a period not to exceed five years and shall in all cases in which probation is granted require as a condition thereof that such person be confined in the county jail for at least 90 days. In no event does the court have the power to absolve a person who violates this section from the obligation of spending at least 90 days in confinement in the county jail.

Under the Influence Defined. If a controlled substance is appreciably affecting the nervous system, brain, muscles, or other parts of a person's body, or is creating in this person any perceptible or abnormal mental or physical condition, such a person is under the influence of a controlled substance.

Opiate Defined *(H & S Code 11020).* "Opiate" means any substance having an addiction-forming or addiction-sustaining liability similar to morphine or being capable of conversion into a drug having addiction-forming or addiction-sustaining liability. It does not include, unless specifically designated as controlled under Chapter 2 (commencing with Section 11053) of this division, the dextrorotatory isomer of 3-methoxy-n-methylmorphinan and its salt (dextromethorphan). It does include its racemic and levorotatory forms.

17.16 MISCELLANEOUS OFFENSES AND PARAPHERNALIA

Unlawful Paraphernalia (H & S Code 11364). It is unlawful to possess an opium pipe or any device, contrivance, instrument or paraphernalia used for unlawfully injecting or smoking (1) a controlled substance specified in subdivision (b) or (c) of Section 11054, specified in paragraph (11), (12), or (17) of subdivision (d) of Section 11054, or specified in subdivision (b) or (c) of Section 11055 or (2) a controlled substance which is a narcotic drug classified in Schedule III, IV, or V.

Drug Paraphernalia—Minors (H & S Code 11364.5). This section restricts sales of any "tobacco related accessory" to minors and restricts display of paraphernalia, excluding rolling papers. It also requires retailers to post a warning that "drug paraphernalia" is for sale on the premises and requires that such paraphernalia be kept in a separate room under certain conditions.

Drug Paraphernalia Defined. As used in this section, "drug paraphernalia" means all equipment, products, and materials of any kind which are intended for use or designed for use in planting, propagating, cultivating, growing, harvesting, manufacturing, compounding, converting, producing, processing, preparing, testing, analyzing, packaging, storing, containing, concealing, injecting, ingesting, inhaling, or otherwise introducing into the human body a controlled substance. (H & S Code 11014.5)

Drug Paraphernalia Listed. Includes, but is not limited to, all of the following:

1. Kits intended for use or designed for use in cultivating, growing, etc. and plant from which a controlled substance can be derived.
2. Kits or devices intended for use in increasing the potency of any plant which is a controlled substance.
3. Kits intended for use in manufacturing, producing, etc., controlled substances.
4. Testing equipment for use in identifying or analyzing the strength or purity of controlled substances.
5. Scales used for weighing controlled substances.
6. Dilutant, etc., used for cutting controlled substances.
7. Sifters, etc., for use in removing twigs, etc., from marijuana.
8. Blenders, containers, etc., for use in compounding controlled substances.
9. Capsules, etc., intended for use in packaging small quantities of controlled substances.
10. Containers, etc., for use in storing or concealing controlled substances.
11. Hypodermic syringes, needles, etc., for use in injecting controlled substances into the human body.
12. Objects for use in ingesting, inhaling, etc., marijuana, cocaine, hashish, or hashish oil into the human body such as:
    A. Pipes with hashish heads, or punctured metal bowls
    B. Water pipes
    C. Carburation tubes and devices
    D. Smoking and carburation masks
    E. Roach clips, used to hold burning material such as a marijuana cigarette
    F. Miniature cocaine spoons and cocaine vials
    G. Chamber pipes
    H. Carburetor pipes
    I. Electric pipes
    J. Air-driven pipes
    K. Chillums
    L. Bongs
    M. Ice pipes or chillers

Unlawful Presence Where Substance Used (H & S Code 11365). It is unlawful to visit or to be in any room or place where any controlled substances which are specified in subdivision (b) or (c) of Section 11054, specified in paragraph (11), (12), or (17) of subdivision (b) or (c) of Section 11055, or which are narcotic drugs classified in Schedule III, IV, or V, are being unlawfully smoked or used with knowledge that such activity is occurring.

17.17 PERSONS REQUIRED TO REGISTER

Convicted Person's Registration With Chief of Police or Sheriff (H & S Code 11590)

a. Any person who, on or after the effective date of this section, is convicted in the State of California of any offense defined in Section 11350, 11351, 11352, 11353, 11354, 11355, 11357, 11358, 11359, 11360, 11361, 11363, 11366, 11368, or 11550, or any person who is, on or after such date, discharged or paroled from a penal institution where he was confined because of the commission of any such offense, or any person who is, on or after such date, convicted in any other state of any offense which, if committed or attempted in this state, would have been punishable as one or more of the above-mentioned offenses, shall within 30 days after the effective date of this section or within 30 days of his coming into any county or city, or city and county in which he resides or is temporarily domiciled for such length of time, register with the chief of police of the city in which he resides or the sheriff of the county if he resides in an unincorporated area.

b. Any person who, on or after the effective date of this section is convicted in any federal court of any offense which, if committed or attempted in this state would have been punishable as one or more of the offenses enumerated in subdivision (a) shall within 30 days after the effective date of this section or within 30 days of his coming into any county or city, or city and county in which he resides or is temporarily domiciled for such length of time, register with the chief police of the city in which he resides or the sheriff of the county if he resides in an unincorporated area.

c This section does not apply to a conviction of a misdemeanor under Section 11357 or 11360.

TERMINOLOGY DEFINED—CHAPTER 17

See the Terminology Quiz at the end of this chapter.
1. Controlled substance: drugs listed in Schedule I-V, H & S Code.
2. Heroin: an opium derivative.
3. Depressants: drugs listed in W & I Code Schedule III and IV.
4. Stimulants: drugs listed in W & I Code, Schedule II.
5. Compounds: combination of narcotic and non-narcotic drugs.
6. LSD: an illegal hallucinogenic.
7. PCP: short for phencyclidine.
8. Marijuana possession offense: defined in H & S Code 11357a.
9. Marijuana sale offense: defined in H & S Code 11360.
10. Heroin possession offense: defined in H & S Code 11350.
11. Dexadrine: an amphetamine, a stimulant.
12. Constructive possession: have a right of control.
13. Actual possession: direct physical control.
14. Marijuana's botanical name: *cannabis sativa L.*
15. Hashish oil: a derivative of marijuana.

TRUE-FALSE QUIZ—CHAPTER 17

1. Narcotics formerly called "dangerous drugs" are now identified as "controlled substances" in the Health and Safety Code.
2. Most narcotics laws are now found in the Welfare and Institutions Code.
3. H & S Code Schedules I-V now identify all currently controlled substances.
4. Heroin is a derivative of opium.
5. LSD and PCP are both hallucinogenics.
6. Cocaine is an opium derivative.
7. Possession of less than one ounce of marijuana is no longer a crime.
8. Methadone is classed as a stimulant in the H & S Code.
9. Barbiturates are classed as depressants in the H & S Code.
10. Dexadrine is a kind of tranquilizer.

ESSAY-DISCUSSION QUESTIONS— CHAPTER 17

1. Define a "controlled substance" for purposes of the H & S Code.
2. What four elements must be proved in the crime of possession under the H & S Code?
3. How many kinds of possession are there, and what are they under the H & S Code?
4. Does the defense or the prosecution have the burden of proof that an amount of controlled substance is sufficient for use?
5. Is it (1) no crime, (2) a felony, or (3) a misdemeanor to unlawfully plant marijuana. What is the penalty, if any?

TERMINOLOGY QUIZ—CHAPTER 17

Match terms and definitions by placing the correct number in the parentheses. Answers may be written on a separate sheet for submission to the instructor at the instructor's direction.

1. H & S Code 11360
2. H & S Code 11350
3. Amphetamine: a stimulant
4. H & S Code 11353
5. Having right of control
6. Direct physical control
7. *Cannabis sativa L.*
8. A derivative of marijuana
9. Hashish oil
10. Any unlawful substance
11. H & S Code 11590
12. LSD
13. H & S Code 11357a
14. Listed in Schedule II
15. Phencyclidine
16. Illegal hallucinogenic
17. Narcotics and nonnarcotics together
18. Listed in Schedule III or IV
19. Opium derivative
20. Listed in Schedules I-V

( ) controlled substance
( ) heroin
( ) depressants
( ) stimulants
( ) compounds
( ) LSD
( ) PCP
( ) marijuana possession
( ) marijuana sale
( ) heroin possession
( ) dexadrine
( ) constructive possession
( ) actual possession
( ) marijuana's botanical name
( ) hashish oil source

TABLE OF CONTROLLED SUBSTANCES AND RELATED HEALTH AND SAFETY CODE SECTIONS

	Drugs	Calif. Sched.	Often Prescribed Brand Names	Health & Safety Code Sec.			Adult
				Possession	Possession For Sale	Sale	Use Of Minor
N A R C O T I C S	OPIUM	II	Dovers powder, paregoric	11350	11351	11352	11353
	MORPHINE	II	Morphine	11350	11351	11352	11353
	CODEINE	II	Codeine	11350	11351	11352	11353
	HEROIN	I	None	11350	11351	11352	11353
	MEPERIDINE (Pethidine)	II	Demerol, Pethadol	11350	11351	11352	11353
	METHADONE	II	Dolophine, Methadone Amidone	11350	11351	11352	11353
	OTHER NARCOTICS	II	Dilaudid, Percodan Numorphan, Leritine	11350	11351	11352	11353
D E P R E S S A N T S	CHLORAL HYDRATE	IV	Noctec, Somnos	11377	11378	11379	11380
	BARBITURATES	III	Amytal, Nembutal, Tuinal Seconal	11377	11378	11379	11380
	OTHER BARBITURATES	IV	Veronal(Barbital) Luminal (Phenobarbital)	11377	11378	11379	11380
	METHAQUALONE	III	Quaalud, Sopor, Parest	11377	11378	11379	11380
	TRANQUILIZERS	IV	Miltown (Meprobromate) Equanil	11377	11378	11379	11380
	OTHER DEPRESSANTS	IV	Placidyl (Ethchlorvynol) Valmid (Ethinamate)	11377	11378	11379	11380
S T I M U L A N T S	COCAINE	II	Cocaine	11350	11351	11352	11353
	AMPHETAMINES	II	Benzedrine, Biphetamine Desoxyn, Dexedrine, Obetrol, Obedrin	11377	11378	11379	11380
	PHENMETRAZINE	II	Preludin	11377	11378	11379	11380
	METHYLPHENIDATE	II	Ritalin	11377	11378	11379	11380
	OTHER STIMULANTS	II		11377	11378	11379	11380
H A L L U C I N O G E N S	LSD	I	None	11377	11378	11379	11380
	MESCALINE	I	None	11377	11378	11379	11380
	PHENCYCLIDINE (PCP)	III	Sernylan	11377	11378.5	11379.5	11380
	OTHER HALLUCINOGENS		None	11377	11378	11379	11380
C A N N A B I S	MARIJUANA HASHISH HASHISH OIL	I	None None None	11357a, b, c 11357a 11357a	11359 11359 11359	11360 11360 11360	11361 11361 11361

This table names each controlled substance, lists its H & S Code Schedule, indicates medical brand names, and identifies the proper booking section for a violation of possession, possession for sale, sale, or use of a minor by an adult for any of these violations.

CHAPTER 18

Forgery—Arson and Miscellaneous Offenses

18.1 FORGERY DEFINED

PC 470. Forgery of Wills, Conveyances. "Every person who with intent to defraud, signs the name of another person or of a fictitious person, knowing that he has no authority so to do, or falsely makes, alters, forges, or counterfeits any...trading stamp, bank bill or note,...check, draft,...contract, promissory note, due bill for the payment of money or property, receipt for money or property...or counterfeits or forges the handwriting of another, or utters, publishes, passes or attempts to pass, as true and genuine, any of the above-named false, altered, forged, or counterfeit matters, knowing the same to be false, altered, forged, or counterfeited, with intent to prejudice, damage, or defraud any person;...is guilty of forgery" (briefed).

Discussion

There are many kinds of forgery defined under PC 470 through 483. Generally, forgery is the false making or material alteration of writing with intent to defraud. The crime consists of either the making or altering of a document described under one of the forgery sections, without authority, or uttering such document with intent to defraud.

One may make a "material alteration" of a document merely by changing a word, a letter, or perhaps even a decimal point. "Writing," as used in forgery, is not limited solely to handwriting but includes any kind of written or printed reproduction. The term "making," as used in forgery also includes any alteration, however slight. "Uttering" is merely giving, offering, or passing.

18.2 INTENT TO DEFRAUD

The specific intent to defraud is an essential element, but it is not necessary to prove that any person was actually defrauded or lost money or property as a result of the forgery. It is sufficient to show that either a specific individual or members of the public would have been injured or defrauded as a result of the defendant's act.

It is not necessary to show that the defendant benefited in any way as the result of his act, nor is it important, in the case of a check, that it was ever presented to the bank.

It is important to remember that forgery consists of two types of acts; either of which is a crime: (1) writing, signing, making, or altering any of the documents described in the section, and (2) passing, attempting to pass, uttering, or giving a false instrument as a genuine one. As mentioned previously, the intent to defraud must be present in each case (see section on credit card theft).

18.3 TYPES OF FORGERY AND FICTITIOUS CHECKS

PC 470 includes any document, check, personal note, will, or writing on which the defendant makes some alteration. It also includes documents which he might prepare in whole or part. Raising the amount of a check, or making out personal or payroll checks or stolen money orders, would be an example.

Forgery of endorsement on a check with intent to defraud is also covered by PC 470. If a person gives another permission to sign his name, it is not a crime. It is not a crime for an employee to sign his boss's name, or a wife to endorse her husband's check, providing there is express or implied permission to do so. Permission to sign another's name need not be in writing. Intent to defraud is the gist of forgery.

Fictitious Name Forgeries. PC 476. This section would be applicable where there is no living person of the name used on the check. It is necessary, under this section, to prove that the telephone and perhaps other directories have been checked and no such person exists. If such person does exist, it would be necessary to subpoena him to court to testify that he did not write the check and did not give the defendant permission to do so. This section also makes it a crime to have in one's possession, with intention to cash it, any check or other instrument in writing for the payment of money. Knowledge of the fictitious nature of the document and intent to defraud are both essential elements of this section.

Issuing Check With Intent to Defraud. PC 476a. This section is used to prosecute nonsufficient fund (N.S.F.) checks, account-closed checks, and no-account checks; the latter being those cases where the defendant uses his true name, but does not have an account in the bank upon which the check was drawn. When one willfully, and with intent to defraud, writes, draws or delivers a check, draft, or money order upon any bank for the payment of money, knowing at the time that he does not have sufficient funds on deposit or credit with the bank, or an account with the bank in question, he is in violation of this section.

Post-dated checks (those dated in the future or after the date they are cashed) may also be prosecuted under PC 476a. If, however, the person cashing the check informs the person who is accepting his check that is post-dated, then there is no deception or intent to defraud and the check becomes a promissory note. The mere fact that the defendant fails to keep his promise and deposit funds in the bank to cover the check on the due date, does not constitute a crime. In such cases the payee would have to take civil action to recover his money or property given for the post-dated check.

PC475a. Fraudulent Possession of Completed Check, Money Order, or Traveler's Check: Punishment. Every person who has in his possession a completed check, money order, traveler's check, or county warrant, whether the parties thereto are real or fictitious, with intention to utter or pass the same, or to permit, cause, or procure the same to be uttered or passed, to defraud any person, is punishable by imprisonment in the state prison, or by imprisonment in the county jail for not more than one year.

Credit Card Forgery: PC 484f, Subdivision (1): "Every person who, with intent to defraud, makes, alters, embosses, or uses a card purporting to be a credit card is guilty of forgery."

PC 484f, Subdivision (2): "Every person other than the cardholder or a person authorized by the cardholder who, with intent to defraud, signs the name of another or a fictitious name to a credit card, sales slip, sales draft, or any other instrument for the payment of money is guilty of forgery."

18.4 PENALTIES—FORGERY AND FICTITIOUS CHECKS

PC 473. Punishment for Forgery. "Forgery is punishable by imprisonment in the state prison, or by imprisonment in the county jail for not more than one year."

PC 476 violations are punishable by imprisonment in the county jail for not more than one year, or in the state prison.

PC 476a violations are punishable by imprisonment in the county jail for not more than one year, or in the state prison for not more than one year.

Exception. If the total amount of all checks that the defendant is convicted of making or uttering does not exceed two hundred dollars ($200), the offense is punishable only by imprisonment in the county jail for not more than one year unless he has been previously convicted in this or any other state of PC 470, 475, 476, or petty theft. If he has been so previously convicted, then the penalty given under PC 476a is applicable.(*PC 476a(b)*).

18.5 ARSON

PC 450. Definitions. In this chapter the following terms have the following meanings:
   a. "Structure" means any building, or commercial or public tent, bridge, tunnel, or powerplant.
   b. "Forest land" means any brush-covered land, cut-over land, forest, grasslands, or woods.
   c. "Property" means real property or personal property, other than a structure or forest land.
   d. "Inhabited" means currently being used for dwelling purposes whether occupied or not. "Inhabited structure" and "inhabited property" do not include the real property (land) on which an inhabited structure or an inhabited property is located.
   e. "Maliciously" imports a wish to vex, defraud, annoy, or injure another person, or an intent to do a wrongful act, established either by proof or presumption of law.

f. "Recklessly" means a person is aware of and consciously disregards a substantial and unjustifiable risk that his or her act will set fire to, burn, or cause to burn a structure, forest land, or property. The risk shall be of such nature and degree that disregard thereof constitutes a gross deviation from the standard of conduct that a reasonable person would observe in the situation. A person who creates such a risk but is unaware thereof solely by reason of voluntary intoxication also acts recklessly with respect thereto.

Punishment for Arson. PC 451. A person is guilty of arson when he willfully and maliciously sets fire to or burns or causes to be burned or who aids, counsels or procures the burning of, any structure, forest land or property.

a. Arson that causes great bodily injury is a felony punishable by imprisonment in the state prison for five, seven, or nine years.

b. Arson that causes an inhabited structure or inhabited property to burn is a felony punishable by imprisonment in the state prison for three, five, or seven years.

c. Arson of a structure or forest land is a felony punishable by imprisonment in the state prison for two, four, or six years.

d. Arson of property is a felony punishable by imprisonment in the state prison for 16 months, two, or three years. For purposes of this paragraph arson of property does not include one burning or causing to be burned his own personal property unless there is intent to defraud or there is injury to another person or another person's structure, forest land, or property.

Discussion

The word "maliciously" imports "a wish to vex, annoy, or injure another person or an intent to do a wrongful act." It is not necessary that the property burned actually be destroyed; it is sufficient if there is but a slight degree of burning with respect to the property damage. However, the offense is complete if the burning is willful and malicious, and is of an intentional or incendiary origin, and proof of the *corpus delicti* of the crime may be proven circumstantially *(People v. Nagy, 199 Cal. 235)*.

All that is needed to establish the *corpus delicti* in a prosecution for arson, in addition to the actual burning, is that the fire was intentional or of an incendiary origin, and this is generally established by circumstantial evidence, such as finding separate and distinct fires on the premises *(People v. Clagg, 197 C.A. 2d 209)*.

Attempt to Burn. PC 455. Any person who willfully and maliciously attempts to set fire to or attempts to burn or to aid, counsel, or procure the burning of any structure, forest land, or property, or who commits any act preliminary thereto, or in furtherance thereof, is punishable by imprisonment in the state prison for 16 months or two or three years. The placing or distributing of any inflammable, explosive, or combustible material or substance, or any device in or about any structure, forest land, or property in an arrangement or preparation with intent to eventually willfully and maliciously set fire to or burn same, or to procure the setting fire to or burning of same shall, for the purposes of this act constitute an attempt to burn such structure, forest land, or property.

Discussion

This section is designed to make "attempt arson" a crime. It would be a violation of PC 455 to place a "firebomb" (see PC 453) or any incendiary device for the purpose of subsequently causing a fire. This section would also cover instances where one arranges with or procures another to burn a structure for insurance fraud purposes. In the latter case, a violation of PC 182 (conspiracy) might also exist.

18.6 UNLAWFULLY CAUSING FIRE

Definition and Punishment. PC 452. A person is guilty of unlawfully causing a fire when he recklessly sets fire to or burns or causes to be burned, any structure, forest land or property.

a. Unlawfully causing a fire that causes great bodily injury is a felony punishable by imprisonment in the state prison for two, four or six years, or by imprisonment in the county jail for not more than one year, or by a fine, or by both such imprisonment and fine.

b. Unlawfully causing a fire that causes inhabited property to burn is a felony punishable by imprisonment in the state prison for two, three or four years, or by imprisonment in the county jail for not more than one year, or by a fine, or by both such imprisonment and fine.

c. Unlawfully causing a fire of a structure or forest land is a felony punishable by imprisonment in the state prison for 16 months or two or three years, or by imprisonment in the county jail for not more than six months, or by a fine, or by both such imprisonment and fine.

d. Unlawfully causing a fire of property is a misdemeanor. For purposes of this paragraph, unlawfully causing a fire of property does not include one burning or causing to be burned his own personal property unless there is injury to another person or to another person's structure, forest land, or property.

Discussion

PC 452 differs from PC 451 in several respects. In PC 451, the burning must be "willful and malicious," such as burning with intent to defraud an insurance company. In PC 452, it is necessary only that the burning be done unlawfully and recklessly (with negligence) to sustain a conviction. Note that PC 452 does not make it a crime to burn one's own property unless there is injury to other persons or their structures (buildings), or to forest land or property. In the latter instances, a violation of PC 452, even if one burns one's own property, is a felony or misdemeanor depending on the damage or injury caused.

18.7 POSSESSION OF FLAMMABLES AND EXPLOSIVES

Combustible Material or Device With Intent to Burn. PC 453

a. Every person who possesses any flammable, explosive or combustible material or substance, or any device in an arrangement or preparation, with intent to willfully and maliciously use such material, substance or device to set fire to or burn any structure, forest land or property, is punishable by imprisonment in the state prison, or in the county jail, not exceeding one year.

b. Every person who possesses, manufactures or disposes of a firebomb is guilty of a felony.

For the purposes of this subdivision, "disposes of" means to give, give away, loan, offer, offer for sale, sell, or transfer.

For the purposes of this subdivision, a "firebomb" is a breakable container containing a flammable liquid with a flashpoint of 150 degrees Fahrenheit or less, having a wick or similar device capable of being ignited, but no device commercially manufactured primarily for the purpose of illumination shall be deemed to be a firebomb for the purposes of this subdivision.

c. Subdivisions (a) and (b) of this section shall not prohibit the authorized use or possession of any material, substance or device described therein by a member of the armed forces of the United States or by firemen, police officers, peace officers, or law enforcement officers authorized by the properly constituted authorities; nor shall those subdivisions prohibit the use or possession of any material, substance or device described therein when used solely for scientific research or educational purposes, or for disposal of brush under permit as provided for in Section 4494 of the Public Resources Code, or for any other lawful burning. Subdivision (b) of this section shall not prohibit the manufacture or disposal of a firebomb for the parties or purposes described in this subdivision.

Discussion

This section of the penal code was added by the legislature for the purpose of better control of incendiary devices such as "Molotov cocktails." Such is referred to in this section as a "firebomb." It should be noted that to constitute a violation of this section, it must be proved that the inflammable or explosive is possessed for the purpose of setting a fire. Specific intent is, therefore, required.

18.8 CRIMES AGAINST INSURED PROPERTY

Defrauding Insurer. PC 548. Every person who willfully injures, destroys, secretes, abandons, or disposes of any property, which at the time is insured against loss of damage by theft or embezzlement, or any casualty with intent to defraud or prejudice the insurer, whether the same be the property or in the possession of such person or any other person, is punishable by imprisonment in the state prison for two, three, or four years.

For purposes of this section, "casualty" does not include fire.

Discussion

This section applies strictly to the destruction, secreting, or disposing of personal property with intent to defraud the insurance carrier. It should be noted the *specific intent* to defraud or prejudice the insurer is a necessary element of this offense. Where the property is destroyed or injured by burning, the act usually involves the crime of arson or unlawful burning (PC 451 or 452). Since this offense and arson are two distinct crimes, they may be jointly charged and tried.

18.9   ABANDONED REFRIGERATORS

Any person who discards or abandons or leaves in any place accessible to children, any refrigerator, icebox, or deep freeze locker, having a capacity of one and one-half cubic feet or more, which is no longer in use, and which has not had the door removed or the hinges and such portion of the latch mechanism removed to prevent latching or locking of the door, is guilty of a misdemeanor. Any owner, lessee, or manager who knowingly permits such a refrigerator, icebox, or deep-freeze locker to remain on premises under his control without having the door removed or the hinges and such portion of the latch mechanism removed to prevent latching or locking of the door, is guilty of a misdemeanor (PC 402b) (briefed).

18.10   DEPOSITING OBJECTS OR MATERIAL ON PUBLIC HIGHWAYS

Throwing Glass, Etc., Upon Highway. PC 588a. "Any person who throws or deposits any oil, glass bottle, glass, nails, tacks, hoops, wire, cans, or any other substance likely to injure any person, animal, or vehicle upon any public highway in the State of California shall be guilty of a misdemeanor; provided however, that any person who willfully deposits any such substance upon any public highway in the State of California with the intent to cause great bodily injury to other persons using the highway shall be guilty of a felony."

18.11   DESTROYING SIGN BARRIERS

Destroying or Removing Authorized Barrier, Sign, or Light on Highway. PC 588b. "Any person who willfully breaks down, removes, injures, or destroys any barrier or obstruction erected or placed in or upon any road or highway by the authorities in charge thereof, or by any authorized contractor engaged in the construction or maintenance thereof, or who tears down, defaces, removes, or destroys any warnings, notices, or directional signs erected, placed or posted in, upon, or adjacent to any road or highway or who extinguishes, removes, injures, or destroys any warning light or lantern or reflectorized warning or directional sign, erected, placed, or maintained by any such road or highway, shall be guilty of a misdemeanor."

18.12   DESTRUCTION OF LANDMARKS, TREES AND SIGNS

PC 605. "Every person who either:
1. Maliciously removes any monument erected for the purpose of designating any point in the boundary of any lot or tract of land, or a place where a subaqueous (underwater) telegraph cable lies; or
2. Maliciously defaces or alters the marks upon any such monument; or
3. Maliciously cuts down or removes any tree upon which any such marks have been made for such purpose, with intent to destroy such marks, is guilty of a misdemeanor."

18.13   INJURING WORKS OF ART OR IMPROVEMENT

PC 622. "Every person, not the owner thereof, who willfully injures, disfigures, or destroys any monument, work of art, or useful or ornamental improvement within the limits of any village, town, or city, or any shade tree or ornamental plant growing therein, whether situated upon private ground or on any street, sidewalk, or public park or place is guilty of a misdemeanor."

18.14   INJURING OR TAMPERING WITH AIRCRAFT

PC 625b. "Every person who willfully injures or tampers with any aircraft or the contents or parts thereof, or removes any part of or from any aircraft without the consent of the owner, and every person who, with intent to commit any malicious mischief, injury, or other crime, climbs into or upon an aircraft or attempts to manipulate any of the controls, starting mechanisms, brakes, or other mechanism or device of an aircraft while it is at rest and unattended or who sets in motion any aircraft while it is at rest and unattended, is guilty of a misdemeanor and upon conviction shall be punished by imprisonment for not more than six months or by a fine of not more than five hundred dollars ($500), or by both such fine and imprisonment.

Anyone who willfully and maliciously damages any aircraft in such a manner as to make it unsafe for flight, is punishable by imprisonment in the state prison or the county jail not exceeding one year or by a fine of five thousand dollars ($5,000), or by both such fine and imprisonment.

18.15   INJURY TO JAIL

PC 4600. "Every person who willfully and intentionally breaks down, pulls down, or otherwise destroys or injures any jail or prison, is punishable by a fine not exceeding ten thousand dollars ($10,000), and by imprisonment in the state prison, except that where the damage or injury to any city, city and county or county jail property is determined to be two hundred dollars ($200) or less, he is guilty of a misdemeanor."

18.16   MISCELLANEOUS OFFENSES

Ticket "Scalping," PC 346. This section makes it a misdemeanor to sell a ticket (1) at a price higher than that printed on the ticket, (2) on the grounds where the event is to be held or where tickets are being sold, (3) without the written permission of the owner or operator of the property where the event is being held, (4) providing the ticket(s) was originally purchased for the purpose of resale. If any one of the above elements is missing, the resale is not a crime.

Poisoning Food, Medicine, Water, PC 347. This section makes it a felony to add any harmful substance to any food, water supply, etc., with the intent that such will be taken by any human being to his injury. The crime is punishable by imprisonment in the state prison for two, three, or four years.

False Telephone or Telegraph Messages, PC 474. Knowingly and willfully sending a false message or knowingly delivering such message is a felony punishable by one year in the county jail, state prison or $5,000 fine, or both.

False Name to Newspaper, PC 538a. It is a misdemeanor to sign and send a letter to a newspaper using a name other than one's own, with intent to cause the newspaper to believe that letter was written by the person whose name was signed.

Vandalism, PC 594. Every person who maliciously (1) defaces with paint or any other liquid, (2) damages, or (3) destroys any real or personal property not his own, is guilty of vandalism. If the amount of defacement, etc., is $1,000 or more, the penalty is six months in the county jail or not to exceed one year and one day in state prison or a fine of $5,000 or both fine and imprisonment. If the defacement damage is less than $1,000, the penalty is not more than six months in the county jail, or by a fine of $1,000 or both.

Aerosol Paint Cans, PC 594.1. This section makes it a misdemeanor (1) for any person (other than legal guardian) to sell or give any person under 18 years of age, any aerosol can (containing more than 6 oz. of paint) that is capable of defacing property, without first obtaining bona fide evidence of age and identity; or (2) for anyone under age 18 to purchase an aerosol can as described; or (3) for any person to carry in plain view an aerosol can as described, in any posted public facility, park, etc.; or (4) for anyone under age 18 to possess an aerosol container of paint (net contents larger than 6 ounces) for the purpose of defacing property while in any public place.

Poisoning Animals, PC 596. Every person who, without the consent of the owner, willfully administers poison to any animal, the property of another, or exposes any poisonous substance, with the intent to poison any such animal, is guilty of a misdemeanor.

Cruelty to Animals, PC 597. Every person who maliciously maims, wounds, tortures, or mutilates a living animal which is the property of another, or maliciously kills an animal which is the property of another, is guilty of an offense punishable by imprisonment in the state prison, or in a county jail for not more than one year.

Fighting Dogs, PC 597.5. Any person who owns, trains, permits or causes any dog to engage in exhibition fighting for amusement or gain, is punishable by imprisonment in the county jail not to exceed one year, or by a fine not exceeding fifty thousand dollars ($50,000) or imprisonment in state prison not exceeding one year and one day, or by both fine and imprisonment. Being present at a dog fight as described above, is a misdemeanor.

Fighting Birds or Animals, PC 597b. Any person who, for amusement or gain, causes any bull, bear, cock, or other animal to fight with any kind of animal or a human being, is guilty of a misdemeanor.

Recording Attorney-Prisoner Conversation, PC 636. Every person, who, without permission from all parties to the conversation, eavesdrops on, or records by any means or device, a conversation, or any portion thereof, between a person who is in custody or who is on the property of a law enforcement or other public agency, and such person's attorney, religious advisor, or licensed physician, is guilty of a felony. Note: This section does not apply to a telephone employee who listens in to such conversations for the limited purpose of testing or servicing equipment.

TERMINOLOGY DEFINED—CHAPTER 18

See the Terminology Quiz at the end of this chapter.

1. Arson: maliciously setting fire to any structure or forest lands.
2. Conveyance: instrument for transferring title to property.
3. Counterfeit: any unlawful duplication of writing with intent to defraud.
4. Debenture: written security for a loan, a type of bond.
5. Defamation: written or spoken words injurious to another.
6. Defraud: breach of legal duty injurious to another.
7. Draft: a check, an order in writing for payment of money.
8. Due process: according to rules for protection of one's rights.
9. Forgery: falsely altering or signing another name with fraudulent intent.
10. Career criminal: third conviction of one twice convicted before.
11. Incendiary: a fire intentionally set, a device for setting fire, arson.
12. Malicious mischief; injuring or destroying real or personal property.
13. Material alteration: any alteration which changes a document's meaning.
14. Payee: one to whom a check or money is to be paid or is payable.
15. Post-dated: dated in the future, after date cashed.
16. Promissory note: an acknowledgment of debt, not a check.
17. Uttering: giving, offering, passing, or presenting.
18. Warrant: type of government check order for payment of money.
19. Will: declaration in writing for distribution of property after death.
20. Writing: in forgery, any duplication or reproduction of words.

TRUE-FALSE QUIZ—CHAPTER 18

1. One can commit forgery merely by changing a word on a document without signing another's name.
2. Specific intent to defraud is an essential element of forgery.
3. One cannot be guilty of check forgery unless it is presented to a bank for payment.
4. Uttering a false instrument in writing constitutes forgery.
5. Fraudulently raising the amount of a check constitutes forgery.
6. Cashing an insufficient funds check is a crime regardless of one's intent.
7. If the payee is not aware of it, it is a crime to cash a post-dated check with him.
8. One cannot be guilty of forgery if one in fact signs the name of a non-existent person.
9. Specific intent to defraud is an essential element of writing a check on a closed account under PC 476a.
10. Forgery is punishable by a sentence in either county jail or state prison.
11. If in fact no one was defrauded, one cannot be guilty of forgery regardless of initial intent.
12. Even if one does not intend to defraud an insurance company, willful and malicious burning of a building constitutes the crime of arson.
13. One is guilty of arson if one accidentally but with gross negligence sets fire to another person's home.
14. One cannot be guilty of arson for willfully burning one's own property.
15. It is a felony to remove one's own property following a fire for the purpose of defrauding the insurance carrier.
16. It is a misdemeanor to abandon a refrigerator one and one-half cubic feet or larger without first removing the lock, hinges, or door.
17. Any person who deposits any material of any kind on a public highway is guilty of a misdemeanor.
18. Removing or destroying any street or directional sign is a misdemeanor.
19. Willfully tampering with any aircraft is a misdemeanor.
20. If one willfully damages jail property, one is guilty of a felony or misdemeanor or depending on the initial charge for which he is serving time.

ESSAY-DISCUSSION QUESTIONS—CHAPTER 18

1. What are the elements of forgery under PC 470?
2. Briefly define the terms (1) "material alteration" and (2) "uttering" as they apply to forgery.
3. Briefly, what is a post-dated check? Under what circumstances is cashing one a crime and when not?
4. What are the elements of arson under PC 451?
5. What does the word "maliciously" mean as it applies to arson? Is specific or general intent required for arson?

6. Discuss whether or not one may be guilty of arson for burning his own property. What effect would the insurance factor have?

7. What size of abandoned refrigerator comes under the purview of PC 402(b)? What must the owner do to avoid a violation of this section?

8. What is the difference, element-wise, between a misdemeanor and felony violation of PC 588a, depositing objects or materials on a public highway?

9. What must the suspect do to constitute "tampering" under PC 625b (injuring or tampering with an aircraft)?

10. What differentiates between misdemeanor and felony injury to prison or jail under PC 4600?

TERMINOLOGY QUIZ—CHAPTER 18

Match terms and definitions by placing the correct number in the parentheses. Answers may be written on a separate sheet for submission to the instructor at the instructor's direction.

1. Arson
2. Conveyance
3. Counterfeit
4. Debenture
5. Defamation
6. Defraud
7. Draft
8. Due process
9. Forgery
10. Career criminal
11. Incendiary
12. Malicious mischief
13. Material alteration
14. Payee
15. Post-dated
16. Promissory note
17. Uttering
18. Warrant
19. Will
20. Writing

( ) one to whom a check is payable
( ) a check or order in writing for payment of money
( ) fire intentionally set, a fire-setting device
( ) injuring or destroying another's property
( ) any unlawful duplication of writing, fraudulent
( ) instrument for transferring title to property
( ) written document for distribution of property after death
( ) type of government check, order for payment of money
( ) written or spoken words injurious to another
( ) written security for a loan, type of bond
( ) any alteration which changes a document's meaning
( ) to give, offer, pass, or present for cashing
( ) dated in the future, after date cashed
( ) an acknowledgment of debt, not a check
( ) breach of legal duty injurious to another

APPENDIX A

Corpus Delicti Chart
Elements of More Frequently Used Penal Code Sections
(In Alphabetical Order by Offense)

CRIME	ELEMENTS	PENALTY
Abduction For Marriage or Defilement 265 PC	1. Takes woman unlawfully; 2. Against her will; 3. By force, menace, or duress; 4. Compels her to marry him or another, or to be defiled.	Felony
Abduction For Prostitution 266a PC	1. Takes any person; 2. Against his or her will and without his or her consent, or with his or her consent, produced by fraud, inducement or misrepresentation; 3. For the purpose of prostitution.	Misdemeanor
Abduction For Illicit Relations 266b PC	1. Takes any person; 2. Unlawfully and against his or her will; 3. By force, menace, or duress; 4. Compels him or her to live with another against his or her consent; 5. In an illicit relationship.	Felony
Abduction of Female Under 18 267 PC	1. Takes female under 18; 2. From parents, guardian, or another having legal custody; 3. Without their consent; 4. For purpose of prostitution.	Felony
Abortion 274 PC	1. Provides, administers, employs; 2. Any means whatever; 3. With intent to procure miscarriage; 4. Except as provided in H & S Code 25950.	Felony
Arson 451 PC	1. Willfully and maliciously; 2. Sets fire to or burns or causes to be burned; 3. Any structure, forest land or property.	Felony
Assault (Simple) 240 PC	1. Unlawful attempt; 2. Present ability; 3. To commit violent injury.	Misdemeanor
Assaulting Peace Officer, Firefighter (Paramedic, Nurse, Doctor) 241 PC	1. Assault on peace officer, firefighter, etc.; 2. Engaged in performance of duties, or; 3. Doctor, nurse giving emergency field care; 4. Assailant knows or should know victim's status.	Felony
Assault With Deadly Weapon (ADW) 245 (a) (1) PC 245 (a) (2) PC	1. Assaults person of another; 2. With deadly weapon or instrument (a)(1) or; 3. Any force likely to produce great bodily injury or; 4. With a firearm (a)(2).	Felony (Wobbler)*

* **Note:** A felony (wobbler) is punishable by either imprisonment in the county jail or a fine or both; or imprisonment in the state prison.

CRIME	ELEMENTS	PENALTY
Assault (ADW) Peace Officer, Firefighter 245 (b) PC 245 (c) PC	1. Assault with deadly weapon or instrument (b) or; 2. A firearm (c); 3. Person of peace officer or firefighter; 4. Engaged in performance of duty; 5. Assailant knows or should know police/fire and on-duty status.	Felony
Assault With Caustic Chemical 244 PC	1. Willfully and maliciously; 2. Places or throws upon another; 3. Caustic chemical of any nature; 4. Intent to injure or disfigure.	Felony
Assault With Intent to Commit Certain Crimes 220 PC	1. Assault with; 2. Intent to commit rape, sodomy or mayhem, oral copulation, PC 264.1, PC 288 or PC 289.	Felony
Battery 242 PC	1. Willful and unlawful; 2. Use of force or violence on person of another. 3. (With serious bodily injury)	Misdemeanor (Felony Wobbler)
Battery, Peace Officer, Firefighter 243 (c) PC	1. Battery resulting in injury; 2. Against peace officer, firefighter, paramedic; 3. Engaged in performance of duty; 4. Assailant knows or should know victim's status.	Felony (Wobbler)
Battery (Sexual) 243.4 PC	1. Touching intimate part of another; 2. Against their will; 3. While restrained by accused or accomplice; 4. For purpose of sexual arousal or gratification.	Felony (Wobbler)
Battery of Spouse, Cohabitant 273.5 PC	1. Willfully inflicts corporal injury; 2. On spouse or cohabitant; 3. Resulting in traumatic condition.	Felony (Wobbler)
Battery, Transportation Personnel 243.3 PC	1. Battery inflicted against; 2. Operator of bus, taxi, streetcar, motor vehicle; 3. Or on ticket or station agent; 4. While victim engaged in duty; 5. Assailant knows or should know victim on duty. (If injury, penalty increased)	Felony (Wobbler)
Breaking and Entering 603 PC	1. Forcibly enters dwelling house, cabin, building; 2. Intended for human occupancy; 3. Without permission owner, lessee; 4. Destroys property of value in, around building.	Misdemeanor
Bribing Officer 67 PC	1. Gives, offers any bribe; 2. To any executive officer; 3. With intent to influence in respect to; 4. Any act, vote, official decision.	Felony
Burglary 459 PC	1. Entry of; (need not be forced) 2. Building or place listed in statute; 3. With intent to commit grand or petty theft or any felony.	Felony First degree — inhabited dwelling house, trailer coach, inhabited portion any building. Second degree — all others.
Burglary With Explosives 464 PC	1. Enters any building; 2. With intent to commit crime; 3. Opens or attempts to open any vault or safe; 4. By use of explosives, torch, burning bar.	Felony
Burglary Tools (Possession) 466 PC	1. Possession of picklock, or tool; 2. With intent to feloniously enter; 3. Any building, etc., described in section; 4. Or knowingly alter any key to unlock a building; 5. Without permission of owner, lessee.	Misdemeanor
Child Abuse 273a PC	1. Any person having care or custody of a child; 2. Willfully permits child to suffer; 3. Or inflicts physical pain or mental suffering; 4. Under conditions likely to produce great bodily injury or death. (If conditions not likely to cause great bodily injury: Misdemeanor)	Felony (Wobbler)

CRIME	ELEMENTS	PENALTY
Child Concealing 280 PC	1. Willfully causes or permits; 2. Removal or concealment of child; 3. In violation of Civil Code 226.10. (If taken out of state—Felony)	Felony—Misdemeanor
Child Molesting **(Under 14)** 288 PC	1. Willfully and lewdly; 2. Commits any lewd or lascivious act upon any part of the body; 3. Of a child under 14; 4. With intent of arousing, appealing to, or gratifying lust passions or sexual desires; 5. Of child or perpetrator.	Felony
Child Molesting **(Under 18)** 647a PC	1. Annoys or molests; 2. Any child under 18. Second conviction or prior conviction of 288 PC (Felony) Violation of this section after having entered inhabited dwelling without consent (Felony, Wobbler).	Misdemeanor
Child Neglect 270 PC	1. Parent willfully omits; 2. Without lawful excuse; 3. To furnish food, clothes, shelter, etc.; 4. Of minor child. (If court has adjudicated matter, penalty: Felony (Wobbler)	Misdemeanor
Child Stealing 278 PC	1. Not having right of custody; 2. Maliciously takes, entices away, detains, or conceals; 3. Any minor child; 4. With intent to detain and conceal; 5. From parent or guardian, or other person having lawful charge.	Felony (Wobbler)
Conspiracy 182 PC	1. Two or more persons conspire; 2. To commit any crime; 3. And do an overt act in furtherance or preparation; 4. To falsely indict, charge, or cause arrest; 5. To cheat any person of any property; 6. To commit any act injurious to public health; 7. To commit any acts injurious to public officials listed; 8. To falsely bring any suit or action; 9. To obtain money or property by false pretenses.	Felony
Contributing to Minor's **Delinquency** 272 PC	1. Commits any act or omits any duty; 2. Causing a person under 18; 3. To come the provisions of W & I Code 300, 601, or 602 (delinquency).	Misdemeanor
Copulation 288a PC	1. Copulates the mouth with sexual organs or anus of another who is under 18, or; 2. Copulation by force or threats; 3. Copulation while in jail or prison; 4. When 10 years difference in age, and youngest party is under 14, or; 5. When one is participating under threat of immediate bodily harm, force, violence, duress or menace; 6. In concert with another by force or violence and against the will; 7. Copulation by person over 21 with another under 16.	Felony—Felony (Wobbler)
Defrauding Hotel, Restaurant 537 PC	1. Obtaining food, credit or accomodations; 2. At any hotel, restaurant, boarding house, ski lodge, campground, etc.; 3. Without paying and with intent to defraud; 4. By use of any false pretense, or; 5. Surriptitiously absconds with intent not to pay.	Misdemeanor (Under $400) Felony (Wobbler) (Over $400)
Defrauding Insurer 548 PC	1. Willfully injures, secretes, disposes of; 2. Any insured property; 3. With intent to injure or defraud insurer.	Felony (Wobbler)
Discharging Firearm at Building 246 PC	1. Maliciously and willfully; 2. Discharges a firearm; 3. At inhabited dwelling, housecar, or camper or occupied building or occupied motor vehicle.	Felony (Wobbler)

CRIME	ELEMENTS	PENALTY
Disorderly Conduct 647 PC	1. Solicits or engages in lewd conduct in public place, or; 2. Solicits or engages in act of prostitution, or; 3. Begging in a public place, or; 4. Loiters about public toilets for purpose of lewd acts, or; 5. Loiters on public streets and refuses to identify self and account for presence to a peace officer, or; 6. Is under influence of liquor or drugs in a public place.	Misdemeanor
Disturbing Public Meeting 403 PC	1. Willfully and illegally; 2. Disturbs any lawful meeting.	Misdemeanor
Disturbing the Peace 415 PC	1. Unlawfully fighting in a public place; 2. Or challenging another person in a public place to fight, or; 3. Maliciously and willfully disturbs another person by loud and unreasonable noise; 4. Or using offensive words in a public place which are inherently likely to produce an immediate violent reaction.	Misdemeanor
Drawing or Exhibiting Firearm or Deadly Weapon 417 PC	1. Not in self-defense; 2. Draws or exhibits firearm; 3. Or other deadly weapon, loaded or unloaded; 4. In rude, angry, or threatening manner; 5. Or in any manner uses same in quarrel. 6. In presence of peace officer: Felony (Wobbler)	Misdemeanor
Embezzlement (Includes theft) 503 PC	1. Fraudulent appropriation of property; 2. By person to whom it has been entrusted. (Penalty same as for theft of like amount.) (If public funds embezzled: Felony.)	Felony—Misdemeanor
Enticing Female Under 18 For Prostitution 266 PC	1. Any person who inveigles or entices; 2. Any unmarried female; 3. Of previous chaste character; 4. Under the age of 18; 5. For prostitution or to have illicit carnal relations with any man; OR 1. Any person who by false pretenses, etc.; 2. Procures any female; 3. To have illicit carnal relations with any man.	Felony (Wobbler)
Extortion (Blackmail) 518 PC	1. Obtaining property from another; 2. With victim's consent, or; 3. Obtaining official act by public officer; 4. By wrongful use of force or fear, or; 5. Under color of official right.	Felony
False Bomb Report 148.1 PC	1. Reports to police, airline, newspapers, etc.; 2. That bomb has been or will be placed; 3. Knowing same to be false, or; 4. Maliciously informs another that a bomb has been or will be placed, or; 5. Maliciously sends false bomb to any person.	Felony (Wobbler)
False Crime Report 148.5 PC	1. Reports to any peace officer; 2. That any crime has been committed; 3. Knowing report is false.	Misdemeanor
False Imprisonment 236 PC	1. Unlawful violation of; 2. Personal liberty of another. (If by means of violence, fraud: Felony)	Misdemeanor—Felony (Wobbler)
Failure to Disperse (on lawful command) 416 PC	1. Assembly by two or more persons; 2. With intent to disturb the peace or commit unlawful act; 3. Fail to disperse on lawful command of public officer	Misdemeanor
Fictitious Check 467a PC	1. Willfully, with intent to defraud; 2. Writes or delivers; 3. Any check; 4. Knowing at time there are insufficient funds or credit in bank for payment in full.	Misdemeanor—Felony (Depends on amount of check)

CRIME	ELEMENTS	PENALTY
Forgery 470 PC	1. Signs name of real or fictitious person; 2. Or alters any document listed in section; 3. Or attempts to pass as genuine; 4. Knowing has no authority to do so; 5. With intent to defraud.	Felony (Wobbler)
Grand Theft 487 PC	1. Takes money, labor, real or personal property of value over $400, or; 2. Domestic fowls, avocadoes, olives, citrus, or deciduous fruits, fruits, nuts, and artichokes, valued over $100 or; 3. From person of another, or; 4. Where money, labor, or property is taken by a servant, agent, or employee from principal or employer and aggregates $400 or more in any 12 consecutive months, or; 5. An automobile, horse, mare, firearm, lamb, gelding, cow, pig, mule, dog, etc., regardless of the value; 6. With intent to permanently deprive.	Felony (Wobbler)
Gratuity, Unauthorized Acceptance 70 PC	1. Executive, ministerial officer, employee or appointee; 2. Of city, county or state; 3. Knowingly asks for or receives; 4. Gratuity, reward or promise of same; 5. For doing an official act; 6. Except as authorized by law.	Misdemeanor
Incest 285 PC	1. Persons more closely related by blood than first cousins; 2. Who marry, or; 3. Commit fornication or adultery.	Felony
Inciting Riot 404.5 PC	1. Commits an act which urges a riot, or; 2. Urges other to acts of force or violence; 3. With intent to cause riot; 4. Under conditions producing immediate danger.	Misdemeanor
Indecent Exposure (Lewd conduct) 314 PC	1. Willfully and lewdly either; 2. Exposes his person or private parts; 3. In any public place, or in any place where there are other persons to be offended thereby, or; 4. Procures another to so exhibit themselves to public view; 5. Such as is offensive to decency, or; 6. Excites lewd thoughts or acts.	Misdemeanor
Kidnapping 207 PC	1. Forcibly steals, takes, or arrests any person in this state; 2. And takes to another location in this state or county; OR 1. Forcibly persuades by false promises; 2. Any child under 14; 3. For purposes of PC 288; 4. To go to another place in or out of the county; OR 1. Hires, persuades, entices, decoys, or seduces; 2. By false promises, misrepresentation, or the like; 3. Any person to go out of the state; 4. With intent to sell him into slavery or involuntary servitude, or otherwise employ him to his own use; OR 1. Abducts or brings; 2. Any person into this state from another state; 3. By force or fraud; 4. Contrary to the law of the place where the act is committed.	Felony
Kidnapping for Extortion, or Ransom 209 PC	1. Conceals, confines, inveigles, entices, kidnaps, or decoys, or carries away; 2. Any person by any means; 3. With intent to hold or detain; 4. For ransom, reward, or extortion. OR 1. Kidnaps or carries away; 2. To commit robbery, or; 3. Aids or abets such act.	Felony

CRIME	ELEMENTS	PENALTY
Kidnapper, Posing as: (Attempt to Profit by Kidnapping) **210 PC**	1. Fraudulently; 2. Represents to be in a position to obtain release of victim; 3. For the purpose of obtaining any ransom, or reward, or money or thing of value.	Felony
Lynching **405-405b PC**	1. Taking any person; 2. From lawful custody of peace officer; 3. By means of a riot.	Felony
Malicious Mischief (Vandalism) **594 PC**	1. Maliciously defaces with paint; 2. Injures or destroys; 3. Any real or personal property; 4. Not his own.	Misdemeanor—Felony (Wobbler) Penalty depends on amount of damage.
Manslaughter (Voluntary) **192(1) PC**	1. Unlawfully, kills a human being; 2. Upon sudden quarrel or heat of passion; 3. Without malice.	Felony
Manslaughter (Involuntary) **192(2) PC**	1. Unlawfully, kills a human being; 2. In commission of unlawful act, not amounting to a felony, or lawful act in an unlawful manner or without due caution or circumspection which might produce death; 3. Without malice.	Felony
Manslaughter (Felony in driving vehicle—involuntary) **192(3)(a) PC**	1. Driving a vehicle; 2. Kills a human being; 3. Unlawful act, not amounting to felony, or a lawful act which might produce death in an unlawful manner; 4. **With** gross negligence; 5. Act must be proximate cause of death; 6. Without malice.	Felony (Wobbler)
Manslaughter (Misdemeanor in driving vehicle—involuntary) **192(3)(b) PC**	1. Same elements as above except **without** gross negligence.	Misdemeanor
Mayhem **203 PC**	1. Unlawfully and maliciously; 2. Amputates, disables, disfigures or renders useless; 3. A member of another's body, or; 4. Slits the tongue, nose, ear, or lip, or; 5. Puts out an eye.	Felony
Murder (first degree) **187-189 PC**	1. Unlawful killing; 2. Of human being or fetus; 3. With malice aforethought; 4. Willful, deliberate or premeditated, or; 5. By poison, lying in wait, torture, or in commission of burglary, arson, robbery, rape, or mayhem, or 288 PC, or; 6. With knowing use of explosives, or; 7. Armor piercing ammunition.	Felony–Possible Death Penalty
Murder (second degree) **187-189 PC**	1. Unlawful killing; 2. Of human being or fetus; 3. With malice aforethought.	Felony
Pandering **266i PC**	1. Procures another for purposes of prostitution, or; 2. By promises, threats, violence causes another; 3. To become a prostitute, or; 4. By threats, promises, violence, causes another; 5. To remain in prostitution, or; 6. By abuse of any position of authority; 7. Procures another for prostitution, or; 8. Receives anything of value for procuring another for prostitution.	Felony
Petty Theft **484-488 PC**	1. Takes money or property; 2. Valued at $400 or less, not listed in 487 PC; 3. With intent to permanently deprive.	Misdemeanor
Pimping **266h PC**	1. Knowing another is a prostitute; 2. Derives support, lives; 3. From earnings of a prostitute.	Felony

CRIME	ELEMENTS	PENALTY
Poisoning Animals 596 PC	1. Without consent of the owner; 2. Willfully administers poison; 3. To any animal; 4. The property of another; 5. Or exposes poison with intent that it shall be taken by an animal.	Misdemeanor
Poisoning Food, Water Supply, Medicine 347 PC	1. Willfully mingles any harmful substance; 2. With any food, drink, medicine, water supply; 3. With intent it be taken by humans to their injury.	Felony
Rape (Victim of unsound mind) 261(1) PC	1. Act of sexual intercourse; 2. Victim not spouse of perpetrator; 3. Victim incapable of giving legal consent due to unsound mind.	Felony
Rape (By force) 261(2) PC	1. Act of sexual intercourse; 2. Victim not spouse of perpetrator; 3. Against victim's will; 4. Accomplished by force or fear; of immediate unlawful bodily injury to victim, or of another.	Felony
Rape (By drugs) 261(3) PC	1. Act of sexual intercourse; 2. Victim not spouse of perpetrator; 3. Prevented from resisting by any intoxicating narcotic or anesthetic substance; 4. Administered by or with knowledge of the accused.	Felony
Rape (Victim unconscious of nature of act) 261(4) PC	1. Act of sexual intercourse; 2. Victim not spouse of perpetrator; 3. Victim is unconscious of the nature of the act; 4. This fact is known to perpetrator.	Felony
Rape (Victim believes perpetrator to be spouse) 261(5) PC	1. Act of sexual intercourse; 2. Victim not spouse of perpetrator; 3. Victim believes perpetrator to be his or her spouse; 4. This belief induced by artifice, pretense or concealment by perpetrator; 5. With intent to induce such belief.	Felony
Rape of Spouse 262 PC	1. Act of sexual intercourse; 2. Accomplished against the will of the spouse; 3. By force or fear of immediate unlawful bodily injury; 4. On the spouse or another, or; 5. When accomplished by threat of future retaliation; 6. Against the victim or another, and; 7. There is reasonable possibility of execution.	Felony (Wobbler)
Receiving Stolen Property 496 PC	1. Buying or accepting stolen property; 2. Knowing property is stolen, or; 3. Concealing, selling stolen property; 4. Knowing property is stolen.	Felony—Misdemeanor (Penalty according to value, same as theft)
Rescuing Prisoner 4550 PC	1. Rescues, attempts, or aids; 2. Prisoner from prison, road camp jail; 3. Or any peace officer having lawful custody.	Felony—Misdemeanor (Penalty depends on rescued prisoner's sentence)
Riot 404 PC	1. Any use of force or violence, or; disturbance of peace, or threat to use such force if accompanied by immediate power of execution; 2. By two or more persons acting together; 3. Without authority of law.	Misdemeanor
Riot (Remaining at riot after command to disperse) 409 PC	1. Remains present; 2. At riot, rout, or unlawful assembly; 3. After lawful command to disperse.	Misdemeanor
Robbery 211 PC	1. Felonious taking of personal property; 2. In possession of another; 3. From person or immediate presence; 4. Against his will; 5. By means of force or fear. Robbery of public vehicle operator, 211a PC.	Felony

CRIME	ELEMENTS	PENALTY
Rout **406-408 PC**	1. Two or more persons acting together; 2. Attempt or advance toward an act; 3. If committed would be a riot.	Misdemeanor
Seduction **268 PC**	1. By promising marriage; 2. Seduces and has sexual relation with; 3. An unmarried female; 4. Of previous chaste character.	Felony
Schools (Loitering about adult schools) **647b PC**	1. Loitering; 2. About any school in which adults attend; 3. And who annoys or molests any person in attendance.	Misdemeanor
Shooting From Highway **374c PC**	1. Shooting any firearm; 2. From or upon a public road or highway.	Misdemeanor
Shooting at Dwelling **246 PC**	1. Maliciously and willfully discharges a firearm; 2. At an inhabited dwelling or occupied building, motor vehicle, camper. (Note: "Inhabited" means currently used for dwelling, whether occupied or not.)	Felony (Wobbler)
Sodomy **286 PC**	1. Contact between the penis of one and anus of another under 18, or; 2. By one over 21 with another under 16, or; 3. With one who is under 14 and more than 10 years younger, or; 4. When accomplished by force, violence, fear, and against will of the other, or; 5. When acting with another is accomplished against victim's will by force or fear of immediate bodily injury on victim or another, or; 6. By anyone in jail or prison, or; 7. When victim is unconscious of the act, and; 8. This is known to assailant, or; 9. Victim is incapable of giving consent due to temporary or permanent unsoundness of mind; 10. And this fact is known to assailant.	Felony
Theft—False Pretenses **532 PC**	1. Knowingly and by false pretense or fraud; 2. Defrauds another of money, labor, property; 3. Or falsely obtains credit, thereby; 4. Fraudulently obtains money, labor, property of another.	Felony—Misdemeanor (Depending on value, as in theft)
Theft—Gas, Water, Electricity **498, 499, 499a PC**	1. Willfully, with intent to defraud; 2. Connects any pipe (or wire); 3. With any service pipe (or wire); 4. For the purpose of taking (gas) (water) (electricity); 5. Without payment.	Misdemeanor
Theft—Phone Calls **502.7 PC**	1. Knowingly, willfully, and with intent to defraud; 2. Avoids or aids or attempts or assists another; 3. Or who uses a code, prearranged scheme; 4. To avoid any lawful charges for service.	Misdemeanor
Ticket "Scalping" **346 PC**	1. Without written permission of owner/operator; 2. Sells tickets to any event; 3. Which were obtained for resale; 4. At any price in excess of that on ticket; 5. While on grounds or place where event is held.	Misdemeanor
Train Wrecking **219 PC**	1. Unlawfully throws a switch, removes a rail, places explosive or obstruction on or near the track of any railroad; 2. With intention to wreck train; 3. And wrecks, derails, or blows up train. (When any person suffers death) Penalty: Death	Felony
Train Wrecking (Intention of wrecking train; Attempt) **218 PC**	1. Unlawfully throws a switch, removes a rail, places explosives or obstruction on or near; 2. The track of any railroad; 3. Or sets fire to any structure or track over which a train must pass; 4. With intention to wreck train.	Felony

CRIME	ELEMENTS	PENALTY
Unlawful Assembly **407-408 PC**	1. Two or more persons assembled; 2. With intent to do unlawful act or lawful act in a violent boisterous or tumultuous manner.	Misdemeanor
Unlawfully Causing Fire **452 PC**	1. Recklessly sets fire to any structure or forest land; 2. Unlawfully causing great bodily injury or property damage; 3. Unlawfully causing inhabited structures or property to burn; 4. Unlawfully causing a fire of a structure or forest land; 5. Other than his own, unless there is injury to others.	Felony (Wobbler)
Unlawful Sexual Intercourse **261.5 PC**	1. Act of sexual intercourse; 2. Female not wife of perpetrator; 3. Female under 18.	Felony (Wobbler)
Vehicle Taking ("Joy-riding") **499b PC**	1. Without permission of owner; 2. Takes any auto, bicycle, motorcycle, or boat; 3. For purpose of temporary use.	Misdemeanor

APPENDIX B

Penal Code Index
In Alphabetical Order by Offense

OFFENSE	SECTION	OFFENSE	SECTION
Failure to disperse	416	Obstructing justice	153
False affidavit	118a	Obstructing sidewalk	647c
False bomb report	148.1		
False crime report	148.5	Pandering	266i
False imprisonment	236	Penetrating genitals, objects	289
False phone messages	474	Perjury	118
Falsification of evidence	132	Perjury, subornation of	127
Falsification, public records	115	Pimping	266h
Fictitious checks	476a	Poisoning animals	596
Fighting birds, animals	597b	Poisoning food, medicine	347
Firearms, possession by felon	12560	Possessing gun, public place	12031
Firearms, sale to minor	12550	Possessing machine gun	12220
Flammables, possession of	453	Principal, in crime	31
Forcible entry & detainer	418	Prisoner mistreatment	147
Forgery	470	Procuring execution	128
Fraud, false pretense (theft)	532	Prostitution	647(b)
		Prowling, property of another	647(g)
Grand theft	487	Punishment for crime, general	18-19
Gratuity, accepting	70		
		Rape	261
Harmful matter, defined	313	Rape, aiding, abetting	264.1
Homicide (see murder)	187	Rape of spouse	262
		Receiving stolen property	496
Impersonating officer	146a	Recording attorney/prisoner meeting	636
Infraction	19c	Refusal to disperse	409
Incest	285	Refusing aid to officer	150
Inciting riot	404.6	Rescue of prisoner	4550
Indecent exposure	314	Resisting executive officer	69
Injury to jail	4600	Resisting public officer	148
Insurance fraud	584	Riot, defined	406
Intent	21	Robbery	211
		Robbery, in dwelling	213.5
Joy-riding (auto theft)	499b	Robbery, pharmacist	213
		Robbery, public vehicle operator	211a
Kidnapping	207	Rout, defined	406
Kidnapping, bodily harm	209		
Kidnapper, posing as	210	Scalping tickets	346
		School official, crime against	71
Lewd conduct	647(a)	Seduction	268
Libel	248	Serial numbers, altering	537c
Loitering, general	647(e)	Sex crime registration	290
Loitering, public toilets	647(d)	Shooting at bus or train	219.2
Loitering, schools	653g	Shooting from highway	374c
Lynching	405a	Shooting, inhabited building	246
		Slander	258
Malicious mischief	594	Sodomy	286
Manslaughter	192	Soliciting crime	653f
Mayhem	203	Switchblade knives	653k
Murder	187		
		Tear gas possession	12403.7
Obscene live conduct	311.6	Theft, aircraft	499d
Obscene matter	311	Theft, defined	484

OFFENSE	SECTION	OFFENSE	SECTION
Theft, electricity	499a	Unlawful arrest	146
Theft, lost property	485	Unlawful assembly	407
Theft, natural gas	498	Unlawful forced entry	603
Theft, phone calls	502.7	Unlawful sexual intercourse	261.5
Theft, water	499		
Threatening letters	523	Vandalism	594
Throwing at bus, train	2119.1		
Treason	37	Weapons, unlawful	12020
Train wrecking	219	Window peeking	647(h)
Trespass	602	Wiretapping	631

APPENDIX C

Penal Code—Key Sections

(With Test)

The following are important or frequently used sections of the Penal Code. Students should know the following and be prepared for a test as directed by the instructor.

SECTION	VIOLATION	SECTION	VIOLATION
148	Resisting arrest	404	Riot
148.5	False crime report	407	Unlawful assembly
182	Conspiracy	415	Disturbing peace
187	Murder	417	Brandishing firearm
192	Manslaughter	451	Arson of dwelling
203	Mayhem	459	Burglary
207	Kidnapping	466	Burglary tools
211	Robbery	470	Forgery
217.1	Assault on judge	484	Theft
220	Assault to rape	485	Theft lost property
240	Simple assault	496	Receiving stolen property
242	Battery	503	Embezzlement
245	ADW	518	Extortion
261	Rape	532	False pretense fraud
272	Contributing	537	Defrauding motel
273a	Cruelty to child	556	Unlawful sign posting
273d	Child beating	594	Malicious mischief
273.5	Spouse/Cohabitant injury	597	Cruelty to animals
278	Child stealing	602	Trespass
286	Sodomy	603	Unlawful forcible entry
288	Crimes against children	647	Disorderly conduct
288a	Copulation	647a	Molesting child (under 18)
290	Sex crime registration	647(b)	Prostitution
311	Obscene matter	647(g)	Prowler
314	Indecent exposure	647(h)	Window peeking
374c	Shooting from highway		

PENAL CODE—KEY SECTIONS QUIZ
(Matching Test)

Match each definition with its code section by placing the number preceding the code section in the parentheses on each of the following.

1.	374c	( )	Resisting arrest
2.	290	( )	False crime report
3.	288	( )	Conspiracy
4.	274	( )	Murder
5.	245	( )	Manslaughter
6.	240	( )	Mayhem
7.	217.1	( )	Kidnapping
8.	207	( )	Robbery
9.	192	( )	Assault on judge
10.	182	( )	Shooting from highway
11.	148	( )	Sex crime registration
12.	148.5	( )	Simple assault
13.	187	( )	ADW
14.	203	( )	Child molesting (under 14)
15.	211	( )	Contributing to minor's delinquency
16.	278	( )	Child stealing
17.	242		
18.	272		

1.	314	( )	Felony child beating
2.	288a	( )	Possession burglary tools
3.	286	( )	Burglary
4.	273a–d	( )	Rape
5.	261	( )	Arson of structure
6.	242	( )	Indecent exposure
7.	220	( )	Brandishing firearm
8.	404	( )	Battery
9.	407	( )	Sodomy
10.	415	( )	Riot
11.	417	( )	Assault to rape
12.	451	( )	Oral copulation
13.	459	( )	Disturbing peace
14.	466	( )	Unlawful assembly
15.	470	( )	Obscene matter
16.	311	( )	Prostitution
17.	647		
18.	647(b)		

1.	647a	( ) Disorderly conduct (a-h)
2.	647(g)	( ) Extortion
3.	647	( ) Receiving stolen property
4.	603	( ) Prowler
5.	602	( ) Fraud
6.	597	( ) Defrauding innkeeper
7.	594	( ) Molesting children (under 18)
8.	556	( ) Theft of lost property
9.	537	( ) Trespass
10.	540	( ) Forcible entry (residence)
11.	470	( ) Theft
12.	494	( ) Unlawful sign posting
13.	496	( ) Embezzlement
14.	485	( ) Cruelty to animals
15.	484	( ) Malicious mischief
16.	532	( ) Forgery
17.	518	
18.	503	

PENAL CODE EXAMINATION

Choose the one best answer in each of the following multiple choice questions.

1. Resisting arrest
   a. 148
   b. 148.5
   c. 217
   d. 240
   e. 242

2. Murder
   a. 182
   b. 197
   c. 192
   d. 203
   e. 207

3. Kidnapping
   a. 288
   b. 273
   c. 278
   d. 203
   e. 207

4. Robbery
   a. 209
   b. 207
   c. 211
   d. 411
   e. 484

5. Assault with intent to murder
   a. 182
   b. 187
   c. 192
   d. 217
   e. 245

6. Assault with intent to rape
   a. 187
   b. 220
   c. 242
   d. 245
   e. 278

7. Simple assault
   a. 217
   b. 220
   c. 240
   d. 242
   e. 245

8. Battery
   a. 217
   b. 220
   c. 240
   d. 242
   e. 245

9. Assault with deadly weapon (ADW)
   a. 187
   b. 217
   c. 220
   d. 240
   e. 245

10. Rape
   a. 217
   b. 220
   c. 261
   d. 278
   e. 287

11. Contributing to delinquency of a minor
   a. 272
   b. 273d
   c. 647
   d. 314
   e. 288

12. Felony child beating
   a. 240d
   b. 242
   c. 245
   d. 273d
   e. 278

13. Child stealing
    - a. 207
    - b. 217
    - c. 273d
    - d. 278
    - e. 647a

14. Molesting child under 14 years
    - a. 278
    - b. 286
    - c. 288
    - d. 288a
    - e. 311

15. Indecent exposure
    - a. 314
    - b. 311
    - c. 288a
    - d. 272
    - e. 261

16. Shooting from a highway
    - a. 602
    - b. 603
    - c. 647(c)
    - d. 347
    - e. 374c

17. Disturbing the peace
    - a. 404
    - b. 407
    - c. 415
    - d. 417
    - e. 447a

18. Brandishing firearm in threatening manner
    - a. 415
    - b. 417
    - c. 447
    - d. 470
    - e. 217

19. Burglary
    - a. 484
    - b. 459
    - c. 466
    - d. 470
    - e. 603

20. Possession of burglary tools
    - a. 484
    - b. 459
    - c. 466
    - d. 470
    - e. 503

21. Theft defined
    - a. 484
    - b. 485
    - c. 496
    - d. 594
    - e. 603

22. Malicious mischief
    - a. 404
    - b. 415
    - c. 647
    - d. 647a
    - e. 594

23. Trespass
    - a. 556
    - b. 597
    - c. 601
    - d. 602
    - e. 603

24. Disorderly conduct
    - a. 148
    - b. 242
    - c. 415
    - d. 642(a-h)
    - e. 647

25. Prowler
    - a. 642 g
    - b. 647(a)
    - c. 647(b)
    - d. 647(g)
    - e. 647(h)

APPENDIX D

Basic Legal Research—Case Law and How to Find It

Introduction. The purpose of this section is to explain the techniques of doing basic legal research. In other words, how to find case law. This ability is important for at least three key reasons:

1. Courts, by their decisions in criminal cases frequently define the meaning of words, phrases, and terms found in the penal code and other codes describing criminal offenses.
2. The courts interpret the intent of the legislature relative to criminal law; i.e., a court decision will frequently explain and define the specific act that the legislature intended to make a crime.
3. The courts also rule on the constitutionality of particular penal statutes; i.e., whether or not all or any part of a specific penal code section is in conflict with the Constitution (U.S. or state).

One must frequently find and read case law (court decisions) in order to fully understand the meaning and scope of a penal code section. One also needs to have some knowledge of case law to determine whether or not a specific act is, in fact, a violation of a certain penal code section. For example, *PC 459*, which defines burglary, reads in part: "Any person who enters . . . any building . . . with intent to commit grand or petit larceny or any felony is guilty of burglary." Let us now assume that someone is caught stealing money from the coin slot in a phone booth. The question may be: did the suspect commit burglary if he or she entered the phone booth with intent to commit theft? In other words, is the phone booth a "building" within the meaning of *PC 459*?

Case Law: An Example. The only way to answer the above question is to research case law pertaining to burglary. We find our answer in *People v. Nunez (1970) 86 Cal Rptr. 707, 7 C.A. 3d 655.* In this case, the court held that a telephone booth with three walls, a door, roof, and floor was a "building" within the meaning of *PC 459*. We now have our answer. A

phone booth may indeed be burglarized, and one who enters same with intent to steal (even if there is no forced entry) can be found guilty of burglary.

The Law Library. When a student is given his or her first assignment to research a case, he or she generally does so with some apprehension. Students may imagine a law library as a confusing collection of large and difficult to understand volumes. Fortunately, this is a gross misconception. Law libraries are well designed, easily understood, and surprisingly simple to use. Following a brief review of the California court system, which will make case law more understandable, we will discuss the actual steps of doing legal research.

THE CALIFORNIA COURT SYSTEM

For case law to have any great effect in modifying criminal statutes (written laws), it must come from either a California court, a federal appellate court, or a Supreme Court. A brief look at the structure and jurisdiction of California and federal courts will give a better understanding of how cases are reported.

Justice and Municipal Courts. Justice and municipal courts have jurisdiction in misdemeanor criminal cases if the maximum penalty for the offense charged is one year in the county jail or a $1000 fine or both, and the crime was committed within the county where the court is established. Additionally, both courts may conduct a preliminary hearing in a felony case to determine whether the defendant should be held to answer in the superior court.

Superior Courts. Each of the 58 counties in California has one superior court, some with many divisions. The superior court has original jurisdiction in all felony offenses, including juvenile offenses. They are also empowered to hear appeals from cases originally heard (tried) in justice or municipal court.

District Courts of Appeal. In California, there are five district courts of appeal. With the exception of the fifth district court, each has two or more divisions. Each division has three judges. The agreement of two is needed for a judgment. These courts are not trial courts; rather, they hear appeals from decisions arrived at in justice, municipal, or superior courts of original jurisdiction.

California Supreme Court. The California Supreme Court is empowered to hear appeals from all California inferior courts: justice, municipal, superior, and district courts of appeal. The Supreme Court meets in San Francisco and consists of a chief justice and six associate justices who may sit in two departments or as a single group (called "sitting in bank"). The chief justice presides when the court sits in bank or may sit with either department during its deliberations.

THE FEDERAL COURT SYSTEM

Federal District Courts. In criminal cases, the federal district courts are principal trial courts for the federal judicial system. A person accused of a federal crime would have his or her case adjudicated in a federal district court. Federal district courts are *not* appellate courts.

Federal Courts of Appeal (Circuit Courts). The federal circuit courts are the federal courts of appeal. When a criminal case originates as an action in a federal district court, the circuit court would ordinarily be the final court of appeal to review the district court decision.

United States Supreme Court. The Supreme Court's judicial power extends to all cases arising under the United States Constitution, laws, and treaties. The Court's appellate jurisdiction is subject to regulations of Congress. The rules governing review of state court decisions distinguish between those cases in which the court *must* review the state court decision (mandatory review on appeal) and those in which the court *may* review the state court decision (discretionary review upon application for a writ of *certiorari*).

Review by the Supreme Court in criminal cases occurs only after a final decision in the highest court of a state. Review by appeal is mandatory where the state court decided against the validity of a treaty or statute of the United States. Mandatory appeal also applies where a state court rules in favor of a state law being challenged as in conflict with the Constitution, treaties, or laws of the United States. Some criminal cases that go from state courts to the United States Supreme Court may be based upon the right to appeal, where a direct conflict exists between a state law and a federal law. But a large number of criminal cases come to the Supreme Court through the Court's discretionary power to grant *certiorari* (a writ from a superior court to an inferior court directing it to send up for review a certified record of its proceedings in a designated case).

An example of this latter discretionary power is found in the case of *Gideon v. Wainwright*. This was a case where the defendant, Gideon, through a writ of *certiorari*, appealed to the United States Supreme Court for a review of his conviction. Gideon claimed the state of Florida has denied him his constitutional right to an attorney as provided under the Sixth Amendment of the U.S. Constitution, and as required of all states through the due process clause of the Fourteenth Amendment. A denial of due process is frequently defined as the failure to observe that fundamental fairness essential to the very concept of justice.

Armed with this brief summary of the California and federal court structure, the student now has an adequate foundation for gaining more insight into case law, its purpose, intent, and effect on statute law.

FEDERAL CASE LAW: DECISIONS OF THE FEDERAL COURTS

The United States Supreme Court. The official reports of the decisions of the U.S. Supreme Court are published in the *United States Reports*. They are also published in the *Supreme Court Reporter* and the *Lawyers Edition, Supreme Court Reports*. The latter contains selected cases that are fully reported and include briefs (written arguments and points of law) filed by opposing counsel.

Since U.S. Supreme Court cases are published in three separate sources, a complete citation of a U.S. Supreme Court case would include citing all three reporters (source books). Thus if we were citing the Gideon case, referred to earlier, we would find it listed in each reporter as follows:

1. *United States Reports: Gideon* [appellant] *v. Wainwright,* [respondent] *372* [volume number]. U.S. [United States Reports] *335* [page number].
2. *Supreme Court Reporter: Gideon v. Wainwright, 83* [volume number] *S. Ct.* [Supreme Court Reporter] *792* [page number].

3. *Lawyer's Edition of Supreme Court Reports:*
Gideon v. Wainwright, 9 L. Ed. [Lawyer's Edition, Supreme Court Reports] *2d* [second series]
799 [page number] *1963* [date].

Discussion

A court decision, as you will note above, is cited by
giving: (1) the names of the parties involved, (2) the
volume number, (3) the name of the reporting publisher (book) in which the case is reported, (4) the
page on which the case begins, and (5) the date of the
decision, where appropriate. Thus in the preceding
example. *Gideon* is the last name of the appellant
(person appealing a decision of a lower court) and
Wainwright, is the last name of the respondent (person or agency who is required to respond to the issue
being appealed).

**The   Federal   Courts   of   Appeal   (Circuit
Courts).** Decisions of the U.S. courts of appeal are
published in the *Federal Reporter.* A typical citation
(case reference) includes (1) the name of the case,
(2) volume and page number where the case can be
found, (3) identification of the circuit in which the
case was decided, and (4) the year the decision was
made.

Example: *Smayda* [appellant] *v. United States*
[respondent] *F. 2d* [Federal Reporter, second series]
251 [page number] *(9th Cir. 1966)* [name of the
court and the date]. When seen as a citation, it would
look like this: *Smyda v. United States, F. 2d 251 (9th
Cir. 1966).*

The Federal District Courts. Even though federal
district courts are trial courts and do not hear
appeals, many of their decisions are reported in the
Federal Supplement. They are cited in the same way
as in the example above.

Example. *Books Inc. v. Leary, 291 F. Supp.* [Federal
Supplement] *622 (S.D.N.Y.)* [Southern District of
New York] *1968.* When seen as a citation the last
example would look like this: *Books Inc. v. Leary,
291 F. Supp. 622 (S.D.N.Y.) 1968.*

Combination Federal and State Reporters. Both federal and state decisions appear in sets of two special-
ized reporters. They are (1) The *American Law
Reports* and (2) the *American Law Reports, 2d.
American Law Reports* are annotated and contain
the full text of selected decisions under which cases
on the same point of law are noted.

American Law Reports, 2d, contain a detailed
discussion on a practical point of current law, followed by a report of a representative case from a state

or federal court involving the problem annotated
(noted). When a case has been annotated in the
American Law Reports, this information is given as
follows: *Mosco v. United States 89 A.L.R. 2d 715.*

This then concludes the essential information
needed for researching cases in the *federal* court system. Let us now turn our attention to how cases are
reported in the California state court system.

CALIFORNIA CASE LAW: DECISIONS OF APPELLATE COURTS

California Appellate and Supreme Court cases are
reported by two different publishers: Bancroft-
Whitney and West Publishing Company. Bancroft-
Whitney publishes two sets of volumes. One is called
California Reports. (Series 1, 2 and 3), which carry
only California *Supreme Court* cases. The other is
California Appellate Reports (Series 1, 2 and 3),
which carry only California *appellate court* cases, as
the title implies. Citations of cases reported in each of
the above series of volumes are written almost the
same way federal cases are cited.

California Supreme Court Decisions: First let us
examine a citation on a case reported in Bancroft-
Whitney's *California Reports. People* [appellant] *v.
Mason,* [respondent] *5* [volume number] *C.* [Califor-
nia Reports] *3d* [third series] *759* [page number].
Without the words of explanation that appear in
brackets in the example above, the citation would
look like this: *People v. Mason, 5 C. 3d 759.* Noting
that this case was reported in the third (3d) series,
indicates that it is relatively recent. Older and very
old cases are reported in the first or second series. The
Mason case was one appealed by the People to the
California State Supreme Court following a motion
to suppress evidence granted by a San Diego Superior
Court under *P.C. 1538.1.* The case was dismissed
against the defendant and the People (San Diego
County District Attorney's office) are appealing to
get the superior court's ruling reversed by the
Supreme Court.

District Court of Appeal. Had this case been heard
by a California district court of appeal, the decision
of that appeal would have been recorded in the *California Appellate Reports* and cited as follows: *People*
[appellant] *v. Nugent,* [respondent] *18* [volume
number] *C.A. 3d* [California Appellate Reports,
third series] *911* [page number]. Again, without the
words of explanation in the brackets, the actual citation would read: *People v. Nugent, 18 C.A. 3d 911.*

Combined California State Supreme and Appellate Court Reports. As mentioned previously, West Publishing Company also reports the decisions of both the state supreme court and the California district courts of appeal. West's publication is the *West California Reporter*, which carries *both* California Supreme Court and appellate court cases in the same series of volumes. A typical *West California Reporter* citation would be: *Mozzetti v. Superior Court, 94 Cal. Rptr.* [California Reporter] *412.*

Because of this dual reporting system, both publishers also cross-cite their cases to give the reader the citation for the same case reported in the other publisher's reports. Thus, a typical case would be cited by West as: *People v. Wilson, 94 Cal. Rptr.* [West California Reporter] *923* and cross-cited in West to Bancroft-Whitney as: *17 Cal. App.* [California Appellate Reports] *3d 598.* A case found in Bancroft-Whitney's *California Appellate Reports* third series, would be cited as: *People v. Clay, 18 C.A. 3d 964,* and would be cross-cited to *West California Reporter* as: *Cal. Rptr. 213.* It is most important to note, in order to avoid confusion, that when a case is cross-cited by *West California Reporter* to Bancroft-Whitney's *California Appellate Reports,* West uses the abbreviation, *Cal. App.* Both C.A. (used by Bancroft-Whitney) and Cal. App. mean the same thing and refer to the same source, which is Bancroft-Whitney's *California Appellate Reports.*

Additionally, both publishers publish advance sheets in paperback form until a sufficient number of cases are adjudicated and collected to publish a hardbound volume to add to the series. It is strongly suggested that students go to their college library or the local county law library and practice finding cases until this rather simple procedure becomes routine.

Case Law Reference Source Review. The following will provide the student with a ready reference to those publications that report federal and state cases. The names of the reference books, along with their standard reference abbreviation is given for each of the courts previously discussed.

Supreme Court Reports

1. *United States Reports,* abbreviated: U.S.
2. *Supreme Court Reporter,* abbreviated: S. Ct.
3. *Lawyer's Edition, Supreme Court Reports,* abbreviated: L. Ed.

Federal Appeals Courts

Federal Reporter (second series), abbreviated: F. 2d

Federal District Courts (not appeals courts)

Federal Supplement, abbreviated: F. Supp.

Combination Federal-State Reporter

1. *American Law Reports,* abbreviated: A.L.R.
2. *American Law Reports,* (second series), abbreviated: A.L.R. 2d

California Supreme Court Reporters

1. *California Reports,* abbreviated: C.
2. *West California Reporter,* abbreviated: Cal. Rptr.

California District Court of Appeals

1. *California Appellate Reports,* abbreviated: C.A. or Cal. App.
2. *West California Reporter,* abbreviated: Cal. Rptr.

SOURCES OF CASE LAW CITATIONS

A most appropriate question at this point might be: where does one find sources for case citations? The answer: in annotated penal codes, legal encyclopedias, legal digests, and in *Shepard's Citator.* All are in either the college library or the local county law library. Each of these will be discussed briefly, below.

Annotated Codes. An annotated California penal code consists generally of several volumes, published either by West Publishing Company as *West's California Codes, Annotated,* or Bancroft-Whitney Company as *Deering's California Codes, Annotated.*

These annotated codes are structured similarly to an unannotated penal code except following each statute you will find excerpts from case decisions that interpret, explain, and clarify the penal statute in terms of its separate components or elements. As an example, take *P.C. 220, Assault with Intent to Commit Mayhem:* "Every person who assaults another with intent to commit mayhem, is punishable by imprisonment for two, four, or six years."

This statute states what the law is categorically. However, to find out whether a specific act meets the requirements of this law, we need to know how courts in the past have interpreted this statute. The annotations will give some help in this regard. Following the statute will be several excerpts from previously decided cases (*stare decisis*) arranged conceptually, e.g., (1) in general, (2) intent, (3) evidence, (4) instructions, (5) methods or means, and (6) defenses. Each contains excerpts from selected cases bearing on that particular element or aspect of the offense, with the appropriate citation to refer the reader to the case in the respective reporter. Thus, under methods or means, one will find: "An assault to commit mayhem is a crime irrespective of the mode or means by which the assault is committed. *People v. Owens (1906) 3 CA 750, 86.*"

Legal Encyclopedias. There are several works recognized as standards in the field of criminal law, two of the best being *Perkins on Criminal Law,* Foundation Press, second edition, and *California Crimes,* Bender-Moss Company, B.E. Witkin, two volumes plus supplement. Both offer quite detailed and thorough information on common crimes and both profusely cite cases for amplification of points made.

A student who wants more information concerning a specific crime should go to the library, find the crime in the table of contents and read the material. Should the student then need to brief a case, he or she can use any of the cases cited by the author on that point of law or criminal statute.

Legal Digests. Every law library subscribes to numerous legal digests, which are structured according to subject matter and deal extensively with legal concepts such as diminished capacity, former jeopardy, defenses, and so on, and stress new or changing philosophies, procedures, and interpretations of the law. They also list numerous case citations on which the student can follow up.

Shepard's California Citations, Statute Edition. This citator is invaluable to the law student. In this volume the student will find all of the codes for the state of California, including the penal code. The student who is interested in finding case citations as assignments, can go to the citator, find the penal code section, and locate the section number he or she is interested in, and find scores of case citations regarding that particular penal statute. Additionally, by referring to the abbreviation key, the student can determine if any particular case had been criticized (c), overruled (o), or reversed (r) to determine if the case is still valid.

REPORTING IN "BRIEF" FORM

Now that you have learned how to find case law, we will proceed to the next logical step—how to read and report case law in a logical and meaningful manner.

Basically, an appealed lawsuit is initiated because one of the parties involved (the appellant) wishes to dispute or contest the adverse ruling of an inferior court. To justify the appeal, the appellant, through an attorney, takes issue either on, for example, a point of law, a constitutional infringement, insufficiency of evidence, or a procedural defect in the trial court proceedings.

We will now look at the standard form that most appeal cases take.

The first item after the citation in a case is a brief statement of the kind of controversy involved. That is, whether it was a criminal prosecution, a tort, or a civil recovery lawsuit. This is followed by a brief accounting of how the case got to this particular court. Such statements may say, for example, "This is an appeal by defendant from an adverse judgment," or "from an order of the lower court denying his motion for a new trial."

Next in order is a short statement of the facts that resulted in the case being brought to trial; who the parties are, what they did or did not do, what happened to them, who brought the action, and what outcome is wanted.

Next comes a statement of the question or questions the court is called upon to decide the various issues (either of law or fact) that must be settled before a decision on the controversy can be reached. An issue can best be understood as a statement of some aspect of a general question of law, such as whether a particular act alleged constitutes the crime charged.

After the issues have been stated, the pro (for) and con (against) arguments by the appellant and respondent are given and discussed by the court. This is where logic comes into play. There are two main kinds of logical reasoning—inductive and deductive. Inductive reasoning involves the formulation of general propositions from a consideration of specific problems or observations. Conversely, deductive reasoning involves the application of a general proposition already formulated to some specific situation or problem so that a conclusion can be drawn from it.

Finally, after the argument on all the issues, the court states the general conclusion to be drawn therefrom; ending with a statement of the court's decision, such as "judgment affirmed"; "judgment reversed"; or "case remanded, new trial ordered."

Some Rules to Follow When Writing Briefs:

1. Read the case through at least once before beginning to brief it. Be certain that you have the facts, issues, conclusions, and findings in your mind before beginning to write.

2. Write the brief in your own words—don't just copy from the case. However, make sure your statements are accurate and pertinent.

3. Organize your brief. Put the essential matters in a logical order, but be as concise as possible. Do not equate a long, rambling brief with a good brief. Use this format:

   a. Facts: what happened to whom, and what was the result. This should be a short resume of the occurrences that precipitated a lawsuit. Generally, this can be adequately done in a paragraph or two.

   b. The facts are followed by a statement of the issues to be resolved by the court.

   c. Next is a restatement of the conclusion that the court has drawn from the facts and issues.

   d. Finally the finding or decision of the court is stated.

   The following is an example of the format to follow:

CASE CITATION

People v. King Kong

1 C. 5th. 69.

Facts: Defendant was convicted of kidnapping [*P.C. 207*], and forcible rape [*P.C. 261(2)*], and is appealing his conviction. Defendant seized one Fay Wray, on the evening of July 4, 1936, from a restraining pedestal outside of the wall surrounding Megetum City, County of Ohwow. From there, he carried her to his cave on Lookout Mountain where he forcibly raped her. Later, she was able to escape and was found by her boyfriend, one Bruce Cabot, wandering aimlessly in the forest.

Issues:

1. The evidence at the trial proceedings was insufficient to prove that the taking was done without the consent of the victim and, therefore, was not kidnapping under *PC 207*.

2. Defendant's sentence of terms prescribed by law on both *PC 207* and *PC 261(2)*, to run concurrently, violates *PC 654* prohibiting double punishment in that kidnapping and subsequent rape were one continuous act—the kidnapping merely being necessary to the act of rape.

Conclusions: As to appellant's claim of insufficient evidence to convict under PC 207, we find the record does support the jury's finding of guilty insofar as there was evidence sufficient to show a taking, without consent of the victim, by considerable force (considering the relative size and strength of the appellant Kong).

As to appellant's claim under *PC 654*, we find that the evidence amply supports his contention that the kidnapping was incidental to his intent to rape and should apply. (Cases cited).

Findings:

1. Judgment affirmed as to conviction of PC 261(2).

2. Judgment reversed as to conviction and concurrent sentencing under PC 207.

Shepards: Not cited.

This admittedly facetious example contains the four areas needed in an adequate brief and hopefully deals with each. Thus, a brief should consist of:

1. **Name** and citation of case

2. **Facts** or summary of occurrence

3. **Issues** to be resolved

4. **Conclusions** drawn from those issues

5. **Findings** of the court relative to the issues and the court's **conclusions.**

This brief narrative, the author hopes, will provide the student with the understanding and skill necessary to meaningfully research case law.

APPENDIX E

Index of Code Sections
Included in *California Criminal Law Manual*
(In Numerical Order)

Penal Code No.	Subject	Text Section	Page No.
261(1)	Rape, victim unsound mind	12.7	166
261(2)	Rape, forcible	12.7	166
261(2)	Rape, penalty enhancement	2.12	22
261(3)	Rape by threat or drugs	12.7	167
261(4)	Rape, unconscious victim	12.7	167
261(5)	Rape by fraud	12.7	167
261.5	Unlawful sexual intercourse	12.7	168
262	Rape of spouse	12.7	169
263	Penetration in rape	12.7	168
261.4	Rape, aiding, statute of limitation	1.7	7
265	Abduction for defilement	12.6	164
266	Enticing, unmarried female	12.6	164
266a	Abducting for prostitution	12.6	164
266b	Abduction for cohabitation	12.6	164
267	Abducting juvenile for prostitution	12.6	164
272	Contributing to minor's delinquency	13.3	177
273d	Cruelty to child	10.15	138
273g	Immoral acts in child's presence	13.4	177
273.5	Battery, cohabiting persons	10.15	137
274	Abortion defined	13.11	183
275	Abortion, soliciting of	13.11	184
276	Abortion, submitting to	13.11	184
278(a)	Child stealing	12.4	162
280	Concealing child	12.6	162
285	Incest	13.6	179
800(b)	Sodomy, statute of limitations	1.7	7
286	Sodomy defined	13.5	178
288	Child molesting, statute of limitation	1.7	7
288	Child molesting, under 14	13.4	177
288a	Oral copulation, statute of limitations	1.7	7
288a	Oral copulation defined	13.5	178
289	Genital penetration, foreign object	1.7	7
290	Sex offender registration	13.10	182
302	Disturbing religious meetings	8.10	104
311	Obscene matter defined	13.1	173
311.2	Sale, distributing obscene matter	13.1	174
311.4	Obscene matter, employing minor	13.1	174
311.5	Advertising obscene matter	13.1	175
311.6	Obscene live conduct	13.1	175
311.9	Obscene matter, penalty	13.1	175
313	Harmful matter defined	13.2	176
314	Indecent exposure	13.7	180
346	Ticket "scalping"	18.16	244
347	Poisoning food, medicine, water	10.6	134
347	Poisoning food, medicine, water	18.16	244
347b	Poisoning alcoholic beverages	10.6	134
402b	Abandoned refrigerators	18.9	243
403	Disturbing public meetings	8.9	104
404	Riot defined	8.6	101
404.6	Inciting riot	8.7	101
405a	Lynching	8.11	104